Economics

Valerie Leonard
BA (Hons) (Econ), BA (Hons) (Russian)
Lecturer in Economics, University of Wolverhampton

Thirteenth Edition

HLT Publications

HLT PUBLICATIONS
200 Greyhound Road, London W14 9RY

First published 1979
Thirteenth edition 1995

© The HLT Group Ltd 1995

All HLT publications enjoy copyright protection and the copyright belongs to The HLT Group Ltd.

All rights reserved. No part of this publication may be reproduced or transmitted in any form or by any means, electronic, mechanical, photocopying, recording or otherwise, or stored in any retrieval system of any nature without either the written permission of the copyright holder, application for which should be made to The HLT Group Ltd, or a licence permitting restricted copying in the United Kingdom issued by the Copyright Licensing Agency.

Any person who infringes the above in relation to this publication may be liable to criminal prosecution and civil claims for damages.

ISBN 0 7510 0522 3

British Library Cataloguing-in-Publication.

A CIP Catalogue record for this book is available from the British Library.

Printed and bound in Great Britain

Contents

Foreword by Brian Heap ix

Preface xi

Acknowledgement xiii

1 Introduction 1

Introduction 3
The economic problem 3
Solutions to economic problems 8

2 The price mechanism 15

Demand 17
Supply 23
The price mechanism 26
Intervention in the market 32

3 The theory of demand 53

Elasticity of demand 55
Consumer's demand 68

4 The theory of production (supply) 75

Introduction 77
Influences on supply 79

5 Ownership and control of firms 97

Introduction 99
The ownership of firms 99
The objectives of the firm 101

6 Market structures and control — 107

- 109 Introduction
- 109 Perfect competition
- 118 Monopoly
- 125 Monopolistic competition
- 128 Oligopolistic competition
- 133 The models compared
- 136 The control of monopoly and merger activity
- 142 Restrictive practices
- 142 EU competition law

7 The market for factors of production — 145

- 147 The factors
- 148 The demand for factors of production (marginal productivity theory)
- 153 The supply of factors and market equilibrium
- 159 Land
- 162 Labour
- 171 Capital
- 189 The distribution of wealth and income
- 199 Minimum wage controls

8 Government involvement in production — 203

- 205 Industrial policy
- 212 Nationalised industries and privatisation
- 226 Public and merit goods
- 228 Housing policy
- 240 Helping markets to work better

9 Money and banking — 247

- 249 The development of money
- 254 The clearing banks
- 262 The Bank of England
- 264 Merchant banks
- 266 Discount houses

10 Inflation, money, interest rates and monetarism — 269

- 271 Inflation (see also Chapter 15)
- 274 Money demand
- 277 Money supply
- 280 Monetary equilibrium and the rate of interest
- 285 Monetarism

11 National income analysis — 293
- Circular flow of income — 295
- Determination of national income — 304

12 The macroeconomic model — 313
- The consumption function — 315
- The model — 321
- Keynesian reasoning — 327
- The multiplier — 328
- The accelerator — 331
- Inflationary and deflationary gaps — 333

13 The unemployment problem — 337
- Unemployment — 339
- Cyclical unemployment — 342
- Structural unemployment — 347
- The natural rate of unemployment — 359
- Measures to help the long-term unemployed — 361
- Trends in employment — 363

14 Public finance — 365
- The budget — 367
- Taxation — 368
- Public expenditure — 379

15 Management of the economy — 391
- The inflation problem — 393
- The Phillips curve — 397

16 International trade theory and the European Union — 407
- Comparative advantage — 409
- The European Union — 416
- International competitiveness — 426

17 The balance of payments — 431
- The accounts — 433
- Methods of control — 439
- UK problems — 441

449 **18 International finance – the world economy**

- 451 Exchange rates
- 458 Recent exchange rate systems
- 462 The IMF
- 466 The Eurocurrency market
- 466 The problems of the Third World
- 468 The World Bank

471 **19 Economic growth**

- 473 Determinants of growth and production possibility frontiers
- 482 The benefits and costs of growth
- 483 Government action
- 485 De-industrialisation

491 **Index**

Foreword by Brian Heap

A-level work, comprising two, three or even four subjects, is a challenging course of study. It follows a period of general education leading to the GCSE in which you have experienced a 'taster' course of up to ten subjects presented to you in a highly structured teaching system. Thereafter, it becomes necessary to make a choice of subject areas for a more concentrated period of study – two years – in which more time will be spent in 'private study' – literally, teaching yourself.

Inevitably, private study is a new experience for most students and the time normally allocated is rarely used to the best advantage. The assimilation of facts, whilst working on your own, can be difficult since it also necessitates identifying the important issues from a range of books and a wealth of information. The framework of your course is naturally vital, not simply in terms of passing your A-level exams but in achieving the right grades you need to enter the university or college degree course of your choice.

My A-level series aims to provide you with this essential framework. This book will give you the support you need to work through your syllabus and to reinforce the knowledge you will need to be sure of success at the end of your school or college career.

Brian Heap

Preface

This textbook covers the core syllabus of all the examination boards offering A-level economics. It is also a valuable text for those taking AS level economics and students who are taking the subject as part of a professional qualification. The student taking an examination with accountancy bodies, such as the Institute of Bankers, and also BTEC courses at Higher and National levels would find the content useful as a course companion.

The textbook is designed to enable students to understand basic economic concepts, and as far as possible to apply these to the latest information and policy changes. The early chapters deal with microeconomic issues, and over half of the text covers macroeconomics. In an attempt to cope with the difficulty of students sometimes having problems appreciating parts of the subject matter without understanding the whole, some use of cross-referencing has been made. There is also treatment of many of the new issues in economics such as recent events in Eastern Europe, the introduction of the council tax, the effects of recent housing legislation, and water and electricity privatisation. The textbook attempts, as far as possible in such a rapidly changing subject, to provide the student with up-to-date coverage of the theory and evidence which is at the heart of modern economics.

In addition, at the end of every chapter, review questions are provided, to enable students to check their understanding and recall of the contents of each chapter. These questions should firstly be attempted without reference to the textbook.

Acknowledgement

All material reproduced from official publications is used by permission of the Controller of Her Majesty's Stationery Office or the Office for Official Publications of the European Communities.

Cover

The author and publishers would like to thank Lloyd's of London, the Bank of England, the Institute of Economic Affairs and the London School of Economics for the loan of pictures and permission to reproduce them on this cover. We would also like to thank George Southall of Peter Van Arden Productions for the photograph of the entrance to the London School of Economics.

Key

1   Lloyd's of London viewed from the south side.
    Photographed by Janet Gill.
2   The Bank of England, © Bank of England. Photograph by Ian Maguire.
3 & 4   The Institute of Economic Affairs.
5   London School of Economics.
6   Crest of the London School of Economics.

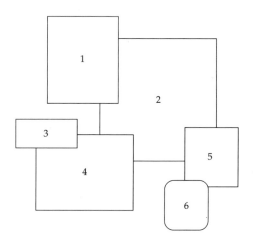

Introduction | 1

Introduction 3

The economic problem 3

Solutions to economic problems 8

Introduction

This textbook has been specifically written to enable you to understand the main economic concepts and their use and relevance in economic analysis. The theoretical basis of economics will be covered, but emphasis will be laid throughout on the 'real' world. The way in which the economy is managed increasingly affects the business environment. Indeed, economics is relevant to so much of everyday life. It can help to answer countless questions and problems. How are the prices of goods really determined? Why – and how – are taxes always being changed? And how is all the money spent? Why it is sometimes necessary for the government to restrict pay increases? Can the government stop the import of Japanese electrical goods if the import bill is too high and, if it can, will it do so? Many of the personal and business decisions which are taken every day depend on a clear understanding of the economic environment.

Very often the teaching and study of economics divide the subject matter into two parts: micro- and macroeconomics. The study of microeconomics looks at *parts* of the economy, such as individual consumer behaviour, and price and output behaviour in markets and industries. Macroeconomics looks at aspects of the economy as a whole, *aggregates*, such as inflation, total output and spending, and unemployment.

Positive economics deals with scientific explanations of the workings of the economy. Normative economics offers recommendations based on personal value judgments. Positive economics is similar to the natural sciences where we can say 'if this is changed then that will happen'. For example, all economists would agree that when the government imposes a sales/indirect tax on a product its price will rise. The normative issue is whether this price rise is desirable or not, and opinions on this will clearly differ.

The economic problem

All economies have the same problem: *their resources are relatively limited while their wants are relatively enormous*. Most consumers can easily imagine happily spending an income twice, ten times or a hundred times their own. Hence the popularity of 'the Pools', Premium Bonds and the lottery. If every individual in an economy such as the UK were to regard these dreams as their economic wants then the demand for the resources of the economy would far outstrip the available resources. Even economies very rich in resources (the major oil producing states who can command great supplies of all resources with their wealth) could still not meet all the material desires of *all* their people.

The scarce resources of a nation are its land, labour and capital (or factors of production). It is these which are used in the production of goods and services. The quantity and quality of these resources determines the level of output in a nation. Goods which are produced using these factors of production usually have a price and are called 'economic goods'. 'Free goods' are sunshine, air and rainwater, whose production does not use scarce resources and involves no opportunity cost.

We will use an unoriginal but useful example to demonstrate the economic problems of most societies: *Robinson Crusoe – the one-person economy*.

Robinson Crusoe was shipwrecked and survived, finding himself on an uninhabited island which, fortunately, has fresh water streams and plenty of vegetation. There are therefore plentiful natural resources but Crusoe has only 24 hours a day and his existing skills with which to feed, house and clothe himself.

He would first establish his needs (a minimum of food, and shelter) and would also sort out, in order of priority, the other 'wants' that he will meet as soon as he is able to. He would then allocate his limited resources of time and skill to get as far down the list as he can.

He must make the fundamental economic decision of *matching extensive wants to limited resources*. If he chooses to spend his time producing more food, he cannot spend the same hours building a shelter to protect himself from the weather. The cost to him of producing the extra food is the shelter he must do without. (The cost of having any good produced with our limited resources is the good we have been obliged to do without as a result. This is the concept of opportunity cost. The *opportunity cost* of more food is less shelter.)

Crusoe will also consider his preference for leisure as opposed to goods. Again, since his time is limited, the opportunity cost of taking the afternoon off to sleep in the sun is the goods he could have produced in the time. The opportunity cost will always be the goods he would *most* have preferred out of all those he could have produced in the afternoon. We might expect Crusoe's preference for leisure instead of more goods to increase, the greater his ability to produce and consume goods.

Crusoe must aim to produce goods as efficiently as possible or he will be wasting his time and producing less goods than would otherwise have been available to him.

Crusoe might also consider the possibility of *saving*. Instead of consuming all the potatoes that he digs up each day, he might choose to pack some away. He will then be able to eat them in the future, giving himself a day off from digging for potatoes. Alternatively, he might choose to save them for the time when potatoes become more difficult to find. The sacrifice of present consumption for the sake of consumption in the future is the economists' definition of *saving*.

Crusoe might also consider the relative advantages of continuing to dig the potatoes up with his bare hands or taking one morning off to produce a spade which would speed up his digging thereafter. Economists make a distinction between *consumption goods* and *capital goods*. The spade is what economists call a *capital good*. A *consumption good* gives direct benefit or *utility* to individuals. We eat food to satisfy our hunger and wear clothes to keep ourselves warm. These are *consumption* goods.

A capital good gives no direct utility but facilitates the production of goods which *do* give utility. A spade is not a consumption good since we cannot eat it or wear it. It does, however, enable Crusoe to produce more potatoes which he can eat. The spade is therefore a capital good. Obviously, the greater the stock of such useful capital goods that Crusoe can build up, the better off he will be for production in the future.

The production of capital goods is what economists mean by *investment*. It is very important that you make sure of the distinction made by economists between saving (refraining from consumption) and investment (the production of capital goods). The words and their meanings are often confused in everyday usage.

Notice that Crusoe has to use his valuable time to produce the spade while he could otherwise have spent it producing potatoes. The opportunity cost of producing the capital good has been the consumption good that could otherwise have been produced in the time.

Crusoe, like any other rational, economic man, wants to get as much satisfaction as he possibly can from the limited resources available to him. He wants to *maximise his total utility*. This is assumed to be the aim of all individuals in any economic model. Since the resources of utility can be assumed to vary enormously between different individuals, this is a realistic assumption to make.

In order to maximise his total utility, Crusoe has a number of problems to solve:

a the choice of priorities out of all the possibilities:

   i the priorities between the available consumption goods;

   ii the choice between producing consumption goods or producing capital goods to increase consumption possibilities in the future;

b matching these priorities to the available resources of time and skill;

c maintaining maximum efficiency so as not to waste those limited resources.

To Crusoe's surprise, after some time, he realises that he is not alone on the island. He and Man Friday decide to work together to solve their economic problems. They must first establish their priorities. If they are to work together and divide activities (as we will see, this decision has great advantages for them), they have to agree on joint priorities. This may, of course, be difficult.

Their productive possibilities are now greatly increased. Some jobs can be more efficiently done by two people than one, eg instead of two of them fishing with lines and doubling their output of fish, they could devise a system of dragging a net up the river held between them, one on each bank. The catch of fish may increase tenfold. They are getting the benefit of *economies of scale*. Since they are catching many more fish (tenfold increase) than the input of labour (doubled), the cost of each fish in terms of the input of labour is greatly reduced.

Each may have specialist skills. Suppose Crusoe is a skilled builder but not very good at farming. Before Friday came, he had both to build and to farm. It happens that Friday is no good at building but good at farming. If Crusoe builds and Friday farms, their output of both building and farming would more than double after the arrival of Friday. Crusoe could not concentrate on building before because he would have starved. This is the advantage of *specialisation and exchange*.

There is, however, a new problem in the two-person economy: how should the output that results from their joint efforts be shared between them? They could agree to share all output equally between them.

However, there are some items that Crusoe values more highly than Friday does, while Friday has different preferences. It seems absurd that they should have equal amounts of all their goods when they would be happier with a different allocation of the same total output. They decide to start out with equal shares of everything and then barter to re-adjust the allocation to suit their personal preferences. So Friday trades some of his share of fish for some of Crusoe's share of fruit.

Friday argues that the equal shares of output used as a starting point for this trade is not fair since he, Friday, works all day while Crusoe goes to sleep for two hours every afternoon. Friday reckons that his share of output should be increased by 20 per cent to reflect the hours of work he does.

Crusoe argues that the work he does, building, is more arduous and unpleasant than farming. He therefore needs a rest in the middle of the day and anyway he is not sleeping but thinking since building is a complicated task requiring some planning. He should be rewarded 20 per cent more than Friday for his work.

Friday argues that Crusoe's work may be difficult but it is more rewarding than Friday's. Crusoe's house will stand for years as a monument to his effort and resourcefulness. Friday's work, on the other hand, is to produce food one day which is eaten and then he must start again the next day. He should be rewarded more highly for this unrewarding work.

Crusoe argues that he spent years training as an apprentice in building to acquire his present skills. It is only right that he should be rewarded for his training by a satisfying job with high rewards. Friday indignantly points out that he, Friday, would have been glad to do a similar training had the opportunity been available to him. Crusoe is lucky to have such advantages and there is no reason why he should be rewarded for his luck. And so on ...! This is the allocation problem common to all economies.

So the two-person economy has both advantages and disadvantages:

a They can enjoy economies of scale and the advantage of specialisation and exchange.

b They may have difficulty establishing or they may disagree about what their collective 'wants' are and about the allocation of output when it is produced.

The situation is further complicated by the arrival, also from a shipwreck, of 50 men, women and children on this quite small island. There are, of course, increased possibilities for disagreement on goals. Establishing the collective priorities is now a more different problem. Should everyone be consulted or just one member of each family and should the collating system weight all first choices equally and all second choices equally, disregarding any differences in people's total valuation of goods? Even then, it is not easy to establish just how much more important first choices are than second choices and the gaps may be different for different people.

There may also be the problem that it is less easy to assess the available resources of skill and intelligence when there are so many more people. It is clearly a waste if these are not exploited to the full but Crusoe (since he is elected as leader) does not know how to discover them and maximise their use. He would prefer some system in which everybody had an incentive to discover and maximise their *own* usefulness in the economy. It occurs to him that this might be linked to the solution of the now much increased difficulty over the allocation of output. Perhaps, if everyone were rewarded according to the society's valuation of their output, that would be fair.

But then there would be the problem of the ill, very young and very old who cannot work. Perhaps it would be better to reward everyone the same regardless of output. However, the economy needs maximum efficiency and this *may* be a problem if people receive no personal reward for being productive.

Crusoe and Friday used to barter their shares of output to re-adjust the distribution of particular goods to reflect their preferences. With 52 people, barter becomes more difficult. Consider the following problem:

There are three people, A, B and C. They each have more than they want of some good:

A has too much of good 1.
B has too much of good 2.
C has too much of good 3.

They each want to swap this excess for another particular good:

A would like more of good 2.
B would like more of good 3.
C would like more of good 1.

It is clear that the bartering is now going to be much more complicated. The only way A can get what he wants is by arranging that C and B trade. B then has what he wanted and C and A then trade to get what they want. The problem is compounded with more people involved.

However, the newly enlarged economy is now much better able to exploit the advantages of the economies of scale and specialisation and exchange. The output of the economy expands more than the population so everyone can be better off than Crusoe and Friday could manage for themselves.

By the time the second generation grows up there is a new problem. Until then, there were more natural resources on the island than Crusoe, Friday and the 50 new arrivals could use. Their 'limited resource' was only their own skills and the time to utilise them. The situation is very different with a population of 100 on this quite small island. The economy begins to suffer from *the law of diminishing returns*.

There is only a limited acreage of cultivatable land. As the labour force increased initially, they were first able to take advantage of the economies of scale so output per worker increased. Now output per worker begins to fall. Total output continues to rise but not proportionately to the increase in workers employed.

The acreage becomes 'overcrowded' and the land exhausted. This is a serious problem for, if it continues, the increase in population will outstrip available output and some would starve. This was the future of the world predicted by Malthus, a nineteenth century economist. What the society must do to avoid this disaster is to develop a new technology so that all scarce resources are used more efficiently, new uses found for previously under-used resources, access to previously unobtainable resources developed and all natural, and therefore irreplaceable, resources conserved. When Crusoe was alone his investment problem was only a question of saving for the winter; now his problem is of how much to save for how many years ahead.

You will, of course, see the correspondence between Crusoe's problem and that of all modern economies. These can be summarised into the problems of:

a *What* to produce? Which consumption goods? Consumption or investment goods?

b *How* to produce it? What should be the method of production? That is, capital intensive or labour intensive?

c *For whom* to produce? Should everyone be given equal shares of output? Should people be rewarded in proportion to their contribution to output?

Solutions to economic problems

The command economy

The state through the central planning authority determines the answers to the above questions.

It decides what should be produced

It decides which consumer 'wants' should be met by output. There is some difficulty here in establishing how much consumers want particular goods. It is obviously fairly easy to do this with an economy which provides a very low standard of living since the available resources are only sufficient to meet the most basic and therefore predictable needs of the consumers. Interestingly, once the economy becomes more productive, a modified version of the price system (see below) has often been introduced to indicate consumers' priorities.

It decides how much output should consist of state consumption goods, eg defence. It decides how much output should be of investment goods and what sort of investment this should be – roads, harbours and airports for transport, education for future productive labour, and machines for industry.

It decides how these goods should be produced

It must know what resources are available to meet the output 'needs' established above and it must know which are scarcest and must be allocated most carefully.

It must know all the most efficient techniques for combining these resources and it must arrange for the resources to be so combined – setting up factories, plants, farms, etc, organising management, moving suitable labour where necessary and ensuring that everything runs to optimal efficiency.

It decides how goods are allocated
It must decide how the output of consumer goods should be allocated to the people. This is obviously a very difficult problem since equity, equality and incentives to efficiency may all be incompatible.

Obvious problems with this system
The enormous amount of information needed, the costs of gathering good information and the time lags likely (see below) in the decision process, making this information out of date. This means that decisions are expensive and unreliable. Decisions can only be as good as the information on which they are based and there is an unfortunate trade-off between economy of collection and reliability of information collected.

Since so many factors are involved in making decisions of this kind, decisions tend to be made by committees. Anyone who has ever worked on a committee will know the enormous time that can be taken and the unsatisfactory decisions that may be the product of committees. It is clearly a problem if the entire economic system is dependent on such bodies.

Command (planned) economies experience a number of problems: poor quality of consumer goods; persistent shortages of consumer goods (caused by bottlenecks in the supply chain); inflexibility of the planning system; and an immense bureaucracy needed to administer the system.

These problems were evident in all of the former command economies of Eastern Europe. (This includes the former USSR, Poland, Hungary, Rumania, Albania, and the former Czechoslovakia.) These economies are now all undergoing the process of transformation from command economies into market economies. This process of transformation is painful and complex. Many problems are being experienced by these economies on the road to becoming market economies (eg rising unemployment and high inflation).

Advantages of this system
Economic decisions are made in the interests of the state rather than the interests of individuals (see discussion on monopoly externalities and distribution of income below) and this may produce a better life for the population. This is most obviously so where the alternative is the concentration of economic power (wealth) in the hands of very few individuals. Often health, education, housing and transport are cheap and universally available.

The market economy

Adam Smith regarded the market system as one in which the private, self-interested decisions of millions of individuals would produce the greatest efficiency of the economy. The miraculous mechanism which did this was the price system. The use of money for all trades in resources and goods gave a common measure against which all costs and values could be compared.

The basic economic problem is one of relating the unlimited wants of consumers to the limited resources of the economy. In the market system, householders who own the resources are linked by firms who organise the production of goods and services. The connections between consumers and firms, and firms and resources are made by prices.

Consumers pay firms a money price for the goods they acquire. The more consumers want the good, the higher the price they will be prepared to pay. The higher the price, the less of the good they will generally want to buy.

When consumers offer to buy a quantity of a particular good at a given price, it is as if they were voting for the good to be produced. Firms receive these 'votes' and use them to bid for resources with which to produce the goods. The greater the number of 'votes', the more resources the firm can afford to buy for the production of the good.

The amount that firms must pay for any particular resource depends on the quantity of the resource that all firms wish to buy in relation to the amount of that resource available. The greater the demand for the resource and the smaller the amount available, the higher the price firms must pay for that resource.

Firms communicate this relative scarcity of resources to consumers in the price firms charge for the good that the consumers want. The greater the relative scarcity, the higher the price and the less consumers will want to buy of goods using that resource.

Suppose consumers decided that they wanted more of a particular good. They would offer more 'votes' for it to the firms. Firms would be able to buy more of the resources with these increased 'votes' and be able to produce more of the good. The increase in consumers preference for the good results in an increased quantity being produced for them.

Suppose a resource became more scarce. Firms would find they had to pay a higher price for the resource. More 'votes' would have to be used to buy the same amount of resources. Firms must therefore ask consumers for a higher price for the good in order to accumulate enough votes. Consumers will want to buy less of the good at a higher price. The increased scarcity of the resource therefore results in a reduction in the amount of goods consumed for which it is required.

The market system therefore deals automatically with changes in consumer preferences and in the relative scarcity of resources. Dealing with such changes can be a big problem for command economies, with their information difficulties.

Firms will try to produce the difference between the revenue received for goods and the costs of resources used, as efficiently as possible since they will be rewarded for efficiency by profits. Firms will therefore aim to supply most of those goods which are most highly valued by consumers and use as little as possible of the resources which are most expensive because of their relative scarcity. These efforts by firms will produce the best use of the economy's scarce resources in terms of the wants of consumers.

The allocation of output produced by the economy is determined by the ownership of resources. Households own resources which they sell to firms. The more they own and the greater the price that firms will pay for them, the more consumers earn from their resources. The money earned is used to buy goods. The greater the consumer's income, the greater his ability to buy and consume the output of the economy. The greater the price offered for any resource, the more of it the owners will generally want to sell since this will increase their ability to buy goods.

The principle advantage of the market system must be that everybody makes independent decisions about what they will pay for good X and how much they must be paid to sell resource Y – there is no committee involved. Similarly independent firms motivated by profit look at the consumers' demands and the scarcity of factors and make independent decisions about what and how to produce – again no committees involved. The only way that firms can be profitable is by being efficient. The outcome is an efficient linking of wants and resources.

There are, however, a number of problems with the market economy. The development of monopoly power so that individual firms or owners of resources gain a disproportionate ability to distort the market to their own benefit. The immobility of resources (especially labour) so that output does not adjust smoothly to changing consumer preferences. There are some goods, known as 'public goods,' which have an undoubted value to society but will not be provided by private firms since it is impossible for the firms to sell them to private individuals. This creates an unequal allocation of resources so that some individuals have a much greater ability than others to determine the output of the economy.

The market economy may, under some circumstances, move into a downward spiral of output and employment so that far less output is produced than would be possible and supposedly 'scarce' resources are idle. These problems with the market system mean that a degree of state intervention is often introduced.

The mixed economy

All economies in the world are mixed economies; that is, they have features of both the market and the command systems. The mixed economies may therefore aim to have the advantages of both systems without their disadvantages. There is a need for governments to get the degree of mixing right.

The economies of the world vary considerably in the way in which they are organised. Some are predominantly command economies with some market features (eg Cuba, North Korea). Some economies are predominantly market economies, with some degree of government intervention in the economy (eg UK, USA, Hong Kong, the member states of the European Union).

All of the economies of the world lie somewhere along a spectrum stretching from a pure command economy to a pure market economy (see following diagram). On the left of the spectrum would lie Cuba, North Korea. On the right of the spectrum would lie the USA, Hong Kong. Even in the economies which lie on the right of the spectrum, the government taxes households and firms in order to provide certain 'public goods' such as defence, and law and order.

Even in the economies which lie towards the left end of the spectrum, it has proved necessary to introduce some elements of the market system; households receive income from the government, with which they make their own choices of their preferred bundle of the goods and services available.

In the following sections, we will look in detail at the operation of the market system and the problems which arise from it. We will then look at the elements of government intervention in the British economy.

The subsistence economy

There are still economies in the world today where vast sections of the community live at a subsistence level (ie they make little enough of their own food to survive and engage in trade). The land and capital is poorly developed and labour is often in need of training. Indeed, the population is often so malnourished that they have little energy to work, which means that food production falls; a vicious circle. Many countries are in this 'subsistence trap', Somalia, Ethiopia, Bangladesh and Mozambique. These countries need political and social organisation, an improved infrastructure, and better farming techniques.

Questions for review

1. What does 'macroeconomics' study?

   What does 'microeconomics' study?

2. What is the difference between 'positive' and 'normative' economics?

3. What do economists mean by 'scarcity'?

   Why is 'scarcity' a problem?

   Are there any goods which are not 'scarce'?

4. What do economists mean by 'opportunity cost'?

   Why is it important?

5. What are the three fundamental decisions which every economy in the world must make?

   How does a market economy make these decisions?

   How does a command economy make these decisions?

The price mechanism | 2

Demand 17

Supply 23

The price mechanism 26

Intervention in the market 32

Demand

Effective demand

There is one problem which is at the core of economic analysis; that is, how people choose *what* needs they are going to satisfy through the use of *which* resources. The examination of this very basic economic problem is carried out through the use of *supply and demand analysis*.

The word *demand* in the economic context has an important additional meaning to that most commonly used. The greengrocer would not be particularly impressed if someone 'demanded' four oranges but did not have any money. In fact, unless he felt generous, it is unlikely he would part with them! It is important to understand that, to the economist, 'demand' means *effective demand*; or a demand that is backed by the *ability to pay*. A poor man may want to buy a large mansion, but his demand for it is not an *effective demand*: he cannot pay for it.

A demand schedule

It is obvious to any experienced consumer that more of a good will generally be sold at a lower price. Consider what happens when one of the airlines offers cheaper flights across the Atlantic. Existing travellers will choose the now cheaper airline instead of their usual choice. People who had not planned to fly because they could not afford to will now find that they can. More airline tickets will be sold. Similarly, if the price of a good rises, consumers will choose to buy less of it. Suppose that a farmer was considering how many oranges he is likely to sell at a number of different prices per orange. Expressed differently, how many oranges will consumers demand at these various prices? His conclusions might be as shown in the following demand schedule.

Demand schedule for oranges

Price (p)	Quantity demanded 000s
12	0
10	5
8	10
6	15
4	20
2	25
0	30

This table shows the number of oranges which will be demanded at prices ranging from 12 pence to 0 pence and it is known as a *demand schedule*. It shows clearly that the demand for oranges rises as the price of oranges falls.

Notice that there is a limited or finite demand for oranges even when the price is zero. This is very important information for industries who sell units of their output for a zero price. If water were supplied for a zero price per unit the demand would not be infinite but some quantity greater than the amount that would be consumed if there were a positive price.

A demand curve

The numbers in the schedule can be transposed onto the graph to give a *demand curve* for oranges over the relevant price range.

Demand curve for oranges

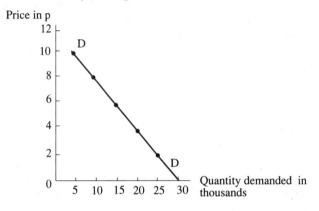

A further point needs to be made for those students who are unfamiliar with mathematical terminology. It is usual to adopt the expression 'curve' for any form of graphical representation, even if the graph happens to be a straight line. In fact, a demand curve will often appear like this:

A demand curve

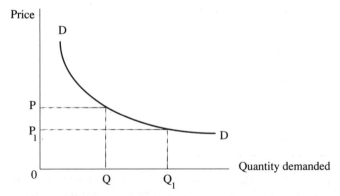

It will also be noticed that the numbered scale used on the axes in the previous graph has not been used. When hypothetical models are used in economics it is easier to omit numerical quantities and prices. For instance, in the graph above, price is represented by 'P' or 'P' with an index, and the quantity demanded is represented by 'Q' or 'Q' with an index. In practical terms, saying 'at a price P, quantity Q is demanded' is just the same as saying 'at a price of 10 pence, the quantity 5,000 is demanded'.

Perverse demand

In a few exceptional circumstances, a demand curve may slope *upwards* from left to right. Demand that *rises* as the price *rises* may occur when consumers expect that there may be a further price rise in the immediate future. It would be natural, therefore, for a consumer to buy at a lower price if possible. It is also likely that the demand curve for status symbols, such as very expensive jewellery, may slope *upwards* from left to right because the more expensive a good, the more a certain section of the community may demand it.

A most interesting and unusual example of *perverse demand* (as this type of demand is called) occurs in the case of very cheap, but necessary, goods such as bread and potatoes. A rise in the price of a very basic food means that the very poor consumer is forced to reduce his expenditure on *other* goods so that he can continue to buy the necessary one. This may, in turn, lead to an increase in the consumption of the more basic food despite its increase in price as the consumer attempts to replace the food which he can no longer buy. An economist who studied the potato famine in Ireland in the nineteenth century noticed this phenomenon among the very poor Irish peasants and his name has been used to describe this type of perverse demand. It is known as the '*Giffen effect*'. A Giffen good will have a demand curve which looks like this:

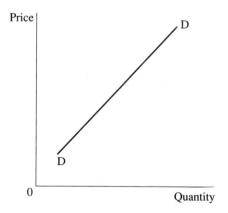

Other influences on demand

It is obvious that the demand for a good is influenced by other factors as well as the price of the good. Suppose that consumers have higher incomes. They will be able to buy more of all goods including oranges. We would therefore expect more oranges to be sold at every price if consumers' incomes rose.

The demand schedule is shown before and after the increase in incomes.

Price (p)	Quantity demanded before the rise in incomes 000s	Quantity demanded after the rise in incomes 000s
12	0	10
10	5	15
8	10	20
6	15	25
4	20	30
2	25	35
0	30	40

We can express this information in a diagram. D_1 shows the demand curve for oranges before the rise in consumer incomes. D_2 shows the demand curve for oranges after the increase in incomes.

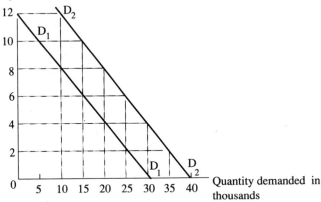

If we take a price such as 6p, we can see that, where consumers used to buy 15,000 oranges at that price, they will now want to buy 25,000 oranges.

More generally, any factor which causes demand to increase will cause the demand curve to shift to the right from D_1 to D_2 in the following diagram. If we take a price P on the vertical axis, we can see that the quantity demanded has increased from Q_1 to Q_2.

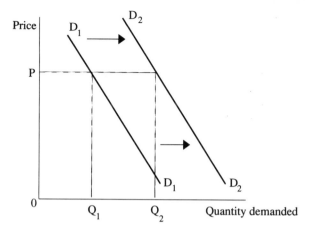

We should consider all those factors which are likely to result in an increase in the demand for a good at any price. An increase in income will result in an increase in the quantity demanded of most goods. There are, however, exceptions which are called inferior goods. These are goods which are only consumed because they are cheap compared to other goods. As soon as income rises sufficiently for them to afford them, consumers choose better goods.

The prices of other goods will influence the demand for a good. We divide 'all other goods' into two groups. *Substitute goods* are those that are alternatives for this good. If we looked at the demand for oil we would expect it to increase if the price of gas, a possible substitute, rose. *Complementary goods* are those that are consumed with this good. The demand for oil would be likely to increase if the price of cars fell. We would also expect demand for a good to increase if the number of consumers was increased or if consumers' tastes changed in favour of the good. When denim jeans became fashionable many more were sold than before.

Demand for a good may be reduced if circumstances change. In the following diagram, the demand curve has shifted from D_2 to D_1. At a price P, the demand for the good had fallen from Q_1 to Q_2.

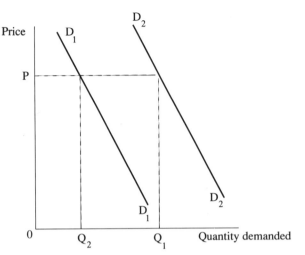

We would expect the demand for a good to be reduced at every price if:

a incomes of consumers fell so that they could afford less goods;

b incomes of consumers rose, if the good we are considering happens to be one of the exceptions, inferior goods;

c the price of a substitute good fell;

d the price of a complementary good rose;

e the population fell;

f consumers' tastes moved against this good, for example, because it became unfashionable.

It is very important for students to understand the difference between:

a a change in the demand for the good because *the price* has changed – this will always appear as a movement *along the demand curve*;

b a change in the demand for the good which results from a change *in some other factor* influencing the demand for the good – this will always appear as *a shift of the demand curve*.

In the following diagram, the demand curve is initially D_1. Any change in the quantity demanded will be a result of a change in price as long as all other factors remain unchanged. (This is known in economics as the 'ceteris paribus' assumption, which means 'all else being the same'. It is an expression which is used very frequently by economists). If the price rises from P_1 to P_2, demand will fall from Q_1 to Q_2 and this point is shown by the existing demand curve D_1. Suppose, however, that the fall in demand from Q_1 to Q_2 is a result of a fall in consumers' income and the price of the good is unchanged at P_1. This situation is shown by a shift of the demand curve from D_1 to D_2.

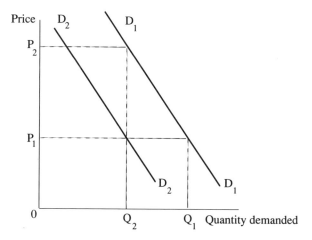

Supply

Willingness to sell

Demand is only one side of the coin. The demand which consumers express through their willingness to buy, needs to be met through the producers' willingness to supply a good. The combination of consumers and producers are the essential ingredients of a market.

A supply schedule and curve

The relationship between price and demand is normally inverse, and the relationship between price and supply is direct. As price rises so does supply. The higher the price, the more will be supplied. This can be illustrated through a supply schedule and then a supply curve, and to enable the development of a theory of relative prices, the market in oranges will again be examined. For convenience it will be assumed that the supply of oranges can be varied easily and quickly, although in real life this is, of course, not the case.

Supply schedule for oranges

Price (p)	Quantity supplied 000s
2	5
4	10
6	15
8	20
10	25
12	30

Supply curve for oranges

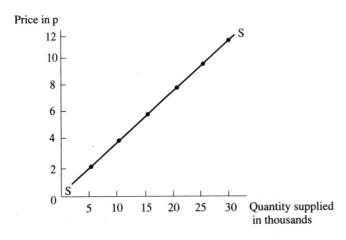

A supply curve usually slopes *upwards* from *left* to *right* because it is natural for producers to seek to maximise their profit. The higher the price they receive for their oranges, the more they are willing to supply.

As in the case of demand curves, supply curves are not always straight lines and a typical supply curve will be:

A supply curve

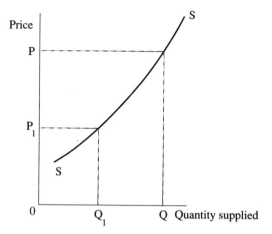

In this graph, price is represented by the letter 'P' and the quantity supplied by the letter 'Q', and so if the price falls from 0P to $0P_1$ the quantity supplied will fall from 0Q to $0Q_1$.

Additional factor

An additional factor in the case of supply curves which is not apparent from the usual graph is that the supply which is represented on the graph is not necessarily the entire stock of the good in question. The actual quantity supplied is only the amount of stock which is drawn into the market by the prevailing price. Producers may well keep some of their stock off the market until the prevailing price is more favourable to them.

Shifts in a supply curve

When another factor apart from price changes, the whole supply curve will shift one way or the other. When it shifts to the right – from S to S_1 – an overall *increase* in supply at each price is indicated, while a shift to the left – from S to S_2 – indicates an overall *decrease* in supply. An increase in supply usually follows a fall in the costs of production, while a decrease in supply follows a rise in the costs of production.

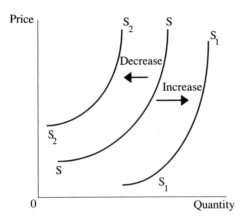

There are again various factors that may cause a change in the conditions of supply:

a changes in the prices of other commodities;

b changes in the state of technology;

c changes in the market structure (eg number of competitors operating in the market);

d changes in Government policy such as taxation and subsidies; and

e changes in the prices of the factors of production, ie the costs of production.

The last factor is very important and will be examined in more detail in the next chapter. However, it should be apparent that if the cost of producing a good rises, then for any given price, a lower quantity of the good will be supplied. The supply curve will have shifted upwards and to the left, because if the cost per unit of production rises by, say, 25 pence, then the producer will expect to receive 25 pence more through his selling price.

The price mechanism

The price

The one common factor in both demand and supply is *price*. It plays a fundamental role in the process of allocating resources within the economy, because the price of any particular good is determined through the interaction of supply and demand.

Equilibrium

When the demand curve which was developed in 'Demand' (above) is superimposed on the supply curve from 'Supply' (above) it can be seen that the supply of, and the demand for, oranges are only equal at one point (ie where the two lines intersect).

The price mechanism

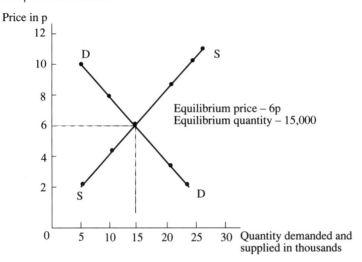

The market for oranges is in *equilibrium* at the point where 15,000 oranges are supplied at a price of 6 pence each. This exactly equals the demand at this price. This can be checked by turning back to the two schedules which were used to construct these two curves. It will be seen that there is no other price at which the quantity supplied exactly equals the quantity demanded.

The forces of supply and demand

If the amount demanded by consumers does not exactly equal the quantity that the producers are prepared to supply, then the market is said to be in a state of *disequilibrium* and the imbalance will cause the price to rise or fall until the market is brought back into equilibrium.

In the graph in 'Equilibrium' (above), for any price *above* 6 pence, the quantity supplied will exceed the quantity demanded, and so the producers will have to lower their selling price if they wish to sell all their stocks. On the other hand, for any price *below* 6 pence, the quantity demanded will exceed the quantity which producers are prepared to sell and so the price will automatically rise as it is 'bid up' by unsatisfied consumers.

The allocation of resources

This process of supply and demand being brought back into equilibrium is referred to as the *price mechanism*. It is of paramount importance in deciding how resources are allocated between different possible uses. If the demand for a good is greater than the current supply then the price will rise. This will encourage producers to divert resources away from production of other 'less profitable' goods into the production of the good which is in demand. In short, the price mechanism not only *allocates* goods between individual consumers; but it also helps to determine what are *actually produced*. This can be illustrated by examining the effects of the price mechanism in a number of specific examples.

Effect of an increase in demand

If the demand curve shifts upwards and to the right, then, assuming the conditions of supply remain unchanged, the equilibrium price will inevitably be affected. This will happen in two distinct stages.

The price mechanism – an increase in demand

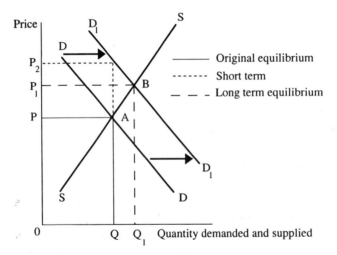

Before the shift in the demand curve, the price and quantity at which the market is in equilibrium for demand DD and supply SS is at the point A (ie where quantity 0Q is demanded and supplied at a price of 0P). The first stage of the price mechanism will happen immediately after the demand curve has shifted, because it is not usually possible to increase the supply of the good in the short term due to the practical problems of increasing production. The price will immediately rise to $0P_2$, because only the same amount of the good will be supplied while more is demanded. However, in the longer term this higher price will lead to an increase in the level of supply and so result in a new equilibrium price. This will be at the point of intersection of the *original* supply curve and the *new* demand curve –

point B. The new price will be $0P_1$ and the quantity demanded and supplied will be $0Q_1$, with the market once again in equilibrium.

The time that it takes for this change to occur will depend partly on the level of stocks which the producers were holding at the moment when the level of demand increased. If stocks were substantial, then the producers would be able to meet the increased demand quickly, simply by releasing stocks onto the market. However, if stocks were low, then the producers would have to increase their production in order to meet the increased demand, and, as will be noted in Chapter 4, this is not always a simple or quick process.

Effect of a decrease in demand

The opposite process of a *decrease* in demand also illustrates the operation of the price mechanism.

The price mechanism – a decrease in demand

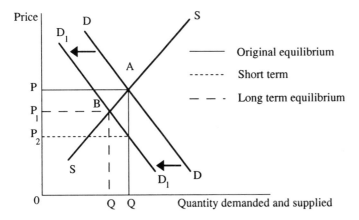

In the short term there is an *excess* of supply over demand. This results in the price falling to the level on the lower demand curve which corresponds to the original quantity supplied ($0P_2$). In the long term, producers would respond to this situation by reducing their production levels (or building up their stocks) so that the quantity supplied to the market is reduced to a level which matches the level of demand. This will raise the price slightly to $0P_1$. The *new* equilibrium position will represent both a lower price and a lower quantity demanded and supplied from the original equilibrium position.

Effect of an increase in supply

The role of the price mechanism in a situation where the conditions of *supply* change should also be examined and for convenience it will be assumed that the conditions of demand remain unchanged.

The price mechanism – an increase in supply

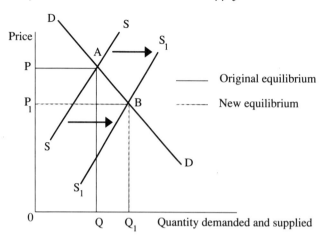

In the graph above, the quantity supplied has increased at all prices through the supply curve shifting from SS to S_1S_1. The price has fallen from $0P$ to $0P_1$ and the quantity demanded and supplied has risen from $0Q$ to $0Q_1$. In most instances this would be a fairly rapid and smooth process, because the level of consumer demand will tend to respond quickly to a change in price and so there is unlikely to be a short- and a long-term position.

Substitute goods and the price mechanism

Now that the simple operation of the price mechanism has been understood it is necessary to examine how the price mechanism operates on two (or more) goods at the same time. This will also illustrate why the price mechanism determines how scarce resources are allocated between different uses. This is illustrated most easily by choosing two goods that are direct or close substitutes for one another. (A substitute good is one that provides an adequate alternative to the original good in the eyes of the consumer. For instance, if butter is unobtainable or too expensive many people consider margarine an adequate alternative.)

So, if the general level of prosperity in the country rises, there is likely to be an increased demand for butter as it is considered to be an improvement on margarine. At the same time, assuming that the *total* level of demand for butter and margarine remains constant, then it is clear that as the demand for butter rises, the demand for its substitute (margarine) must fall. These events can be shown using simple supply and demand graphs (see overleaf).

The price mechanism

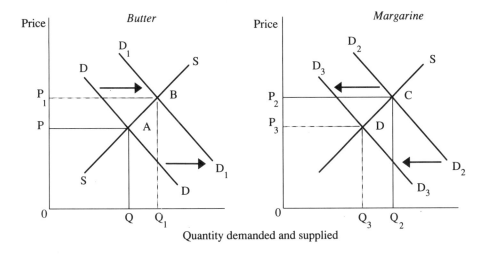

Quantity demanded and supplied

For convenience, the graphs only show the long-term position after the conditions of demand have changed. The price of butter has risen to $0P_1$ from $0P$, while the quantity demanded and supplied has increased to $0Q_1$ from $0Q$, and the opposite process has occurred in the market for margarine, with the price falling to $0P_3$ from $0P_2$ and the quantity demanded and supplied fully to $0Q_3$ from $0Q_2$. In short, after the conditions of demand have changed, the revised preferences of the consumers have effectively forced the producers to alter both their outputs and their prices. This has been achieved efficiently and quickly through the price mechanism. In this instance, more resources have been drawn into the production of butter in response to the increased level of demand, while fewer resources will be necessary for the production of margarine.

Profits play a very important part in this adjustment process, as they are directly affected by price movements. It is mainly because profits are rising or falling that producers increase or decrease production and so the price mechanism encourages certain industries to expand while other industries contract. In short, the price mechanism causes and reflects changes in the *relative prices* of goods. It can be said therefore, that *the price mechanism enables the economic system to adjust itself constantly to changes in the **relative** scarcity of different goods and that 'scarcity' is determined primarily by the respective levels of supply and demand.*

This type of adjustment could also have arisen from changes in the conditions of supply but in either instance the price mechanism ensures that resources are allocated primarily in accordance with the preferences that prevail at any given time in the market place.

Markets are interdependent

No single market is an island, because all markets are interdependent. For instance, if the price of wool in this country rises due to a shortage of sheep abroad, then the price of land for sheep-rearing will rise due to the increased demand for it. At the same time, the price paid to the men who look after sheep in this country will also rise. However, as people attempt to reduce their expenditure on higher-priced woollen products, it is probable that the price of possible substitutes (eg cotton products) will rise as people shift their demand away from woollen goods. This would then reduce the earnings of wool-spinners and reduce the profits of those clothing manufacturers who used wool.

Intervention in the market

Introduction

We have seen that the quantity of a good demanded depends on the preferences of consumers, their money incomes and the price of this good in relation to the prices and characteristics of all other goods. The supply of the good depends on: the availability, prices and productivity of factors of production (the costs of production per unit produced); the profits to be made by supplying alternative goods; and the price of the good. The price which influences both demand and supply is determined by the interaction of demand and supply.

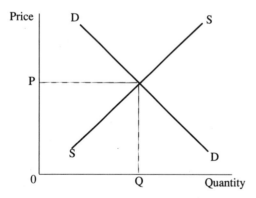

However, there are few markets that operate independently of intervention. There are many reasons for this intervention and many different methods of intervention.

Fluctuations in supply and buffer stocks

We have seen that supply can change and that this will, ceteris paribus, lead to fluctuations in price. The market shown in the following diagram is the world market for wheat. The supply in any year depends to a large extent on the weather. Thus G may be the quantity supplied in a good harvest year while B may be the quantity supplied in a bad harvest year. With the demand curve as shown, the supply G would be sold at a price per unit of L while the supply B would be sold at a unit price of H. Thus because of the varying weather conditions there may be substantial variations in price and quantity from one year to another and the price and quantity in any year may be uncertain until the harvest is gathered in.

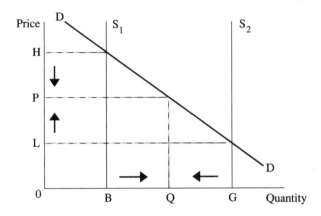

These fluctuations and the level of uncertainty make it difficult for consumers to make purchasing plans. The high prices of a bad harvest year may be too high for low income families so that they are unable to buy the good. The government can stabilise the market price and quantity and keep prices below the high level of a bad harvest year through a buffer stock scheme.

In the diagram above, the supply curves are shown as vertical to show that the supply of wheat cannot be increased in the short run (as is the case with much agricultural produce).

In the diagram above, the expected average supply of wheat over the next few years (assuming the normal variation in weather conditions over that time) is Q. This level of output will be sold at price P. Suppose there is a good harvest so that the amount of wheat produced is G. The government buys the excess over Q (G–Q) from the suppliers at the price P and keeps this quantity in stock. The supply actually reaching the market will then only be Q and the market price will be P. In a bad year, when output is only B, the government uses its stocks to boost market supply to Q (supplying Q–B from stocks) so that price and quantity remain at their normal level.

The problem with a buffer stock system is in anticipating average output correctly. In the following diagram, the government decides that the average output will be Q over the next few years and that the price should therefore be P. In fact, the average supply turns out to be Q_1 so the government finds that the level of stocks accumulated are never used up in the bad harvest years. For each year of the scheme the government will on average accumulate excess stocks of Q_1–Q. This is how the 'butter mountain' of the EU was accumulated.

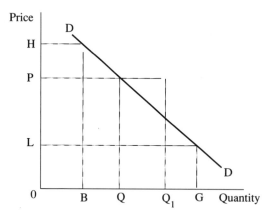

Buffer stocks used to stabilise suppliers' incomes

The buffer stock scheme used above can stabilise prices and market supply in the interests of consumers. However, it means that there may be great fluctuations in the incomes of producing firms. For example, in the diagram below, the price selected is P. However much output is produced, the firms will always receive a price of P for each unit produced. The output is either sold at this price to consumers or it is bought by the government and added to the stock. The income of the firms from selling these goods will be the output produced times the price at which it is sold. Thus in the following diagram, if the EU farmers produce Q output, the revenue they receive will be PQ (or the rectangle 0PAQ). If they have a good harvest and produce output G, their income will be PG (or the rectangle 0PEG).

The more they produce, the higher their income. As a result of the EU buffer stock scheme for farm produce, there has been substantial over-production of many products as the farmers seek the maximum benefit from the scheme. This is against the interests of consumers (who pay higher prices than they would if there were no buffer stock scheme) and taxpayers (who provide the funds which are used to buy the excess output from the farmers).

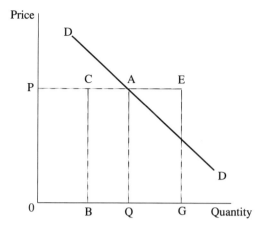

If there is a bad harvest, the income of the farmers falls to PB (or the rectangle 0PCB). With such a sharp fall in incomes, many farmers may wish to close down their farms. This will reduce the potential output of the farming industry so that the average output Q will not be produced in the future.

A buffer stock scheme can be used to stabilise the incomes of producers so that they neither make excessive incomes in good years nor disastrously low incomes in bad years. The necessary scheme to achieve stable incomes would be as shown in the following diagram. Suppose that the average output is going to be Q and that, given market demand, the market price will then be P. The average income of farmers would then be PQ (the rectangle 0PAQ). The government wishes to maintain incomes at this level. Suppose output is B, then the price needs to rise high enough so that P_bB = PQ (the rectangle 0PAQ has the same area as the rectangle $0P_bCB$). If the output is G then the price must fall low enough so that PgG = PQ (the rectangle 0PAQ has the same area as the rectangle $0P_gEG$). We can construct a demand curve such that the rectangle of income is the same whatever the output. This demand curve is a 'rectangular hyperbola'. Whatever the output, Q, G or B, the price will adjust so that price x quantity always gives the same total.

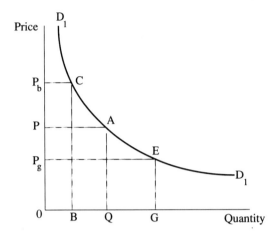

Now suppose that the actual demand curve is DD in the diagram below. The rectangular hyperbola which gives constant income is shown by D_1D_1. If output is B, the government should boost farmers' incomes by using government purchases to push the price up to P_b. If the output is G, the government should use the stocks to boost supply to bring the market price down to P_g.

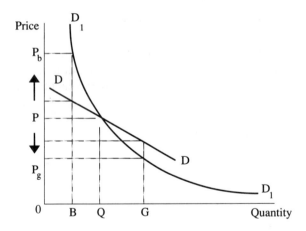

Notice that in this example the farmers' incomes are stabilised but market supply for consumers and price are even more unstable than they would be without government intervention. The government strategy depends on the relationship between the actual market demand curve and the rectangular hyperbola that gives stable incomes. In the following diagram, the actual demand curve is DD and the rectangular hyperbola is D_1D_1. In this case, the government should boost the price by buying stocks when output is G and should use stocks to depress the price when output is B.

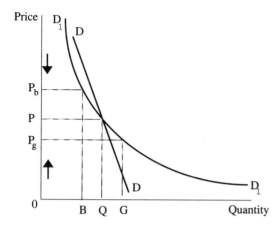

In this example, the government policy to stabilise farmers' incomes also leads to a greater stability of price and market supply than if there were no government intervention.

Buffer stocks and fluctuations in demand

In the following diagram, the demand curve is shown shifting from DD to D_1D_1. As a result the equilibrium output for this industry falls from Q to B. Firms will have to cut production or close down and make employees redundant. In a subsequent period, the demand might shift back again to DD so that equilibrium output increases back to Q. However, the industry may be slow to react to the changed circumstances. There will be delays before firms can set up, expand production and employ new staff.

The government may wish to produce more stable conditions in this industry. Suppose it is decided that the ideal output of the industry is Q so supply is to be maintained at this level. The supply curve is shown fixed at Q. If demand is D_1D_1, the government should buy stocks of Q–B so that output is maintained at Q. If demand rises to D_2D_2, the government should release G–Q stocks so that industry output is maintained at Q.

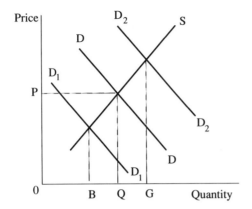

Notice that with this scheme price and firms' incomes are stabilised, with supply responding to changes in demand because of the use of government buffer stocks.

Limits on supply

Where there are many suppliers in an industry, they may produce a level of supply which is so great that price is very low and the incomes of suppliers are correspondingly low. For example, the large number of small farmers in the USA were producing so much agricultural output that agricultural prices were very low and the living standards of many small farmers were at poverty level.

The government reduced supply by reducing the amount of land under cultivation and thus the number of farmers. The farmers were paid compensation for their land. As a result of this policy, the supply of agricultural output was reduced and the prices rose, increasing the incomes of the remaining farmers.

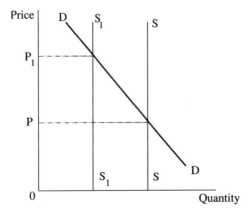

The price mechanism

A very similar strategy was adopted by the oil producing states in the 1970s when they collectively limited their output of oil so that the price of oil was forced up, increasing the incomes of OPEC (Organisation of Petroleum Exporting Countries) members.

Subsidies on goods and services

The effect of a subsidy on a market price of a good is shown below. Suppose that the following table gives the existing supply and price relationship before the subsidy is applied. For example, at a market price of £4, the firm will supply 10 units of the good.

Market price	Quantity supplied before subsidy (units)	Quantity supplied at each market price after the subsidy of £2 per unit is introduced
£1	4	8
£2	6	10
£3	8	12
£4	10	14
£5	12	16
£6	14	18
£7	16	?
£8	18	?

Now suppose that the government puts a subsidy on the good of £2 per unit sold. What this means is that, for each unit sold, the government will pay the firm £2 in addition to the price paid per unit by the consumer. So if the firm sells units at a market price of £4, it will receive an additional £2 from the government. Its total revenue per unit sold will then be £6.

Since the firm is now receiving £6 when the market price is £4, the firm will expand supply to 14 units at the market price of £4. Similarly it will supply not 14 units when the market price is £6 but 18 units because the firm is actually receiving £8 including the subsidy of £2 per unit. At any market price, firms will supply as if the market price were £2 higher.

The following diagram illustrates this. SS shows the original supply curve before the subsidy and S_1S_1 the supply curve when the subsidy is paid. Notice that the supply curve has shifted down vertically by £2, the amount of the subsidy per unit.

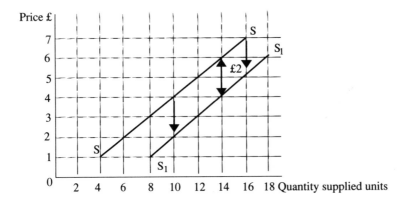

We can now examine the effect of a subsidy of this type on the market equilibrium price and quantity.

Market price	Quantity supplied before subsidy (units)	Quantity supplied after subsidy (units)	Quantity demanded (units)
£1	4	8	16
£2	6	10	14
£3	8	12	12
£4	10	14	10
£5	12	16	8
£6	14	18	6
£7	16	?	4
£8	18	?	2

Before the subsidy is used, we can see that the market equilibrium price is £4 where quantity demanded and quantity supplied are equal at 10 units. After the subsidy is applied, the new market equilibrium price is £3 where quantity demanded and quantity supplied are equal at 12 units.

The following diagram illustrates the same demand and supply curves and the change in market equilibrium. Firms are now prepared to supply an extra 4 units at the existing market equilibrium price of £4. (Supply has expanded from 10 units to 14 units at that price.) Consumers will only want to buy 10 units at a market price of £4. The excess supply of 4 units causes the market price to fall with demand increasing and supply reducing until a new equilibrium is reached at £3.

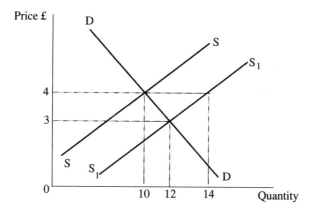

So, the effect of the subsidy has been to reduce equilibrium price and increase the market equilibrium quantity.

We can list a number of reasons for this government policy of putting a subsidy on a good.

First, the good is a *merit good*. The demand curve reflects the consumers' preferences for this good. Merit goods are goods that society thinks everyone ought to have regardless of whether they are wanted by each individual. Examples of merit goods are education and health. Since society (represented by the government) often places a higher value on these goods than the individual, it follows that individual choice within a free market economy will lead to a different allocation from the allocation which society/government wants. In order to encourage more consumption of merit goods they are usually subsidised by the government, often to the extent of 100 per cent.

Secondly, when consumers choose to buy a certain quantity of a good, they make this decision on the basis of their own preferences for this good compared with all other goods. They do not consider the effect that this decision has on others.

For example, suppose a householder were considering planting roses in his front garden. He will buy the roses on the basis of his own preference for them in relation to their price. He will, rationally, ignore the potential enjoyment to his neighbours of seeing the roses in his garden. This enjoyment would be the *external benefit* resulting from his decision to buy the roses. (The benefit is external in that it comes to individuals who are not directly involved in the decision to buy the roses.)

Since the state is interested in the utility of all consumers, it will want to encourage the consumption of goods that produce external benefits. A subsidy on the good would have this effect. A subsidy on roses would lower the price and therefore increase consumption.

Other examples of goods producing external benefits would be the restoration of houses of historical interest and the consumption of education and medical treatment. These last two are greatly subsidised in Britain. Education produces external benefits in that the better educated the population, the greater the productivity of the workforce and the more goods and services are produced for us all to consume. Medical treatment produces a more productive workforce and also controls the spread of infectious disease.

Thirdly, many goods are subsidised in order to increase the real incomes of the consumers of those goods. If goods are cheaper, consumers are able to buy more goods and services with any given money income so their *real income* (their ability to consume goods and services) is increased.

Additionally, the government may subsidise a good so that it becomes sufficiently cheap for consumers who could not otherwise afford them to buy these goods. For example, some families may be unable to afford to send their children to school at the current price for education. The subsidy will, by reducing the price, enable these families to buy education for their children.

The government may also be concerned to *re-distribute income* from rich to poor thus creating a greater equality of real incomes among consumers. One way of doing this is to use money paid in taxes by the rich to subsidise goods typically consumed by the poor. Goods which are typically consumed by the poor are *inferior goods* (see Chapter 3). An example would be public transport, especially bus services. Senior Citizens travel free on buses in the Greater London area. This naturally increases their real income at the expense of the tax payers who cover the cost of losses made by the operators.

Many goods which are subsidised (housing, education, medical treatment) are not specifically inferior goods and are consumed as much or even more by the rich. However, since the rich pay more taxes than the poor, there is still generally an element of income redistribution in the subsidies on these goods.

Fourthly, some suppliers of goods suffer from *fluctuations in the demand* for those goods (see above). This causes disruption in the industry as shown in the following diagram. When demand shifts from DD to D_1D_1, the equilibrium output falls from Q to Q_1. In a subsequent period, demand may return to DD so output must be expanded again. This scale of adjustment may be beyond the industry without widespread firm closures and unemployment followed by delays before the industry readjusts again to greater demand. Capital goods industries (for example, the building industry) are particularly vulnerable to this type of problem.

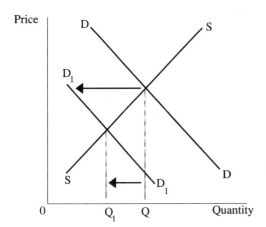

The government can stabilise this industry by using subsidies. In the diagram below, when demand is contracting from DD to D_1D_1, the government puts subsidies on the output of the industry. As shown in the following diagram, this can bring industry output back to its equilibrium level at Q. The increase in quantity demanded in response to the subsidy (moving along the demand curve D_1D_1) counteracts the shift of the demand curve from DD to D_1D_1.

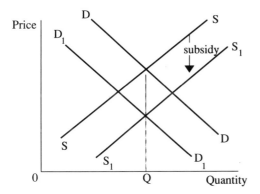

Fifthly, the government may wish to *maintain or increase employment* in an industry. The government has a basic concern for the level of employment nationally, locally and in industry. Thus it might want to boost the level of employment of workers in a particular industry, because it may be concerned about the level of unemployment in that industry, and about the high level of unemployment in areas where that industry is concentrated.

One way of doing this is to subsidise the good which those workers produce. The subsidy will result in increased demand for the good. The greater the demand, the more workers will be employed in producing it.

Taxes on goods

The imposition of a tax on a good has the opposite affect to the subsidy discussed above. Given the existing supply schedule which follows, firms will be prepared to supply, for example, 10 units if the market price is £4. Now suppose the government imposes a sales tax of £2 per unit. This means that for every unit sold, the firm must pay £2 over to the government. Thus, with a selling price of £4, the firm will be left with only £2. As a result, the imposition of the tax will reduce the amount that firms are prepared to supply at any market price. After the imposition of the tax, the firms will only supply 6 units at a market price of £4.

Market price	Quantity supplied before tax is imposed (units)	Quantity supplied after tax is imposed (units)
£1	4	?
£2	6	?
£3	8	4
£4	10	6
£5	12	8
£6	14	10
£7	16	12

In the following diagram, the supply curve is shifted to the left as a result of the imposition of a tax. It shifts vertically by the amount of the tax per unit.

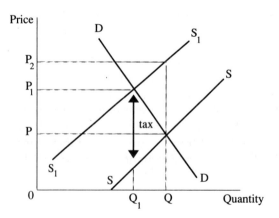

At the existing equilibrium level of output Q, firms will want to be paid a higher price (P_2). Consumers are not prepared to buy Q output at price P_2. The firms will find that the new equilibrium in the market is when price is P_1 and quantity is Q_1. Compared with the original equilibrium, the imposition of the tax will typically increase the market price and reduce the market equilibrium output.

We can list a number of reasons for imposing a sales tax on a good. Firstly, the good may be a *demerit good*. The government feels that consumers overestimate the utility of this good to them. An example would be alcohol. Consumers may buy and consume too much alcohol given the health risks involved. They underestimate these health risks. The government discourages consumption by imposing a sales tax. Another example of a demerit good is cigarettes.

Secondly, the consumption of the good may produce *external costs*. When a consumer decides to smoke a cigarette he rationally considers only the expected enjoyment of the cigarette compared to the price of that cigarette. However, the smoking of that cigarette will force others to breathe polluted air. The cost imposed on these others is the external cost. Since the government is concerned with the utility of all consumers, it will want to discourage the consumption of cigarettes by imposing a sales tax.

Other examples of goods producing these consumption externalities are alcohol and petrol. A car driver who has drunk too much alcohol may impose excessive costs on other road users by endangering their lives. The use of petrol in cars imposes noxious fumes on residents and road users in the surrounding area. The lower rates of taxation on lead-free petrol is designed to *raise* the consumption of this fuel by motorists.

Thirdly, the government may tax a good in order to encourage the consumption of substitute goods (see Chapter 3). The most obvious example of this is in discouraging the consumption of imported goods in order to increase the consumption of domestically produced goods. The sales tax would be imposed on the imported goods. This increases their price so that consumers tend to switch to the substitute goods which are domestically produced.

Another example of this is the use of a tax on labour to encourage firms to buy the alternative capital goods. These factors of production are substitutes for each other. The higher the price of labour, the more firms will want to use capital goods.

Fourthly, taxes on goods become *revenue* for the government. They may use sales taxes as a general source of revenue. For example, the taxes on alcohol, cigarettes and petrol all provide substantial revenues for the government. They use this revenue to add to the general funds for all types of government expenditure.

The government may also collect sales taxes in order to pay for particular services. For example, petrol taxes are collected from car drivers and these funds are used to pay for part of the building and maintenance of the roads that motorists use.

The taxes on goods can also be used as a way of *re-distributing income* from rich to poor. The government can put a tax on goods which are typically consumed by the rich rather than the poor. Examples of such goods are cigars, champagne, fur coats, Rolls Royce cars. The revenue collected comes from the rich since they are the consumers buying these goods. The revenue could then be used to provide services specifically for the poor, the sick or the elderly.

Imposition of a maximum price

In the following diagram, the market equilibrium price is P. The government may fix a maximum price for this good which is below this equilibrium price. This maximum price is P_m in the diagram below.

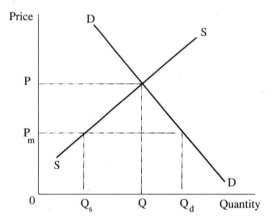

At this lower price P_m, the demand increases from the equilibrium of Q to Q_d. At the same time, the quantity supplied falls to Q_s. The imposition of a maximum price below the equilibrium will therefore impose disequilibrium on the market. The price cannot legally rise above P_m, but at that price the quantity demanded exceeds the quantity supplied. The disequilibrium will be dealt with in a variety of ways.

Firms may use a rationing system to share a supply of Q_s out among the consumers who want to buy Q_d. The rationing may be 'first come, first served', or supplies going to favoured customers, or a queueing system where all consumers eventually get their turn of X units per customer whatever their individual demand. Alternatively, the suppliers and consumers may trade illegally at a price above the legal maximum price. This is known as a 'black market'. In this illegal market, prices are likely to be far higher than the original equilibrium price P because of the reduced supply of the good.

There are a number of reasons for a government imposition of a maximum price below the equilibrium.

The price mechanism

First, the government may aim to reduce the price that consumers pay for the good in order to raise the real income of these consumers. An example of such a policy is the controls on the maximum price of private sector rental housing which have been in place in the UK for most of this century. Rent controls were first introduced after the First World War, in an attempt to ensure that rents were reasonable and affordable. These controls have continued in one form or another until the 1988 Housing Act came into force. The decades of maximum price controls had resulted in a severe drop in the available private sector rental housing. What was available was in very short supply, and showed all the characteristics of a black market (prices much higher than the legal maximum; allocation by seller's preferences).

The Thatcher government wished to ensure a greater supply of private sector rental housing. The 1988 Housing Act removed some of the previous controls (including the maximum price) in order to achieve this.

Secondly, the government may also fix maximum price in order to check excessive profits being made by firms supplying the good. Price controls were put on many products during the Second World War. The war and particularly the blockade of British ports had greatly reduced the supply of food. As a result the equilibrium price rose dramatically. In the following diagram, the reduction in supply from SS to S_1S_1 causes a price increase from P to P_1.

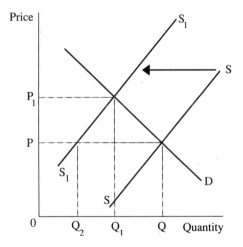

The suppliers of food products in this country were therefore able to make greatly increased profits. These profits were seen as being made at the expense of the consumers who were forced to pay the much higher prices.

The government fixed prices at the pre-war level. The maximum price was therefore P. This further reduced the supply as domestic firms reduced their output along the new supply curve S_1S_1. A system of rationing had to be operated with everyone having ration cards which allowed each consumer X units each. In addition, a thriving 'black market' operated with goods trading at illegal prices.

Imposition of a minimum price

In the following diagram, the market equilibrium price is P at which price the quantity demanded is equal to the quantity supplied at Q. The government may fix a minimum price for this market at P_m which is above the current equilibrium price P.

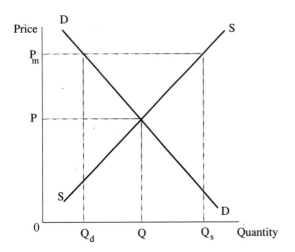

At this higher price, the supply in this market will increase to Q_s while demand is reduced to Q_d. The price control therefore imposes disequilibrium on this market with price held at a minimum level which gives excess supply.

The obvious example of this type of policy is minimum wage legislation. The firms will employ more people the lower the wage. As the wage rises from P to P_m, the demand for labour (the number of people the firm will employ) falls from Q to Q_d. At the same time, the higher wage level will attract more people to seek the jobs. (The supply of labour increases from Q to Q_s). There are thus many more people seeking jobs than there are jobs available.

Minimum wage legislation can be introduced to increase the wages of low-paid workers so that their standard of living rises. It benefits the workers who are able to get jobs at the now higher wage. However, $Q-Q_d$ workers could have had jobs at a lower wage of P and are now unemployed. They will, ceteris paribus, be worse off as a result of this policy.

Rationing systems will have to be introduced to reconcile the greater supply of labour (Q_s) with the reduced availability of jobs (Q_d). Again this may involve a 'first come, first served' system or discrimination as employers give jobs to favoured employees. An illegal market may develop where workers offer to work at lower than the legal minimum wages in order to get a job. Employers will obviously gain from this 'black market' in labour since they will be paying lower wages.

Note: a minimum price will have no effect on the market if it is fixed at or below the market equilibrium price. Similarly, a maximum price will have no effect on the market if it is fixed at or above the market equilibrium price.

The effect of advertising on demand

The government may use advertising to change consumer preferences for a good. In the following diagram, the demand for cigarettes is shown by DD so that, given market supply SS and the resulting equilibrium price of P, Q cigarettes are consumed.

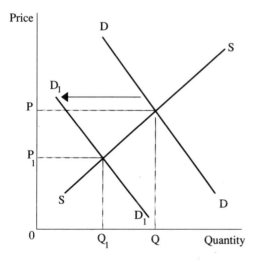

The government introduces an advertising campaign which points out the health hazards of smoking. As a result, consumer demand is reduced to D_1D_1 and market equilibrium consumption falls to Q_1.

Similarly, advertising can be used to encourage consumption of a good. The advantages of dental care and treatment have been advertised by the government. As shown in the following diagram, the consumption of dental care and treatment at any price would therefore tend to increase.

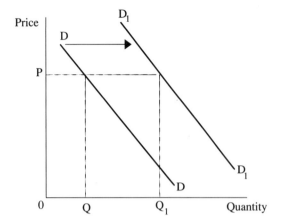

Firms naturally use advertising to promote their products. For example, the manufacturers of butter may produce advertisements arguing that butter is a wholesome, traditional, healthy product. This, if successful, will persuade consumers to buy more butter at any market price.

Firms may also use advertising to reduce the demand for substitute goods in order to promote the consumption of their own goods. For example, the margarine manufacturers have financed a great deal of medical research which argues that butter is full of poly-saturated fats which are thought to contribute to heart disease. If this persuades consumers that butter is bad for them, they will buy margarine (a close substitute) instead. This boosts the demand for margarine at any price.

Legal controls on consumption

The government may also legislate to limit or prohibit the consumption of goods. The consumption of alcohol in certain circumstances is limited by legislation. Thus, while it is not an offence to drink any amount of alcohol as long as the individual then stays quietly at home, there are laws against driving while having more than a prescribed maximum of alcohol in the blood.

In the following diagram, an individual's consumption of alcohol within a few hours of driving a car is limited to Q_x; given the market price of alcohol and the consumer's preferences, he would otherwise consume Q_e.

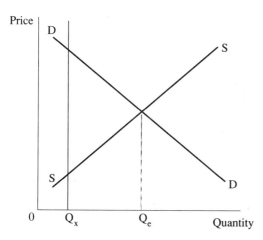

There are some goods whose consumption is illegal. Examples are the so-called 'hard' and 'soft' drugs. Here the consumer's consumption is limited to zero consumption in the diagram above, even though his preferences would indicate that he would buy a positive amount of this good at a prevailing market price. (Trading in such goods is, of course, illegal, but a market does exist with an equilibrium price indicated by the demand and supply conditions.)

The government may also legislate to ensure some minimum level of consumption. For example, full-time education for children between the ages of 5 and 16 years is compulsory in Britain. Thus, this minimum consumption of education services is required by law.

Questions for review

1 What does a demand curve represent?

 What does a supply curve represent?

 What does the point of intersection of the demand and supply curves represent?

2 Why do demand curves normally slope downwards?

 Are there any exceptions to this?

3 Why do supply curves normally slope upwards?

 What would a vertical supply curve represent?

4 What are the determinants of demand?

5 What are the determinants of supply?

6 Give some examples of goods which are substitutes for each other.

7 Give some examples of goods which are complements to each other.

8 Explain why governments often intervene in agricultural markets.

   Explain some of the problems of buffer stock schemes.

9 Why might the government wish to subsidise some goods and services?

   What would be the effect of such a subsidy?

   What goods and services might be involved?

10 Why might the government wish to tax some goods and services in particular?

   What would be the effect of such a tax?

   Give some examples.

11 Why might the government wish to place a maximum price on a good or service?

   What would be the effect of such a price ceiling?

12 Why might the government wish to place a minimum price on a good or service?

   What would be the effect of such a price floor?

13 What does the expression 'ceteris paribus' mean?

The theory of demand | 3

Elasticity of demand   55

Consumer's demand   68

Elasticity of demand

Introduction

The previous chapter discussed elementary supply and demand analysis and developed a number of guidelines about supply and demand curves and the price mechanism. However, the only firm rule that was developed was a general one which stated that *'as the price of a good falls, the demand for it rises'*. This general rule only becomes useful if we know *how much* demand will respond to a change in price.

Suppose London Transport were considering reducing bus fares in an attempt to increase the number of passengers travelling on buses. They would want to know whether a 10 per cent reduction in fares would result in an increase of 5 per cent or 50 per cent in the number of passengers. They need, therefore, to know the *responsiveness* of demand to the change in price.

Elasticity of demand

The measure that economists use to indicate the responsiveness of demand to changes in price is the *elasticity of demand*. This is established by comparing the amount by which the price has changed (10 per cent or 50 per cent) with the resulting amount by which the quantity demanded has changed (10 per cent or 50 per cent).

$$\text{The elasticity of demand } (E_d) = (-1) \frac{\% \text{ change in quantity}}{\% \text{ change in price}}$$

In mathematical terminology, the elasticity of demand is negative as shown here. This is because an *increase* in price is accompanied by a *decrease* in demand; and a *decrease* in price is accompanied by an *increase* in demand. Mathematically, because one factor is negative, the fraction itself must be negative. However, this observation is not relevant to this level of study and so in what follows the negative sign will be ignored.

Types of elasticity

We can define a variety of degrees of responsiveness to demand to changes in price and then use the concepts of elasticity of demand to identify them.

Suppose demand were completely unresponsive to changes in price. Demand is exactly the same whether the firm charges a very high or very low price. The demand curve would be vertical as shown in the following diagram. Demand is then said to be *completely* or *perfectly inelastic*.

If we calculated the elasticity of demand using the formula below the answer would always be zero.

$$E_d = \frac{\% \text{ change in quantity}}{\% \text{ change in price}} = \frac{0}{X}$$

Demand might alternatively be extremely responsive to changes in price. Suppose the firm could sell an infinite quantity of the good at a particular price but none at all at any higher price. The demand curve would be horizontal as shown in the following diagram. If price rose from P to any higher price, demand falls from infinity to zero and so is extremely responsive to price changes.

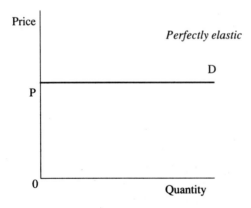

Demand is then said to be *perfectly elastic*. If we calculated elasticity using the formula:

$$E_d = \frac{\text{\% change in quantity}}{\text{\% change in price}}$$

$$= \frac{\text{infinity}}{x}$$

ie E_d = infinity

In between these two extremes is the normal demand curve. A change in price results in a change in the quantity demanded by something between zero and infinity. The greater the reaction of demand to some change in price, the more elastic the demand curve is said to be. The smaller the reaction, the more inelastic the demand curve. The degree of elasticity is indicated by the formula:

$$E_d = \frac{\text{\% change in quantity}}{\text{\% change in price}}$$

Suppose we consider two situations where the price of a good is reduced by 10 per cent. In the first situation, the 10 per cent reduction in price results in a 10 per cent increase in quantity demanded. Demand is not very responsive to changes in prices. Calculating elasticity will give us $E_d = 1$. In the second situation, the 10 per cent reduction in price results in a 50 per cent increase in the quantity demanded. Demand is much more responsive to changes in price. Calculating elasticity will give us $E_d = 5$.

The more responsive demand is to changes in price, the higher the value of the elasticity. Very elastic demand curves have elasticities of high numbers (approaching infinity which is the extreme case of high elasticity). Very inelastic demand curves will have elasticities of low numbers (approaching zero which is the extreme case of inelasticity).

The degrees of elasticity between zero and infinity are categorised into three types. First, when the change in price results in a *less than proportional* change in the quantity demanded, demand is said to be *relatively inelastic*. A 10 per cent increase in price might result, for example, in only a 5 per cent reduction in quantity demanded ($E_d = 1/2$). Demand would be defined as relatively inelastic if demand had been reduced by anything *less* than 10 per cent. (The E_d will be less than 1.)

Secondly, when the change in price results in a *more than proportional* change in the quantity demanded, demand is said to be *relatively elastic*. A 10 per cent increase in price might result, for example, in a 20 per cent reduction in quantity demanded ($E_d = 2$). Demand would be defined as relatively elastic if demand had been reduced by anything *more* than 10 per cent. (E_d will be greater than 1.)

Thirdly, if the change in price results in an *exactly proportional* change in the quantity demanded, demand is said to have *unit elasticity*. A 10 per cent increase in price would result in a 10 per cent reduction in quantity demanded ($E_d = 1$).

Summary of different types of elasticity

It will be useful at this stage to summarise the text so far by listing the types of elasticity which can exist:

Numerical value	General description	Economic terminology
Zero	Quantity demanded does not change at all despite changes in price	Perfectly or completely inelastic
Greater than zero, but less than one	Quantity demanded changes by a smaller percentage than price changes	Inelastic
One	Quantity demanded changes by the same percentage as price changes	Unit elasticity
Greater than one, but less than infinity	Quantity demanded changes by a larger percentage than price changes	Elastic
Infinity	People will buy all they can at a given price, but none at all at a slightly higher price	Perfectly or completely elastic

Slopes do not show degree of elasticity

An inexperienced student may be tempted to suggest that the degree of change could be judged from the gradient of any given demand curve, but this is not necessarily true.

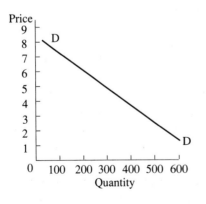
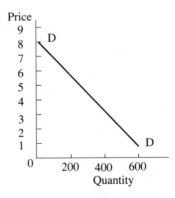

It would appear in the first instance that the graph on the right shows that the quantity demanded increases relatively little as the price falls and that the graph on the left shows that demand increases a great deal for every small fall in price.

However, a more detailed examination will reveal that the numbers plotted along the horizontal axis are the same. The difference is that the scale on the left has been *compressed* to give the scale of the right. In short, both the graphs show the same demand curve and so it is incorrect to assume that the slope of a demand curve *necessarily* indicates the responsiveness of demand to a change in price.

Absolute vs relative changes

It is very important when discussing elasticity not to confuse *absolute* changes in either price or demand with *relative* changes. Suppose we are told that the price of petrol has risen by £1 per gallon while the price of cars has also risen by £1. While both prices have risen by the same absolute amount, the proportional change is much greater for the good with the lower starting price, petrol.

If we were then told that the demand for both goods had halved as a result of the change in price, we are obviously not looking at similar elasticities. Elasticity is much higher for cars since a smaller percentage increase in price results in a comparable reduction in demand. Comparing the absolute changes in price leads to the wrong conclusions about relative elasticities.

The importance of concentrating on proportionate not absolute changes is demonstrated by looking at elasticity at different points along a straight-line demand curve. At each point the same absolute adjustment is made to price and this results in the same absolute change in quantity demanded but the elasticity is different at each point.

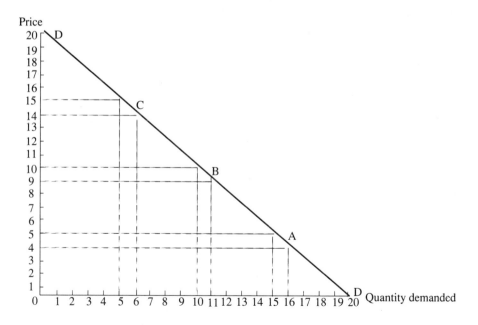

Elasticity at point A
The proportionate change in price = 1/5
The proportionate change in quantity demanded = 1/15
Therefore, the elasticity of demand = $\dfrac{1/15}{1/5}$ = ⅓ or 0.33 (ie inelastic)

Elasticity at point B
The proportionate change in price = 1/10
The proportionate change in quantity demanded = 1/10
Therefore, the elasticity of demand = $\dfrac{1/10}{1/10}$ = 1 (ie unity)

Elasticity at point C
The proportionate change in price = 1/15
The proportionate change in quantity demanded = 1/5
Therefore, the elasticity of demand = $\dfrac{1/5}{1/15}$ = 3 (ie elastic)

It can be seen, therefore, that the elasticity of a demand curve can vary over its length. The above analysis illustrates the principle of point elasticity.

The connection between elasticity and revenue

The concept of elasticity has an important practical application. The elasticity of demand determines what happens to the total revenue of the firm when price is adjusted. If London Transport were considering reducing fares their interest is more likely to be in increasing the revenue received from selling tickets rather than in the number of passengers travelling by bus.

Suppose they are considering reducing the fare per passenger mile from 20p to 10p. If demand is very elastic, there will be a large increase in the number of passengers and an increase in the revenue raised from fares. For example:

Fare per passenger mile x Number of passengers = Total Revenue

    20p   5,000   £1,000
    10p   12,000 £1,200

If, on the other hand, demand had been quite inelastic, revenue would have been reduced as a result of the fare reduction. For example:

Fare per passenger mile x Number of passengers = Total Revenue

    20p   5,000   £1,000
    10p   7,000   £700

This information can also be shown in a diagram. The left-hand diagram shows the increase in revenue that results from the price reduction with the more elastic demand curve. The right-hand diagram shows the reduction in revenue that results from a price reduction with a less elastic demand curve.

Elastic	Inelastic
Total revenue At A = 20p x 5,000 = £1,000 At B = 10p x 12,000 = £1,200	Total revenue At A = 20p x 5,000 = £1,000 At B = 10p x 7,000 = £700

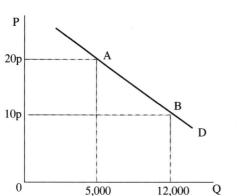 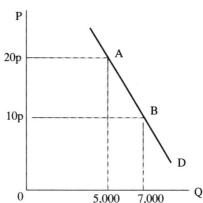

Calculations of elasticity from revenue changes

In the 'objective test' paper for A-level, students are likely to be asked to identify elasticity from a demand schedule. The formula for expressing elasticity is, of course,

$$E_d = \frac{\% \text{ change in quantity demanded}}{\% \text{ change in price}}$$

However, this formula can only be depended on to produce the correct answer when price is changed only marginally (that is, by tiny amounts). It often produces the wrong answer if the price change is larger.

Students should, for this type of question, deduce elasticity from the effect of price changes on the revenue of the firm. This method will always produce the correct answer.

The demand schedule might be shown as follows:

Price £	Quantity demanded
10	120
8	120
6	150
4	225
2	500
2	700

Consider what happens when price is reduced from £8 to £6. The quantity demanded increases from 120 to 150. The total revenue therefore reduced from £960 (£8 x 120) to £900 (£6 x 150). The firm have reduced the price of the good but have found that there is little reaction from the quantity demanded so that total revenue is reduced. Demand is relatively inelastic or unresponsive to changes in price.

If the firm had increased the price from £6 to £8, there would only be a small reduction in quantity demanded so that the total revenue increased. Demand is relatively inelastic. The rule is that *demand is relatively inelastic when firms find that reductions in price lead to a lower total revenue and increases in price lead to a higher total revenue.*

We must use the same method to determine a situation of unit elasticity. *Demand has unit elasticity when changes in price result in no change in total revenue.* Whether the price is £6 or £4, the total revenue is £900 (£6 x 150 and £4 x 225). When the price is reduced from £4 to £2, there is a substantial increase in the quantity demanded so that total revenue increases from £900 to £1,000 (£4 x 225 to £2 x 500). The demand is relatively elastic or responsive to changes in price. If the price increases from £2 to £4, there is a large reduction in quantity demanded so that there is a reduction in the total revenue. The rule is that *demand is relatively elastic when reductions in price lead to greater total revenue and increases in price lead to lower total revenue.*

Cases of perfectly inelastic demand and perfectly elastic demand can be identified directly from the demand schedule. Demand is *perfectly inelastic* when there is no change in the quantity demanded in spite of some change in price. When the price is reduced from £10 to £8 or increased from £8 to £10, the demand stays at 120 units. Demand is *perfectly elastic* when the quantity demanded may vary from zero to infinity at a particular price. For the firm this means that they can sell any quantity at that price. In this schedule this appears to be true when demand can be 500 or 700 at the price of £2.

Elasticities and goods

There are certain goods which people tend to want whatever their cost. When the price of food rises people will still continue to buy it. Conversely, if the price of food falls, it is unlikely that people will buy much more of it. So, it should be clear that food will have an inelastic demand, because the quantity demanded does not change very much even when its price changes. In short, the necessities of life will usually have inelastic demand curves. However, a particular *type* or *make* of food may have an *elastic* demand. If the price of bread rises significantly, people may well eat less bread and more potatoes.

With goods which are not necessities, people will probably consider the cost quite carefully before buying them and so such goods will tend to have elastic demand curves. Luxuries, by definition, will always have elastic demand curves, because if the price of a luxury good rises or falls, the demand for it will vary quite considerably.

However, the elasticity of demand for a product is not a static or rigid concept, because as was noted above, a demand curve can have different degrees of elasticity over its length, and it is now necessary to develop that observation.

When enough of a good has been bought to satisfy the usual requirements of an individual consumer his demand for more of that good will be negligible. For instance, if he regularly drank one pint of milk a day, his demand for that pint would be relatively *inelastic* – he would tend to buy it whatever the price. However, his demand for an extra pint would be relatively *elastic*, because he would have had enough milk to satisfy his usual requirements, and so he would not buy another pint unless its price fell considerably and made it more attractive relative to other possible goods.

Influences on elasticity

We can list the factors which will explain why some goods will generally have high elasticities of demand while other goods have lower elasticities of demand.

Availability of substitutes

This is the most important influence on price elasticity of demand. Suppose that a good has many close substitutes. If the price of the good rises, consumers will switch to the alternative goods which are very similar but whose prices are unchanged. There will be a very large drop in demand for the good whose price goes up. The price elasticity of demand is high. Similarly, if the price of this good fell, the consumers of the many other similar goods will buy this good instead since it is now cheaper. Demand will greatly increase and the price elasticity of demand is high.

We can compare this with a good which has no close substitutes. When its price goes up consumers have no option of switching to close substitutes so the elasticity will tend to be low. Similarly, if the price falls, there are no consumers of similar goods who will now switch to this good so elasticity tends to be low.

We will see in Chapter 6 that where a firm operates in a market in which there are a large number of competing firms producing identical goods (perfect competition), the firm will face a perfectly elastic demand curve. In monopoly (where there is only one firm operating in the market with no competing firms producing similar goods), demand will tend to be relatively inelastic.

Students should also note that the more precisely a good is specified, the greater the price elasticity of demand. The wider the definition of the good, the more of the potential substitutes have been included in the definition of the good so the elasticity of demand is lower. For example, the elasticity of demand for one soap powder (Persil) will be very high because there are so many alternative brands. However, if we look at the elasticity of demand for soap powder (including all these brands) the elasticity of demand will be lower. There are many substitutes for Persil but few for soap powder.

Time

The price elasticity of demand will tend to increase as time passes after the price increase. For example, when OPEC increased the price of oil in 1974, the demand was initially very inelastic. People with high fuel consumption motor cars and no alternative means of transport could only reduce their petrol consumption by a small amount. As time passed, people bought lower fuel consumption cars and found alternative means of transport so the price elasticity of demand increased.

Expenditure as a proportion of consumers' incomes

Suppose a consumer spends one per cent of his income on a good and the price of that good goes up by one per cent. The consumer's real income has only been reduced by 0.01 per cent and he is hardly likely to notice or react to the price change. Suppose however that a good takes up 30 per cent of the consumer's income and its price goes up by one per cent. The consumer's real income has been reduced by a much greater amount (0.3 per cent) and the consumer is likely to react to this by reducing his consumption of this good.

The price elasticity of demand for many goods will therefore be higher in countries with low money incomes than in countries with high money incomes. In the high income countries, any price increase is a smaller proportion of consumer incomes so the elasticity of demand will be less.

Necessity or luxury goods

Necessary goods tend to have less elastic demand than luxury goods. For example, consumers have to buy food and will buy a minimum quantity whatever the price (to the maximum limit of their money income) so demand is very inelastic. Consumers can manage without colour television sets so if the price rises substantially, demand will be greatly reduced for this luxury good.

Durable and non-durable goods

Demand will tend to be less elastic for non-durable goods. If the price goes up, consumers can go on using their existing durable items instead of replacing them. The demand for replacement, new goods will fall substantially. Non-durable goods do not offer this alternative to replacement since they are used up in consumption.

For example, we would expect the demand for petrol (a non-durable good) to be less elastic than the demand for motor cars (a durable good).

Advertising

Firms would generally prefer to face a less elastic demand curve since it presents the possibility of raising price and increasing revenue and profits. They may use advertising to reduce the price elasticity of demand for their product. Advertising increases 'consumer loyalty' to a product so that they go on buying it even when the price goes up and in spite of the fact that there may be many similar goods available at lower prices.

Income elasticity

The discussion so far in this chapter has been solely concerned with a change in demand in response to a change in *price*. We need now to turn our attention to two other elasticity concepts.

Income elasticity measures the extent, as well as the direction of, changes in demand which are the result of a change in consumer income. We calculate it by finding *the % change in demand and then dividing it by the % change in the level of consumer income.*

$$\text{Income elasticity} = \frac{\text{\% change in } Q_d}{\text{\% change in Y}}$$

As consumer incomes grow, demand for most goods and services in the economy will grow (these goods and services are known as *normal goods*). Examples of this for the UK include books, watches. furniture, cars, services of solicitors, hairdressers.

For some goods and services, demand is very responsive to changes in the level of consumer income. These goods and services are said to have *income elastic demand*. This means that a 10% change in consumer income will lead to a more than 10% change in demand for these goods and services. These are classed as *luxuries*. Examples would include high performance cars, designer clothes, good quality wines, exotic foods, upmarket foreign holidays. As consumers become richer, they will have more money available to spend on such luxuries. This is true both of individual consumers and households, and of society as a whole. The flip side of this for manufacturers and suppliers of such goods and services is that when the economy is in recession, with high unemployment, demand for such luxuries will fall more than in proportion to the change in consumer incomes, as consumers reign in their spending on non-necessities. The numerical value of elasticity for goods and services for which demand is income elastic will be positive and greater than 1.

For some goods and services, demand is not very responsive to changes in the level of consumer income. These are said to be in *income inelastic demand*. This means that a 10 per cent change in consumer income will lead to a less than 10 per cent change in demand for these goods and services. These goods are *necessities*. Examples include basic foodstuffs (food as a whole is a necessity, but individual types of food are not necessarily so, some are luxuries), basic clothing, basic housing. As consumer income increases, more will be demanded of these goods and services, but not very much more. If the economy is in recession, demand for these types of goods and services will fall, but not by very much. The numerical value of income elasticity for goods and services which are in income inelastic demand will be positive but less than 1.

For some goods and services, as consumer income increases, demand will actually fall. These are known as *inferior goods*. As consumers become/society becomes richer, people are able to switch their spending from cheaper items into more expensive alternatives. Examples include remould tyres (as consumers become richer, they can afford new tyres), potatoes (as consumers become richer, they are able to switch some of their food demand away from cheap basic items into more expensive types of food). If consumer income falls, eg during recession, then demand for inferior goods may actually increase, as consumers can no longer afford the more expensive alternative. The numerical value of elasticity for inferior goods and services will be negative.

There are three factors which determine income elasticity:

a The level of income of consumers.

b How necessary is the good or service.

c The rate at which consumer desire for a particular good or service is satisfied as consumption grows.

Cross-elasticity

Cross-elasticity (or cross-price elasticity) measures the responsiveness of demand for one good or service to a change in the price of another good or service.

$$\text{Cross elasticity} = \frac{\text{\% change in quantity demanded of good X}}{\text{\% change in the price of good Y)}}$$

Some goods are *substitutes* for each other, eg public transport and private transport, rice and potatoes, CDs and audio tapes. For such goods and services, as the price of one rises, the demand for its substitute will also rise (the sign of the numerical calculation will be positive). For example, as the cost of cars rises, this will lead to an increase in demand for public transport (ceteris paribus). The extent to which demand for one good will be affected by changes in the price of its substitute depends on how close substitutes they are for each other. If they are very close substitutes, then demand will respond strongly (eg two brands of baked beans). If they are not very close substitutes, then demand will not be strongly affected.

Some goods are generally consumed together; they are *complements* for each other. Examples include cars and petrol, pen and paper, computers and floppy disks. As the price of one of these goods changes, demand for its complement will also change. For example, if the price of petrol rises, then demand for cars will go down. The numerical calculation will have a negative sign. Again, the extent of the response will depend on the degree of complementarity.

Sometimes changes in the price of one good or service can have an effect on demand for apparently unrelated goods and services (ie which are not substitutes for each other). This may happen if the good or service which changes price represents a large percentage of consumers' average income. An example of this happened when the cost of mortgages rose sharply, thus reducing many consumers' real incomes, and leaving them with less money available to spend on other goods and services.

It is important for manufacturers/suppliers to keep an eye on changes in the prices of goods and services which are substitutes or complements for their good or service. They will thus be able to predict changes in demand. They will also need to know the degree of responsiveness (or how close substitutes/complements they are) to predict the extent of changes in demand.

Elasticity and tax policies

The degree of *price* elasticity of demand for a product has important implications for taxation policies. Some of the taxes raised by the government come from *indirect* taxation levied on consumer spending. This type of taxation raises the price of a good. For instance, if the rate of indirect taxation is 10 per cent then a good originally costing £1 will, after the tax, cost £1.10, with the 10 pence going to the government. Clearly, the government needs to consider the elasticity of demand for a good when it is contemplating raising the rate of indirect taxation. If it raises the rate by too large an amount, it may well *lose* rather than *gain* revenue, because, as was noted earlier, a substantial price rise in a good with an elastic demand will result in a fall in total revenue. A price rise is a price rise, whether it is caused by an increase in the producer's selling price or by a rise in indirect tax, so it is obviously wiser to place an indirect tax on a good with an *inelastic* demand rather than on one with an elastic demand. Pursuing the latter course may be self-defeating. Admittedly, it is not always a simple task to decide which goods have inelastic demands. On occasions, governments have found that goods which have traditionally had inelastic demands have suddenly changed to having elastic demands after the price has risen beyond a certain point. Indeed, it is unlikely that a good will have an inelastic demand permanently, because there will usually be a price when people begin to think about the cost and so attempt to reduce consumption.

Consumer's demand

We have been concentrating until now on the problem of the demand for goods as the firm or government might observe it: the problem of how many of this good consumers will buy under certain circumstances such as the prices of the good, the prices of other goods, the incomes of consumers, etc.

We must now consider the demand for goods from the individual consumer's point of view. Each consumer must decide which of the available goods he wishes to consume and how many of each he wants to consume.

Consumer rationality and the income constraint

Economists assume that all consumers behave rationally. They must do this in order to be able to predict consumer behaviour. Each consumer is assumed to want to *maximise his total utility* (or satisfaction) from the consumption of goods and services. The constraint on his total utility is his limited income. He is only able to buy a limited amount of goods and services.

Marginal utility and opportunity cost

Since income is the constraint, the consumer will allocate it carefully. He must consider the utility derived from each unit of each good that he can buy so as to allocate his income optimally. This means that he must consider *marginal utility* which is the additional utility derived from the consumption of an extra unit of a good.

He should never buy a unit of a good if, by doing so, he is then not able to buy a unit of another good that would have given greater additional utility. In other words, he should never buy a unit of a good if the resulting marginal utility does not exceed the opportunity cost of buying it.

Marginal utility and total utility

Generally, the more of a particular good the consumer has the greater his total utility, the sum of utility for each of the units consumed. An ardent tea drinker will get greater total utility from the consumption of three cups of tea compared with two or one.

However, we generally assume that marginal utility (the additional utility derived from the consumption of each successive unit of a good) will decline as more of the good is consumed. The tea drinker probably enjoyed the third cup less than the first and would enjoy a fifth cup less than the third. As long as the marginal utility is positive, the total utility will continue to rise as more cups are drunk but it rises by smaller and smaller amounts.

Eventually marginal utility may become negative and, if the consumer drank that cup, his total utility from the cups of tea would be reduced. When marginal utility is negative this is called disutility.

If we could measure utility in, for example, money terms, a utility schedule might look like this. Utility is often measured by utils although this is rather arbitrary.

Number of cups drunk	Total utility	Marginal utility
1	10	10
2	18	8
3	24	6
4	27	3
5	28	1
6	27	-1

Total utility

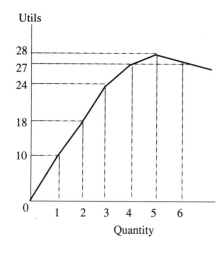

Marginal utility

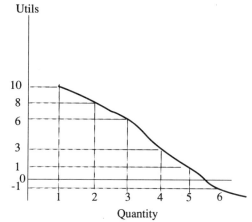

The Marginal Utility schedule and graph above illustrate the principle of *diminishing marginal utility*. Consumption of each additional unit (in this case, a cup of tea) provides our consumer with extra utility, but at a decreasing rate. This is assumed by economists to be true for virtually all goods and services. As we consume more and more units, they each add less and less to our total utility (satisfaction), until we reach a point when consuming another unit would provide no additional utility.

Utility is a concept which is very useful as a way to help explain the process of consumer decision-making. However, it is solely a theoretical concept. Utils are unobservable and unmeasurable. We are not in reality able to calculate our consumer's total and marginal utility from consumption.

Another problem is that the amount of utility which each of us gets from consuming units of any particular good or service is not the same. Different consumers have different preferences. For example, many consumers love chocolate; chocolate provides such people with high levels of utility, and they will consume many units before their marginal utility from it becomes negative. However, migraine sufferers will get disutility from consuming one unit (it will make them ill). Utility is therefore a very subjective matter.

There is an exception to the principle of diminishing marginal utility described above. There are some (few) goods which are assumed to provide *increasing marginal utility*; each additional unit provides not less marginal utility, but more marginal utility. This is only true of highly addictive substances, such as heroin and other hard drugs.

Consumer's decision

The analysis above discussed the process of consumer decision-making with respect to one good only. Our consumer only had to make a decision about how many cups of tea to buy. We did not consider either our consumer's income, or the possibility that he may wish to spend some of it on other goods and services.

We will now move on to incorporate both of these factors into our analysis. Every consumer has a limited amount of income (this is what economists refer to as the consumer's *budget constraint*). Within this budget constraint, our consumer aims to maximise his total utility gained from consuming his own preferred bundle out of all the available goods and services in the economy (as mentioned above, each of us will have a different preferred bundle).

Marginal Utility Theory assumes that rational consumers will select their preferred bundles, and the quantities of each good and service within it, such that they maximise their total utility. In order to achieve this, our consumer needs to ensure that the marginal utilities of each good and service in his bundle, divided by their prices, are equal. Our consumer maximises their utility (otherwise put, our consumer is in equilibrium) when:

$$\frac{MU \text{ good A}}{P \text{ good A}} = \frac{MU \text{ good B}}{P \text{ good B}} = \frac{MU \text{ good C}}{P \text{ good C}} ----- = \frac{MU \text{ good N}}{P \text{ good N}}$$

The opportunity cost of each unit of each good consumed is the marginal utility which could have been gained by consuming a unit of the best alternative.

What if the price of one good changes, relative to the prices of the other goods and services in our consumer's preferred bundle? (eg, the price of a cup of tea goes up, while the prices of everything else stay the same). Our consumer will no longer be in equilibrium. He will need to recalculate his preferred bundle, and the quantities therein, to take account of the price change. He will need to recalculate a (different) equilibrium, until he is again maximising his utility.

As we have seen in the last chapter, an increase in the price of a good normally leads to a decrease in the demand for it. Otherwise expressed: an increase in the price of good A leads to a decrease in demand for good A and a decrease in the marginal utility provided by good A.

Utility can be maximised by switching (some of) consumption of good A into something else which will provide higher utility.

Clearly, in reality consumers do not sit down and make calculations as this theory specifies. This is not important, as long as consumers behave as if they are doing so. The end result of many thousands/millions of consumer decisions made each day will be more or less in line with the predictions of marginal utility theory.

Advertising and preferences

The market system allows consumers to choose their optimal allocation of goods and services according to their own preferences. The allocation of output therefore takes account of the varying tastes of consumers. This is its great advantage over the command system of allocation of goods.

However, it is sometimes argued (see Galbraith, *The Affluent Society*) that consumers' tastes are manipulated by firms through extensive advertising. The choice made by consumers does not then reflect their 'real' preferences.

It is obviously difficult to measure the extent of any distortion of demand by advertising. If all advertising were banned this might solve the problem but advertising does serve a useful information function in the economy as well as occasionally being entertaining. The government has made some steps in this direction. Alcohol can not be advertised in such a way as to imply that its consumption will transform the consumer into a more successful, sociable and attractive person. The advertising of cigarettes is banned on television, and health warnings are printed on the sides of cigarette packets.

Illegal preferences

Some goods that consumers would choose are made illegal by the government. The so-called 'hard' and 'soft' drugs are an example. The debate on the question of whether the consumption of cannabis should or should not be legalised centres around the right of the state to dictate the consumer's choice of goods regardless of his preferences.

Redistribution of income

The ability of consumers to buy goods and services is determined by their income. This income will depend on the resources they own and their value in the resource markets. The market allocation of income has tended in the past to produce a very unequal allocation of income. Some individuals, therefore, can command a large amount and range of goods and services and achieve a very high level of total utility. Others, however, are limited to a very low level of total utility by their incomes. The government reallocates income (and therefore the ability to buy goods and services) through taxation and subsidies.

As well as changing the ability of individuals to buy goods, taxation will also change the type of goods bought. A very unequal distribution of income will produce a high demand (from the small, very rich sector) for luxury cars such as the Rolls Royce. There will be little demand for medium and low-priced cars since the rest of the population must use their much lower income for buying necessities such as food, housing and clothing. As income is redistributed, fewer of the rich can afford Rolls Royce cars, so demand will fall. More of the poor, however, will now be able to buy a car. There will be an increased demand for medium- and low-priced cars.

Externalities

Each consumer decides on his own consumption behaviour. His aim is to maximise his own total utility. However, the consumption behaviour of some customers may affect the total utility enjoyed by other customers. It is not rational for the consumer to consider the impact of his actions on the utility of other consumers, but only on his own utility.

Society might, however, consider that the total utility enjoyed by the population might be greater if consumers were forced to modify their consumption behaviour according to its impact on others. It will be rational for society to control individual consumption accordingly.

For example, smokers decide whether or not to have a cigarette on the basis of their own marginal utility compared to the price of cigarettes. They do not consider the *external costs* they impose on the people near them by forcing them to inhale polluted air. Thus we have 'No Smoking' carriages on trains and areas in cinemas.

Drivers may prefer to drive their car at maximum speed through urban areas. They may not consider the noise, fumes and danger they impose on the occupants of that area. Society imposes speed restrictions to check this externality.

Society is interested in maintaining old houses but the weighting of the costs and benefits of the maintenance may be the decision of an individual consumer. He might not consider the external benefit for everyone else when he spends money on the house. Society passes this *external benefit* on to the individual consumer through grants for the maintenance of 'historic buildings'.

Questions for review

1. What is meant by Price Elasticity of Demand?

    Why is it important?

    Give the formula used to calculate it.

2 Illustrate a demand curve which is:
   a   perfectly inelastic
   b   perfectly elastic.
3 Why does elasticity vary throughout the length of a straight line curve?
4 What factors influence price elasticity of demand?
5 Explain income elasticity.

   Give the formula used to calculate it.
6 What are 'normal' goods?

   What are 'inferior' goods?
7 Explain the concept of cross-elasticity.

   Give the formula used to calculate it.
8 Explain 'substitutes' and 'complements'.
9 What is 'utility'?
10 Distinguish between 'marginal' and 'total' utility.
11 Explain the process by which consumers are assumed to maximise their utility.
12 What happens if the price of one good changes?

The theory of production (supply) | 4

Introduction 77

Influences on supply 79

The theory of production (supply)

Introduction

The price mechanism and production

It was noted in the previous chapter that the interaction of demand and supply curves is the basis of the price mechanism and that when demand and supply match each other an equilibrium price exists. This theory can now be extended so that the role of the price mechanism in the pricing system of an economy can be examined.

First, the price mechanism has a *static* function. It allocates a good that is in a fixed supply to the consumer with the greatest effective demand; that is, the consumer who is prepared to pay the highest price for the good. This is why goods that are in short supply, and rare or unique goods, are 'bid up' in price.

Secondly, the price mechanism has a *dynamic* function as it allocates resources *through time*. If demand exceeds supply, then in the long run supply will be increased to meet this excess demand, as producers will be encouraged to reallocate resources to the production of the good in question. The length of time which this increase in production takes to occur must be examined in detail.

Elasticity of supply

The concept of elasticity can be applied to the forces of supply in a similar way in which they are applied to the forces of demand. The elasticity of supply is defined as the *proportionate change in the quantity supplied over the proportionate change in the price of the commodity*, or:

$$\text{Elasticity of supply} = \frac{\text{\% change in quantity supplied}}{\text{\% change in price)}}$$

As in the case of demand, if the proportionate changes in quantity and price are equal then elasticity is unity, while if the elasticity is greater than 1 the supply is said to be price elastic and if less than one the supply is said to be price inelastic. The elasticity of supply is influenced by two principle factors: the production process itself, and time.

Unlike demand elasticity, supply elasticity is easy to describe in a diagram if straight-line supply curves are used. A supply curve of unit elasticity ($E_s = 1$) will always pass through the origin. A change in price will always result in a proportional change in quantity supplied (see following diagram).

Supply curves of unit elasticity

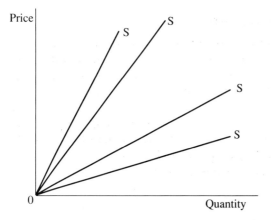

A supply curve which is relatively inelastic will cut the horizontal axis. A change in price will always result in a smaller change in quantity supplied than if the curve had had unit elasticity. A supply curve that is relatively elastic will cut the vertical axis. A change in price will always result in a larger change in quantity supplied than if the curve had had unit elasticity.

Relatively inelastic supply curves   *Relatively elastic supply curves*

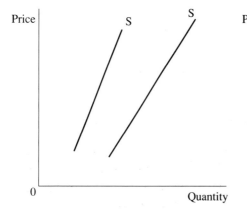
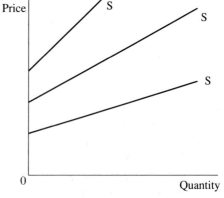

Influences on supply

Influences – production process

The production process directly governs the extent to which companies can respond to price changes, and the major factors can be divided into three main sub-headings:

Surplus capacity
Most manufacturing companies do not operate at maximum capacity continuously and so, by arranging overtime, increasing the usage of machines, avoiding unnecessary waste and improving operating methods, it should be relatively easy to increase output. The greater the amount of 'organisational slack', the easier it is for a company to respond to price changes in the short term. When there is considerable surplus capacity supply is relatively elastic, whereas if there is only a small amount of surplus capacity, supply will be relatively inelastic in the short term.

Length of production process
The speed at which goods can be manufactured is naturally also an important factor in the determination of elasticity of supply. The quicker goods can be made, the more likely it is that supply will be elastic. However, many goods take a considerable time to produce and this inevitably results in an inelastic supply. For instance, most foodstuffs are produced through an annual cycle (eg in 1976 because of a drought in Britain it was just not possible to increase the supply of potatoes in the short term despite a massive increase in price), and many capital and some semi-durable goods can take many months to manufacture.

Resources have limited uses
Resources of one sort or another cannot be switched to different areas of production easily or quickly. For example: machines have a limited number of uses; workers cannot often be retrained quickly; and there are many restrictions on the movement of manpower, some natural (geographical and physical) and some man-made (union rules and traditions). The ease with which resources can be switched will therefore affect the elasticity of supply.

Influences – time

The key to understanding the elasticity of supply is to appreciate the effect of time on the production process. It is inevitably true that supply must be elastic in the long term, but this is not a very helpful statement because the 'long term' varies from industry to industry. However, for the sake of analysis, the three stages – the immediate, the short term and the long term – may be examined without putting a precise timescale on the process.

The immediate effect
An immediate increase in supply can only come from stocks and business stocks are not often large enough to meet the needs that arise from a permanent shift in demand. As a result the price of the product will tend to rise as in the graph, from OP to OP_1. (The graph shows the special case where stocks are zero.)

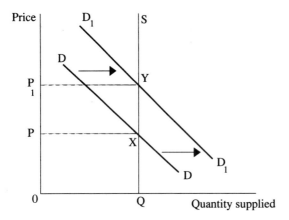

The short-term effect
In the short term some increase in supply can take place, as producers are able to utilise their surplus capacity. Although supply can, therefore, begin to increase, it will not be elastic. As supply increases (from SS to S_1S_1), the equilibrium price falls from the OP_1 of the previous graph to OP_2. It should be noted, however, that this price is still higher than the original price and that the equilibrium quantity produced is also higher at OQ_1.

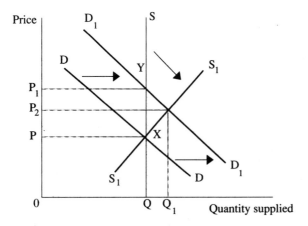

The theory of production (supply) | 81

The long-term effect

Eventually, the whole supply position will change as existing producers adjust their production to meet the new demand conditions and new suppliers enter the market in an effort to increase their own incomes. This final change in supply – to a point where it has become elastic – is shown on the final graph:

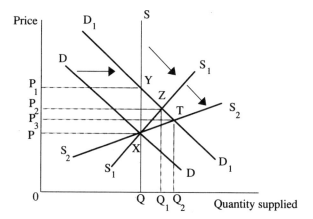

This time the price falls further to 0P3, but it is still higher than the original price (0P) and equilibrium output is higher still at 0Q2. This shows that the quantity supplied to the market and the equilibrium price are both higher at the end of the process than they were before. It is possible to follow the process through on this last graph by studying the price and quantity levels at each of the four consecutive stages – X, Y, Z and T.

Movements in the supply curve

By definition, an increase in demand must have an effect on the level of supply, but it is not always realised just how profound such an effect might be. In the diagram above it was assumed that the conditions of supply remained unchanged (ie the supply curve only pivoted around point X rather than shifting one way or the other). It is, in fact, likely that over time the actual conditions of supply will alter. It could be that new technology reduces the cost of production. Some producers may respond to these opportunities more quickly or more effectively than others and some may even gain an upper hand in the competitive process. Similarly, if potential profits are exceptionally high, due to a substantial increase in demand, larger and more efficient businesses may be attracted into the particular market. The end result of any of these events will be that the supply curve shifts to the right:

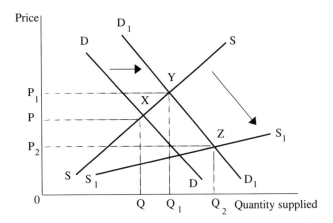

Point X again represents the original equilibrium position while point Y shows the immediate or short-term position. As the supply curve shifts from SS to S_1S_1, the price *falls* to a level *below* the original price and the quantity supplied increases considerably.

This type of situation has arisen in recent years in a number of consumer durable markets, such as washing machines, television sets and vacuum cleaners. As a result of demand rising rapidly, new production and marketing techniques have been used and longer production runs organised to meet the steadily increasing demand.

The dynamic flows of supply and demand

It should not be forgotten that the rather simple analytical models that have been used here cannot possibly illustrate the real complexity of movements in supply and demand. After all, such movements are primarily dynamic and these models are static. The models consider only one step at a time and also assume that all the other possible influences remain unchanged. However, the principles which have been outlined should provide a guide as to the influences and general trends in the determination of supply and demand which affect real-world situations.

Influences on the supply curve itself

A supply curve is primarily influenced by the costs of production and yet so far only generalisations have been made about how the costs of production influence how much of a good is supplied. Obviously, as it is these costs that ultimately determine the level of production and supply, it is important to analyse the cost structure of an individual company carefully.

The more business a company transacts, the more resources it has to pay for, so, its management has to assess with a fair degree of accuracy the extent to which any extra business will result in extra costs. Management needs to be able to classify and measure costs and there are two basic types of costs – *fixed costs and variable costs.*

The first category of costs are fixed costs which relate to the costs of those factors of production whose input cannot be varied according to the level of output produced. Fixed costs only exist in the short run. Indeed the existence of these fixed costs in the firm's framework for decision-making is what defines the short-run situation for the firm. For example, suppose a firm has given six-month contracts to a number of employees and has paid six months' rent in advance for the factory and its equipment with no possibility of sub-letting. Suppose that it is also impossible for the firm to acquire additional workers or extra capital inputs until after the six-month period. Now, within those six months (the short run for the firm) the firm cannot change the inputs of these fixed factors of production and therefore must bear the costs associated with these inputs, whatever the level of production during that period. Even if the firm produced and sold no goods at all, it must pay these fixed costs.

During that six-month period (the short run), the graph of fixed costs at each level of output would be as shown in the following diagram. They are the same whatever the level of output of the firm.

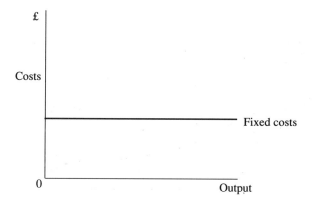

Typical fixed costs are rent, interest payments on capital inputs, costs of heating, lighting and insurance, and wages of certain workers, usually key administrative or maintenance workers.

In the long run, the inputs of all these factors can be varied and so their costs are no longer fixed costs. The long run is therefore that period sufficiently long for there to be no fixed costs of production. For example, a firm selling no output could close down, getting rid of all factors of production.

Variable costs vary in a direct relationship with the actual level of output. Obviously, if a company increases its output from 100,000 units to 150,000 units, it will require more materials and more labour to produce the extra 50,000 units (ie variable costs increase as output increases).

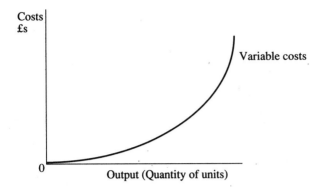

The following diagrams show total and average cost curves. Notice that the total cost curve is the vertical sum of the fixed cost and variable cost curves. The firm incurs substantial costs (the total fixed costs) even at zero output.

The average cost curve is the vertical sum of the average fixed-cost curve (which falls as output rises) and the average variable-cost curve (which typically falls and then rises – see the right-hand chart). The average cost curve is therefore typically U-shaped, first falling and then rising as output is expanded.

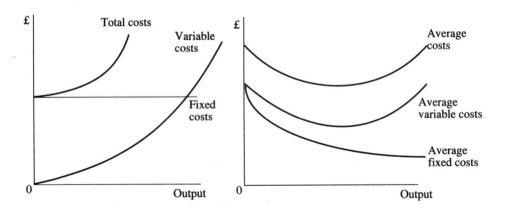

There are three factors which explain why the short-run average cost curve is generally U-shaped.

First, as output is expanded, *the fixed costs of production are being spread over more units of output*, so that fixed costs per unit of output get less. For example, with fixed costs of £1,000 and the firm only producing 10 units of output, the average cost will be an average fixed cost of £100 plus any average variable cost. If the firm produces 100 units of output, the average cost will be an average fixed cost of only £10 plus any average variable cost. The decline of average fixed costs as output is expanded therefore exerts a downward pressure on average costs. However, note that the decline of average fixed costs gets smaller with successive increases in output. An increase of output from 1 to 2 units will halve the average fixed costs but an increase of one unit from 100 to 101 units will reduce the average fixed costs by only a small percentage.

Secondly, the expansion of output can only be achieved in the short run by increasing the inputs of variable factors of production. The *law of diminishing returns* states that as successive extra units of a variable factor are used with a fixed stock of other factors, the increase in output that results from each successive addition of the variable factor will eventually decline. For example, suppose extra labour is used in a workshop with a fixed stock of equipment.

In the following table, the second worker is able to add more to output than the first worker, as the workers increase their productivity by specialising in different jobs. The third worker is not able to add so greatly to output since the advantages of specialisation have been exhausted.

The fourth worker adds even less to output, as by now the workshop is becoming over-crowded and there are insufficient tools and machines so time is wasted queueing. The law of diminishing returns is operating.

Number employed per week	Total output per week	Marginal output	Wage bill per week	Average variable cost (wage bill total output)
1	10	10	£100	£10
2	25	15	£200	£8
3	30	5	£300	£10
4	32	2	£400	£12.50

The marginal output column (the change in output resulting from the employment of each extra worker) shows the 'returns' from the employment of each extra worker. These returns are diminishing after two workers have been employed. The wage is assumed to be £100 per worker per week so the wage bill is rising proportionately with employment. The average variable cost therefore first falls (while marginal returns are initially rising) and then rises (as marginal returns are diminishing).

Thirdly, the elasticity of supply of variable factors may not be perfectly elastic (as it is in the example above). The employment of additional workers may require the payment of higher wages to attract these extra factors. The following table shows what happens to average variable cost when the wage bill is rising more than proportionately with the numbers employed.

Number employed per week	Total output per week	Wage bill per week	Average variable costs (wage bill/total output)
1	10	£100	£10
2	25	£250	£10
3	30	£450	£15
4	32	£640	£20

Thus, in conclusion, the average variable costs will tend to fall initially (if marginal returns are initially rising) but then will rise as the law of diminishing returns begins to apply and because the price that must be paid for variable factors may be rising as more workers are employed. Average fixed costs fall as output is expanded but by smaller and smaller amounts. The average cost curve (the vertical sum of the average variable-cost curve and the average fixed-cost curve) will therefore fall and then rise.

Marginal costs

Marginal costs, like the 'marginal' utility discussed earlier, are the *extra costs incurred by a company when it increases its output by one unit*. If a company produces 1,000 units of a good at a total cost of £1,000 and then increases its production by one unit (to 1,001) and as a result increases its total costs to £1,000.50, then the marginal cost of the extra unit of output is 50 pence, or the difference between the two levels of total costs.

The cost structure

Costs of a hypothetical company at varying levels of output:

(1) Annual production (units)	(2) Fixed costs (£s)	(3) Variable costs (£s)	(4) Total costs (£s)	(5) Average costs (£s per unit)	(6) Marginal costs (£s per unit)
100	1,000	900	1,900	19.00	9.00
200	1,000	1,600	2,600	13.00	7.00
300	1,000	2,200	3,200	10.67	6.00
400	1,000	2,800	3,800	9.50	6.00
500	1,000	3,400	4,400	8.80	6.00
600	1,000	4,050	5,050	8.42	6.50
700	1,000	4,750	5,750	8.21	7.00
800	1,000	5,550	6,550	8.19	8.00
900	1,000	6,500	7,500	8.33	9.50
1,000	1,000	7,650	8,650	8.65	11.50
1,100	1,000	9,050	10,050	9.14	14.00

This table shows how the costs of a hypothetical company vary over a range of output levels. Column 1 details the range of output. Column 2 shows the fixed costs which remain stable at £1,000 throughout the output range. Column 3 lists the variable costs incurred at each level of output, while column 4 simply totals the fixed and variable costs. Column 5 introduces a new concept – *average cost* which is the total cost divided by output. Finally, in column 6 the marginal cost of each increase in output is shown. (In fact, it is not strictly correct to calculate it by dividing the increase in cost by the increase in the number of units. The actual cost of producing *only one more unit* may well be slightly higher than the figure shown but is a near enough approximation. Furthermore, it is unlikely that production would be increased by only one unit. As in the table, production increases will usually be in reasonable jumps.)

It should be apparent from the table that the active component is *variable costs*. The first 100 units incur a variable cost of £900, while the second 100 units incur a much lower variable cost, only £700. Once work has actually been started, it is much easier to increase production as machines are simply kept working a little longer, or workers are encouraged to work a bit harder or more efficiently, or materials are bought in larger quantities. All these factors mean that average costs fall as production is increased from low levels.

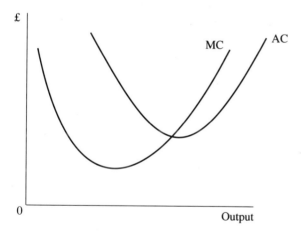

The diagram above depicts the normal situation of the marginal cost curve cutting the average cost curve at its lowest point.

Government intervention

It is rational for firms to consider only their own profits in making their production decisions. They should aim for the widest gap between costs and revenues. Business is often highly competitive with no room for the firm that does not keep its costs as low as possible.

If firms can reduce their costs by pouring noxious fumes and chemical-laden effluent into rivers, they should do so if they want to profit-maximise. However, by doing so they are imposing external costs on society – the people who must breathe the air, who might want to drink the water. The government checks these externalities through regulations and fines.

Firms might also reduce their costs by increasing the danger of accident or illness for their employees. It is, of course, surprising that employees will work in these conditions. Often they are ignorant of the danger or have no alternative employment. Employees may be protected from these dangers by government regulations. All these regulations will increase the costs of the firm.

Determination of output

The firm will decide how much to produce on the basis of producing the maximum profit. This is rational since the profit is the income of the owners of the firm. Profit is the difference between total cost and total revenue. The *marginal revenue* is the addition to total revenue from selling one more unit of output.

The revenue depends on the market price at which the firm can sell the output produced. The costs of the firm vary with the output. The firm will maximise profits if it expands output, as long as the additional output adds more to revenue than it adds to costs. If each additional unit of output can be sold for the market price, the firm should expand output as long as the marginal cost is less than the price.

The situation is illustrated in the following diagram.

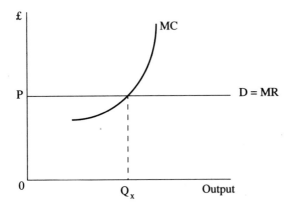

The firm can sell any amount of output for price P. The marginal cost curve is shown first falling and then rising. Up to output Q_x, the price is greater than the marginal cost so the firm should expand output increasing its profit. It should not produce more than Q_x because those additional units will add more to costs than they do to revenue. The profit maximising output is therefore Q_x, where marginal cost is equal to the price.

The theory of production (supply)

As we shall see in Chapter 6, the firm may find that the market price at which output is sold may vary according to output. The profit maximisation rule should therefore be stated more generally. The firm should expand output as long as the marginal cost is less than the marginal revenue (the addition to total revenue that results from selling an extra unit of output).

Profit maximising output will then be when marginal revenue is equal to marginal cost.

Calculation of profits

With the costs above and the price of the good at £10, how much output should the firm produce and what will the profits be?

The profit-maximising rule is that firms should produce the output at which marginal cost = marginal revenue. In fact, there is rarely a level of output for which this is true. More generally, firms should expand output as long as marginal revenue exceeds marginal cost. An extra unit should not be produced if it increases costs by more than it increases revenue but should be if it adds more to revenue than costs.

With these figures, that rule applies for an output of 900 units. Producing 1,000 units instead would add £11.50 per extra unit produced to costs but only £10 per unit to revenue.

At an output of 900 units, total costs are £7,500 while total revenue is £9,000 (900 x £10). The total profit is therefore £1,500. An alternative way of calculating profit is to take an average revenue (the price of £10) minus the average cost (£8.33) and multiply it by the output to give £1.66 x 900 or £1,500.

Losses

Suppose that the price of the good is such that it is impossible for the firm to be able to make a profit; that is, there is no output at which total revenue will be sufficient to cover total costs at that output, or no output at which the price exceeds the average cost at that output.

This situation might be as shown in the following table.

Output (units)	Fixed costs £	Variable costs £	Total costs £	Marginal costs £	Average costs £	Price £
1	100	100	200	100	200	110
2	100	260	360	160	180	110
3	100	380	480	120	160	110
4	100	460	560	80	140	110
5	100	500	600	40	120	110
6	100	740	840	240	140	110
7	100	1,020	1,120	280	160	110
8	100	1,340	1,440	320	180	110
9	100	1,700	1,800	360	200	110
10	100	2,100	2,200	400	220	110

To apply our previous profit maximising rule, the firm will produce maximum profits by producing output as long as marginal revenue (the price of the good) exceeds the marginal cost of producing it. With these figures that is true for an output of 5 units. If the firm produced the 6th unit, it would add £240 to its costs and only £110 to its revenue.

However, at that output average costs (£120) exceed average revenue (£110) which means that at this 'profit maximising' output will produce losses of £50 (total revenue is £550 ie 5 x £110 while total costs are £600). Should the firm produce this output?

We assume that firms will, if they cannot profit maximise, aim to *loss minimise*. The marginal cost-marginal revenue rule will give us the best output for the firm to produce if it produces any at all. Average costs exceed price by even greater amounts at all other levels of output listed.

However, the firm might consider the option of producing no output at all. At zero output, the firm will have no variable costs but will still have to pay the fixed costs. Its losses would then be £100, the fixed costs. In this situation, it would obviously be better for the firm to produce 5 units since it will make least losses then.

Suppose, however, that the price of the good were £90. The marginal cost-marginal revenue rule will not give us loss minimising output at 5 units. In this case, the losses will be £150 (total revenue will be 5 x £90 = £450 while total cost is £600). The firm would now have lower losses (£100) if it produced no output at all, as at any level of output losses would be greater than £100 (fixed costs).

The rule for a loss-making situation is:

a the firm should produce where marginal cost = marginal revenue as long as at that output the total revenue covers the total variable cost (or price is greater than average variable cost);

b the firm should otherwise produce zero output in which case the firm's losses will be the fixed costs.

In the first example, with price at £110, total revenue of £550 exceeded the variable costs of £500 so the firm should produce 5 units. The justification for this is that the firm is able to pay the labour, raw material and power costs of producing output and has some money left to contribute to its fixed costs.

In the second example, with the price at £90, this was less than the average cost of £100 (£500/5) so the firm increased its losses by producing output.

Economies of scale

Until now we have been considering the short run situation for the firm. The firm has had fixed costs which relate to the inputs of the firm which cannot be altered – the rent of the factory, etc.

In *the long run* (defined in economics as that period of time sufficient for the firm to have no fixed inputs) the firm can sell the factory and buy a new one. All factors, and therefore all costs, are variable.

The theory of production (supply)

Generally, it seems that the average costs of production will tend to fall as the size of the operation is increased. When a firm can reduce its costs by expanding its operations it is said to benefit from *economies of scale.*

Technical
A greater specialisation of labour becomes possible so that people do only those tasks in which they are most skilled.

Specialised machines with a minimum output for economic use can be justified by the larger output. Larger machines and buildings may be proportionately cheaper to run.

Managerial and administrative
Many management and administrative processes can be simplified or streamlined through the use of machines and computers, providing there is a large enough throughput to justify the investment. Furthermore, increases in output do not usually require a proportionate increase in management and administrative staff and so the costs related to these areas will fall as output increases.

Purchasing, marketing and sales
Similarly, costs in these areas tend to fall as output increases (eg bulk buying, more cost effective advertising).

Financial
Larger organisations find it cheaper and easier to raise finance. Small operations may be limited to borrowing fixed interest finance from commercial bank managers who are unlikely to take risks in their loans. Large organisations can raise finance from a new issue of shares. This provides them with finance on high risk ventures which need never be repaid and only earns 'interest' when profits are made.

Diseconomies of scale

While these various influences are helping to reduce marginal and average costs, other influences may begin to work forcing up marginal and average cost. These influences are principally the management and labour problems that large organisations run into.

A larger organisation is more difficult to run. The number of managers can be increased to cover the larger organisation but this increases the communication difficulties between the managers. While two department heads can meet regularly to exchange informal and formal views on the firm's path, twenty department heads are likely to be reduced to formal interaction only, often greatly reducing the extent and usefulness of the information exchanged.

Computer technology has greatly increased the capacity of firms to store and communicate information making larger organisations easier to run. However, success in business is concerned with the accurate anticipation of the essentially uncertain future. The 'hunch', which is often enormously important in business decisions, cannot easily be transferred into data suitable for analysis on a computer.

Secondly, larger organisations tend to run into labour problems. There is considerable evidence to show that larger organisations suffer from more workdays lost from absenteeism and labour disputes. There is also some evidence that larger organisations suffer from higher labour turnover, increasing training costs.

Opinion surveys have shown that employees in large organisations emphasise income rather than 'job satisfaction' or social factors as important in their job. Large organisations are then much more likely to suffer from strikes over pay than small organisations. Labour disputes may arise because of poor communication between work-force and management. These are likely to be more difficult in large organisations.

The very advantages of large organisations, such as mass-production, may be a problem. Mass-production is a system of a particular product being produced by a sequence of operations by different groups of workers. Any one of those groups can bring the whole process to a halt. Thus, the machine minders at Rover Group can paralyse the whole operation.

An interesting point about diseconomies of scale is that the factors involved are difficult to anticipate in detail. It is difficult to estimate what sort of problems the management team are likely to develop, or the adjustment of the labour force from small to large operation. The factors causing economies of scale are, however, easy to identify.

A firm's decision about internal growth may therefore be dominated by cost reducing factors resulting from larger size. Once greater size is achieved the firm may discover the unexpected problems. Firms may therefore tend to grow beyond their most efficient size.

Relationship between short-run and long-run costs

Under the flexibility of the long-run situation, there will be a maximum cost associated with the ideal mix of factors of production for that output. This point for each level of output forms the long-run average cost curve.

Let us assume that as output is expanded, there are economies of scale until such factors as loss of management control begin to be more important than technical economies, so that there are diseconomies of scale for any further expansion of output. This will give us the U-shaped long-run average cost curve.

The theory of production (supply) | 93

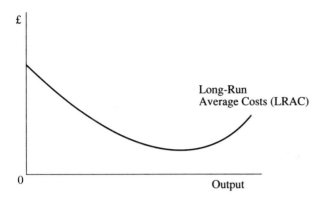

There is some evidence suggesting that long-run cost curves are generally U-shaped but alternative evidence suggests that, in some industries, long-run cost curves are L-shaped – economies of scale giving falling costs initially and then constant returns to scale (unchanged average costs at each level of output) for any further expansion.

Suppose the firm has expanded so that the ideal output for the current plant is Q_x. The firm is then in a short-run situation. It cannot vary the size of the plant quickly so any adjustment of output will mean that the plant is running with excess capacity or over capacity. Costs will then tend to be higher than if the firm had been able to adapt the plant, moving along the long-run cost curve. The point x on the long-run cost curve therefore has a short-run cost curve associated with it. Short-run costs are only the same as long-run costs when the plant is actually producing output x.

The relationship of the long- and short-run cost curves

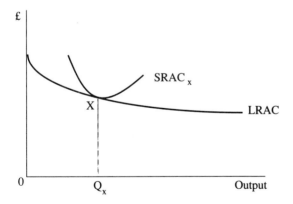

For each and every size of plant, there will also be a short-run average cost curve, and a long-run average cost curve envelopes a series of short-run average cost curves. So remember, each *short-run average cost curve* represents the *average costs of production for different levels of output with a specific and fixed level of plant* and the *long-run average cost curve* represents *the optimum level of costs associated with different sizes of plant*. In the following diagram, if a firm increases output from $0Q_1$, to $0Q_2$ it would be cheaper to employ the plant size corresponding to $SRAC_2$. The average cost would then fall from E to B.

Long- and short-run average cost curves

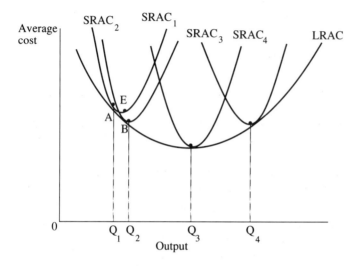

The optimal size of firms

Clearly, optimal efficiency is reached if each firm in an industry is operating at the output where long-run costs are minimised. The resource costs of producing output will then be as low as possible. At output $ØQ_3$ in the above diagram, LRAC are minimised.

This optimal size of firms will obviously vary from one industry to another. In some industries the possibilities for technical economies and the large initial costs of research and development and advertising will produce substantial economies of scale over a large output. Motor car manufacturers and pharmaceuticals are possible examples. The optimal size of firms will then be very large.

In other industries there may be few economies of scale and diseconomies of scale may be very significant at low levels of output. The optimal size of firms may then be very small. In the above diagram diseconomies have set in at output $ØQ_4$.

Scale of plant vs scale of firm

It is often important to distinguish between optimal *plant size* and optimal *firm size*.

Many industries are characterised by large firms owning many small plants. The explanation for this may be that diseconomies of scale (loss of management control, labour problems) become relevant at low output levels in each plant but economies of scale (research and development, advertising, bulk buying, finance) make the optimal size of firms quite large.

The constraint of the market

Some industries are characterised by small firms, not because of economies or diseconomies of scale but because the demand for output is quite low. The small corner grocery and general store is an example. The shop is small because the population it serves is small. There are economies of scale in retailing (the success of supermarkets shows that) but they can only be exploited with the large markets of urban centres.

The great advantage of the increased communications within and between countries is that they expand the potential market for goods making it possible to exploit economies of scale.

Questions for review

1 Explain the concept of 'elasticity of supply'.

   Give the appropriate formula.

2 Explain why elasticity of supply may change over time.

3 Explain some of the factors which influence supply.

4 Explain the possible impact of new technology on the supply curve.

5 Explain the following concepts:

   a   fixed costs;

   b   variable costs;

   c   average costs;

   d   marginal costs.

6 Explain and illustrate the Law of Diminishing Returns.

7 Why are short-run average cost curves generally U-shaped?

8 Explain why the profit maximising level of output will be where marginal cost = marginal revenue.

9 What are economies of scale?

   Identify the main sources of these.

10 What are diseconomies of scale?

   Identify some of the sources of these.

11 Explain the relationship of short-run average cost curves to long-run average cost curves.

   Illustrate this with a diagram.

Ownership and control of firms | 5

Introduction 99

The ownership of firms 99

The objectives of the firm 101

Introduction

Up until now, we have treated 'the firm' as a sort of black box, and we have not really looked inside that black box. We have made the traditional assumption that the objective of every firm is to maximise profits. We have also not so far examined different forms of ownership of firms.

The form of ownership of a firm may well have some impact on its objectives and on its economic performance. Hence we now need to turn our attention to this topic. Having examined the impact of different forms of ownership, we will be in a position to look again at the profit maximisation objective and some of its limitations. We will then look at possible alternative objectives of firms, and the impact which these may have on a firm's performance.

The ownership of firms

There are a number of different types of ownership of firms which may have important influences on the operation of the firm.

The sole proprietor

About 45 per cent of the firms in the country are owned and often run single handed. The owner has complete control over the operation of the company and can be assumed to profit maximise since the profits are his income. However, some owners may be in business for other reasons – enjoyment, philanthropy, the satisfaction of producing a good product, etc, and so may choose not to profit maximise. The owner of the business is liable for all the debts of the business. Hence the term 'unlimited liability'.

An important point about one-man companies is their lack of financial resources. These may be limited to their private capital plus loans from commercial banks whose lending policies are generally extremely cautious. This lack of finance may seriously constrain the growth of the firm. The owner may solve this problem and also expand his management resources by taking in a partner.

The partnership

A partnership is a firm owned by two or more people (usually up to twenty). Each partner's share in the business determines how much each can draw in profit. If a partner owns 30 per cent of a business then he/she is entitled to 30 per cent of any profit which is distributed.

A partnership has advantages over the sole proprietorship in that more owners means greater potential capital and more opportunity for skills/ideas to be used for the good of the business. Partnerships are common among professions such as dentists, opticians and solicitors. In most cases all the partners are still personally liable for all the debts of the business.

Private joint-stock company (private limited company)

These are an extended form of partnership. The firm may have an unlimited number of shareholders who have bought a share in the assets of the company and therefore have a claim on the profits of the company (dividends). This greatly increases the financial resources of the company and so its capacity for growth.

The owners (shareholders) are now certain to be in favour of profit maximisation since larger profits increase their incomes and the expectation of high profits in the future increases the value of their assets when they want to sell them. The owners, since there are more of them, are less likely to be directly involved in the running of the company. This may create a divergence of interests between the owners of the company and the executives involved in running it – see below. The shareholders' liability in the business is limited only to the investment in the company: hence the term 'limited liability'.

The public joint-stock company (PLC)

Most large companies are public joint-stock companies. The great advantage for firms is the greatly increased potential for acquiring capital for investment. The shares in the company are quoted on the Stock Exchange which provides the link between millions of individuals who have money to lend and the firms who want to use it for investment.

The Stock Exchange solves the problem of the essentially incompatible nature of saving and investment. Savers are usually saving in order to consume in the future. They therefore wish to be repaid in the future. (It is important to remember that the bulk of the money invested on the Stock Exchange comes from millions of people who have contributed to insurance, trade union and pension funds which are then invested by these institutions in securities.) Firms who borrow money for capital investment would prefer never to repay it. This would mean selling productive assets. With the facilities offered by the Stock Exchange, lenders can recover their funds by selling to new savers. The firm is never involved in repayment. Most of the trading on the Stock Exchange is the reselling of existing securities. The certainty of being able to resell increases the security of shareholders. Shareholders in private, joint-stock companies (whose shares cannot be sold on the stock market) may feel less secure.

These owners will, like the shareholders in private joint-stock companies, want the firm to profit maximise. They are, however, likely to have little influence over the operation of the company. They are not there when decisions are made so know little of the realistic alternatives to the decisions made. They may vote against the board at the annual general meeting of shareholders but only an attack by a large number of shareholders is likely to have any impact. The disgruntled shareholder is much more likely to 'vote with his feet', ie sell his shares. This is again only a serious threat if a large number of shares are sold. The owners, the shareholders, are distinct from those who control the company, the board of Directors. This problem is known as the 'divorce of ownership and control'.

The professional executives who typically run these companies may therefore decide that their optimal strategy is to 'profit satisfice' (produce enough profits to satisfy shareholders but not necessarily to profit maximise). Instead of profit maximising, the executives may then maximise their own utility. Their utility depends on their current income, status, satisfaction and their anticipation of increases on these in the future. These may depend not on profit so much as on the size of the turnover, employment and market share of the company and on the rate of growth of any of these. We may then see firms apparently maximising growth rather than profit. This is a very important qualification of the usual profit maximisation assumption to predict the behaviour of firms.

Co-operatives

The firm is owned and run by its consumers or producers or workers. The Co-op (now a retail company with many branches) was set up by consumers to cut out the profits of the middle-man (the wholesaler/retailer) who bought goods from producers and then sold them at a much higher price to consumers. The Co-op bought directly from producers and then sold the goods to its members at cost price. The members/shareholders of the Co-op are largely its customers who receive a share of the profits according to their number of purchases at Co-op shops.

French vineyard owners formed a number of co-operatives to organise the production and sale of their wine to the market. This organisation had previously been done by middlemen who could exploit the farmers, paying minimal prices for grapes, and then making large profits from the final price for which the wine was sold. The vineyard owners wanted this profit for themselves. A large co-operative community has been built up at Mondragon in Spain.

During the 1970s Britain saw the development of worker co-operatives usually as a consequence of failure by existing management in declining industries. The Meriden motor-cycle co-operative and others such as the Scottish Daily Express were to survive only for a short time: short of both cash and management expertise. More recently worker co-operatives have successfully re-emerged in Britain on a small scale, particularly in service industries including 'growth' sectors such as retailing and 'high tech'. They usually employ less than 20 people. The Co-Operative Development Agency and the government have encouraged the expansion of the co-operative sector.

The objectives of the firm

In Chapter 4 we made the assumption that firms will decide on their optimal output by choosing the output at which profits are maximised. This is the traditional assumption made in economics about the behaviour of firms; it is based on the argument that the owners of firms wish to maximise incomes in order to maximise utility, and do this by maximising the profits of the firms.

However, as we have seen above, when we look more closely at the characteristics of the structure of firms, the assumption of profit maximisation seems less realistic. The single owner of a health food shop may be more interested in spreading the benefits of better nutrition to a maximum number of consumers than in maximising profits. The directors and executives of a public joint-stock company may choose to maximise employment, sales, revenue, market share rather than to maximise profits. (We would, however, expect that the constraint on the choice of company strategy is the need to produce enough profit to satisfy the shareholders.) A co-operative of the Meriden type may be more interested in maintaining employment than in maximising profits.

The following diagram illustrates the difference that certain alternative strategies make to the firm's output decision. The firm's total costs are shown rising proportionately with output (constant average costs and marginal costs and no economies or diseconomies of scale) while the demand curve is a straight line sloping downwards (initially relatively elastic but becoming relatively inelastic as output is expanded where marginal revenue is equal to zero when total revenue is maximised). Total revenue, therefore, first rises and then falls as output is expanded.

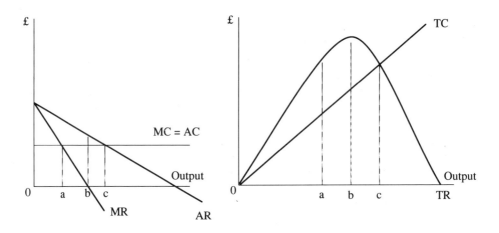

Profit maximising output is at 0a in both diagrams. Marginal revenue is equal to marginal cost and the difference between total revenue and total cost (total profit) is greatest at that output. Revenue is, however, maximised at output 0b in both diagrams. It is the highest level of the total revenue curve and is where marginal revenue is zero (that is, where changing output adds no more to revenue). A revenue maximising firm will therefore choose 0b not 0a, the profit maximising output. Maximising unit sales would imply producing an infinite output even if this required selling at negative prices (where the firm pays consumers to take the good). Losses would then be enormous.

More realistically, it is likely that the firm operates under some profit/loss constraint. Let us assume, for example, that the firm must provide shareholders with a reasonable return on their investment. At this point, we need to diverge to explain that there is a difference between how an economist defines 'profit' and how an accountant does so. This is illustrated in the following diagram.

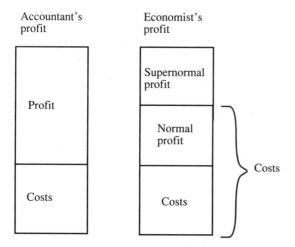

As shown in this diagram, part of what an accountant calls 'profit' is counted by economists as part of the operating costs. The rationale for this is that a 'normal' rate of return is needed to keep a firm in that industry; if returns are below the 'normal' level available elsewhere, then firms will leave the industry for more profitable ones. Hence what an economist means by 'profit' is in fact profits over and above the 'normal' level.

Returning to our discussion on the need to provide shareholders with a reasonable return on their investment: this reasonable return is, of course, included in the cost function.

The shareholders will, therefore, be satisfied as long as the firm 'breaks even', where costs (including a reasonable profit) are covered by revenue. The firm will then maximise sales within this profit/loss constraint by producing output Oc which is the largest output possible while avoiding losses.

The divergence of firms from the objective of profit maximisation is likely to depend on the firm's competitive situation. In the next chapter, the various competitive situations are discussed. In highly competitive industries, each firm must profit maximise in the long run or it will be making losses at the prices fixed by other profit maximising firms. In less competitive situations (monopoly and oligopoly), the firms have less pressure on them and therefore can choose alternative strategies. In oligopoly, we typically find a great emphasis on maintaining and increasing market share (which effectively means maximising unit sales) rather than on profit maximising.

Additionally, we might find that the strategy for maximising long-run profits is different from that for maximising profits over the next year's trading. For example, a high-price strategy may maximise profits in the short run since demand is likely to be inelastic. However, in the long run, consumers will find alternative sources of supply so that sales are lost and profit is reduced. A firm might therefore prefer to keep prices low in order to maximise long-run profits. The choice of the short-run strategy will probably be determined by pressure from the firm's creditors to settle debts immediately.

An additional problem with the profit maximising assumption (or indeed any other assumption about the behaviour of firms) is the degree of uncertainty under which firms must make decisions. Firms must consider the future in making their decisions (future demand conditions, the likely behaviour of competitors, the future prices of inputs and likely changes in the technological environment) but the future is uncertain. Firms may therefore be presented with a range of possible profit-maximising strategies (or strategies for the maximisation of any other variable) made on the basis of different assumptions about the future. A simple assumption about the objectives of firms may not, therefore, be very useful in predicting their behaviour.

In view of these problems with using the profit maximisation assumption as a way of predicting the behaviour of firms, economists have looked at the actual decision-making behaviour of firms. A common method used by firms in fixing prices and output is to use 'a mark-up on costs' to fix the price and then sell however many units consumers want at that price.

In the following diagram, the firm's average cost is shown by the curve AC which indicates that average costs are constant over a range of output. The firm expects to sell a quantity within this range of output given its expectations about demand conditions. It prices at some fixed 'mark-up' on these average costs. This mark-up would be likely to be sufficient to produce normal profits if the firm is operating in a competitive situation but perhaps more than normal profits in a less competitive situation. (See the discussion of competitive models in Chapter 6.) The price is therefore fixed at P in the diagram.

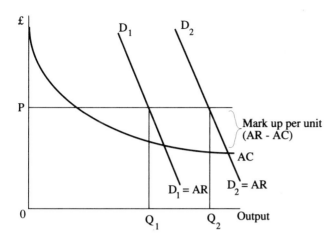

The volume of sales depends on demand at this price. The firm may expect demand to be anything between D_1 and D_2. If demand is D_1 the firm will sell Q_1 but if demand is D_2 the firm will sell Q_2.

The firm may, of course, find it difficult to adapt its output to these extremes of demand. In that case there may be surplus goods produced (if demand is only Q_1) or a shortage of goods (if demand is Q_2). The firm may then alter its pricing strategy in order to clear excess stocks or to ration a shortage. It may alternatively choose to maintain a consistent pricing policy which may be preferred by consumers. Which strategy the firm chooses may depend on its competitive situation. Where there is an element of consumer loyalty to a product (important in monopolistic competition and oligopoly, discussed in the following chapter) the firm may prefer to maintain a consistent price strategy at the cost of dealing with accumulating stocks or shortages. Where there is no element of consumer loyalty (perfect competition, discussed in the following chapter) the firm would rationally adjust price to equate output to demand.

This section has examined the problem with making a single assumption about the objectives of firms. Not only may firms be opting for some objective other than the most obvious choice of profit maximisation but they may be working with a number of objectives (eg profit maximising while maintaining a certain minimum market share; increasing sales at a certain minimum rate while producing reasonable profits and maximising employment). Actual decisions will then depend on the weights given to each objective.

An added problem is the difficulty of uncertainty which forces firms to choose from a range of probabilities. In reality firms seem to apply certain 'rules of thumb' to guide their decisions in an uncertain world.

Nevertheless, it is necessary for economists to make some assumptions about the objectives of firms in order to predict their behaviour. In Chapter 6, we will persist in assuming the objective of profit maximisation, and students should remember that the predictions of the behaviour of firms in various competitive situations are only sound if firms are choosing the single objective of profit maximising in a situation of certainty about the commercial world in the present and future.

Questions for review

1 Explain the concept of 'divorce of ownership and control'.

2 What possible alternatives to the profit-maximisation assumption are there?

Market structures and control | 6

Introduction	109
Perfect competition	109
Monopoly	118
Monopolistic competition	125
Oligopolistic competition	128
The models compared	133
The control of monopoly and merger activity	136
Restrictive practices	142
EU competition law	142

Introduction

In some industries there are many firms, which compete vigorously for business. These industries are *highly competitive*. In such industries, there are no large dominant firms. Examples in the UK include some types of farming, where there are a large number of small firms producing identical produce/livestock.

In other industries, there are only a handful of firms, which do not compete as vigorously as those in competitive industries, or who compete in different ways. These industries are *imperfectly competitive*. Examples in the UK include petrol, beer, and washing powder.

In some industries, there is only one firm. Such industries are *monopolies*. Examples include the UK rail network.

These are all different *market structures*. Economists use four different models of market structure as a framework for analysis. These different models are examined in detail in this chapter.

Perfect competition

Maximisation of profits

As a company *maximises its profits when its marginal revenue is equal to its marginal cost*, whatever type of market structure is considered a company will usually try to equate its marginal revenue with its marginal cost. It is important, therefore, that this concept is kept clearly in mind in any study of the different types of competitive structure.

Another key to understanding the behaviour of the company in any market is found in the relationship between the company and the consumer. In practice, that really means discovering the amount of influence that the company can exercise over its pricing and output policies.

Necessary assumptions

At one extreme, the company has no alternative but to accept the prevailing market price and so it is a *price-taker*. This type of competition is called *perfect competition*. For perfect competition to exist, a number of conditions must be satisfied, or, in economic jargon, a number of *assumptions* must be made:

a both buyers and sellers must have complete information about the market as a whole;

b the good being sold must be standardised (or homogeneous);

c any company must be able to move into, or out of, the industry freely (there are no barriers to entry and exit);

d no individual consumer or producer is able to influence the price level or the output level through his own actions; and

e consumers, as well as producers, must be free to allocate their resources any way they wish.

Perfectly elastic demand curve

So, under the conditions of perfect competition, the company is a price-taker and therefore it has to accept the equilibrium price as set by the normal forces of supply and demand. If the equilibrium price in the market is 0p, then the demand curve for the output of the individual company will be:

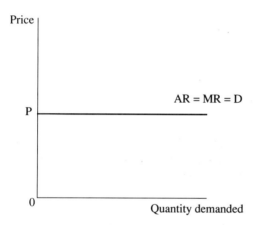

The company can sell as much as it likes at a price of 0p, but it cannot sell any at all at any other price. So, the demand curve for the output of the individual company will be a horizontal straight line at the price 0p. In effect, the demand curve is *perfectly elastic*. Furthermore, if the company receives a price of 0p for each and every unit it sells, its *average revenue* must also be its *marginal revenue*.

Determination of output level

A company will always try to equate its marginal revenue with its marginal cost as it wishes to maximise its profits. In this example, the company will maximise its profits at the level of output where its marginal cost curve cuts its demand curve, or where its marginal cost equals the selling price. However, under the conditions of perfect competition, if any companies make larger than normal profits, then more companies will enter the industry to take advantage of those profits. It follows that the equilibrium position under perfect competition can only be where a company is making a *'normal'* level of profit.

Normal profit is that level of profit which is necessary to keep a company in the line of production in question. Consequently, 'normal' profit is a genuine cost of production as without it there would be no production. So, it must be included in the cost curves of the company. Having said that, it can be seen that the company will be in equilibrium at the point where it is just covering its average costs of production (ie where the average cost curve, the marginal cost curve *and* the marginal revenue curve all meet).

At that point, the company is in equilibrium and its output will be 0Q:

Equilibrium under conditions of perfect competition

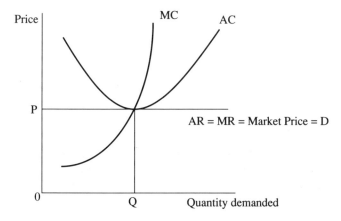

Free market mechanism

The process of each company being forced to accept the forces of supply and demand under conditions of perfect competition must be clearly understood. If the demand for the good in question suddenly increases, then its price will also rise. This, in turn, will cause the demand curve for each individual company to rise, as it is directly connected to the market price (see following graphs).

Sudden increase in demand leading to supernormal profits for company

Return to equilibrium due to new companies entering industry and increasing supply

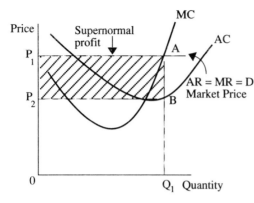
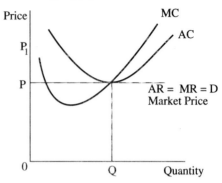

This means the resources have been ideally allocated:

a Suppose less of any particular good had been produced. The additional utility that consumers would derive from extra units of the good (marginal utility) would exceed the additional resource costs of producing those extra units (marginal cost). More of the good should be produced.

b Suppose more of any particular good had been produced. The resource costs of the extra units exceed the utility derived from their consumption so they should not have been produced.

The identity of marginal cost and price under perfect competition therefore indicates that exactly the right amount of all goods have been produced given the relative resource costs and the relative preferences of consumers. This conclusion is very important for the study of monopoly where firms tend to sell output for a price greater than marginal cost.

Students should note that even perfect competition only produces the ideal allocation of resources when there is no divergence between social and private costs and benefits. The existence of *externalities* in the production or consumption of goods will mean that perfect competition will produce the wrong allocation of resources. Externalities occur when the production or consumption of a good imposes some cost or benefit on individuals or institutions not directly involved in the transaction taking place.

Suppose we examine the long-run equilibrium of a perfectly competitive industry. Every firm in the industry will be producing where its marginal cost is equal to price. The *industry demand curve* is, of course, downward sloping since the more output the industry produces the lower the price at which it must be sold if consumers are to buy it.

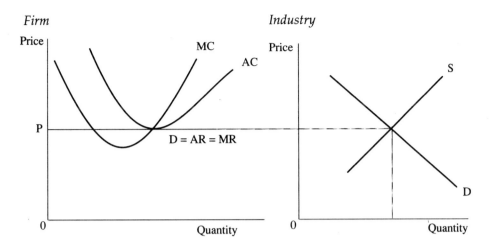

The diagram above shows the long-run equilibrium in perfect competition for the firm and the industry.

Let us now introduce the problem of externalities into the analysis. For example, a perfectly competitive industry may be minimising its costs by pouring waste chemicals into the atmosphere. The consumers of the good produced benefit from this cost-reducing pollution but this pollution imposes costs on the people who must breathe the polluted air. In this situation, what is the 'right' output and price for this good and how does it differ from the price and output produced by a perfectly competitive industry?

In the following diagram, the industry's average and marginal cost curves show the benefit of the cost-reducing pollution (AC_p and MC_p). The industry will, in the long-run equilibrium, be producing output Q_p and selling price P_p.

The true costs of producing these goods should, however, include the external cost of pollution. Including these costs, the social costs of producing these goods are shown by AC_s and MC_s where the difference between these social costs and the private costs is the value of the external cost of pollution.

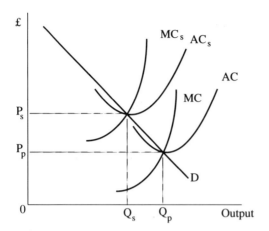

The 'right' output in this good should be where price is equal to the social marginal cost in which case the industry would produce only output Q_s and sell it at a higher price P_s.

Thus, if there are external costs, a perfectly competitive industry will produce 'too much' output and sell it at too low a price for allocative efficiency in the economy. Conversely, if there are external benefits resulting from the production or consumption of a good, a perfectly competitive industry will produce too little of the good and sell it at too high a price.

Perfect competition rarely exists in the real world. Buyers and sellers do not have complete information about the market nor are they always numerous, particularly in the case of sellers. There usually are differences in the quality and specification of products and it is not always easy for new companies to enter an industry quickly just because excess profits are being made. Similarly, just because losses are being incurred, firms will not necessarily leave an industry in the short term and, in real life, both individual buyers and sellers can influence prices directly. Buyers can obtain substantial discounts through bulk buying and sellers can enforce price levels if there are not many alternative suppliers. So, economists have constructed other models in an attempt to reach a close approximation to the type of markets found in the real world. They all come under the general heading of *imperfect competition*.

A firm's supply curve in perfect competition

Having demonstrated the equilibrium of a firm, the derivation of its supply curve can be considered. It will be recalled that the supply curve shows how supply varies in response to changes in price. No matter how the *market price* changes, the *demand curve* always appears to be a horizontal line (perfectly elastic) to the individual firm under perfect competition.

Market structures and control

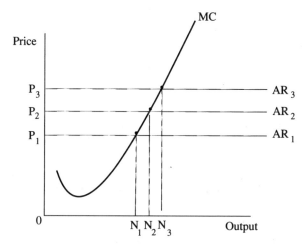

Therefore as price goes up or down the firm always tries to equate price with marginal cost in order to maximise its profits. As price increases from OP_1 to OP_2 to OP_3 the firm expands output from ON_1 to ON_2 to ON_3. This, therefore, shows how the firm varies output in response to changes in price; in other words, it is a supply curve. Thus it can be concluded that: under perfect competition the firm's MC curve, above AVC, is its supply curve. However, this analysis only applies to the short run. In the long run a firm must cover its long-run average costs (LRAC).

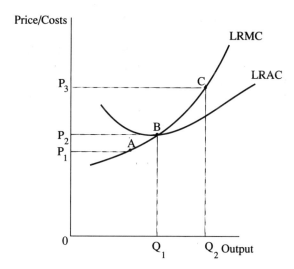

The perfectly competitive firm produces at that level of output at which P is equal to marginal cost, provided it makes more profit by producing some output than none at all. It therefore chooses points on the LRMC curve. At any price above

P_2 the firm makes profits because price is above long-run average cost (LRAC). At any price below P_2 such as P_1, the firm makes losses because price is below long-run average cost. It therefore will not produce any output at prices below P_2. The long-run supply curve is the LRMC curve above point B.

The resurgence of the small firm?

Much has been written recently about small businesses and the revival that they are apparently undergoing in the UK. Poor statistics make it difficult to discern the exact pattern of this revival, but it is clear that after a long period of decline the number of small businesses is increasing and relatively more people are working in them. What is not immediately clear is the extent to which this revival is a temporary response to the recession, with its growth of business counselling.

Technological as well as social change now strongly favours small firms and even higher prices favour decentralised production to avoid rising transport costs and the disruption associated with unionisation in large scale plants. We may yet see a return to a brewery and a bakery in every small community and certainly telematics and microprocessors will allow more and more people to work at home in what has been called the 'electronic cottage'.

Studies on technology, industrial structure and scale of production in the UK centred during the 1960s and 70s on the concept of 'minimum efficient scale' (see below). A common conclusion of such studies was that, in most industries, minimum efficient scale (MES) of production was above the average size of operating plants, that scaled-up plants would bring cost reductions, and that economies of scale were increasing over time. These analyses were tentative in nature and their value for policy has been questioned.

The concept of MES suggests that there is in many industries a level of output (or scale of production) below which it would be inefficient to produce. The following diagram illustrates this. It would not be efficient to produce at output levels below the level labelled MES, because long-run average costs are still falling.

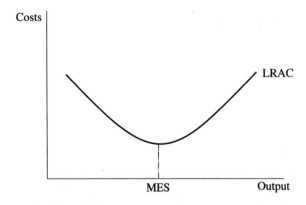

Since the early 1970s major technological and economic changes have taken place and these have implications for small-scale production and the general role of small firms. In 1971 the Bolton Committee of Enquiry was set up by the then Conservative Government to examine the state of small businesses in this country. Its report highlighted the burdens of taxation and bureaucratic regulation laid on small firms and the difficulties they faced in raising adequate capital; it concluded that the small business sector was in long-term decline. Since 1979, however, that trend has been reversed, and small businesses are now playing a more important part in Britain's economy.

There is no universally accepted definition of a small business. The Bolton Committee defined it as having up to 200 employees in the manufacturing sector, and elsewhere as operations to which certain arbitrary limits regarding turnover applied.

Over 95 per cent of all UK businesses employ fewer than 20 people. They account for 35 per cent of total employment outside central and local government. These figures make a significant contribution to Gross National Product (the total output of the economy). Since 1979 there has been rapid growth in the number of small firms. Between 1979-89 the overall number of small firms in the UK rose by around two thirds. On average, nearly 500 additional firms were created each working day. It is important however, to remember that the small firm sector suffers from many more business failures than do larger operations.

A recent Conservative party document representing closely the views of the government said:

> 'We believe that the health of small firms is vital to the future of the economy. In times of social and industrial change, flexibility and innovation are essential; it is the small and independent business community that often has these qualities. Small firms are run by individuals, unhampered by tradition, and suffer less from restrictive union practices. They only survive if they can react to the challenges of the market – their condition therefore reflects the performance of the free enterprise system as a whole. They provide variety and diversity, thus ensuring a wide range of choice for consumers. They stimulate employment, since more business means more jobs. They are the basis for future prosperity.'

The present government has done much to promote the revival of small business. It is through small business that incentive and initiative should flourish in a free market economy according to the monetarist theory. The reform and reduction of taxation, the loan guarantee scheme, the business expansion scheme, the enterprise allowance scheme, the business improvement scheme are but a few of the present government initiatives designed to stimulate small business development.

Small firms will always have a role in a modern economy. They often cater for local markets particularly when the product is perishable (ie florists). They cater for specialist markets or ones with a low demand (specialist custom built cars or hand-made furniture). High-technology industries have many specialist areas within which the small business can flourish.

Monopoly

Necessary conditions

Monopoly is at the other end of the market spectrum to perfect competition and is also a limited extreme. Two basic conditions are required for it to exist:

a the production of the commodity or service must be undertaken by one producer and one producer only; and

b the commodity or service must have few or no substitutes.

Although it is not impossible for these two conditions to be met, it is extremely unlikely that they will be. Condition (a) can be – and sometimes is – easily met (eg there is only one supplier of rail transport in each area in this country), but condition (b) is effectively an impossibility because there will always be some kind of substitute for a product. (Road transport may not be a close substitute for rail transport in the sense that it is not exactly the same, but it is, after all, an effective substitute – you can still get from A to B.)

Demand in a monopoly situation

The absolute monopolist may be able to control the supply of the product concerned, but he cannot completely control the demand. As there is usually at least some form of substitute for his product, if the monopolist tries to raise his selling price too high, the demand for his product will fall. As a result – unlike the situation found under perfect competition where the demand curve was a horizontal line – the demand curve for the product of a monopolist will slope *downwards* from left to right. However, as there is only one supplier of the product, the curve will still represent the average revenue (or price) curve as well.

In fact, the monopolist faces a choice. He can either:

a *determine the price* at which he will sell his output and then accept the quantity demanded at that price by the consumers; or he can

b *determine the output* that he will supply and then sell that output at whatever price the consumers are prepared to pay.

This can be summarised by saying that the *monopolist can determine the price of his product or its output, but not both*. The important point is that, in the final analysis, the monopolist is still subject to some degree of *consumer sovereignty*.

Marginal revenue can be negative

The essential point to grasp about a monopolist is that his demand curve is the same as the demand curve for the product as a whole, because whatever the quantity demanded in the market, he is the only person who can supply it. So the demand curve for his product also represents his average revenue curve, but the problem for the monopolist is to decide the most profitable price/output combination on that demand curve. He does this by the same process as the company operating under conditions of perfect competition – he equates his marginal cost of production with the marginal revenue from sales. However, the marginal revenue of a monopolist is *not* equal to his selling-price. If the monopolist wants to sell more units, he will have to lower the price on *all* the units he sells. The amount of revenue he gains from the sale of the last additional unit – his marginal revenue – will therefore be less than its price. For instance, suppose the monopolist can sell 50 units for £1 each. If he wants to sell one more unit he may have to lower his price to 99 pence. This price not only applies to that extra unit, but to the other 50 units as well. So, although his *gross* marginal revenue for the last additional unit is 99 pence, his *net* marginal revenue is, in fact, 99 pence *minus* 1 pence for each of the other 50 units. Consequently, his net marginal revenue is 49 pence, which is significantly less than the selling price.

For a company operating under conditions of perfect competition, an increase in its level of sales has no effect whatsoever on the selling price, but if the monopolist increases his level of sales, the market price will inevitably be depressed. Indeed, a monopolist's two revenue curves diverge and fall apart as he increases his output, although the actual extent of this is dependent upon the elasticity of demand of his product.

The monopolist's marginal revenue can be negative

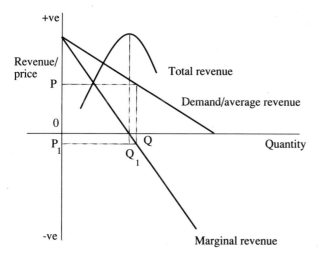

It will be remembered that when demand is *elastic*, total revenue increases after a reduction in price, but it falls when demand is *inelastic*. Now the connection between *total* revenue and *marginal* revenue is obvious. When total revenue is increasing as output increases, marginal revenue must be positive, but once marginal revenue becomes negative, total revenue must fall. When 0Q units are sold, average revenue is OP, but the marginal revenue of the $0Q'$th unit is OP_1 which is negative. In fact, total revenue starts to fall once the marginal revenue of a monopolist changes from being positive to being negative. This is at output $0Q_1$ on the graph, and the monopolist will restrict output to below $0Q$, so as to maximise profits. At $0Q_1$ total revenue is maximised. A useful guide to memorising this fact about a monopolist's total revenue is that when the demand for his product is *elastic*, his *marginal revenue* will be *positive*, but when his *marginal revenue* becomes *negative* – causing total revenue to fall – the demand changes from being elastic to being *inelastic*.

Profit maximisation for the monopolist

The technological 'facts of life' are the same for a monopolist as they would be for a producer under perfect competition. As a result, a monopolist's cost curves are the same as those experienced elsewhere: the difference lies in the demand conditions. However, the profit maximising position of the monopolist will still be where marginal cost equals marginal revenue:

Monopoly profits

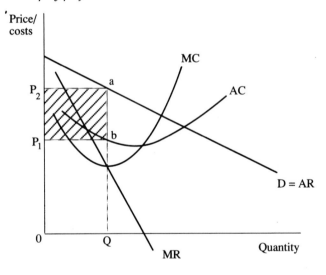

The output at which the monopolist will maximise his profits is $0Q$, where marginal revenue equals marginal cost. The price at this point is $0P_2$ (the price that consumers are prepared to pay for that particular output) and the average cost per unit is $0P_1$. It follows, therefore, that the average profit per unit is $0P_2$ minus $0P_1$. The total revenue derived from this output is represented by the rectangle $0P_2aQ$ and the total profit is P_1P_2aB (the shaded area).

This monopoly profit situation should not be confused with the supernormal profit of perfect competition. Although both are effectively the same in the short term, the former is unlikely – due to the nature of the market – to draw new entrants into the market in the long term. Monopolies tend to arise in industries which experience considerable economies of scale, or in industries which have decreasing long-run average costs. Such industries require enormous amounts of capital and have large distribution and service networks. As a result, it is not easy for new companies to enter the industry just because excess profits are being made. Furthermore, the monopolist will not wish to increase his output as his marginal costs will exceed his marginal revenue if he does.

Decreasing long-term costs

The long-term equilibrium position of a monopolist who has decreasing long-term costs will probably be:

Monopoly long-term equilibrium

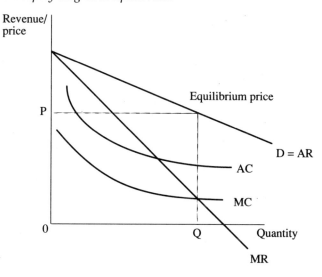

If a monopolist followed a policy of pricing his goods in accordance with the level of marginal cost, he would inevitably incur substantial losses as average cost is above marginal cost. No matter how much the economist might argue that a company should always follow a policy of marginal-cost pricing, the evidence in both this graph and the previous graph shows that a monopolist will not operate such a policy. However, there is no justification for the monopolist to reap quite such a high level of profit as is shown on both graphs. Some practical controls and restraints are clearly necessary and these will be studied in 'The models compared' below.

Theoretical objections

The economist's fundamental *theoretical* objection to monopoly is that by holding down production to a level where marginal cost equals marginal revenue, while charging the consumer considerably more, the monopolist is wasting economic resources. A simple numerical example will clarify this. If the marginal cost of producing an extra unit of output is £1 while the price the consumer is prepared to pay is £1.50, then by letting this discrepancy prevail the monopolist is putting a false signal into the operation of the price mechanism. As far as the consumer is concerned, he is really indicating that the opportunity cost of paying £1.50 for the monopolised good is the sacrificed goods valued at £1.50, but to the producer the opportunity cost of economic resources is only £1. Clearly, the difference of 50 pence constitutes a waste of resources. Either the monopolist should only charge £1 – the true cost of the resources used – or he should increase his level of output to the point where opportunity costs are equal. Only by doing one or the other will economic resources be used as efficiently as possible. As it is, under monopoly conditions the consumer may be forced to buy too little of the monopolised product, and too much of other products which may be produced less efficiently due to the higher cost in terms of resources.

Externalities and the monopolist

Note that if there are external costs associated with the production or consumption of this good, the monopolist may actually produce the *right* output for allocative efficiency in the economy. This is an example of Lipsey and Lancaster's 'Theory of the Second Best'. Suppose that, considering only private costs, the monopolist produces a profit-maximising output of Q_p and sells at price P_p. Since price exceeds the private marginal cost at this output, the monopolist is apparently selling too little of this good at too high a price for allocative efficiency. With externalities the 'right' output would be at Q_e and the price would be P_e, which is, incidentally, the output and price that a perfectly competitive industry would produce.

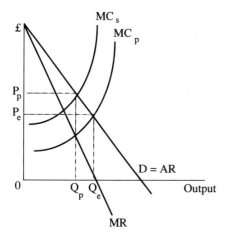

Now suppose that there are external costs associated with the production of this good, as discussed earlier. The social costs then may be shown by MC_s which is higher than MC_p by the value of the external cost. The 'right' output and price for this good is then Q_p and P_p. The effect of including externalities may be greater or less than the monopolist's distortion of output but it remains true that, if firms ignore external costs, it may be better to have a monopolist than a perfectly competitive industry for allocative efficiency.

Price discrimination

Another problem that may occur with monopoly is the distortion produced by price discrimination. Consider the problem facing the monopolist. He is currently selling output Q_a at price P_a. He would like to sell more output, Q_b, but he can only do so by lowering the price on *all* the units he sells. He will be selling Q_b output at P_b. What he would prefer is to be able to continue to sell Q_a at price P_a and only sell the extra $Q_b - Q_a$ units at P_b. His revenue would then be much greater. The monopolist may be able to manage this through a policy of price discrimination.

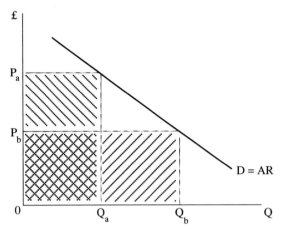

He must be able to divide his market into two or more different groups in terms of their demand for his goods. The significant difference between the groups will be their elasticity of demand for the goods. For example, the monopolist would find it profitable to charge a high price to a group with low price elasticity and a low price to a group with high elasticity.

An example of this type of selling is the railway companies' policy of charging high prices for commuter trips into and out of London and offering 'cheap-day returns' to travellers in the middle of the day. Having identified the groups and fixed discriminatory prices, the monopolist must be able to keep them separate. It obviously would not work if the high-price group could pretend to be low-price people. This is easy for the railway operating companies since the passengers are distinguished by their time of travel (generally before or after 9.30 am). The groups must be prevented from trading among themselves. If the high-price groups could buy goods from the low-price group, the monopolist would lose his high-price sales. This is again easy for British Rail. Cheap tickets can only be used for the specified journey times.

The final condition for price discrimination is that the firm should have no competitors who will offer to sell at lower prices to his high-price group from whom he is obviously making excess profits. Since monopolists are protected from competition, this condition will be satisfied.

The equilibrium pricing and output decision depends on the demand and cost conditions in the usual way but the price discriminator has two markets. If the marginal cost of supplying each group is the same, he should equate marginal cost to marginal revenue for each group. That is the marginal revenue for each group will be the same. Otherwise the monopolist could increase his profits by moving output into the market with the higher marginal revenue.

Price discrimination as practised a few years ago by British Gas against industrial consumers was seen as an anti-competitive practice and subject to a Monopolies and Mergers Commission investigation. The company sold gas to industrial consumers at a higher price than to domestic consumers.

Equilibrium for the price discriminating monopolist with identical marginal costs

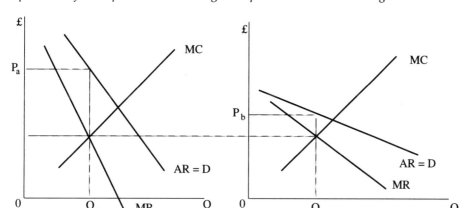

The monopolist might alternatively be facing a situation of zero marginal costs for his low price group. This applies for the spare seats on airliners and in theatres. The firm should then sell for maximum revenue which will be where marginal revenue is zero.

Monopolistic competition

Principle of minimum differentiation

Monopoly is a limiting extreme and so economists have developed a market theory which is a nearer approximation to the situation which exists in the real world. It is usually referred to as *monopolistic competition* because although there is an element of competition, there is also an element of monopoly power. The main characteristics of monopolistic competition are:

a *many companies* in the industry, and

b slightly *differentiated products*.

Each company therefore has a small degree of monopoly power while still being in competition with all the other companies in the industry. Consequently, the AR curve of the company (the demand curve for its product) is elastic, although not perfectly. If the company cuts its prices then it will gain some sales from other companies, but only to a limited extent, whilst if it raises the prices then it will lose some, but not all, of its sales.

It is, therefore, the differences that exist between the products within an industry that are the key to understanding the *theory of monopolistic competition*. Consumers do, in fact, tend to believe that a particular product from a particular company within an industry is genuinely different and so assume that no other similar product will be an adequate substitute. This belief is encouraged by the producers as they recognise its value to them. The three main ways in which producers encourage the belief are:

a use of *trade-marks*;

b *advertising*; and

c *brand-names*.

Packets of washing-powder may have almost identical ingredients, but if the consumer can be persuaded by the producer that its own brand-name has unique washing qualities, then he/she will buy that brand in preference to others. The demand curve, therefore, for a branded product does tend to slope downwards from left to right, but it will show signs of some inelasticity depending on the degree of brand attachment by the consumer to the product. Some economists summarise the main characteristics of monopolistic competition by the *Principle of Minimum Differentiation* which states that 'producers will make their own product as like existing products as possible without destroying the difference'.

Short-term excess profits

Under monopolistic competition a company will, in the short term, usually experience a high level of profit similar to that found in a monopoly situation:

Monopolistic competition (short term)

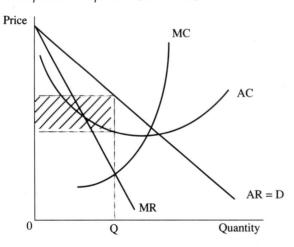

The shaded area represents this high profit.

Market structures and control | 127

Eventual position

However, in monopolistic competition the company is *in competition* with others and so it cannot, in the long term, prevent the entry of new competitors into the market. The situation will be similar to that prevailing under perfect competition. The high profits that existing suppliers are receiving will tend to attract new entrants into the market and they will seek to manufacture products which are very close substitutes. Once this happens, the degree of product loyalty (to the original producers) will tend to decline. This will cause the demand curve (average revenue curve) to become most elastic and also move to the left as the individual share of the total market falls.

In fact, as more and more competitors enter the industry, the level of excess profits will fall and eventually disappear, until all companies are only just covering their costs.

Monopolistic competition – eventual position

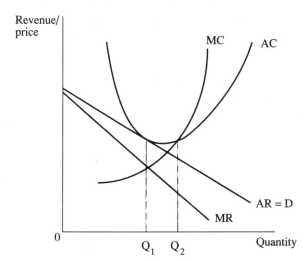

The only output worth producing is output $0Q_1$. Here at least average revenue covers its average cost. If output is raised beyond this point the company will not be covering its cost. Indeed, if it attempted to produce at its maximum capacity – where average cost is at a minimum – $0Q_2$ on the graph – it would be incurring substantial losses. It is a characteristic of monopolistic competition that a company will *restrict its output considerably*, and is operating sub-optimally.

Predictions of theory

First, the theory shows how there will be a continual tendency towards excess capacity or wasted resources. *Second*, it predicts that prices will be higher than they would be under perfect competition, simply because selling prices are above marginal costs.

Third, the theory of monopolistic competition explains why one observes firms making very different profits in the same industry. This would be impossible in perfect competition where all firms make only normal profits (ie more, and they would be competed away by other firms; less, and the firm would be making losses). Monopolistic competition allows for many firms in the same industry, but not producing identical goods. It is therefore possible for individual firms to dominate a particular area of the market and earn excess profits.

For example, a corner grocery store has a particularly good location compared to other similar firms in similar situations. The grocery store therefore makes excess profits. However, no firm will set up in competition because the market of that area is too small to support another shop and the best location is already occupied. The firm therefore keeps its excess profits. These excess profits are known as 'economic rent', and are due in this case to the good location.

The theory of monopolistic competition was developed some 40 years ago in response to the valid argument that the theory of perfect competition was irrelevant to the vast majority of markets in the real world, and at least it recognises that there is a considerable amount of genuine (as well as contrived) product differentiation. It also recognises that companies can, and do, influence consumers through the use of advertising. In short, the principle benefit from this theory compared to the theory of perfect competition is that the assumptions are more relevant to the real world. However, although it is not possible to test the theory as such due to the economist's difficulty in conducting controlled experiments, it does lead us to an interesting and more relevant theory.

Oligopolistic competition

Domination of an industry

An apparent example of monopolistic competition is the washing powder industry. There are countless washing powders under various brand names, but they all perform the same basic function. However, the different brands are always presented to the consumer as having 'unique' qualities, although they are really very similar to one another. So this would appear to be an excellent example of the principles of minimum differentiation and monopolistic competition. In fact, nearly every brand of washing powder is produced by one of two companies. Between them, Procter & Gamble and Unilever produce the vast majority of washing powders. The companies have discovered that consumers show distinct preferences for a particular 'brand' and so they continue to produce a multitude of brands instead of just two. The end result is an industry which is effectively controlled by two companies. Clearly the theory of monopolistic competition cannot be relevant in such a situation. In fact, competition amongst a small number of firms – or *oligopoly* – is very common today. Many industries are dominated by a handful of firms. Although there are a number of small motor car manufacturers, the UK car industry is effectively dominated by 4 major firms. There are only two major firms in the safety match industry and the electric wire and cable industry, the tyre industry and the chemical industry all show similar characteristics. Where *two* firms dominate a market this is called a *duopoly*.

Fundamentally different

Oligopoly is not a compromise between perfect competition and monopoly as monopolistic competition tends to be. It is fundamentally different. In all the other types of market structure examined so far, there has been one common factor: the company has always faced impersonal and anonymous market forces. A company under conditions of perfect competition knows that it cannot affect the behaviour or profitability of other companies through its own actions. A monopolistic company knows that none of its customers can have an appreciable effect on either its sales or its profits, but an oligopolistic company has a very different relationship with both its competitors and its customers. An oligopolist has only a handful of competitors. Whenever he changes his price or alters his level of output or changes the specification of his product his actions are immediately noticed by those competitors and they will react accordingly. Above all, an oligopolist wants to maintain his market share. He wants to keep his customers loyal to *his* product rather than to the products of his competitors and, wherever possible, to attract customers away from competitors. As in monopolistic competition, this involves maintaining differences (both real and imagined) between his product and those of his competitors, but these differences may well be more pronounced in an oligopolistic market.

Above all else, oligopolists have reason to fear price competition. They and their competitors are currently making excess profits (the greater the barrier to new entrants, the larger those profits are likely to be). If they start competing on price, a price war between them may eliminate their excess profits. They will only 'win' if they can drive their competitors out of business but they risk being driven out of business themselves. (The battle between the big airlines over the North Atlantic routes is an example of this type of potentially destructive battle.) Much safer to be satisfied with current profit levels and prices.

Sales strategy

The prime concern of an oligopolist is his sales strategy. He will prosper or perish through his success or failure in attracting and maintaining sales levels, without necessarily changing his price levels. His principle problem is that his competitors will not stand idly by while he increases his market share. If he produces a new product variation, his competitors will follow suit. If he increases his level of advertising expenditure, so will the others. Those of you who play board games like chess will already be aware of how important it is to try to be one or two moves ahead of your opponent. Despite your natural concern about your own next move, you must also think about the next move of your opponent. In this way, you might be able to counter it before he has a chance to make it. Oligopolists are in a very similar situation.

Complex relationships

The complexities of such a relationship between competing companies are obvious. For instance oligopolists are likely to spend enormous sums of money on advertising in an attempt to persuade customers to buy their products. It might be the case that in an industry dominated by two companies that each company spent £1 million a year on advertising, in order simply to maintain its current sales levels. Similarly, it might be possible for both companies to reduce their advertising budgets to £200,000 without harming their sales levels, *provided that both did so at the same time*. However, it is probable that if one company cut its budget while the other did not, that the second company would gain sales at the expense of the other. (This naturally works the other way as well.) The problem is simple. Both companies *could* save £800,000 by cutting their advertising budgets, but neither is prepared to do so in case the other does not follow suit. In short, one company could cut its advertising budget and save £800,000 but in the process it would lose, say, sales worth £400,000 while its competitor would raise its sales by £400,000 without lifting a finger! The dilemma for each company is obvious.

Similar examples could be given for the price and output levels of oligopolistic firms. Indeed, even more complicated examples could be envisaged. An oligopolist does not only need to consider very carefully what he *thinks* his competitors might do. He also needs to consider what his competitors expect him to do, or even what he thinks his competitors think he expects them to do! The possible outcome of such thinking is clearly indeterminate. The obvious solution for an oligopolist is to co-operate with his competitors, either openly or secretively. This used to be common practice on both sides of the Atlantic, but governments of all persuasions now effectively limit the freedom of action of companies, and particularly those which show signs of being oligopolistic.

An example of just such a complicated situation is where we observe an industry dominated by very few, very big firms with a 'fringe' of many much smaller firms. The price level is the same throughout the industry while the profit levels vary enormously – the big firms making excess profits and the small firms just covering their costs.

Non-price competition

If outright cooperation is not permitted, then oligopolists will try to preserve their advantages in other ways. They engage in a great deal of *non-price competition*. This includes such things as a personal delivery service, free trial offers, glamorous and expensive public relations and, above all, advertising. It is this last item in particular which effectively ensures that new entrants find it difficult to survive in the industry. As the very nature of oligopoly enables companies to reap supernormal or excess profits, the main problem for an oligoplist is the prevention of new competitors entering the industry in response to the high profit levels. Advertising on a grand scale not only helps to maintain sales levels against immediate competitors, but it also makes it difficult for new entrants. The prohibitive cost of advertising is a real deterrent. Indeed, it is not unusual for an oligopolistic industry to spend around 10 per cent of its gross sales revenue on advertising. A new company entering the industry would need to spend even more than that just to break into the market. However, this fact does not always prevent new competition. There are various examples of new companies entering traditionally oligoplistic markets. For instance, General Electric and Xerox invaded the computer market in the United States, while Golden Wonder Potato Crisps – backed by its American parent company – eventually provided effective competition to Smith's Crisps in the UK. Indeed, Smith's had a stranglehold on the entire market before Golden Wonder arrived. It must be admitted, though, that the majority of new companies entering an oligopolistic market are already large established firms in other fields. It is very rare for a new small company to 'break into' an oligopoly situation.

No simple rules

It is impossible to construct a model for a typical oligopolistic industry. Any model would have to take into account the complexities of each individual industry and each industry is unique. They do not exhibit a uniform equilibrium position as such because price and output levels are indeterminate in the conventional sense. They are entirely dependent on the views taken by individual companies based on their own assessments of likely action by competitors, and these are not quantifiable in any precise way.

The pricing strategy of oligopolists (in theory at least) is constrained by the kinked demand curve that operates in both stable and buoyant conditions.

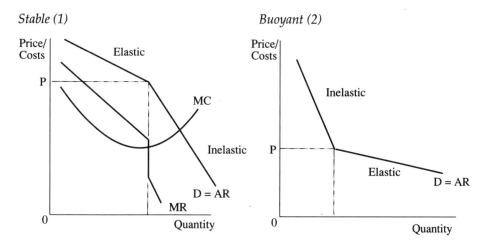

In a market which is not growing, any sudden price change by *one* of the oligopolists will not be to that firm's advantage. If price is at P in diagram (1) in the depressed market no one firm will rush to raise or lower its price. The upper part of the kinked demand curve is elastic, and if a firm raised its price its total revenue would fall because other firms would not follow its lead in a depressed market. On the other hand, if an oligopolist lowered its price the other firms would follow down the inelastic section of the demand curve. Thus all firms would see their total revenue fall. In a buoyant market (2) demand is rising and will mean higher pricing is possible. If one firm either lowers or raises its price higher total revenue is possible. However, lower prices could lead to a price war. It is thus in the interests of oligopolists not to engage in price competition. Non-price competition is much more likely.

Empirical evidence

Many oligopolists maintain that their prices are decided by estimating their long-term costs and adding a mark-up to give a reasonable profit on invested capital. This 'rule' is too vague to be of much use to the economist. It does not define a 'reasonable' return, let alone indicate the volume of sales on which estimates are based. Indeed, the rule implies that when sales are at a low level the oligopolist will *raise* prices in order to cover his fixed costs. A very unlikely event! Most important, the rule does not indicate how the rigid price structure common to oligopolistic markets is preserved, when the price which is appropriate for one company is either excessive or insufficient for others.

When oligopolists are pressed on these matters, it is usually discovered that the 'rule' is always interpreted 'in the light of the prevailing competitive conditions'. In short, although the rule of estimating costs and adding a mark-up may provide a vague approximation to the pricing policies of oligopolists it has to be adapted to the prevailing strategic considerations. The main consolation to the consumer is that the continued threat of competition from outside the industry helps to keep an oligopolist's prices moderately competitive. It is indeed possible that oligopolists maintain prices at a level which is reasonably profitable to them, but not so profitable as to attract outsiders.

Why don't the big firms eliminate the fringe of small firms through slightly lower prices so that they then have the whole market to themselves and can increase their profits? They do not do this because the price competition to eliminate the small firms might set off a price war between the big firms as they fight over the larger markets. Since price competition between the big firms is to be avoided, the large firms allow the small firms to survive.

The real world

The vague rule which oligopolists appear to follow regarding their pricing policies is also probably true of most industrialists in the real world. Few – if any – spend hours constructing complicated graphs of all the relevant cost and revenue curves, so it is unlikely that any industrialist would consciously equate his marginal revenue with his marginal cost. However, it is a fair assumption that in his attempt to maximise his profits, an industrialist would probably reach the same approximate conclusion. Furthermore, in today's mechanised and automated world, many companies are utilising computers and the like in their management processes. Increasingly, as you progress through the world of management, you will come across statistical and mathematical techniques such as operational research and linear programming, which are used to help the industrialist reach a very similar profit maximisation level of output to the one the economist reaches with his geometrical curves. However, due to the imperfect or oligopolistic nature of many markets today, it is also probable that firms take more notice of their *average* cost levels than their *marginal* ones. This is also partly due to the 'stickiness' of prices and costs. They are not nearly so variable as many an economist makes out, so it is much easier to determine total or average costs and then add a 'reasonable' mark-up.

The models compared

Advantages of competition

From the economist's viewpoint a high level of competition has three potential advantages:

a There will be a higher level of economic efficiency as resources are allocated in accordance with the free operation of the price mechanism.

b There will be a higher level of satisfaction among consumers as prices are equal to marginal costs, so *real* incomes remain as high as possible.

c The competition and assumptions of perfect competition – particularly free entry for producers – allow consumers a wide choice of suppliers.

Disadvantages of competition

However, these claimed advantages tend to ignore the state of modern technology and the highly complex and integrated nature of an industrialised society. Indeed, it is possible to make a strong case for *less* rather than *more* competition:

First, the need for mass production techniques requires companies wherever possible to utilise the economies of scale. It just would not be possible to meet the demand for the family motor car at a competitive and realistic price if there were numerous small manufacturers. In fact, the average cost curve of a large manufacturer is usually lower than the overall average cost curve for a competitive industry.

Secondly, many technological developments would not have been possible if there had not been the opportunity for large companies to exist side-by-side with small ones. The costs of research and development in modern industry are often very high and the advances in pharmaceuticals and motor cars, for instance, would not have been possible had the industries been highly competitive in the economist's sense.

Thirdly, the implications for employment from a high level of competition are also important. One of the assumptions for the existence of perfect competition is free entry for new companies into the industry, but the converse also applies. If the demand for a product declines then, under perfect competition, the marginal company will leave the industry. (The marginal company is the one that is just covering its costs before the decline in demand.) If it does leave the industry, this will result in a decline in employment within the industry. It is true that the economist would argue that under perfect competition all resources are mobile between different industries, but in real life this is not the case. It is unlikely that a worker who had been working in one industry all his life will find it easy to change to an unrelated industry. So, it is probable that employment prospects are more stable in an industry where companies are able to influence the demand for their product through advertising and so forth rather than in a perfectly competitive industry.

Fourthly, another point which some economists prefer to ignore is the possibility of having *too many* companies in a perfectly competitive industry. In fact, many industries do have an excessive number of companies, most of which do a very small volume of business and only remain in the industry until they have gone bankrupt. However, just as fast as one company goes out of business, another company springs up. Small grocery stores, pubs, restaurants, petrol stations, clothing manufacturers and undertakers are typical examples. These small concerns do not sell cheaply as they are often grossly inefficient and they rarely utilise their plant to its full capacity. For example, it has been estimated that 40 per cent of petrol stations in the UK could disappear without detracting from the service given to consumers. Indeed, those remaining would make more efficient use of their resources. In addition, a sharp reduction in the number of stations would free many resources for more 'profitable' lines of production.

Empirical research on economic loss

A considerable amount of research has been undertaken into the economic loss caused by monopoly and oligopoly. The extent of the loss depends on two main factors:

a the amount by which the price of the product has been raised above the (so-called) competitive price; and

b the amount by which output has been restricted by the same token.

These two factors are, of course, inter-related through the elasticity of demand (ie the percentage rise or fall in the quantity demanded after a one per cent fall or rise in price). So, if the elasticity of demand was 2 – which is on the high side for most goods – and an oligopoly resulted in prices being one per cent higher than the competitive level, then the reduction in output caused by the oligopoly would be 1 times 2, or 2 per cent. In fact, surveys in the United States indicate that at the outside, prices in oligopolistic markets are 15 per cent higher than the comparable competitive market. This would indicate that output in such industries is around 30 per cent lower – assuming an elasticity of demand of 2.

However, this does not represent the actual economic loss. Although output may be 30 per cent lower, the resources that would have been used to produce that missing 30 per cent are now in fact freed from other activities. Admittedly, according to the price mechanism, the resources will be used in producing less valued goods, but they will still be used. The calculations from here onwards in the published research are complicated, but the conclusions show that the cost of both monopoly and oligopoly is between 5 per cent and 7 per cent of the value of output for those industries concerned. As these industries themselves account for about a quarter of the entire industrial output of the United States, it would seem that the overall economic loss to the country in terms of the value of output is only about 1 per cent or 2 per cent. Despite protestations to the contrary by some politicians and economists, imperfect competition is a surprisingly minor source of economic inefficiency!

However, it must be emphasised that this is probably the result of the strict controls that are now applied to the majority of oligopolies and monopolies.

Summary

In conclusion, it will be useful to summarise the various types of market structure in tabular form:

Types of market structure

Type	No of producers	Product Differentiation	Example	Influence over price	Marketing Methods
Perfect competition	Many	Identical	A few agric products	None	Market exchange or auction
Monopolistic competition	Many	Real or minor imagined differences	Retail trade	Some	Heavy advertising (product differentiation)
Oligopoly	Few	Some differences	Banks, confectionery, car manufacturers	Considerable, but with restraints	Heavy advertising and administered prices
Duopoly	Two	Used extensively	Detergents Telecommunications	Considerable	Heavy advertising
Monopoly	One	Unique product with no close substitutes	Gas, area water boards	Very considerable but dependent on existence of indirect substitutes (eg road v rail or oil v coal)	Promotional advertising

Many monopolies face competition from either substitutes or imports. Many face foreign competition which dilutes their power in the market place. The privatised companies such as BT and British Gas have considerable amounts of monopoly power. The water supply industry is a further example of a monopoly, in that each Water Board has a monopoly in its area.

Students should be aware of monopsony where there is a single buyer of a product which is often produced by many suppliers. A monopsonist's power can be quite considerable when he can take his custom to any of a number of producers, possibly negotiating quite large documents. Governments are often monopsonists – sole buyers of certain items such as defence products.

The control of monopoly and merger activity

Economists can identify certain *market structures* and certain types of *market conduct* by firms that *may* lead to a poor industrial performance in terms of efficiency.

a A highly *concentrated* industry (where there are only a few firms or where some firms produce an output which is a large part of industry output) may give firms the power to reduce output, forcing up price and increasing profits at the expense of the consumer. *Concentration* is usually measured by taking, say, the few largest firms in the industry and calculating what percentage of the output or sales they control. For example, a four-firm concentration ratio of 85 per cent means that the four largest firms control 85 per cent of the market.

b If firms are resisting the entry of new firms into the market this is likely to lead to higher prices and less efficient production than if the firms had to face the pressure of competition.

A government wishing to promote efficiency in industry might therefore decide that it should prevent industry from becoming too concentrated and should outlaw certain types of industrial conduct.

However, these high levels of concentration and types of market conduct do not *necessarily* lead to undesirable results in terms of efficiency.

a A highly concentrated industry may be necessary if economies of scale are to be fully exploited.

b Protection from the entry of new competing firms may give the existing firms the security and profits likely to encourage a high rate of innovation.

The government might, therefore, be wiser to look directly at *industrial performance* so that they can judge the net advantage or disadvantage of particular industrial situations. These performance indicators could be:

a the level of profit earned on capital invested compared to average profit levels;

b the level of expenditure on advertising;

c the rate of innovation of new products and processes.

It should be noted that performance indicators are not particularly easy to apply to real industries.

a It may be that average profit levels are being distorted by structural decline in some large sectors of the economy. A higher profit level may therefore only indicate a relatively successful and expanding industry.

b We would expect rates of innovation to vary between industries since technological advances are not necessarily evenly spread. How can the government establish whether the actual rate of innovation in an industry is less than it might have been if there had been some alternative market structure?

The British government has typically chosen to use a pragmatic approach towards monopoly power that looks at each case on its merits. This section covers the legislation enacted in this area over recent years and some of the cases examined.

The Monopolies and Mergers Commission (MMC)

The Commission is a statutory body set up to inquire into and report on matters which are referred to it. These references include questions relating to specific mergers, monopolies, anti-competitive practices and the performance of some public sector bodies.

The Commission was first set up as the Monopolies and Restrictive Practices Commission in 1948. Its present title and many of its current responsibilities are derived from the Fair Trading Act 1973. The Competition Act 1980 is the other main piece of legislation governing the Commission's activities. There are several different types of issue that may be referred to the Commission for inquiry and report, but the Commission has no power to initiate its own investigations.

Under the 1973 Act, the Secretary of State may refer specific *mergers* and *monopoly situations*, or make what are called *general references*. Monopoly situations may also be referred by the Director General of Fair Trading (who heads the Office of Fair Trading, a separate, independent, government agency) and it is generally he who does so.

The 1980 Act contains powers for the Director General to make *competition references* to the Commission, and for the Secretary of State to refer questions relating to certain *public sector* bodies. Since 1984 the Commission has also been given responsibility for investigating questions referred to it relating to certain privatised undertakings.

Merger references

The 1980s brought an increase in the amount of merger activity. Mergers can be classified into a number of groups.

Horizontal mergers
The integration of two or more firms in the same industry and operating at the same stage in the productive process, eg two supermarket chains merging. The advantages for the firms are the exploitation of economies of scale and the elimination of competitors by merging with them. The British Airways/British Caledonian merger is a horizontal merger in airline services.

Vertical mergers
The integration of two or more firms operating in the same industry but at different stages in the productive process, eg a chain of shoe shops merging with a shoe manufacturer. The advantages for the firm may be certain technical advantages (eliminating packaging, for example) but also the elimination of competition for markets or suppliers through the acquisition of an exclusive market or supplier.

Conglomerate mergers
The diversification of a firm by its acquisition of a firm from a different industry.

The advantages for the firms may be certain financial economies of scale and also greater security in fluctuating economic conditions. An additional advantage may be the elimination of competition through cross-subsidisation of products. The Imperial Group is a result of conglomerate mergers.

Lateral mergers

The integration of two or more firms who make products in roughly the same broad product market (ie food and drink, Brooke Bond – Oxo).

The assumption underlying the 1973 Act is that some mergers may have economic, social or other effects which go beyond the interests of the shareholders concerned and merit examination on grounds of the public interest.

It is important to note that there is no presumption in the Act that a merger is undesirable, and even if it is referred to the Commission the bidder does not have to show that the merger will be beneficial, although he will hope to show that it may be expected not to operate against the public interest.

Section 84 of the 1973 Act requires the Commission when considering the public interest to *take into account* 'all matters which appear to them in the particular circumstances to be relevant'; and among other things to *have regard to* five points:

a maintaining and promoting competition in the United Kingdom;

b the interests of consumers;

c the development of new products and the reduction of costs;

d the balanced distribution of industry and employment; and

e competitive activity by United Kingdom companies in overseas markets.

Since 1984 it has become apparent that the government has allowed mergers to proceed as long as competition in the market is unaffected. The broader criteria of the 'public interest' have been given a lower priority by the DTI/OFT. Many economists and politicians were surprised that the Rowntree/Nestlé and British Airways/British Caledonian mergers were not investigated by the MMC.

Before a merger can be referred the criteria that have to be met are that two or more businesses (at least one of which is carried on in the United Kingdom) must cease to be distinct enterprises; and that one or both of the market-share test and the assets test are satisfied. These are, respectively, that as a result of the merger the enterprises which cease to be distinct will together supply or receive at least one-quarter of the goods or services of a particular description supplied in the United Kingdom or a substantial part of it; and that the gross value of the worldwide assets taken over exceeds £30 million.

If these criteria appear to be satisfied the Office of Fair Trading (OFT) endeavours to establish the likely effects of the merger, primarily upon competition, but also upon any other matter that might be of concern to the public interest. OFT's function here is to assist the Director General in deciding whether to advise the Secretary of State that there are sufficient public interest reasons for an in-depth investigation of a particular case by the Commission.

Only a small minority of mergers scrutinised by OFT are referred to the Commission. It should also be remembered that the proposals which OFT considers are themselves only a proportion – about one-third or less – of all mergers.

It has been argued that one of the major weaknesses of UK merger legislation is the need for the MMC to 'prove guilt'. A merger is not considered to be against the public interest unless the MMC can actually prove it. Parties to a merger are seen to be 'innocent until proved guilty'. The cost and time involved for the MMC have severely curtailed its effectiveness here.

Monopoly references

In this context it is not what a dictionary may say it is, ie 'exclusive possession of the trade in some commodity'.

Under the Fair Trading Act 1973 (sections 6 and 7) a monopoly situation arises where a company supplies or receives at least one-quarter of all the goods or services of a particular description in the United Kingdom, or in a specified part thereof. There can similarly be a monopoly reference in respect of exports.

These are often known as 'scale' monopolies. There may also be a 'complex' monopoly, where two or more persons (or companies which are not part of the same group), who supply or receive at least one-quarter of all the goods or services of a particular description in the United Kingdom, so conduct their affairs, whether by agreement or not, as to prevent, restrict or distort competition in connection with those goods or services.

There is no presumption in the legislation that it is wrong to be a monopolist. For example, if a person invents and patents a new gadget and sets up a firm to make it, he is perforce a total monopolist – but he may well have performed a public service. The 1973 Act merely recognises that when over one-quarter of the supply or receipt of particular goods or services is in one pair of hands, or is shared in a 'complex' situation, the possibility exists of that power being misused in ways that prejudice the public interest. That possibility can only be confirmed by investigation.

Competition references

A monopoly reference necessitates the Commission investigating a whole market and – if they are there to be found – identifying any anti-competitive practices and their effects, etc. The Competition Act 1980 introduced a speedier process which could focus on a specific practice. For the first time an individual practice by an individual firm can be thoroughly investigated and if it is an anti-competitive practice it can be stopped should that practice be against the public interest.

To establish whether there is a course of conduct which restricts, distorts or prevents competition the Director General conducts his own examination and publishes a report of his findings. If these establish that the conduct amounts to an anti-competitive practice he may accept undertakings from any person the report has named, if he finds those undertakings to be a sufficient remedy. He must then publish the undertakings and keep their observance under review.

Examples of references made include, in 1982, the London Electricity Board and its sale of domestic electrical goods through its retail showrooms in such a way as to give rise to losses; and, in 1984, the policy of the Ford Motor Company of not granting licences to manufacture or sell in the United Kingdom certain replacement body parts for Ford vehicles.

Public sector references

Section 11 of the Competition Act 1980 empowers the Secretary of State to refer to the Commission any question relating to the efficiency and costs of and the service provided by nationalised industries and certain other public sector bodies such as the Post Office, the Civil Aviation Authority, etc, or any abuse by them of a monopoly situation.

With very few exceptions such bodies are not accountable, as is a public limited company (plc), to shareholders. In the public sector there is often little effective competition, and even where a public body has no monopoly it is not subject to the full rigours of the market place and the commercial incentives to efficiency which that can provide.

Parliament therefore considered it important that what are in effect efficiency audits of such bodies should be carried out periodically. At present up to six such references are made to the Commission each year, and they now represent a major and important part of the Commission's work.

The terms of reference for each inquiry may also require the Commission to report on whether the body concerned is pursuing a course of conduct which operates against the public interest; this is usually included since an adverse public interest finding is the trigger to the use, if appropriate, of statutory follow-up powers contained in section 12 of the Act.

Privatised undertakings

Since 1984 a new duty has been laid upon the Commission, that of conducting inquiries arising under statutes designed to effect the privatisation of undertakings formerly in the public sector.

Under the Telecommunications Act 1984, the Director General of Telecommunications may refer certain questions relating to telecommunications to the Commission. Under the Airports Act 1986 certain aspects of the economic regulation of airports may be referred by the Civil Aviation Authority. Powers for the Director General of Gas Supply to refer specific matters relating to the supply of gas to tariff customers are included in the Gas Act 1986.

Restrictive practices

The Restrictive Practices Act 1976 and the Resale Prices Act 1976 consolidated the legislation of 1956, 1964 and 1968. Restrictive practices legislation applies to the supply of both goods and services. It is concerned with agreements which restrict prices, conditions of sale and quantities to be supplied, and which lead firms to exchange information on prices and costs. Restrictive agreements have to be registered, and are presumed to be illegal and against the public interest unless the parties can establish a case for exemption before the Restrictive Practices Court. Firms are thus guilty until they can prove their innocence. This puts the pressure for an agreement on the parties concerned, who may find merging easier than fighting it out in the Restrictive Practices Court.

To be exempted, an agreement has to pass through one or more of eight gateways. For example, it has to be shown that an agreement protects the public against injury; that it provides substantial benefits to the public as purchasers, consumers or users; that it acts as a countervailing power against the anti-competitive practices of third parties; or that its removal would result in local unemployment or a reduction in exports. However, even if an agreement passes through the gateways, it still has to satisfy the 'public interest' test. The Court has to determine whether, both currently and in the future, on balance the benefits to the public outweigh the detriments or costs.

EU competition law

As a member of the EU, the UK is subject to European competition law, reflected in articles 85 and 86 of the Treaty of Rome which are enforced by the European Commission. Article 85 prohibits restrictive agreements and practices which prevent, restrict or distort competition within the EU and which affect trade between member states. Examples include price-fixing, market-sharing and limitations of production, technical progress and investment. Agreements may be exempted where they improve production, distribution or technical progress, subject to the requirement that these benefits must not be outweighed by other detriments associated with reduced competition. The European Commission has the power to impose heavy fines.

Article 86 originally applied to monopolies but has since been extended to mergers. It deals with situations where trade between member states might be affected by one or more enterprises taking 'improper advantage of a dominant position'. Examples of improper practices include the imposition of inequitable purchase or selling prices, or limiting production, markets or technical developments. However, questions arise as to what constitutes a firm with a dominant position. In the case of mergers, the position is clearer. The European Commission can prohibit mergers which hinder competition beween member states and where the combined turnover of the companies exceeds ECU 200 mn or where they share 25 per cent or more of a national market. Firms and member states can appeal to the European Court of Justice against decisions of the European Commission. Clearly, European competition policy and its relationship with national policy will become a more important issue with the creation of the Single European Market in 1992.

Questions for review

1 Explain the term 'market structure'.
2 What are the characteristics of perfect competition?
3 What are the characteristics of monopoly?
   Why does the government seek to control monopolies?
4 What is meant by price discrimination?
   Under what conditions is such discrimination possible.?
5 What are the main characteristics of monopolistic competition.
   Give some examples of this market structure.
7 Define the following terms:
   a   imperfect competition;
   b   product differentiation;
   c   barriers to entry.

The market for factors of production 7

The factors	147
The demand for factors of production (marginal productivity theory)	148
The supply of factors and market equilibrium	153
Land	159
Labour	162
Capital	171
The distribution of wealth and income	189
Minimum wage controls	199

The factors

Previous sections have dealt with the market in goods and services and their production. In a market economy another market operates for the allocation of factors of production, the resources of the economy, to make production of goods and services possible.

These resources are *land* (which, in economics, includes the natural resources found on or under the land – oil for example), *labour* and *capital*. 'Enterprise', the risk-taking function of pulling factors together for production, is also sometimes included in the list. It can alternatively be seen as a special type of labour input.

In the private sector of the economy resources are owned by households and institutions. They sell these resources to firms for production in return for the payment of rent, wages or interest. This payment provides an income for the owners of factors. If we assume that households and institutions wish to maximise their utility by maximising income, they will find the highest-income use they can for the factors that they own.

Again in the private sector, privately owned firms employ factors for the production of goods. It is important to note that the demand for factors of production is a *derived demand*. Resources are only employed by firms because they can be used to produce goods and services which are demanded by consumers. If there is no demand for the goods, there will be no demand for the resources that produce them. If demand for goods increases, so will demand for the associated factors of production. The chain of derived demand may be very long in a developed industrial economy. For example, coal-miners are required because they can produce coal which is used to produce electricity which, in turn, is used by industry to produce capital and consumption goods. The *consumption goods* are demanded by households, while the *capital goods* (machines, buildings) are used to produce consumption goods which are demanded by households. If the demands by households of consumption goods change, this will change the demand for coal miners through this chain of linked markets.

Firms will, in order to maximise profits, employ factors according to the productivity of those factors (the value of the output of goods and services that they can produce) compared to the incomes that must be paid to the owners of the factors for their use, and compared also to the productivity and prices of alternative factors.

In *the public sector* of the mixed economy, resources may be owned by the state (local and central government and the public corporations own a large part of the land in Britain) or they may be employed by the state. Considerations other than maximising profits from the use of resources or maximising income from making them available will probably apply in the public sector. The sections below which deal with the markets in each of the factors of production include a discussion of the considerations relevant for the public sector.

The demand for factors of production (marginal productivity theory)

The concept of marginal physical product

Suppose a farmer has a field and one tractor (his inputs of land and capital are fixed) and he is considering how many workers to employ. The addition of extra workers will generally increase his output, but the amount by which each additional worker increases output (the marginal physical product of that worker) will vary according to how many workers are already employed. (Note that this variation is assumed to depend not on the individual characteristics of the workers – some being more skilful than others – but on the conditions in which they are working.)

We might suppose, for example, that the second worker employed will more than double output since the two workers can be more efficient working together than one can be working alone. The third worker may only be able to increase output by one-half since the efficiency gains are less. The fifth worker may only increase output by 10 per cent since five men working in the field get in each other's way and have to waste time waiting to use the tractor. Additional workers would increase output by smaller and smaller amounts since these problems would increase.

The marginal physical product curve is shown in the following diagram to illustrate the situation. It initially rises and then falls as more workers are employed. This diagram illustrates *the law of diminishing returns* which states that if successive units of a variable factor (labour in this example) are added to fixed inputs of other factors (land and capital in this example), the increases in output resulting from these successive additions of the variable factor will eventually decline.

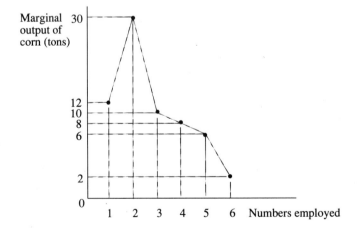

The general shape of the marginal physical product curve will then be as shown in the following diagram.

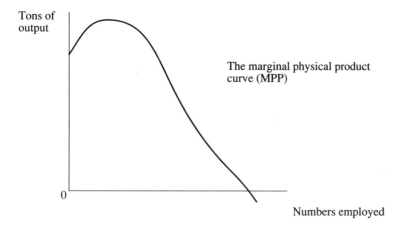

It is intuitively obvious that marginal physical product must eventually decline. It would otherwise be possible for the farmer to produce infinite quantities of output from this one field with one tractor simply by employing an infinite number of workers on the field.

The concept of marginal revenue product

This additional output produced by successive additions to the workforce is only worth producing because it can be sold. The price at which each unit produced can be sold depends on the relevant demand and supply conditions in the goods market. The value of the additional output produced by each successive employee is the marginal revenue product of that employee.

There are two possible market situations in the goods market in which the firm operates.

First, suppose the firm is operating in perfect competition in the goods market. It can sell every unit of output produced, irrespective of how much it produces, at the current market price. The firm is a *'price taker'*.

In that case the marginal revenue product of each successive worker is his marginal physical product, measured in units of the good multiplied by the price per unit of the good.

MPP x Price = MRP

Secondly, if the firm is operating in other market situations it becomes a *'price maker'*. The more output the firm produces the lower the price at which that output will be sold since the firm faces a downward-sloping demand curve for the good. If the firm employs an extra employee, any extra output resulting from this extra employment must be sold at a lower price and will (unless the firm can price discriminate between consumers) force down the price at which the previous level of output is sold. The marginal revenue product of an additional worker is then the marginal physical product of the employee multiplied by the marginal revenue resulting from the sale of the extra output.

MRP = MPP x MR

Since in perfect competition, discussed above, price is equal to marginal revenue, this is the general rule.

The marginal revenue curve is downward-sloping reflecting the law of diminishing returns. As more men are employed the value of the additional output produced by each will decline since the addition to output is declining.

If the price at which the output can be sold also declines as more workers are employed and more output is produced, then the marginal revenue product curve will fall more steeply. Therefore, in the following diagram MRP^1 represents the marginal revenue product curve for a firm operating in perfect competition in the goods market. MRP^2 represents the marginal revenue product curve for a firm operating under the same production conditions but operating as a price maker in the goods market.

Note that a firm operating in imperfect competition whose demand curve becomes more elastic will find that the marginal revenue product curve becomes flatter.

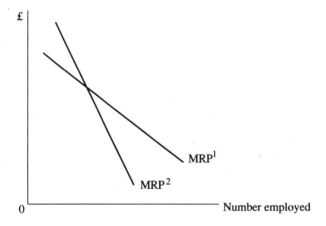

The demand for factors of production

Exactly as in the determination of optimal output for a firm, the determination of the optimal employment of factors will depend on the comparison of the effects on revenue and on costs. The firm will employ an additional unit of factors of production as long as the resulting addition to revenue is greater than the

The market for factors of production

corresponding increase in costs. To know what will happen to costs as employment of factors is increased will depend on supply conditions in the relevant factor market. This will be examined in the next section.

It should be noted that the decline of the marginal physical product of a factor was made on the assumption that the input of this factor was being changed while the inputs of other factors were held constant. It was therefore possible to measure the productivity of each unit of a particular factor precisely.

It is often impossible to vary the input of one factor alone. For example, suppose the firm is employing window cleaners, each one needing a bucket, ladder, cloth, etc. An extra window cleaner means extra capital equipment must be employed. It is then impossible to apportion the resulting marginal revenue precisely to either factor.

In fact firms would be likely to increase output by varying the inputs of other factors as well, in order to *avoid* the problem of diminishing returns. If all factor inputs can be expanded by equal amounts, then diminishing returns will not apply. This is of course the long-run situation for the firm.

Nevertheless, it seems obvious that, 'ceteris paribus', if the price of a factor of production rises, a firm will use less of it. The higher price will make it more expensive compared to other factors; we would expect the firm to substitute other factors for the one whose price has risen.

This substitution of factors must mean that the costs of production have increased. Otherwise, this combination of factors would have been chosen before in preference to the original combination. If the costs of production rise, the firms must sell their output at a higher price in order to maintain their profit margins. Assuming that demand for the good is not completely inelastic, the higher price will cause demand to be reduced. The firm's output must then be reduced, causing a reduction in demand for all factors including the one whose price has risen.

Thus, the higher price of a factor is, ceteris paribus, likely to lead to a reduction in demand for it. A lowering of the price of a factor will similarly result in an increased demand for it. The demand for factors is therefore likely to be downward-sloping.

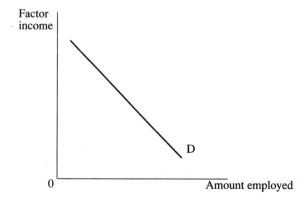

The elasticity of the demand function

This depends on a number of factors. Demand will tend to be more elastic for a factor:

a the easier it is to substitute other factors for this one;

b the greater the proportion of total cost this factor represents (because a rise in the price will then have a greater effect on firms' costs and thus on prices for the good);

c the greater the elasticity of demand for the good.

Shifts of the demand curve

The downward sloping demand curve for a factor will shift upwards if:

a there is an increase in the productivity of the factor (shifting the MRP function);

b there is an increase in the selling price of the good produced (shifting the MRP function);

c a rise in the price of other factors causing firms to substitute more of this one for the same level of output.

In this case the firm will employ more of this factor, at any price for that factor.

Alternative factor combinations

We assumed above that the firm could only vary the input of one factor of production while the other factors were held constant, which resulted in the problem of diminishing returns. This is a common situation for a firm varying output in the short run. However *in the long run*, the firm can vary the inputs of all factors of production and, in these circumstances, the profit maximising firm will choose that combination of factors which minimises unit costs of production.

The table below gives the alternative combinations of factors of production which can be used to produce 100 units of output per week.

Inputs:	Land (acres)	Labour (workers employed)	Capital (machines employed)
Method A	10	5	10
Method B	15	4	12
Method C	12	5	10

We can see that method C cannot possibly be the *least-cost method of production* if any positive price must be paid for land use. Method C uses the same amount of labour and capital as method A but 2 more acres of land.

Method A is the *more labour-intensive method* of production while method B is more *land and capital intensive* as a method of production. We cannot say which of these would be the least-cost method of production until we know the amount that must be paid for these inputs. Suppose that the prices that must be paid for inputs are as shown below:

Land rent per acre per week	£10
Labour wage per worker employed per week	£100
Rent paid per machine per week	£20

With these prices, method B is the least-cost method of production.

Now suppose that the rent paid on the land goes up to £15 per acre per week. Ceteris paribus, the least-cost method of production is now method A.

Let us consider these results. The rise in the price of land has persuaded the profit maximising firm to choose an alternative method of production which uses less of the factor whose price has gone up. By switching from method B to method A, in response to the increase in the price of land, the firm chose a less land-intensive method of production and uses 10 instead of 15 units of land. Thus, even in this more realistic long-term situation we can show that a firm will generally use less of a factor of production whose price has increased.

The supply of factors and market equilibrium

We can imagine a firm being in a variety of situations with regard to the supply of factors of production.

It may be that there is a *fixed supply* of the factor. For example, the government may find that there are only 100,000 qualified teachers available or a firm may find that only X million tons of some raw material is available. In this case supply is completely inelastic.

The firm can only employ the quantity available. In the following diagram the supply is fixed at quantity Q_e and the firm will employ Q_e units of this factor with the marginal revenue product curve shown.

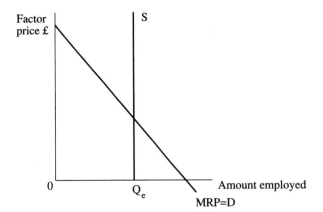

In this situation, output can only be expanded by using more of other factors in combination with this one, and the firm will then be certain to incur diminishing returns.

For most factors this completely inelastic supply is likely to be only a short-run situation. Generally, in the long run, more teachers can be trained and more raw materials produced.

Alternatively, supply of a factor may be *perfectly elastic*. In the following diagram any amount of this factor can be employed at a price for that factor of £P per unit employed. This situation may occur when a firm is a very small employer of a factor in a comparatively very large factor market.

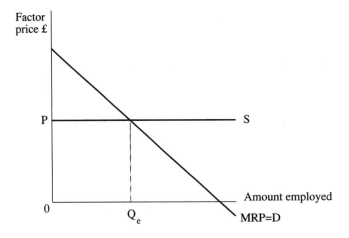

The profit maximising firm should decide how many units of this factor to employ by comparing the extra cost of employing each unit to the additional revenue that will result from that employment. Since MRP indicates the effect on revenue of additional units employed and the factor price per unit employed (£P in this example) indicates the effect of costs of employing additional units, the firm should employ Q_e units. All the units up to Q_e add more to revenue than costs since MRP is greater than P. Any additional units increase costs by more than they increase revenue (MRP is less than P), and so should not be employed.

Finally, the firms may be in the situation where they can employ extra units of a factor but only by offering a higher price for the factor per unit employed.

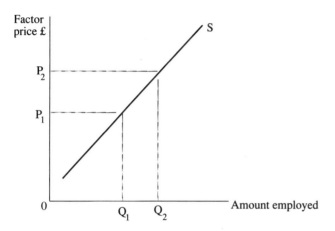

The supply of the factor is then upward sloping. If the firm wants to employ Q_1 it must pay P_1 to those factors. If it wants to increase employment to Q_2 it must raise the price paid to P_2. Assuming that the firm must pay this higher price to all the factors employed (including those that were previously employed at P_1), the additional cost that results from employing the extra units is greater than the costs that relate only to those extra units.

To give a numerical illustration: suppose a firm is currently employing 5 workers at a wage of £100 per week. The wage bill is £500. It now wants to employ an extra worker who demands a wage of £120 per week. The fact that the 6th worker is getting £120 per week means that this higher wage must be paid to the 5 workers already employed. The wage bill is now £720 (6 x £120) and has increased by £220 as a result of employing the additional worker. Of that £220, £120 has gone to pay the extra worker while £100 is needed to bring the existing 5 workers up to this higher wage level. The extra cost that results from employing the 6th worker is therefore greater than his wage.

The situation is illustrated in the following diagram.

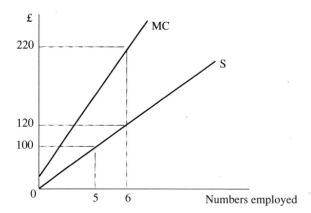

It would obviously not be profit maximising to employ this 6th worker unless he adds more than £220 to revenue. If his marginal revenue product is only £150 (which is greater than his wage but less than his marginal cost) the firm should not employ him.

In this situation the firm should employ factors only as long as the MRP associated with them exceeds the marginal cost (the increase in the total wage bill) that will result from their employment. In the following diagram, the profit maximising firm should therefore employ Q_e units of this factor.

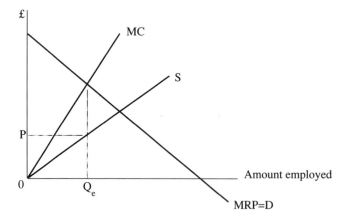

The price paid to the factor at this level of employment will be P.

The income earned by factors of production is, in economics, regarded as having two distinct elements.

One of these is *transfer earnings*. Transfer earnings are that part of the income which is just sufficient to persuade this factor to accept this employment and just sufficient to prevent it from accepting some alternative employment. Transfer earnings will therefore be slightly more than the income that could be earned in the best alternative employment. (In the numerical example above, the £100 per week that was being paid to the existing workers might be the transfer earnings of the 5th worker. The firm wanting 5 workers had needed to pay £100 per week in order to attract this 5th worker.)

The rest of the income is *economic rent*, ie the difference between transfer earnings and the total income is economic rent. (In the example above, when employment was increased to 6 men employed, the wage rate paid to all workers had to rise to £120 because this was the required transfer earnings for the 6th worker. The 5th worker was prepared to work for £100 so he is now receiving an economic rent of £20.)

The income that a factor receives may not be only the money payment paid to a factor. *Real income* from employment may include both money and *non-money income*. For example, if a person derives enjoyment from his job (satisfying work, in comfortable surroundings, with congenial companions) then the utility he derives from that job exceeds the money payment he receives for working. He may then be prepared to work for less than his money transfer earnings (the money income available for working in the best alternative job) if the non-money income from this job brings the total real income to a level higher than that in the best alternative job.

Similarly, an owner of a piece of land may derive utility from seeing it used for agricultural purposes rather than for housing. In this case the land may be used for agriculture even when the money income from that use is less than the money income for its use as housing land, as long as non-money income more than makes up the difference. Note that non-money income may be positive or negative. A negative non-money element might be a very unpleasant or dangerous job. In this case we may find someone accepting an alternative job even though the money wages are less than in this unpleasant/dangerous job. We can assume that all owners of factors will seek out that use for the factor which yields the highest real income in order to maximise utility. The supply of any factor at any money wage rate will then depend on the number of factor owners willing to make their factors available, given the real income available from alternative uses and given any non-money components of this use.

The *equilibrium price* operating in any factor market depends on the interaction of demand and supply in that factor market.

The demand will be the sum of the demand curves of all the firms interested in using that particular factor, while the supply curve will be determined by the willingness of the relevant factor owners to make these factors available at any price, given the alternatives available and any non-money elements (see following diagram).

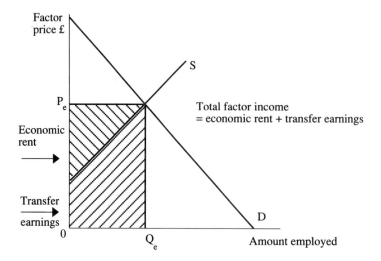

The demand and supply are equal at price P_e where Q_e units of the factor are being supplied. Any lower price would cause some factor owners to withdraw their factors from the market, while the firms would want more of the factor at this lower price. Excess demand would force the factor price back towards the equilibrium. Similarly, too high a price would cause excess supply which would force prices down.

If demand increases, perhaps because of increased demand for the final good, equilibrium price would rise and more units would be employed, attracted from other factor markets. If supply was reduced, perhaps because of higher incomes being offered in alternative uses, factor incomes in this market would be forced up since fewer factors are available.

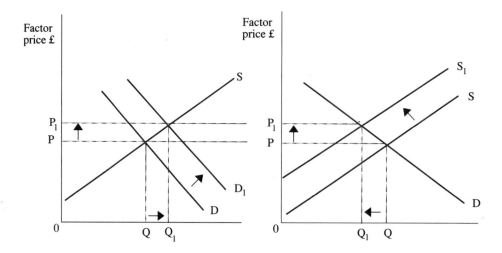

Land

There are a number of different *definitions* of land.

First the *surface of the planet* (including land, sea, lakes and rivers) which is obviously fixed in supply. The supply of land available to any one economy may, of course, be increased by conquest or treaty. For example, the international agreements on each country's exclusive right to the sea off its coasts makes a significant difference to the 'land' available to those economies.

This supply of land will not, however, vary according to the rent paid on it, so it is unresponsive or completely inelastic to changes in price. In this case, the fixed supply will be available even at zero prices which means that the transfer earnings are zero.

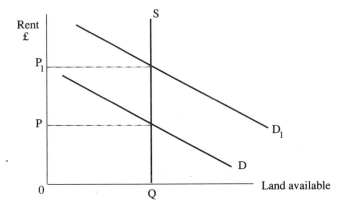

The rent paid on this land is therefore determined *entirely* by demand, and the whole of the price is 'economic rent'. Governments might see this as a justification for taxing away the whole of landowners' rent from their land. Such a tax would, unlike most taxes, result in no change either in the supply of land or in the price paid for it by the firms using it.

Secondly, the supply of land suitable for economic use. This supply is obviously more elastic. The supply of cultivatable land can be increased by irrigation, drainage, and the use of fertilizers, and this will tend to happen as the value of such land rises. For example, if the price of food rises, then the potential value of cultivatable land increases and owners will respond by taking steps to make more available through the application of investment to land.

Thirdly, a wider definition of land may include *all natural resources* found on and under the surface including, therefore, minerals and metals. The supply of these resources is ultimately fixed. There are only a fixed amount of fossil fuel sources in the earth and when these are used up no more can be acquired at any price. With the accelerated use of such resources because of the spread of industrialisation, there is now an increasing debate on the dangers of exhaustion.

However, until we reach that limit, the supply of these resources does respond to higher prices. It only became worth extracting the oil from the North Sea fields when the price of oil from more easily accessible areas rose. As a result of the exploitation of this new source, more oil is now becoming available. New sources become available as a result of investment and technological advance. There may be oil under the Atlantic which is now unavailable but which could be acquired, given the appropriate technology, investment and sufficiently high oil prices.

Any increase in availability of such resources is, however, a lengthy process. Short-term supply may therefore be very inelastic. In addition, the suppliers of these irreplacable resources may limit supply in order to conserve the stocks for the future. As a result, the prices of these commodities are extremely volatile to changes in demand conditions. During the early and mid-1970s, commodity prices rose dramatically in response to a boom in the industrialised countries. This boom was suddenly reversed by the oil crisis of 1974 and commodity prices fell equally dramatically. Copper, for example, rose in price from about £500 per ton in 1972 to a peak of £1,400 per ton in mid-1974, and then fell back to £500 per ton by the end of 1975. The following graph shows the erratic price of copper on a week-to-week basis in the spring of 1988.

Copper

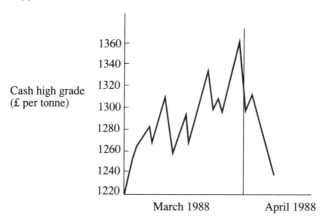

The mobility of land

Land is physically very immobile. It is not possible to increase the acreage available in the City of London by transporting vacant land from the Scottish Highlands.

Land is, however, quite mobile between uses. Land used for growing wheat can be switched to vegetable growing if relative prices change. Land that has been used for farming can be used for building houses. Once land has been built on, the mobility between uses may be reduced. However, unused industrial sites can be reclaimed for other uses.

A land tax intended to eliminate all earnings of landowners (see Chapter 6) would have the disadvantage of reducing the mobility of land between uses. For example, suppose the demand for housing land is increasing. Under normal market circumstances, landowners would make more housing land available by switching land from currently less profitable uses. Their incentive to do so will be greatly reduced if the government taxes away the whole of any rent they earn. A policy of taxing all rents on land would have to be accompanied by the state direction of land from one use to another in response to changes in demand conditions. A tax on only a proportion of the landlord's earnings would not have this disadvantage of checking mobility.

Land use planning

In Britain the use of land is closely controlled by the government. Britain is a small and densely populated island. This congestion means that the *externalities* associated with land use are substantial. For example, people living on a large housing estate will suffer considerable external costs if the currently high value of land in industrial use results in the building of a noisy and smelly industrial plant right next to them.

Similarly, the use of additional land in central London for commercial development in response to the high demand for office space will result in increased congestion on the transport system which brings office workers in to these new jobs. This increased congestion imposes an external cost on all existing commuters.

The demand for land changes, but once applied to one use it becomes more difficult to apply it subsequently to some other use. Suppose boom in the commercial sector of the economy causes office rents to rise sharply. Landowners sell their land for office development. The demand for office space may then fall because commercial circumstances change, leaving a large number of empty, newly built offices. This is obviously undesirable when the land could otherwise have remained in housing, farming or retailing uses.

As a result of these problems, the government intervenes in the allocation of land to particular uses. No land can have a change of use without *'planning permission'* from the local authority. Any disputes over planning permission are dealt with by the Department of the Environment.

Thus the government can decide to zone land into particular uses with one area used for industrial building while another is for housing. No new industrial use will then be allowed in the housing zone. This reduces the pollution externalities.

The government may decide that cities should not be allowed to spread untidily over the countryside, so they designate a zone around the present city limits as a *'green belt'* where no currently agricultural land can be converted into use for housing, offices or factories. The government can control the number of commuters travelling into London to work by controlling the amount of office building. It can check the tendency for land use to respond to short-term changes in demand by denying planning permission for this change of use.

In a free market, an increase in demand for a particular use of land (eg commercial) would lead to higher rents/prices for the existing stock in that use. These higher rents/prices would encourage landowners with suitable land to switch it from its existing use (eg agriculture) into the higher-price use, thus allowing supply to respond to increased demand. We would then expect there to be similar rents/prices for similar pieces of land (same location and conditions). If prices were different, land would be re-allocated until prices fell into line.

With the government controlling the allocations of land between uses, the market system cannot operate. Land is not automatically reallocated according to changing demand conditions. It is important that the government, giving due consideration to social costs and benefits, allows land to be reallocated appropriately. Otherwise, the expansion of rising industries would be checked by a shortage of land while land was underused and wasted in other uses.

Government controls also mean that similar land may have quite different prices. Two areas of land, identical in all respects with similar locations, may be earning quite different rents/prices for their owners. Suppose one has been designated as commercial land, of which there is currently a shortage. The price/rent will be very high. The other is designated for agricultural use, for which prices/rents are much lower. Obviously, the second landowner would, ceteris paribus, want to transfer his land from one use to the other. He is prevented from doing so by the government controls. The prices will therefore stay at their different levels. (With these government controls, the supply of land for any particular use is fixed and completely inelastic to changes in prices/rents. As discussed above, price in each use is then determined entirely by demand and consists of 'economic rent' alone.)

Land-use planning is a good illustration of an area where government intervention in the market mechanism was needed but where these controls have created a number of problems for government.

Labour

The total supply of labour resources

Population: The supply of labour resources in the economy is ultimately dependent on the size of the population. Changes in a country's population depend on the birth rate, the death rate and net migration. As a country develops, it is usual for the death rate to fall as advances in medical treatment check previously fatal illnesses and improvements in living standards raise the level of nutrition. The fall in the death rate is then eventually followed by a fall in the birth rate as family size adjusts to increased expectations of survival. The fall in the birth rate may also be a result of changed economic circumstances. Higher-income families appear to choose to be smaller families. If people could migrate freely between countries, we would, ceteris paribus, expect a net inflow into countries with higher living standards. Improved economic circumstances in a country would then result in an increase in net immigration. In fact, there are many legal restrictions on labour migration between countries.

Supply of labour inputs – quantity

The proportion of any given population that looks for employment depends on a number of factors. There may be legislation or conventions about the age at which children accept paid employment. In Britain, all children between the ages of 5 and 16 have to be in full-time education and may not accept paid employment for more than a few hours a week. In many jobs there is compulsory retirement at 65. The provision of old-age pensions by the State reduces the need for people to continue working after they reach these ages. Married women, particularly those with children, were not until recently expected to accept paid employment. Many factors have resulted in an enormous increase (to over 60 per cent of married women) in this source of labour resources. The 'Women's Movement' in the early 1970s changed women's expectations and stressed the potential satisfaction to be had from working ouside the home. Rising living standards and technological changes have resulted in an enormous increase in the availability of machines which reduce the work involved in keeping house and looking after a family, thus freeing women from some of their domestic responsibilities. The rapidly expanding economy of the 1950s and 1960s generated employment possibilities for women, particularly in the service sectors of the economy. With more and more well-educated women available on the labour market, the 1990s will see many occupy positions of responsibility in large organisations.

The quantity of labour resources available depends not only on the number of workers but also on the hours they work. The longer the working day and the shorter annual holidays and weekend breaks, the more the labour inputs provided. Industrial advance has, in Britain, been accompanied by a shortening of the working day, the working week and the working year. People now work fewer hours in the year for more real income than they did 100 years ago.

This tendency can be illustrated in the following diagram. As wage levels rise up to wage level W, the number of hours worked increases. Labour is prepared to give up leisure in return for these higher wage rates. If wages rise further, the workers prefer to reduce their hours of work so that their money income is unchanged (they have apparently reached their target money income) and they take extra leisure which gives them extra utility.

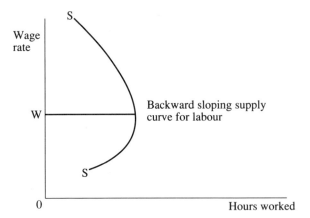

With a fixed number of workers, an increasing demand for labour and a higher wages rate may therefore result in a *reduced* supply of labour.

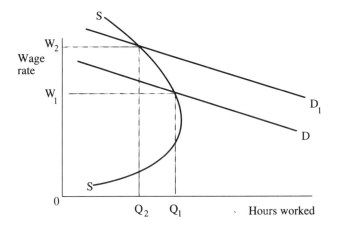

In mining (which is dangerous and unpleasant) or assembly line work (which is boring), increasing wage rates have actually resulted in an immediate increased rate of absenteeism so that fewer hours are worked.

Supply of labour inputs – quality

The supply of labour inputs also depends on the quality of labour. Some of the quality characteristics of the labour force might be regarded as inherent, such as intelligence, but most are acquired through education and training. The education and training may be done by privately owned firms selling education services, it may be provided free by the state or it may be provided by firms to their employees.

It is important to remember the concept of opportunity cost in relation to education and training. The economy, in using resources to increase the quality of the work-force, cannot then use those same resources for the production of other goods and services. This is, of course, true whether the education and training is provided by private firms for profit or by the state. The benefits that result from this use of the economy's resources are the improvement in the quality of the work-force and thus in its productivity.

Similarly, a private individual will choose whether or not to pursue further education (a basic education is compulsory in Britain) by considering the associated costs and benefits. The costs are fees, if any, and the opportunity cost of lost earnings. The time spent in full-time education cannot also be used for earning money. The benefits are the increase in earning potential in the future, plus any non-money benefits that result from access to more interesting or satisfying work, plus any non-money benefits derived directly from pursuing education (enjoyment of study, for example).

Labour sub-markets and the mobility of labour

Labour has alternative uses. With changing demand conditions in the different goods markets, we would expect that the wages offered in different uses would diverge. If all units of labour were identical, labour would move out of the lower-paid jobs into the higher-paid jobs until real wages were equalised. Only then would the movement of labour stop and equilibrium be achieved.

Note that in considering the reward to be earned in alternative jobs, workers consider both money and non-money rewards, where non-money rewards may be positive or negative (for example where the job is unpleasant or requires the working of inconvenient hours). In fact all units of labour are far from identical. Certain workers may be particularly suited to particular jobs because of inherent characteristics, education, training and work experience. Supply of labour between different uses may then not be perfectly elastic but quite inelastic, particularly in the short run. In this case we may expect different wages to persist in different labour sub-markets. For example, suppose there is an increased demand for computer engineers since computers are in increased demand. As a result, wages rise for these employees. People in lower-paid jobs would naturally now want to get a job as a computer engineer, but they lack the required qualifications. The wages, therefore, stay disproportionately high for computer engineers. Eventually, of course, more people would train as computer engineers, and labour supply in this sub-market would expand and wage levels would fall.

The mobility of labour between labour sub-markets may also be limited by trade union action which will be discussed below. Another factor limiting *labour mobility* is the specific location of jobs. Real wages may be very high in London compared to the wages available doing a similar job in Newcastle. However, the movement of labour from Newcastle to London may be greatly limited by family ties and responsibilities. More seriously, the very rigid housing system in this country generally makes it extremely difficult for a family to move from one area to another. Moving to the South East/London from the North means bridging a very wide house-price gap. The immobility of labour will be discussed in more detail in Chapter 13.

The determination of equilibrium wages

We will concentrate on the factors determining wages in a particular labour sub-market.

The demand for this type of labour is determined by those firms interested in employing labour with these specific characteristics. The number they will want to employ at any level depends on the marginal revenue product functions of the firms. Demand for labour would increase if there are increased prices for the goods produced or if the price of alternative factors rose or if there was an increase in the physical productivity of labour.

The supply of this type of labour depends on the number of people with the appropriate characteristics in the labour force and the rewards (including both money and non-money benefits) available in alternative jobs. Supply would increase, for example, if the costs of acquiring the appropriate characteristics were reduced or if the rewards from alternative jobs were reduced.

Equilibrium
a *initially* b *with increased demand* c *with increased supply*

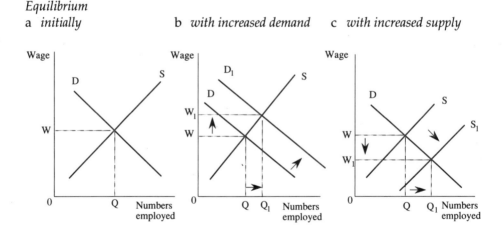

The effect of trade unions on wage levels

There are a number of ways in which trade unions and similar bodies can influence wage levels.

Firstly, they can check the supply of labour so that equilibrium wages are increased.

For example, the Law Society limits the number of solicitors entering the labour market by requiring that certain minimum standards of general education are achieved (two A-level passes) and that candidates pass specific law exams where the percentage passing can be controlled by the institution. This permanently limits the supply of solicitors.

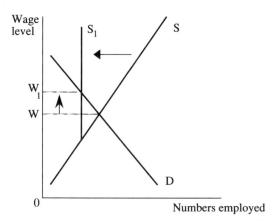

Similarly, a trade union might require that its members had been through a specific apprenticeship scheme or it might just control the number of union members numerically. For this system to work the union must have a 'closed shop' agreement with its employers. In the case of solicitors, consumers (the direct employers for most solicitors) are not given the choice of employing alternative labour since it is illegal for anyone to set up as a solicitor without being a member of the Law Society. In the case of the trade union, the employing firms must be forced (usually through the threat of strike action) to agree to employ only union members. Otherwise, the union could raise wages no higher than the level at which non-union members would be prepared to work, ie the equilibrium wage in the labour market if there were no trade union.

Secondly, 'productivity agreements' generally seek to secure increased wages through some change in working practice which it is argued will increase the output per worker employed. Higher productivity would cause a shift in the demand for labour as discussed above.

Thirdly, trade unions may also use their industrial power to push wages above the market equilibrium level. In the following diagram, the market equilibrium wage is W_e with Q_e people employed. The trade union bargains for a minimum wage of W_t. No union member will work for any wage below W_t. With the demand curve as shown, the level of employment in this labour market will fall to Q_t.

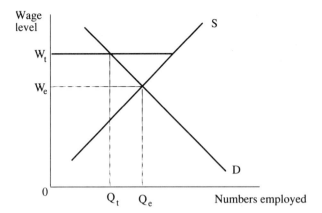

The higher wage is thus achieved at the cost of reduced employment opportunities in the labour market. Is this a rational strategy for a union to pursue?

The union may believe that the individuals whose jobs are lost will be those who joined the union most recently. The union feels least loyalty to these late members.

The union may be uncertain about the shape of the demand curve for labour. Wage negotiations typically deal with wage levels for the year ahead. The commercial future is uncertain. The union may have expected the curve to be at D_1 for the coming year and therefore put wages at W_t in the expectation of this being the equilibrium wage for Q_e employees.

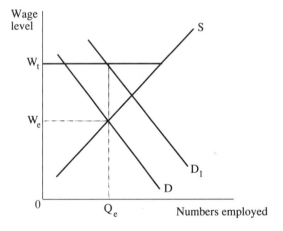

It may be that the higher wage level of W_t may itself cause the demand curve to shift from D to D_1. If the wage rise is general through the economy, incomes have generally been increased, and therefore demand for all goods and services may be increased. This is quite likely in a situation where the various unions look at the wage increases achieved by other unions in fixing the wage for which they will bargain.

The union may feel itself to be in a sufficiently strong position to impose the wage increase on the employers without any redundancies resulting. The strength of the union depends on the proportion of the potential work-force that are members of the union, the financial resources of the union for paying 'strike-pay' and the financial resources of their members to deal with the fall in incomes that always results from a strike. A strong union can impose wage increases without redundancies by using the threat of prolonged strike action.

The long term success of this action depends on the market position of the firm. If the firm is making excess profits, it can afford to pay higher wages at the cost of reduced profits. This is most likely to be the situation if the firm is operating in monopoly or oligopoly. If the firm is not making any excess profits, the wage increases will reduce those profits below a normal return on the capital. In the short term, the firm may choose the higher wage costs, since their losses will be smaller than if they are faced with a long strike. In the long term, employment will be reduced as the industry responds to lower profit levels.

Recent policies by the government toward trade unions

The Thatcher government elected in 1979 carried out major reforms in the labour market throughout the 1980s. Powerful trade unions were seen as a hindrance toward a free market for labour. Legislation has meant that strike ballots are compulsory, secondary picketing illegal, and closed-shop agreements subject to periodic ballots. Besides reducing industrial action these reforms were designed to make the labour market less inflexible (see Chapter 8), and to improve the 'supply side' of the economy.

Wage levels in the public sector of the economy

The important points that should be noted about the factor market operating in the public sector in Britain are: first, the employees can choose whether to work for the government or not. There is no direction of labour and workers can therefore be assumed to allocate their labour according to where it will earn the highest reward. (Both monetary and non-money factors will be considered.) They will work for the government as long as the reward exceeds the reward in the best alternative job.

Secondly, the government is often a *monopsonist employer*. While teachers, doctors and nurses can work using their skills in the private sector, civil servants, post-office workers and train drivers cannot. In state teaching and medical services the transfer earnings are high since workers can earn high wages in the alternative private sector. The government must pay a higher reward to these employees if it is not to lose all the best doctors, etc, to the private sector.

This is not true for many other government employees. They could not use their skills in private industry, so their transfer earnings are quite low (at the level of unskilled labour or general clerical work). The government could, therefore, easily 'exploit' its monoposonist position and pay wages to skilled workers which just exceed their unskilled value in the private sector's labour market.

The government is, therefore, very vulnerable to arguments about what 'should' be paid to their employees, eg 'the wage level for comparable skill levels in the private sector', 'a reasonable wage for a working man with dependents', etc. The *Clegg Commission* in 1978 was set the task of recommending wage levels in the public sector which would be comparable with wage levels earned by individuals of similar education, training and age who had similar work experience and responsibilities in the private sector. The calculations are complex and the Clegg Commission made a well publicised error which resulted in the teachers being offered a pay increase which was later shown to be well in excess of the 'comparable' wage in the private sector. Clegg was abolished in 1979 when the incoming Conservative government wanted public sector pay linked to what could be afforded by public spending targets. For instance, in 1988 the government allocated £300m for pay rises for teachers. This effectively limited teachers' pay rises to 4 per cent.

Thirdly, where the output of the government service is *not* directly sold (the Civil Service, the Health Service, Education, Social Services) there is no obvious way of measuring the marginal or even the average revenue productivity of employees. It is important to remember that the present government has tried to improve the efficiency of Health and Education by introducing 'market forces' to a limited degree. Self-managed hospitals and schools with an 'opting out' opportunity could mean employees in these sectors finding their pay related directly to 'performance'.

How much utility will be lost by the public if the government closes one university? Obviously some people will argue that the loss is enormous, while others will argue that it is quite small, given that many other universities remain. The argument about the size of the loss will be based largely on value judgments. Now suppose the university lecturers put through a pay claim which greatly increases labour costs. Where is the marginal revenue product curve? Can the current level of employment be justified with these wage costs, or not? This is a political decision. The public sector employees in these services may feel that the loss of any of their jobs as a result of an increase in wages depends on the political situation.

If the wage claim is accepted with no redundancies, there is a transfer of income from the tax-payers (if taxes are increased to finance this increased expenditure) or from the consumers of other services (if, for example, medical services are reduced in order to finance the increased costs of the education services).

Fourthly, where the output is sold to consumers, eg the Post Office, the government is often an effectively monopolist supplier of a good or service which has a very inelastic demand curve. For example, the demand for the standard letter delivery is inelastic.

Like any other monopolist the Post Office can exploit its position and charge high prices to its consumers. Suppose the Post Office unions secure a large pay increase for their members. The Post Office is in a position to pass the whole of this increase in costs on to consumers. The higher price for postal services will cover the increased wages bill, so there will be no drop in employment. These public sector unions can therefore be confident that increased wages will not result in job losses. Higher wages and higher prices will, of course, mean a transfer of income from the consumers to the Post Office employees.

Fifthly, in other government industries there is no such monopoly power because of competition from other domestic and foreign producers *or* the monopoly power is limited by the existence of possible substitutes. In these cases, increased wage costs will result in losses, since the cost cannot be passed on completely to consumers. An example of this was the former British Coal, when coal was a government industry.

There is no effective limit to the amount of losses that government industry, unlike private industry, can bear. When a private firm would go out of business, the government still has sources of finance. It can shift funds from one area to another in order to cover losses. (Given the size of total government expenditure, the government's ability to do this greatly exceeds that of most private firms.) Alternatively, it can raise taxation to cover the losses, shifting income from taxpayers to employees. Or it can increase its borrowing (the security of loans made to the British government is much greater than that of loans made to a privately owned firm in financial difficulties).

Increased wages, therefore, need not result in job losses but in increased government subsidies for this industry.

Sixthly, the service provided may be of such importance to the economy of the government that, regardless of wage costs, the service must be maintained. For example, the government cannot govern without the Civil Service. The coal-miners in 1974 used their demonstrated ability to bring British industry to a standstill (through their ability to stop electricity supplies) to ensure increasing real wages for their members without job losses. The coal strike of 1984-5 did not produce the same results, primarily because electricity generation was less dependent on coal, and also many miners did not join the strike.

Seventhly, the government is concerned about employment levels in the economy; and it also has to pay redundancy and unemployment pay to those who lose their jobs as a result of high wage costs. It may therefore prefer to subsidise increased losses in government operations rather than see jobs lost as a result of excessive wage claims.

Capital

Definition of capital

Capital is a man-made factor of production. It includes most obviously machines, buildings, motor vehicles, ships, aircraft (where these are not consumption goods), railway lines and trains, roads, airports, and docks. It may also include stocks of raw materials and semi-finished goods.

The greater the stock of capital goods in an economy, the greater the potential production of goods and services. The opportunity cost of producing capital goods is the sacrifice of the consumption goods that could have been produced with the resources used. The more of an economy's production that is of capital goods, therefore, the lower the current standard of living (availability of consumption goods), but the greater the potential for the production of consumption or capital goods in the future.

Mobility of capital

Capital is a stock of machines, buildings, etc, which were designed for a particular technology for the production of a particular range of goods. Technological advance continues and the preferences for goods change. The mobility of this capital stock then becomes important. How easily can the existing stock of capital goods be adapted to changed preferences and technology?

Where demand is changing, the important characteristic of capital is its adaptability to different uses. For example, a fleet of lorries may have been accumulated by a firm producing cotton goods for transporting raw cotton to the spinning factories. The demand for these cotton goods collapses, so these lorries are no longer needed in their present use. However, they can be taken up by an expanding industry (for example, a pharmaceutical company) and used for transporting their goods. The spinning machines are, however, less adaptable.

The wider the range of industries in which a piece of capital can be used, the greater its mobility and its ability to adapt to changing demand conditions.

When technology changes, certain types of capital equipment become non-optimal for their present use. The more functions they can be used for, the more likely it is that a new use can be found for them. For example, a computer can be used for many functions. Suppose one is currently employed in stock-keeping for a company, but a technological advance produces a new computer that can handle this function more easily. The old computer could then be switched to dealing with the employees' wages.

Geographical mobility is an important factor. While vehicles such as ships, aeroplanes and lorries can be used in a different location, the docks, airfields and roads that served them cannot. If the location of economic activity changes, fixed capital equipment may become obsolete because it is immobile geographically. Alternatively, the cost of moving it may be so high, compared with the value of it in an alternative use, that it is not worth moving it.

Investment

Investment is the process of increasing the stock of capital goods. It is made up of increases in the stock of machines, buildings, etc, and also any addition to the stock of raw materials and semi-finished and finished goods. Expenditure on capital goods has a value of about 20 per cent of the total expenditure in the British economy, although this percentage can vary widely according to economic circumstances (discussed below).

Note that investment is *not* buying stocks and shares; or buying an existing house off someone else; or putting money into a building society or deposit account in a commercial bank. All these activities could be defined as *'saving'*. These two activities *must* be distinguished clearly. Saving does have an important function in providing funds for investment which will be discussed below, but it is *not the same thing* as investment.

A distinction is made between replacement investment (which restores the value of the existing stock of capital after its depreciation as it is used) and net investment (which adds to the stock of capital).

Gross investment (total expenditure on capital goods) = Replacement investment + Net investment

Motives for investment: the rate of return

Concentrating initially on the private sector, the incentive for investment is, for private firms, the possibility of increased profits. The usual reasons may be to respond to expanding demand by increasing capacity, to introduce some new technology which lowers costs or improves the product, or to prevent a fall in profitability as capital stock deteriorates or as competing firms introduce new capital stock.

The incentive for investment might then be measured as the expected return on the investment compared to the costs of investing. The expected *rate of return* is one way of measuring anticipated profits. Suppose a sum of £1,000 is invested in an investment project and after one year produces a revenue of £1,100. £1,000 of this revenue is needed to repay the initial investment. The money may have been borrowed from another individual/institution and they will want it repaid. The remaining £100 is the profit from the investment and, in this case, the rate of return is 10 per cent, ie:

$$\frac{\text{Profit}}{\text{Sum invested}} \times 100\%$$

(The rate-of-return method of measuring the profitability of investment is, in practice, rather unreliable, and the alternative 'discounted cash flow' system is discussed below. Nevertheless, the rate of return is the most useful for illustrative purposes.)

Now suppose that a firm is faced with a series of independent investment projects. The expected rates of return will obviously vary on these projects. The rational, profit-maximising firm will choose to do the highest-expected-return project first and will then work through the others in the order suggested by their expected rates of return. Thus, the more money the firm invests, the lower the rate of return on the last project. A marginal efficiency of capital schedule, such as the one shown in the following diagram, could then be constructed. If the firm invests I, then the return on the last £ invested is R, and every £ in previous projects earns a higher reward than that. If the firm increases its investment to I_1, the return on the last £ invested falls to R_1, with all previous projects exceeding this lower rate of return.

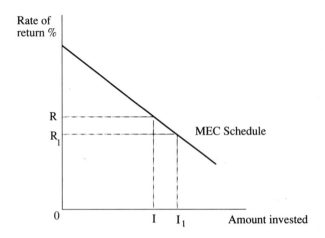

The amount invested: the rate of interest

The amount that the firm should invest depends on the cost of acquiring the funds for investment. Suppose the firm borrows the money from some other individual or institution. As well as having their loan repaid, they will expect some reward for letting their money be used for this period. Loaning the money means that they must delay consumption, and consumers are expected to be myopic (short-sighted) about future consumption compared to present consumption, valuing future consumption now at a lower value than present consumption. In times of inflation the individual/institution that loans the money will want a larger repayment in order to cover the fall in the value of money during the period of the loan. Anyway, since firms can earn profits from investing, the individuals/institutions who provide the funds will expect some share of this profit. The market in funds is competitive like any other, and to obtain funds the firm must offer a reward to the providers of those funds which is at least as great as the reward they could get by lending the funds to other firms. This reward paid to the lenders of the funds is called the *rate of interest*.

The firm may not have borrowed the money but may be using its own funds ('internal' as opposed to 'external' sources of finance). In this case the concept of *opportunity cost* is important. Instead of using the funds for its own investment, the firm could have lent them to another firm, in which case a rate of interest would have been earned. The firm must take account of this opportunity cost before deciding if investment is worthwhile.

Suppose the current rate of interest at which money can be borrowed for investment is R in the following diagram. If the firm has a MEC (*Marginal Efficiency of Capital*) schedule as shown, it should invest I since all investment projects up to that point produce a yield greater than the cost of borrowing the money. It should only invest as much as I_1 if the interest rate is lower than R_1. Note that the return on the investment projects between I and I_1 is positive but insufficient, given the cost of borrowing the money.

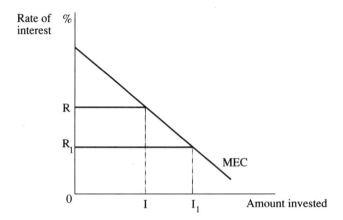

Thus, if the rate of interest falls from R to R_1, the amount of investment will increase.

The demand for investment

As we have seen above, the amount of money invested by an individual firm will tend to be inversely related to the rate of interest. Referring back to marginal revenue product theory (see above), we could produce a similar result by arguing that, if additional units of capital are applied to stock of other factors of production, the return on the marginal £ invested will decline as more investment is undertaken. This follows from the law of diminishing returns. If we assume that there is a cost associated with each £ invested (the rate of interest), the firm should only invest in those projects which exceed the cost of borrowing. Investment will then increase as the cost falls.

Alternatively, we would expect investment to be reduced as the cost rose, since extra capital goods would be less competitive with other factors of production at their current prices, while the higher price of capital would push up firms' costs, causing demand for the product to fall and thus the demand for all factors of production.

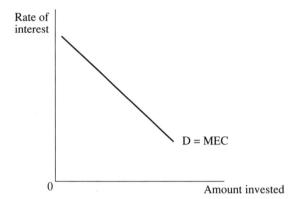

Influences on the demand for investment

If the expected return from investment increases, then the demand for investment curve will shift upwards so that more is invested at any rate of interest. Referring back to the MEC schedule above, the MEC schedule would shift upwards so that at any rate of interest more investment projects can be justified.

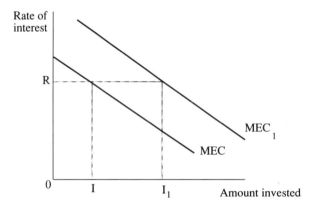

We should now examine the possible explanations for a change in the level of investment in the private sector other than the explanation of some change in the rate of interest.

Business expectations

The return on investment is only an *expected* return. The firm investing cannot be certain of the return since the commercial future is always uncertain. As a result the MEC function may not be a simple line but a range where the return may be anything between MEC and MEC_1 in the diagram above, depending on whether commercial circumstances in the future are good (MEC_1) or quite bad (MEC).

An improvement in business expectations will result in an increase in investment at current rates of interest, since firms are expecting an MEC function at MEC_1 rather than at MEC. MEC_1 will possibly become more elastic than MEC.

An indication of changes in business expectations occurs in the rise in the share price index that always follows the election of a Conservative government (generally expected to be sympathetic to the interests of private business), while the index usually falls when a Labour government is elected. The individuals and institutions dealing in stocks and shares expect average profitability to rise. The share price index is generally used by commentators as an indicator of business confidence.

A high level of demand in the economy

If demand in the economy is high, then each firm will be faced with a high level of demand for its products, and thus the return on investment high. More will, therefore, be invested than when demand in the economy is low.

A change in the level of demand: the accelerator process

An important influence on the level of net investment is any increase in the level of stocks held by firms. The higher the volume of sales, the larger the stocks of raw materials, semi-finished and finished goods the firm will need to hold.

Many firms use a rule of thumb to adjust their stocks to changing demand conditions. Suppose they feel that £1,000 of stock in a shop is necessary to maintain a level of sales of £200 per week. Now, if sales increase to £300 per week the firm will feel that this level of sales justifies a stock holding of £1,500. Thus, investment (increase in stock holding) responds to change in demand. *The accelerator* principle is a slightly more complex version of the same story.

Suppose a factory producing overalls needs 10 machines in order to produce 1,000 overalls per year. The output of each machine is then 100 overalls per year (a capital output ratio of 10:1). The machines depreciate at the rate of each machine lasting 5 years, which means that, in any year, 2 machines must be replaced in order to spread out the costs of depreciation while maintaining the stock of machines. The current rate of gross investment (entirely replacement investment) is 2 machines a year.

Now suppose that demand in year 2 for overalls increases so that production of 1,100 is required. In order to produce this level of output, the firm needs to have an extra machine. Therefore, it will buy in this year its usual 2 replacement machines plus one extra machine in order to expand output. Gross investment has therefore increased by 50 per cent (from 2 to 3 machines) in response to an increase of 10 per cent (from 1,000 to 1,100) in required output. When demand remains unchanged in year 3 investment falls to 2 machines. Demand for overalls would have had to go up to 1,200 in year 3 for there to be the same total demand for 3 machines. Unless the demand for overalls goes up at the same rate per year there will be unemployment in the capital goods industry.

Year	Goods produced (consumer goods)	Machinery required (capital goods)	Replacement investment	New investment	Total
1	1,000	10	2	0	2
2	1,100	11	2	1	3
3	1,100	11	2	0	2
4	900	9	0	0	0
5	900	9	2	0	2

The conclusion to be drawn from the accelerator principle is that any increase in demand in the economy will result in a much larger increase in the level of gross investment by firms. Similarly, if the level of demand falls in year 3 firms may stop investing altogether. They will want to run down their stock of machines in line with reduced demand. Suppose, in the example above, demand for overalls fell to 900 units per year, the firm would not need to replace the depreciated machines and would allow its gross investment to fall to zero. An 18 per cent drop in sales therefore results in a 100 per cent drop in investment (see year 4 above).

In year 5 despite consumer demand staying at only 900 machinery demand has recovered slightly because the decline in consumer demand has stopped.

It should be noted that the theory of the accelerator is unlikely to match reality. It assumes that while the consumption goods industry has no excess capacity to deal with a 10 per cent increase in sales, the capital goods industry has sufficient excess capacity to deal with a 50 per cent increase in sales (in the example above). In fact, the overall producers may have some machines that are being underused and it may be able to increase output entirely by employing more labour or by employing its existing labour force for longer hours. In this case there is no need to buy extra machines. Alternatively, the industry producing the machines may be unable to expand output to meet increased demand. They may therefore ration their existing output by raising the price for capital goods in which case the increased investment will be choked off.

It should, therefore, be noted that increased investment as a result of increased demand for the product may be less than the accelerator theory might predict.

The accelerator principle is useful in explaining the aggravated response of the economy to any changes in the level of demand (discussed in Chapter 12), and also in explaining the observed instability of capital goods industries. For example, the building industry has one of the highest rates of bankruptcy because it must expand rapidly in response to any increase in demand for building, but then must contract rapidly as soon as demand begins to fall.

Supply of other factors

As discussed above, there is likely to be more investment in capital equipment if the factor prices of alternative inputs rise, so that firms substitute capital for these other factors. Thus, one of the reasons for the investment by newspaper producers in computerised type-setting machines is the high level of wages secured as a result of industrial action by the print unions.

Technological change

Technological change responds to changing factor prices. Research and development will be concentrated on producing a technology which minimises costs, given the new ratios of factor prices. Thus, technology has responded to higher real wages in industrialised countries by producing labour-saving machines.

Additionally, technological change may produce spontaneously labour- or capital-saving machines. The introduction of this new technology by cost-minimising firms will mean, at least initially, an increased rate of investment. New products may also be developed which require production equipment, again increasing investment.

The supply of funds

We have so far assumed that firms are able to borrow for investment if they are prepared to pay the current market rate of interest in order to attract the necessary funds. In fact, the availability of funds may vary according to the firm's situation and the general economic situation.

The provision of funds for investment in an economy requires saving. Money that might have been spent on consumption is instead made available for the purchase of capital equipment. This saving may be done by the firm itself (through retained profits) or by other individuals or institutions. The determination of the level of saving in the economy is discussed in Chapter 12, but generally the higher the level of activity in the economy, the higher the rate of saving. Households save an increasing proportion of their higher incomes, and higher demand and higher prices yield bigger profits for firms and therefore a larger source of internal finance.

The amount of saving may respond to higher interest rates since this increases the reward for saving. However, in reality, saving appears to be very interest-inelastic, responding more to expectations, income levels and institutional factors than to interest changes. It is true that higher interest rates may attract increased funds from abroad, but these funds tend to go into government stock rather than into investment projects in private industry.

The availability of funds for investment is also influenced by government monetary policy (discussed in Chapter 10). When the government adopts an expansionary monetary policy (plenty of money available with low interest rates) there is plenty of money for the banks to lend to firms, and this money is available at low interest rates, so investment tends to increase. On the other hand, if the government runs a 'tight money' policy, the banks will make very little money available and interest rates will tend to be high, discouraging investment.

The investment by private firms may also be influenced by the competition for available funds. If the government is itself borrowing an increased amount to fill the gap between its income and its expenditure (the Public Sector Borrowing Requirement), there will be less money available for private firms unless the government at the same time increases the total amount available (with the expansionary monetary policy).

Government taxation policy (discussed in Chapter 14) may also influence the level of investment. High rates of tax on households' incomes leaves less money available for saving, and high rates of tax on company profits leave a smaller supply of internal funds for investment.

The access of the individual firm to the funds available depends on the firm's situation. The Stock Exchange channels funds from savers (generally through intermediaries such as insurance or pension funds) to the firms whose issues of shares are sold on the Stock Exchange (discussed above). Merchant banks perform a similar function, channelling their clients' money into productive investment projects. Many firms, particularly smaller operations, are unable to get access to these sources of finance. Their remaining source is the commercial banks whose managers traditionally take a very conservative view of commercial investment projects.

Since investment cannot proceed without funds, the government and financial institutions have taken a number of steps to widen the availability of finance, particularly to small firms. For example, the commercial banks and the Bank of England set up Finance For Industry (FFI) in 1975 using its assets for investment in industry. The National Enterprise Board (discussed in Chapter 8) used its funds for acquiring equity in companies in return for investment funds. Many of the firms involved were quite small. Since 1979 direct government funding for industrial investment has largely disappeared. The Department of Trade and Industry has sought to create the right conditions for industry to invest by a policy of administrative deregulation and simplification of corporate taxation. The government have sought to create the right economic conditions for private sector industry (enterprise) to flourish. The DTI is also now called the Department for Enterprise.

Given the difficulties of convincing potential suppliers of funds of the viability of a commercial project, funds for investment still remain a problem, particularly for smaller firms. A crucial element in investment, therefore, becomes the availability of internal funds. These internal funds come from profits. Profits will be boosted in the short term by expanding demand in the economy. In very competitive industries the supply of internal finance will be limited in the long term. In less competitive industries firms may earn excess profits, protected by barriers to the entry of competing firms. These accumulated profits provide the source for investment funds. As a result, Schumpeter has argued that it is firms operating in monopolistic and oligopolistic situations who produce the highest rates of investment and accompanying innovation.

The importance of the rate of interest in determining the level of investment

It has been argued that the rate of investment by private firms is influenced very little by the rate of interest in the economy. Its responsiveness to changes in expectations, changes in demand and changes in the availability of finance is much greater.

A large part of investment at any time is in new stocks of raw materials, semi-finished and finished goods. The costs of holding stocks are high. They must be insured; night-watchmen may be needed; the stocks may need to be kept in special conditions such as temperature or humidity. Given these high costs of stock holding whatever the rate of interest, firms will generally try to keep their stock holding at a minimum level consistent with the current level of demand. They will not be able, therefore, to reduce their stock holding if interest rates rise; nor will they want to increase it when interest rates fall.

We have discussed the uncertain nature of commercial investment. The return may be estimated to be 200 per cent under ideal conditions but *minus* 50 per cent if circumstances are as bad as is possible. Faced with this range of expected returns, the firm will be unlikely to respond to a change in the interest rate from 12 per cent to 14 per cent. It will invest if it is optimistic about the future, and will not if it is not, whatever happens to the rate of interest.

The rate of interest frequently changes, if only by relatively small amounts. Firms plan their investment generally over a medium-term or long-term period. In planning that investment they will consider the likely commercial circumstances and also any likely changes in the rate of interest over that period. Having made the decision, the investment plan will not be changed by the predicted change in the rate of interest.

It is, however, probably true that for small operations the rate of interest on their borrowing for investment is a central element in their cash-flow problems. They may, therefore, be forced to adjust their investment expenditure to changes in the rate of interest.

Discounted cash flow method

As mentioned above, the rate of return method of measuring the benefits of investment can be unreliable. A better alternative is the discounted (or internal) cash flow method.

Money generally has a lower value in the future than now. Note that this is not because of inflation. Money received this year is preferred to the same sum received next year because it can be invested for one year in some interest/profit earning project. Similar money received in two years time has a lower value than the same sum received in one year.

So, if a firm were to choose between two alternative streams of receipts from projects where the total cost and total receipts are the same but the time at which the receipts are received varies, it would generally prefer project A to project B in the example below:

	Project A	Project B
After 1 year	£30	£10
After 2 years	£20	£20
After 3 years	£10	£30

Similarly, any firm making payments would rather make them next year than this. If the payment is made now, money must be borrowed and interest paid. By delaying payment until next year, the firm can avoid one year's interest payments. Thus, we should discount (or reduce) the value of money paid or received in the future. The money received or paid should be discounted by a larger amount the further in the future is the time of payment and receipt. The usual discount rate is the current market rate of interest.

Suppose there is a project which involves a stream of payments and receipts over three years. The *Net Present Value* of the project is found by the formula:

$$NPV = NR_0 + \frac{NR_1}{1+r} + \frac{NR_2}{(1+r)^2} + \frac{NR_3}{(1+r)^3} + \ldots + \frac{NR_n}{(1+r)^n}$$

where NR is the net receipt occurring at any time (ie receipt minus out-payment); NR_0 is the net receipt at the beginning of the project; NR_1 is the net receipt after 1 year; NR_2 is the net receipt after two years and so on; r is the discount rate.

Using this formula, a firm can identify a project which is worth undertaking where the net present value of the project is greater than zero. For example, suppose a firm is considering a project which involves an out-payment now of £1,000 in return for a receipt after one year of £1,200. If the discount rate is 10 per cent we will find that the Net Present Value of the project is $-£1,000 + \frac{£1200}{1.1}$

$= -£1,000 + £1,091$

$= £91$

Since the Net Present Value is positive at this discount rate, the firm should undertake the project.

Notice that at higher discount rates the NPV would become negative as the higher discount rates reduce the present value of the later gain from the project. For example, with a discount rate of 30 per cent, the NPV of the project would be –£77. Thus, we would expect firms to undertake more projects if they use lower discount rates. If the discount rate is related to market interest rates, lower market interest rates would result in more investment.

Note also that more optimistic expectations about the commercial future would increase the expected receipts, so more projects would become viable with any discount rate. Suppose, for example, that the net receipt after one year was expected to be £1,500 instead of £1,200. The Net Present Value would then be £154 with a discount rate of 30 per cent.

The firm should also use the Net Present Values of projects as a way of choosing between alternative projects. Suppose, for example, that the firm can choose between project X and project Y, where the NPV of project X is £500 while the NPV of the alternative project Y is £700: the firm should choose project Y.

Cost benefit analysis

The growing size of the public sector and its significant use of society's limited resources has increased the need for *a rational approach* to the allocation of resources in the public sector and between the public and private sectors. Given our limited resources, any resources used on a project in the public sector have an *opportunity cost* of the benefit from the best alternative use in some other project in the public sector or in the private sector.

The rational approach for the appraisal of projects in the private sector is *discounted cash flow* analysis. The costs and benefits associated with the project are adjusted or *discounted* according to the time at which they occur, so that all costs and benefits are expressed at their *present value*. The Net Present Value of the project is then the total of benefits minus costs, all expressed at their present values.

The costs and benefits considered by a profit maximising firm appraising a project in the private sector will be the *private costs* (wages, rents, payments for raw materials and components) and the *private benefits* (the revenue) resulting from the projects. Only these private costs and benefits have any impact on the firm's profits.

In the public sector, decision-makers have wider responsibilities. It is necessary to take *a wider view* of the project, in the sense that the decision-maker in the public sector must consider the effects of the project on everyone – households, firms, local, regional, national and international interests. Many of these effects will be *externalities or spill-overs*. The decision-maker in the public sector should also take *a longer view* than might be considered appropriate in the private sector. He must consider the repercussions of the project in the distant as well as the near future, since a responsible society must take account of the welfare of future generations.

The general principles of Cost Benefit Analysis (CBA) require the answering of four *basic questions*:

a Which costs and benefits should be included?

b How should these be valued?

c What discount rate should be used?

d What relevant constraints exist?

Which costs and benefits should be included?

Let us take an example of a public works scheme such as building a by-pass road to carry traffic around a busy city or town centre. (The M25 was this type of scheme.)

The obvious or *direct costs* of such a scheme are the costs of buying the land needed for the road and the materials such as concrete and tarmac, the costs of the capital equipment used such as earth moving equipment, and the wage costs of the labour employed on the scheme.

Similarly, there are some obvious or *direct benefits* from the scheme: ie the benefits enjoyed by road users of a shorter time spent travelling on a less congested road; and the benefits in the town centre of reduced congestion caused by through traffic.

There are more remote costs and benefits which should also be included. For example, people who live near the new road may suffer from noise and other pollution while the road is being built and will also suffer from noise and air pollution caused by the traffic on the road when it is completed. Some households may suffer the loss of a pleasant view because of the siting of the road (social costs).

On the other hand, the increased accessibility provided by the road may raise house prices in the area generally (local benefits). Local businesses may have reduced or increased profits because of the new road. Petrol stations near the town centre may have less business while those near the new road may have more business.

The region may benefit generally from the new road. Increased accessibility may bring new businesses and households into the area. Employment and incomes will be increased, with the associated multiplier effects on the income of the region.

Many of the costs and benefits listed above are external costs or benefits and would not normally be considered in a private sector project. Private sector projects are only concerned with private costs and benefits.

There are two important principles that should be borne in mind in deciding on the costs and benefits to be included in the CBA study: *double counting must be avoided*. For example, the increased profits enjoyed by petrol stations near the new road and the higher values of houses in the area are a reflection of the benefits to travellers of the new road. If the study includes an estimate of the benefit to travellers of the new road it should not also include the pecuniary advantage to local businesses and households. A *cut-off point* will, in practice, have to be established. Some costs and benefits will be extremely remote from the project, and at this remoteness from the project thousands of households and firms may, in

The market for factors of production

some way, be affected by the project. These effects may be very slight. The problems of listing and assessing these remote, slight and widely spread effects may be great; their significance may be small. The decision-maker will need to define the scope of the study if it is to be practicable.

How should these costs and benefits be valued?

The process of CBA requires that all costs and benefits be valued by some *common yardstick* so that they may be summed to calculate the Net Present Value of the project. The common yardstick is *money*. So money values need to be placed on all costs and benefits.

Since the project is being viewed from society's point of view, it should be society's valuation of costs and benefits which should be used.

There are two problems:

a Where *market prices* exist for the goods and services which are relevant costs and benefits in the scheme, are these market prices a reliable indication of society's valuation of these goods and services?

b If there are no market prices for relevant goods and services, can *'imputed'* or *'shadow' prices* be derived which reflect society's valuation of these goods and services?

Problems associated with the use of market prices:

Firstly, where there is *monopoly power* in the market, the market price will exceed the marginal cost of providing the good. So if the market price is used in the CBA, this will overstate society's valuation of the good (the cost of the resources used in producing the good). Secondly, if there are any *externalities* associated with producing the good or service, the market price will be greater or less than the value that society places on the good.

Thirdly, the total benefit to society of a unit of any good or service exceeds the price by the amount of *consumer surplus*. Suppose the following demand curve indicates the marginal utility of visits to Kew Gardens. At a price of P, there will be Q visitors per day. The total benefit or utility from the visits is the area ABC (society's valuation of Q units of this good) while the revenue (market price x quantity) is APDQ. Society's valuation of this good therefore exceeds the value indicated by market price by the consumer surplus of PBD.

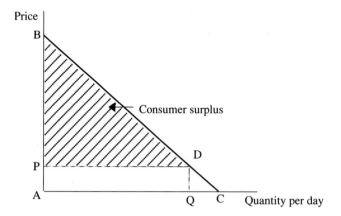

There may be *uncertainty* about the market prices of costs and benefits occurring in the future. This is a problem which occurs in investment analysis in both the public and private sector. Probability or sensitivity techniques can be used to take account of uncertainty.

Finally, if the project is a very large one, it may itself influence market price. In the following diagram, the market equilibrium is shown for the tarmac market. The equilibrium price is P and the quantity Q. The project planned is a motorway network for Britain. This project is so large that it will significantly increase the demand for tarmac. The demand curve shifts to D_1 in the diagram. The market equilibrium price as a result rises to P_1. Now the analyst has the problem of deciding which is the appropriate market price, P or P_1.

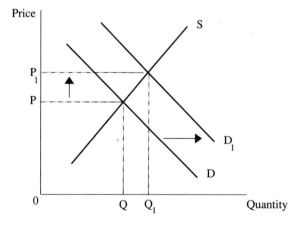

Problems associated with deriving shadow prices:

There are no markets in such things as pollution, amenity, time, life. There are, therefore, no market prices. However, if these variables are to be included in the CBA, these *intangibles* require *shadow prices*. This is especially so when these intangibles are major costs or benefits in the scheme. For example, the major benefit from a road scheme is the time saved by travellers.

Many public sector schemes involve the production of *public goods*: for example, public open space, lighthouses, the cleansing of rivers and the Thames Barrier. The essence of these goods is that they are supplied to the whole of society and no individual can be excluded from their consumption. There is thus no market in these goods and no market prices.

There are a number of techniques for imputing prices to these intangibles.

a   There may be markets for similar goods and services or markets in other countries which may be used to indicate the appropriate shadow price. Obviously, different circumstances may yield dissimilar social values, so this technique must be used cautiously.

b   Direct enquiry or survey may indicate shadow prices. For example, householders might be asked how much money they would be prepared to pay to avoid a particular cost (pollution for example), or how much they would be prepared to pay to acquire a particular benefit (amenity for example). The form of the questions may determine the answer, so care needs to be taken with this technique. Additionally, different people put different values on money. This largely depends on their income. If only low income people are questioned, the shadow price will be too low for society as a whole.

c   Shadow prices can be inferred from observed behaviour. Suppose that passengers are prepared to pay £100 more for an air-ticket on a plane which reduces the journey time by 1 hour. This implies that those passengers value their time at at least £100 per hour. However, this may be misleading, since there may be more luxury on the faster plane or greater status associated with travelling on it. Some of the £100 is then being paid for luxury and status rather than time-saving.

d   Finally, the analyst may abandon all attempts to put money values on certain intangibles since any money value would be arbitrary. For example, the Roskill Commission put no money value on the loss of wildlife and the destruction of a medieval church in assessing the costs and benefits of the alternative sites for the proposed third London Airport. Instead, the analyst might present the CBA with its Net Present Value stated in money terms, with a note on the significant intangibles. For example, 'the NPV of the proposed project is £10m but it involves an intangible item of the destruction of the environment in this area.' The decision-maker can then consider whether the £10m NPV justifies the loss of environment.

What discount rate should be used?

The discount rate used for adjusting the values of all costs and benefits to their present values should in CBA reflect the *social time preference rate*. This is the rate at which society values future benefits and costs as compared with present benefits and costs. For example, if society placed a zero value on any costs or benefits occurring more than 50 years into the future, we would need a discount rate which reduced those costs and benefits to zero.

The *private time preference rate* is perhaps indicated by the rate of interest earned on savings. This rate of interest is sufficient to compensate individuals and institutions for the sacrifice of present consumption for future consumption.

It is argued that the social time preference rate should be lower than the private time preference rate as indicated by the interest paid on savings, since individuals may be myopic and irrational about the future while society must take a greater responsibility for the future than individuals do.

Alternatively, it might be argued that future generations will be richer than we are and so they will place a lower value on their benefits and costs than we might on their behalf. This would indicate that a high discount rate should be used.

An alternative way of considering the appropriate discount rate to be used is to look at *the marginal cost of borrowing*, which indicates the disadvantage of benefits coming in later rather than sooner and the advantage of costs being paid later rather than sooner. This is the discount rate which would be used in calculating Net Present Values in the private sector. Firms would look at the marginal cost of borrowing the funds needed for the scheme.

The government's cost of borrowing for public sector schemes might be taken as *the government's gilt edged rate* (the rate of interest paid on bonds). This will be similar to the cost of borrowing in the private sector since the market will bring long-term interest rates into line with each other. Using the cost of borrowing is therefore a useful way of ensuring that similar discount rates are used on private sector and public sector. If this were not so, there would be a misallocation of resources between the public and private sectors. For example, suppose a lower discount rate were used in the public sector than that used in the private sector. Projects could be justified and funds used to finance them in the public sector which would be rejected in the private sector. Similarly, the private sector would be rejecting projects which would produce a higher NPV than projects accepted in the public sector. Since there is only a limited supply of finance for long-term investment in society, we would prefer to see it allocated rationally and fairly.

The capital market is far from perfect, so there is no reason to suppose that the marginal cost of borrowing will be the same as the private time preference rate, let alone the social time preference rate. Thus, we have contradictory arguments for the choice of the appropriate discount rate to be used in CBA. Should the discount rate be the same as the marginal cost of borrowing, in which case it is likely to exceed the social time preference rate since that may be less than the interest rate paid on savings? *Or* should the discount rate be a social time preference rate which will almost certainly be less than the marginal cost of borrowing in the private sector, and thus cause a mis-allocation between the public and private sectors?

There is no right answer to the discount rate problem.

A useful technique for getting round this problem is to calculate that discount rate which reduces the NPV of the project to zero. This rate is known as the *Internal Rate of Return* (IRR). The IRR can then be compared with various potential discount rates. If the IRR exceeds the marginal cost of borrowing and the social time preference rate, then the project is obviously worthwhile.

What relevant constraints exist?

There is no point in working through a lengthy and costly CBA if the analysis ignores the realistic constraints.

These constraints may be:

a physical, eg the site is too small for the proposed scheme;

b legal, eg there is a public right of way across the site;

c financial, eg the scheme may be impracticable if its costs exceed government expenditure limits;

d distributional, eg all the benefits of the scheme go to high income households while low income households suffer most of the costs. This might be unacceptable to a government committed to redistributing from rich to poor.

Conclusions

CBA works best when used to indicate the choice between two or more well-defined projects when these projects have few intangibles. The option with the highest NPV can then be chosen with some confidence.

A single option with many wide repercussions and significant intangibles provides greater problems, since a positive NPV may be considered insufficient to justify the project, given the inevitable doubts about the choice of relevant costs and benefits, their valuation and the choice of the discount rate.

CBA is obviously not an exact technique since it involves so many subjective and potentially controversial decisions. It might be thought that these problems make the technique a costly and time consuming irrelevance. However, it does provide a rational framework for decision-making and is more complete than any other technique available.

The distribution of wealth and income

The ownership of resources

The amount of income earned by an individual under the market system will be determined by the resources he has to sell and the value of those resources when sold to firms. The more resources and the higher their market value, the higher the individual's income. These resources may be land, labour or capital, and their incomes rent, wages and interest respectively.

Wealth is a *stock of assets* which produce a *yield of income* which may be *pecuniary* or *psychic*. The pecuniary or money income earned is *'unearned income'*. Wealth includes land, buildings, furniture, accumulated savings, stocks and shares, pension rights. Almost everyone owns some wealth and earns some income from wealth even if this is just their consumer durables such as houses, furniture, motor cars and the consumer benefits that can be derived from them. Wealth can be termed anything with monetary value.

Income may be either *earned income* from the use of labour/resources or *unearned income* from the consumption of the yield from wealth. The income whether earned or unearned may be pecuniary or not. For example *pecuniary earned income* would be the wages or salaries paid for work. *Non-pecuniary earned income* would be the benefits resulting from unpaid housework, care of children, home repairs and decorating, and gardening. Benefits, taxation and spending on government services help the lower income groups.

The distribution of wealth

The main determinant of wealth inequalities is still the pattern of inheritance. But the distribution of earnings also has an influence, through differences in ability to accumulate savings and investments out of earned incomes.

Until the late 1970s there had been a long-term trend towards a marginal redistribution of wealth. However, this historical trend was from the very rich to the rich, rather than from rich to poor. Redistribution since the inter-war period failed to reach downwards much beyond the top 20 per cent. During the Thatcher years even that small amount of redistribution has been halted. The effect of current government policy has been to buttress extremes of wealth. For example:

a in 1990 over half (51 per cent) of all marketable wealth was owned by the richest 10 per cent;

b just less than a fifth (18 per cent) of marketable wealth was concentrated in the hands of the richest 1 per cent;

c in stark contrast the bottom 50 per cent of the population control just 7 per cent of marketable wealth.

Even if the definition of wealth is widened to allow for occupational and state pension rights, 84 per cent of wealth remains controlled by the richest half of the nation.

Distribution of wealth

United Kingdom	Percentages and £ billion			
	1976	1981	1986	1990
Marketable wealth				
Percentage of wealth owned by:				
Most wealthy 1%	21	18	18	18
Most wealthy 5%	38	36	36	37
Most wealthy 10%	50	50	50	51
Most wealthy 25%	71	73	73	72
Most wealthy 50%	92	92	90	93
Total marketable wealth (£ billion)	280	565	955	1,689
Marketable wealth less value of dwellings				
Percentage of wealth owned by:				
Most wealthy 1%	29	26	25	27
Most wealthy 5%	47	45	46	51
Most wealthy 10%	57	56	58	63
Most wealthy 25%	73	74	75	78
Most wealthy 50%	88	87	89	92
Marketable wealth plus occupational and state pension rights (latest valuation)				
Percentage of wealth owned by:				
Most wealthy 1%	13	11	10	11
Most wealthy 5%	26	24	24	26
Most wealthy 10%	36	34	35	37
Most wealthy 25%	57	56	58	60
Most wealthy 50%	80	79	82	84

(Source: *Social Trends 23*, 1993, Table 5.20)

The distribution of income

Income is more evenly distributed than wealth. However, between 1979 and 1989 inequality in both disposable and final income grew wider. The top 20 per cent of income earners increased their share of incomes during the 1980s largely at the expense of other income groups.

Distribution of household income

United Kingdom	Percentages Quintile groups of individuals					
	Bottom fifth	Next fifth	Middle fifth	Next fifth	Top fifth	Total
Net income before housing costs						
1979	9.9	14.2	18.1	22.9	34.8	100
1981	9.7	13.9	17.8	22.9	35.7	100
1987	8.6	12.8	17.1	22.6	39.0	100
1988-89	7.9	12.4	17.0	22.7	40.0	100
Net income after housing costs						
1979	9.6	14.1	18.1	23.1	35.1	100
1981	9.0	13.6	17.8	23.1	36.5	100
1987	7.6	12.3	17.1	22.9	40.1	100
1988-89	6.9	12.0	17.0	22.9	41.1	100

(Source: *Social Trends 23*, 1993, Table 5.17)

Most of this income comes from earnings, as established above. Differences in earnings from the sale of labour resources depend on a number of factors, as discussed above. Other things being equal, we would expect that workers will earn more if they are more productive, are doing a more difficult, dangerous or unpleasant job, have had to undertake a long or difficult training on a low income, can earn high incomes in alternative jobs, or belong to a union with a strong bargaining position.

To look at a few examples from statistics of earnings:

a non-manual workers earn more than manual workers, presumably reflecting differences in productivity and initial training;

b furnacemen earn more than plumbers, presumably because, with similar skill levels, their job is done in a more unpleasant environment;

c bricklayers earn more than general labourers, presumably because of the apprenticeship system which keeps trainee bricklayers on very low wages while they learn their skill;

d firemen earn more than security guards, presumably because of the greater danger involved in their work;

e teachers in further education earn more than secondary school teachers, presumably because of their alternative job opportunities;

f lorry drivers are paid more the larger the vehicle they drive, presumably reflecting their higher productivity and the skill involved.

The following chart shows differences in earnings across a range of occupations. In general, the more skilled earn higher pay than the unskilled.

Average gross weekly pay (males) 1993

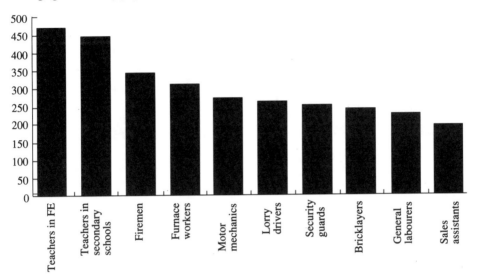

(Source: *New Earnings Survey*, 1993, Part A, Table 8)

Earnings differentials between ethnic groups

People from ethnic minorities now make up almost 6 per cent of the working age population, according to the 1993 Labour Force Survey. Of the economically active working age population, people from ethnic minorities make up 4.9 per cent. In spite of this contribution to the workforce, people from ethnic minorities suffer disadvantage and discrimination in the labour market.

Rates of unemployment are higher on average for people from ethnic minority groups than they are for comparable white people (see following chart).

Unemployment by ethnic group, men and women 1994

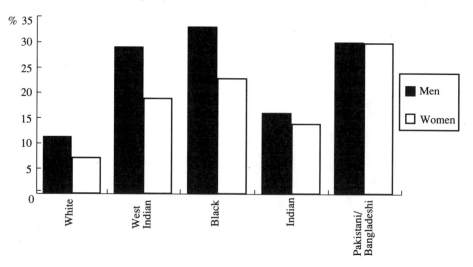

(Source: *Employment Gazette*, May 94)

The following graph shows trends in unemployment rates (ILO definition) for white people and for people from ethnic minorities in Great Britain from spring 1984 to autumn 1993.

Trends in ILO unemployment rates by ethnic origin: Great Britain, spring 1984 to autumn 1993

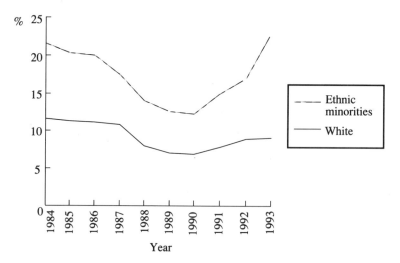

(Source: *Employment Gazette*, May 1994)

In addition, ethnic minority workers are more likely than white workers to be employed in occupations below their qualification level (underemployment). With regard to earnings, on average white workers are paid more than ethnic minority workers; white women are paid more than ethnic minority women, white men are paid more than ethnic minority men. Within the ethnic minority groups themselves, some workers are more disadvantaged than others: Pakistanis and Bangladeshis earn less than West Indians, who earn less than Indians.

With regard to skill level and qualifications, the following chart shows broad occupational groups by ethnic origin in spring 1993, for men and women separately.

Percentage of population with no qualifications, by ethnic origin and age, Great Britain, spring 1993

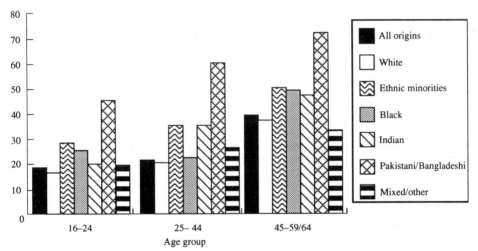

(Source: Labour Force Survey, *Employment Gazette*, May 1994)

The Race Relations Act, passed in 1968, aimed to eliminate discrimination in employment, housing, and the provision of goods and services. The Commission for Racial Equality, set up in 1976, was established in order to further the aims of the Act and to reduce inequalities.

Earnings differentials between men and women

In every occupation and industry in the UK, men earn on average more than women. This is also true of the other member countries of the European Union, and of all other OECD countries. There is a variety of explanations for this situation.

It has historically been the case in the UK, as in other developed countries, that women participated less in the labour market than did men, due to the domestic roles which our culture assigns to women. Until World War 2, UK women normally dropped out of the labour market on marriage. Indeed, in some occupations such as teaching, women were required to leave upon marriage. Following the large contribution which women made to the war effort, by working in factories and on the land, women in post-war Britain have participated more. Most women drop out of the labour market temporarily on the birth of their first child, and rejoin when the youngest child reaches school age. This discontinuity of labour market experience disadvantages women vis a vis men in two ways: firstly, whilst they are out of the labour market engaged in childrearing, their male colleagues are moving higher up the incremental pay scales, and/or moving into higher grades of work which pay more, and also gaining valuable occupational experience; secondly, employers may be reluctant to employ a woman of childbearing age, in case she should leave to have a baby, or require maternity leave.

The relative scarcity and high cost of good childminding also makes it difficult for many women to find and afford it (bearing in mind that many women are low paid). Many women are thus obliged to take only part-time work, which is on average lower paid than comparable full-time work, and in which opportunities for progression to higher paid work are fewer.

The following table shows the average gross hourly earnings of full-time men and women in selected occupations.

Average Gross Hourly Earnings for full-time men and women in selected occupations, excluding overtime (in pence)

	Men	Women
Medical practitioners	1858	1500
Solicitors	1693	1314
FE teachers	1482	1334
Nurses	837	787
Admin/clerical officers in civil service/local govt	623	561
Police officers	1083	992
Sales assistants	456	409
Assemblers/lineworkers (electrical/electronic goods)	550	442
Postal workers	598	577
Cleaners	445	399

(Source: *New Earnings Survey*, 1993, Part D, Table 87)

Until 1975 in the UK it was perfectly legal to pay men and women different rates for doing exactly the same jobs. The Equal Pay Act was passed in 1970, but not implemented until 1975. This stated that men and women doing exactly the same job in the same enterprises must be paid the same. The effects of this piece of legislation can be seen by looking at the chart below: in 1975 there was a sudden rise in the average pay of women relative to men. This piece of legislation had however a fairly limited impact, in that it only covered the jobs in which both men and women worked. The UK labour market is strongly horizontally segregated (this means that, by and large, men and women do different jobs; there are 'men's jobs' (eg plumbers) and 'women's jobs' (eg secretaries)).

In 1983, following pressure from the European Community, the UK government passed the Equal Value (Amendment) Regulations. This required that men and women doing jobs which were of equal value to their employer should be paid the same amount. Women are now allowed to compare themselves to a man doing different jobs for the same employer in the same enterprise. If they can prove that the skill levels are the same, they should be paid the same.

Another important piece of legislation passed in 1975 was the Sex Discrimination Act. This made illegal discrimination in hiring/firing/training and promotion.

The effects of these pieces of legislation and other factors can be seen in the chart below. There has, since 1975, been a gradual slow rise in the average earnings of women relative to men, but there is still a gap.

Women's pay as a percentage of men's, 1970 to 1993

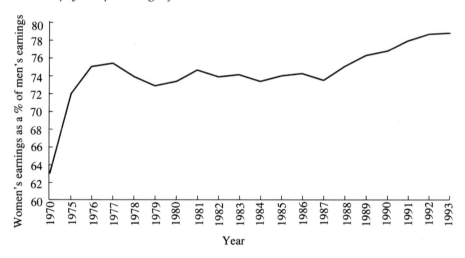

Average gross hourly earnings, excluding overtime, of full-time employees aged 18 and over whose pay was not affected by absence.
(Source: *Employment Gazette*, November 1993)

Another factor which has affected the relative earnings of women has been the increasing education of women. It has historically been the case that women received less education and training than did men. This situation has been changing in recent years. Now, there are almost as many women in higher education as there are men. But the subjects which they study are to a great extent different. This is clearly seen in the following chart, which shows a selection of different subjects. Education is heavily female dominated, with 80 per cent women. Engineering, however, is heavily male dominated, with approximately 15 per cent women. This situation is changing, but slowly.

Female students as a percentage of all students: by selected full-time degree courses, 1981/82 and 1990/91, UK (%)

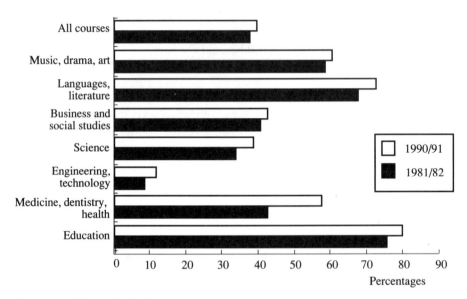

(Source: *Social Trends* 23, 1993)

Summing up this section on earnings differentials between men and women, we can say that the differentials still exist, but are being gradually eroded. There are several reasons for this erosion: legislation, changing cultural values, increasing education and qualifications, increasing participation rates, and the realisation by employers that women have much to offer.

Poverty

In Britain, poverty is defined as households whose income falls below the income support level. This is itself a very low level of income.

There are four main groups which form the overwhelming majority of such poverty line households: people who work but whose earnings are very low; lone-parent households (the majority being female-headed); old-age pensioners without occupational pensions; and households whose adult members are unemployed.

The government redistributes resources from taxpayers and local council tax payers to these very low income groups. This takes the form of a wide variety of means-tested benefits: income support, family credit, unemployment benefit, housing benefit. Nevertheless, these groups still live in poverty.

There is much debate as to whether relative poverty or absoluted poverty should be the reference level. Relative poverty means that people have an income level which is well below the average for Britain, such that they are unable to participate fully in the society in which they live.

The following table shows how far below average income for their particular group, different types of households fall.

Proportions of individuals below various household income thresholds for 1990/91: by family type – income after housing costs

Family type	Percentage with income below a given proportion of the average					
	Below 40%	Below 50%	Below 60%	Below 70%	Below 80%	Below 100%
Pensioner couple	15	31	43	54	62	75
Single pensioner	11	44	55	63	68	78
Couple with children	16	23	31	42	53	69
Couple without children	7	10	13	18	24	38
Single with children	30	60	69	76	83	91
Single without children	13	19	25	31	37	51

(Source: *Social Security Statistics*, 1993, Table H3.03)

Because of the complexity of the tax and benefit systems in the UK, and due to the fact that they are not co-ordinated, many households become caught in what is known as the *poverty trap*. Many benefits are means-tested (including income support, family credit, housing benefit, which means that any income from earnings is deducted on a £ for £ basis after a certain (very low) threshold is reached. Households in such situations find it difficult to get themselves out of poverty because of their marginal tax rates if they were to take on work would be very high. The same problem exists with unemployed households with children: these households are unable to accept low paid work, as their total income from all benefits might actually decrease.

Minimum wage controls

A minimum wage is a threshold level below which employers are not legally allowed to pay. Britain does not have an across-the-board statutory minimum wage. The other members of the European Union do have one. One of the reasons for the current government's unwillingness to sign up to the Social Chapter of the Maastricht Treaty is that it includes provision for such a minimum wage. The current government has pursued a hands-off stance to the labour market, believing that a deregulated labour market, in which social protection for workers is low, is the best policy for Britain, and will enable us to be competitive internationally.

Although we do not have a statutory minimum wage, we have had for most of this century Wages Councils which set (very low) minimum wage levels for certain low paying industries. These wages councils were first established in the early years of this century to regulate pay in the 'sweated trades'. Until recently, 26 Wages Councils had survived, setting wage levels for some of the worst-paid occupations in Britain. The Thatcher government wished to remove the Wages Councils, but the outcry from the anti-poverty lobby was so great that they were retained for a while longer. However, the Wages Inspectorate whose job it was to police these industries, to ensure compliance with the legal wage rates, was under-resourced. The Wages Councils have now finally been abolished.

Prior to the last general election, there was a widespread debate as to the effects which the introduction of a minimum wage would have on employment and competitiveness. The Labour Party was advocating a Minimum Wage of £3.60 per hour. The Conservative Party alleged that this would cost many jobs: as the price of workers rises (as wages go up) then, using standard demand and supply analysis, we would expect that the demand for workers would go down. This is particularly the case if it is easy to replace the now higher-paid workers with capital (machines) and/or the wage costs are a high part of the final product cost. This is illustrated in the following diagram.

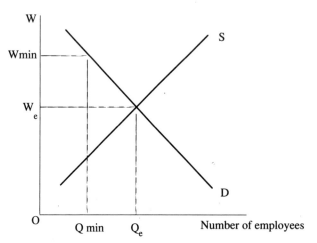

Note: in the diagram, W = wage; O = origin.

As the diagram shows, if the minimum wage is set above the equilibrium wage rate, then demand for workers falls, and some of the workers lose their jobs. Clearly, the higher the minimum wage, the more workers will be unemployed.

The extent to which this analysis is the whole of the story is debatable. The government believed that our industries would be unable to compete with such a minimum wage in place, that workers would be 'priced out of jobs'. Nevertheless, our European Union partners have minimum wages, and are able to compete with us (although it must be admitted that there is currently much concern over the cost of the high level of social protection for EU workers).

Questions for review

1. What are the four factors of production? Explain each one.
2. a Explain Marginal Productivity Theory.
   b What is marginal physical product?
   c What is marginal revenue product?
3. Why is the demand for factors of production a 'derived demand'?
4. What influences the elasticity of demand for a factor of production?
5. Explain 'economic rent'.
6. Explain 'transfer earnings'.
7. Why does the UK government impose restrictions on the use of land?
8. What does a backward bending supply curve for labour demonstrate?
9. Explain how education and training are relevant to the process of wage determination.
10. How can trade unions influence wage levels?
11. What is a 'monopsonistic employer'?
12. Explain the difference between saving and investment.
13. What are the main influences on the demand for investment?
14. Explain the accelerator model.
15. Explain what you understand of cost-benefit analysis.
16. What is 'consumer surplus'?

Government involvement in production | 8

Industrial policy 205

Nationalised industries and privatisation 212

Public and merit goods 226

Housing policy 228

Helping markets to work better 240

Industrial policy

Reasons for government intervention in privately owned industry

The government becomes involved in privately owned industry because of market failures and externalities. It may also be concerned about the effect of market operation on unemployment, income distribution and the balance of international payments.

In a perfectly working market there is perfect knowledge, no uncertainty, no immobility of factors of production and no monopoly power. Firms will be motivated by profit maximisation under the pressure of competition to operate at maximum efficiency. They will react swiftly to changes in market conditions by reallocating resources in line with consumer preferences. They will select worthwhile investment projects, both for replacement and for innovation, and will raise the appropriate finance from the finance markets. Firms will seek the most efficient form of production through adjustments of scale or mergers with other firms. Less efficient firms and declining industries will disappear under these competitive pressures, releasing the resources for the more efficient firms and expanding industries.

Government intervention is needed because the market does not always work as well as this, for the following reasons:

a Firms are uncertain about the future and output cannot necessarily be adjusted very swiftly when changes have occurred. As a result, delays and bottlenecks occur in the productive process.

b Not all firms are profit-maximising, and many industries give firms significant monopoly power. As a result, it cannot be assumed that firms will produce at optimum efficiency.

c As a result of monopoly power and excess profits, there may be substantial inertia in industry where firms fail to respond to changes in market conditions or technology.

d Firms may be unaware of the potential of scale economies, or of the existence of firms with whom they can merge in the interests of efficiency and profits.

e Firms may have worthwhile investment projects, but be unable to find appropriate finance because of failures in the market in loanable funds. Lenders may be uncertain and therefore behave non-optimally, or there may be monopoly power, which may mean that lenders become prejudiced in their choice of projects.

f Resources may be immobile, so that, instead of transferring from declining to expanding firms and industries, they simply become unemployed.

Additionally, the government may be concerned about the effects of the operation of the market on unemployment, the balance of payments and income distribution, for the following reasons:

a If resources are not reallocated from declining to expanding industries, unemployment occurs with all its associated social, economic and political consequences discussed in Chapter 13.

b If British industries close down because of their inefficiency compared with foreign competitors, this reflects the correct working of the market system, but it may also mean that Britain's payments to foreign suppliers exceed her earnings from the sale of British goods to foreign customers. (The problems created by this are discussed in Chapter 17.)

c The prices charged for goods and the earnings paid by firms may leave some individuals with an unacceptably low real income.

The government therefore has a number of policies designed to adjust the operation of the market, as follows:

a It may use indicative planning (discussed below) to reduce delays and bottlenecks.

b It controls the development and exercise of monopoly power (see Chapter 6).

c It may itself invest or encourage investment in innovation, in order to speed industry's adaptation to change (see below).

d It may inform firms of investment possibilities and may 'introduce' firms that may benefit from merging with each other.

e It may directly make funds available to firms for investment where the finance market is thought to be operating inefficiently (see below).

f It has a range of policies to speed the reallocation of labour resources in order to limit unemployment (see Chapter 13). It may also use government funds to maintain a declining industry in order to check the creation of unemployment (see below).

g It may similarly use government funds to maintain an uncompetitive domestic industry or limit the entry of cheaper imports into the country in the interests of the balance of payments (see Chapter 17).

h It may fix maximum prices for goods (see Chapter 2), or set minimum wage levels (see Chapter 7) in order to protect the real income of the poor.

Indicative planning

Also called central planning, this type of government involvement in industry is thought to have contributed greatly to the greater relative success of the French economy in the post-war period. In the 1960s it became an important feature of government policy towards industry.

It was felt that rapid economic growth and the efficiency of the economy was often limited by delays in the adjustment of some sectors to changes generated elsewhere. Suppose that one sector expands rapidly. If this expansion is unexpected, the sector's suppliers will find themselves operating inefficiently as they try to stretch their capacity to meet demand, and bottle-necks may develop.

To correct this, the government should anticipate the expansion of the economy so that all relevant sectors can be geared up to the changes. The key to the process is to predict the anticipated rate of growth in the economy, and then inform the various industries of the expansion that will, on the basis of this growth rate, be expected of them.

In 1962 the National Economic Development Council was set up to apply this exercise to 17 selected industries on the basis of a rate of economic growth of 4 per cent per year. Later, in 1965, a National Plan was drawn up which extended the exercise. Unfortunately, in both cases the plans turned out to be irrelevant since the economy failed to grow at the required rate. Indeed, only ten months after the publication of the National Plan, an economic 'freeze' was forced on the government because of rising inflation rates and an increasing balance-of-payments deficit. The freeze effectively checked economic growth.

Since then, any indicative planning has tended to relate only to specific industries. In 1975 the Industry Act set up the National Economic Development Council, which has members representing government, management and trade unions. They study key industries, looking for potential bottle-necks which might check the economy's expansion and for any investment policies and mergers that might increase efficiency. This type of planning links in with the policy for industrial restructuring discussed below.

Industrial restructuring

Specific Acts have been passed to deal with the restructuring of certain declining industries (their problem is discussed in more detail in Chapter 13). The Cotton Industry Act of 1959 and the Shipbuilding Industry Act of 1967 attempt to increase the efficiency and competitiveness of these industries through the investment and rationalisation of the industries into fewer, larger operations. This intervention implies that the restructuring of the industries under market pressure (more efficient firms taking over or eliminating less efficient firms) will be too slow or will produce the wrong industrial structure. For example, the pressure of a diminishing market may lead to the elimination of efficient as well as inefficient firms.

The *Industrial Reorganisation Act of 1967* was a more general attempt to improve the efficiency of industry. In particular, the Industrial Reorganisation Corporation was to act as a 'marriage broker', encouraging mergers between firms where these would lead to greater efficiency and competitiveness. It could also make loans to support this rationalisation. For example, it concentrated a large part of its energies and funds on the automobile industry, and its efforts greatly contributed to the concentration of that industry into British Leyland. The conspicuous problems of that firm since then are a powerful illustration of the difficulties created by increasing concentration and scale of operation in industry.

The *Industrial Expansion Act of 1968* made provision for assistance to be made available on projects that would promote efficiency, technological advance and productive capacity. It resulted in some concentration of the British computer industry with the formation of ICL. The most famous project initiated under this Act was Concorde. This project was set up with initial loans and credit guarantees of £100m which then needed to be greatly increased as the project continued, and it is said to be the biggest loss-maker in commercial history! While brilliant technologically, the project produced a high-speed, high-fuel-consumption, small-payload aeroplane which could not be justified in a world of rising fuel prices. Market conditions now make fuel cost per passenger more important than speed. Only British Airways and Air France 'bought' the plane. Although it now makes an operating profit for these airlines, the fact remains that sales of the plane never recouped the R and D costs.

The Industry Act 1972
Initially introduced by a Conservative government it was used more extensively by the following Labour government to extend direct government involvement in industry. The government was enabled to take control wholly or partially of companies in financial difficulties. An example of such a step under this legislation was the government's acquisition of British Leyland.

The Industry Act 1975
The National Enterprise Board (now abolished) was set up as a publicly owned industrial holding company. It took over the assets acquired in private industries under previous legislation. These included holdings in Rolls Royce, British Leyland (Rover Group) and Ferranti. The available funds for further acquisitions were greatly extended. In the first year after the Act the NEB acquired shares in over a dozen small and medium-sized companies. It also considered ways in which the performance of industries could be improved through co-ordination by off-shoots of the NEB. For example, it set up a number of operations in the rapidly expanding computer/electronics field to co-ordinate the design of systems and marketing of products.

As British industry moved into the recession of the late 1970s, the government was forced to use funds intended for industrial restructuring for what were really last-ditch attempts to stop large employers from closing down. For example, government funds kept Chrysler (now Talbot cars) operating in this country.

Industrial Development Act 1982
This Act of Parliament gave the Secretary of State at the DTI powers to provide direct financial assistance to an industry if this assistance will:

a benefit the UK economy, and

b produce benefits which are in the national interest.

Effects of government involvement in industry

Given the spectacular problems of some of the results of government intervention in private industry (eg British Leyland, Concorde) it is important to look at the justifications for intervention again. For example:

a Civil servants are not necessarily good at commercial decisions which – inevitably, because of the element of uncertainty – involve a measure of 'hunch' or instinct. Businessmen certainly seem to dislike the intervention of the government in their affairs. Many companies resisted the funds of the NEB because of the intervention that would have resulted.

b The government may have too many, sometimes conflicting, objectives to be able to run its operations efficiently. For example, Inmos, a company involved in the production of computer 'chips' under the aegis of the NEB, was forced to locate its operations in South Wales where there was high unemployment, rather than in Bristol where the company believed it could operate most efficiently. It may, therefore, be better to leave industry to choose its own single-minded path in the interests of industrial efficiency.

c In the short-run interest of protecting employment or the balance of payments, the government may be ensuring the long-run survival of inefficient firms which may never be genuinely competitive. Inefficiency remains, and resources are not transferred into more promising sectors.

d If industry is aware that the government will provide funds to cover losses in order to protect employment or the balance of payments, there is no incentive for those firms to be efficient.

Recent developments

Encouraging the smaller firm

The Conservative government (1979-) has given greater emphasis than its predecessors to the encouragement of small businesses, and during the last few years initiatives have been taken in the provision of long-term finance for such companies; these are as follows:

a The Stock Exchange has introduced an Unlisted Securities Market to help smaller firms benefit from a full Stock Exchange listing.

b The government, in collaboration with the clearing banks, has introduced a Loan Guarantee Scheme.

c A number of finance institutions have been involved in the provision of finance to managers wishing to buy out firms for which they work.

The main problem for the small firm is the inability to obtain sufficient funds to promote growth. The smaller the firm, the larger proportionate increase in the capital base required to respond to an increase in demand, but the lower its ability to command loan and equity finance.

In essence, they have been unable to raise equity finance, and possess inadequate collateral to obtain debt finance. Yet small firms should be encouraged as a source of employment; many introduce innovations and compete successfully with foreign industry. In recent years, there has been a growing demand for finance by managers wishing to purchase (and perhaps save) the firm for which they work.

The acknowledgement of this need is not new, but previous attempts to provide finance have not been entirely successful, and the reasons for this may include the following:

a Relative to the needs of smaller firms, the funds actually provided have been inadequate.

b Some of the financial institutions imposed relatively high minimum-size cut-off points.

c For those institutions not dealing exclusively with small firms, the disproportionately high cost of processing applications and the higher risks involved would lead them to prefer larger projects.

d Small firms are often reluctant to allow interests into their organisation, because of the diminution of control which might result.

e Too much loan capital would raise the gearing ratio of the firm to one of high risk. Therefore, the ability to take both types of finance from the same source can be advantageous. The Industrial and Commercial Finance Corporation has been successful in this respect.

Of the *three* initiatives recently taken to alleviate these problems, the introduction of the *Unlisted Securities Market (USM)* in November 1980 was intended to fill a gap in the provision of venture capital for small and medium-sized firms on the London Stock Exchange. By reducing the proportion of equity funds required to be in public hands, from at least 25 per cent for a full listing to 10 per cent on the USM, and by lowering the cost of entry, it was hoped that small firms would be able to raise external finance more easily than before.

An analysis of the Unlisted Securities Market shows that it is going some way to meet the needs of both young, fast-growing firms and those of lower growth rate needing to replace equipment. Such areas of the economy least hit by recession are well represented, such as oil exploitation, financial services, and professional services (including computing and North Sea Oil services).

In addition, the *Loan Guarantee Scheme* was introduced in the Finance Act 1981. It provided for a total of £50m annually for three years. It was extended in the 1986 budget for a further three years. The period of the loans may be from two to seven years, at a commercial rate of interest plus a premium of 2½ per cent. Loans of up to £75,000 are guaranteed up to a limit of 70 per cent by the DTI.

The initial shortcomings of the scheme were:

a The amount available is relatively small.

b The loan period is only of medium term.

c The interest rate may be regarded as excessive.

d The upper limit of £75,000 on individual loans.

Despite these problems, the scheme appears to have been successful, and since 1981 over £565m has been made available with 17,270 businesses receiving loans.

Thirdly, on the provision of finance for *management buy-outs*, the number of such buy-outs has increased in the last few years for several reasons:

a The current economic recession has often forced companies to sell subsidiaries.

b A number of financial institutions have recognised the opportunities and provided finance on favourable terms to managers.

c Recent changes in the legislation regarding divestment have made it more attractive financially.

The three types of buy-out schemes comprise Asset Purchase, Holding Company Loan Funding and Share Purchase. Typically, the financing takes the form of a combination of loan and equity funds, normally with the majority equity stake lying with the management. However, the taking of an equity stake by the financial institution helps reduce the size of fixed-interest loan payments and lends credibility to the business.

Prices paid for buy-outs vary from £30,000 to £53 million. At the top end of the range, the amount of finance and risk involved has usually resulted in consortia of institutions funding the venture. Industrial and Commercial Finance Corporation is the market leader in terms of the number of deals completed, but, on average, the size of these buy-outs is relatively small. Candover Investments concentrates upon the larger end of the market. In value terms, management buy-outs are only one-third as important as other non-financial divestments. Compared with total liquidations, both are insignificant.

It is important, also, to remember that initiatives such as the *Business Expansion Scheme*, the *Enterprise Allowance Scheme*, and the *Business Improvement Scheme* have been part of recent government policy to encourage enterprise among small firms. The Business Expansion Scheme offers income tax relief to individuals investing up to £40,000 in unquoted UK companies. The Enterprise Allowance Scheme is designed to encourage people to create their own jobs. Unemployed people receive £40 per week in lieu of benefit for up to a year while they start their own business. The Business Improvement Scheme offers 55 per cent grants towards consultancy costs which will enhance the management skills of small firms. This scheme operates in steel, shipbuilding and textile closure areas.

In conclusion, it should be pointed out that, in terms of the amount of funds provided, finance for management buy-outs is the largest, followed by the Loan Guarantee Scheme and the USM. The level of involvement of the clearing banks in the Loan Guarantee Scheme and in management buy-outs is encouraging, but there remain the twin problems of high interest rates and taxation rates to impede the progress of smaller firms.

Encouraging industry in general
There still exists the apparatus in statutes to provide substantial direct financial help to industry, but the present government wants to foster growth through less intervention. To make the market work freely and to improve the 'supply side' of the economy, the government has tried to create the right economic conditions for industry and commerce to prosper (the creation of an 'enterprise' culture). This means deregulation, tax reform and schemes to promote initiative, enterprise and competition. Straightforward aid to industry is out, and policies to create an efficient, dynamic, free, competitive market are in. Indeed, the DTI is now called the 'Department for Enterprise'.

At the time of writing (July 94), the confidence of the corporate sector in the recovery seems to be growing, albeit slowly. Manufacturing output was up by 2.3 per cent over the previous 12 months. Investment by companies was up by 3.4 per cent over the previous 12 months. This investment however has played only a small part in the recovery. According to the latest CBI Industrial Trends Survey, the major factors limiting capital expenditure by companies are uncertainty over future demand, or an inadequate rate of return (low profits). On the positive side, the ratio of debt to income in the corporate sector has fallen sharply from its peak in 1991 during the recession. Companies are continuing to adjust to the high debt levels they took on in the late 1980s. This has also impacted upon investment.

Nationalised industries and privatisation

History
The phrase 'nationalised industry' refers to any industry or company which is wholly owned by the government. The *nationalised industry sector* of the economy inextricably affects all government economic policies.

The 'public corporation' has existed in embryo form for many years. Early in the nineteenth century many local water and sewerage undertakings were controlled by the local authorities, and in the inter-war years in the United Kingdom the British Electricity Authority was established as well as the London Transport Board. It was considered to be both more sensible and more economic for services such as water supply and electricity to be supplied by one national authority rather than by many individual private companies, and this principle was naturally extended to cover other basic supplies such as gas. (Obviously, it would indeed have been a tremendous waste of resources to allow innumerable power cables or pipes to be laid by different companies to individual houses in an area, not to mention the probable confusion and danger.)

However, nationalisation became a really important economic and political issue when the Labour government was returned to power after the Second World War. They were committed – partly for pressing economic reasons, but mainly for ideological reasons – to taking into public ownership the so-called 'commanding heights of the economy'. In the period between 1945 and 1951, the coal mines, the railways, the major airlines, the gas industry, the steel industry and the electricity industry throughout the United Kingdom were all nationalised. (As will be noted below, the industries which were nationalised tended to be the industries of the *past* rather than those of the *future* and so, despite an obvious need for such industries, the government failed to secure the ownership of the (future) 'commanding heights of the economy'.) Since 1951 the political swings and roundabouts have led to some industries such as steel being de-nationalised and then re-nationalised, and other industries or companies being taken into public ownership either for political reasons or out of economic necessity (ie Rolls Royce and British Leyland). Between 1974 and 1979 the Labour government nationalised shipbuilding and aerospace, but the election of the Conservative government in 1979 changed policy once again. The Thatcher administration elected in 1979 was mandated to privatise large areas of the nationalised sector. Indeed the re-election of the same administration in 1983, 1987 and 1992 has meant still fewer nationalised industries remaining by the early 1990s. (See later section on privatisation.)

Reasons for nationalisation

Certain governments have nationalised industries for the following reasons:

a To control key (vital) areas of the economy (either for planning or political purposes).

b To prevent an industry declining or disappearing completely (ie coal, rail). The loss of such industries could have seriously affected the performance of the rest of the economy.

c To provide long-term capital investment which private industry would not have undertaken.

d To allow an industry to operate as a monopoly (thereby avoiding duplication) without abusing its monopoly power.

e To promote industries which are vital to the security of the nation, especially in the high-technology sector.

f To provide the government with a source of revenue. Some of the high profits of gas, electricity, and telephones were often taken by the government to supplement tax revenue.

g To bring together an industry on a national basis in order to gain the maximum economies of scale.

h To preserve jobs in a high-unemployment area when a private sector company would have closed.

The nationalised industries today

All the industries are autonomous public corporations which are run by a Board of Directors and are self-financing to a very large degree. The directors are responsible to a government minister. This is usually the Minister for Industry, but this is not always the case. For instance, the power industries are responsible to the Minister of State for Energy. Parliament also exercises a limited degree of control through the Select Committee on Nationalised Industries, although this tends to be 'retrospective' (ie the committee examines events a considerable time after they have occurred). It should be noted that companies such as the Rover Group (BL) (before its takeover by British Aerospace) were still plcs. Although the government owned most of the shares, private shareholders still existed.

At the end of the 1970s nationalised industries (NIs) as a whole were performing badly, after years of financial problems and subsidisation. The government's main response has been to privatise. So far 16 main businesses have been returned to the private sector. For those still in the public sector the government has tightened up financial disciplines, exposed their activities wherever possible to market competition and generally demanded higher standards of management and efficiency. The NIs now account for some 3 per cent of total UK output compared to 9 per cent in 1979. And they employ around 750,000 people, under 2.9 per cent of total employees in the United Kingdom.

Taking the sector as a whole, labour productivity has gone up sharply, due both to cutting out overmanning and to increases in output. Over the past few years it has outstripped the high increase in private manufacturing industry. This higher productivity has helped to increase profits, and there has been less need for grants, subsidies and loans. NIs' total requirement for external finance (that part of their needs for finance which cannot be met from their own internal resources) fell sharply from £3000m in 79/80 to only £449m in 89/90 (due to a combination of reduced levels of government support and the privatisation of some industries, and also a gross trading surplus from the electricity industry), but then rose again to £2672m in 91/92 (partly because the electricity industry had by then been privatised). In 1993/94 the NIs borrowed £1,503m from central government and repaid a net total of £81m borrowed from other sources. Each industry which remains nationalised is now set an External Financing Limit (EFL) and tight financial targets. Borrowing by the nationalised industries forms part of the Public Sector Borrowing Requirement (this is the total borrowing by central government, local authorities, and the nationalised industries).

The *output* in the NIs was flat or falling during the 1970s and early 1980s. At that time, there were long-standing problems which had not yet been tackled effectively, among them overmanning, financial problems, inefficient working practices, and difficult labour relations. Also, the beginning of the 1980s was in any case a time of relatively low growth for industry generally.

Since 1983 there has been some recovery in NI output. However, the average growth rate, at 1¼ per cent over the three years to 1986/87, was well below that in either private manufacturing or the economy as a whole. The sector includes several long-established basic industries, such as coal and shipbuilding, with demand for their products declining or flat. In the early 1980s nationalised industries and private manufacturing alike sharply reduced their labour forces.

The size of the reductions in NI employment reflects both the former extent of overmanning and the unsatisfactory working practices, and also the effectiveness of the management's recent efficiency drive. While experience has obviously differed from industry to industry, *productivity levels* in all the major industries have improved significantly since the early 1980s.

Nationalised industries' labour productivity

Year	Annual percentage change		
	Nationalised industries	Manufacturing industries	Whole economy
79/80	1.7	0.9	1.2
80/81	-0.4	-5.3	-3.7
81/82	0.9	6.9	3.6
82/83	2.0	6.3	4.8
83/84	1.3	8.4	4.1
84/85	6.3	4.5	1.7
85/86	6.7	2.0	2.2
86/87	9.6	5.4	4.6
87/88	8.9	5.9	3.5
88/89	8.2	5.8	1.4
89/90	3.7	2.7	0.4
90/91	1.8	-0.1	-0.1

Output per person employed (adjusted for coal strike).
Industries in the public sector at 31 March 1992, excluding all electricity.
Excluding North Sea sector and non-trading public sector.
(Source: *Public Expenditure Analysis to 1994-95*, Cm 1920)

Management and cost control have greatly improved during the 1980s, both for industries such as steel, which are facing keen market competition, and those which are not. The government have set demanding targets for cost reductions and profitability. And they have been helped by the efforts of managements to improve efficiency. Industries facing privatisation have been impelled by that prospect to increase efficiency. Even those expecting to remain in the public sector indefinitely have been stimulated by the example set by private businesses.

Cutting costs has enabled the NIs to improve *profitability*. This has been done without raising prices in aggregate faster than the general inflation rate. Since then their real prices have in fact fallen. The progress made on cost reductions, in particular the productivity gains, has brought about a much needed improvement in the sector's gross trading surplus (trading profits).

Total nationalised industries financing 1991/92

	1991/92 est out-turns)	1993/94 (plans)
Total capital requirements	3,222	3,852
Total internal resources		
of which:	550	997
Current cost operating profit	-1,051	-785
Other	1,601	1,782
Total external finance		
of which:	2,672	2,855
Borrowing (net)	323	147
Subsidies	1,769	1,324
Capital grants	580	1,383

(Source: *Public Expenditure Analysis to 1994-95*, Cm 1920)

However, the *profitability* of the NIs is generally still well below that of private industry, in terms of real rate of return on capital. Nationalised industries are required to aim at a *rate of return* on their new investment programmes of 5 per cent in real terms (before payment of interest and tax). A required rate of return was first set in 1978, following a period when their capital spending had been running high. In retrospect, the 1970s were, for some industries, a time of overinvestment relative to demand, and led to serious overcapacity in some industries.

The nationalised industries

The list of nationalised industries which remained in the public sector in the summer of 1994 is as follows:

British Coal
Post Office
Girobank
British Rail
British Waterways Board
Scottish Transport Group
Civil Aviation Authority
London Regional Transport

The following industries have been privatised since 1979:

British Telecom
British Gas Corporation
British National Oil Corporation
British Airways
British Airports Authority
British Aerospace
British Shipbuilders (Warships)
British Transport Docks Board
National Freight Company
Enterprise Oil
National Bus Company
Electricity
Water
Steel

There has been an improvement in many aspects of nationalised industries' performance. Gains in labour productivity have helped to cut costs substantially. So profitability has increased and demands on public expenditure and borrowing have been reduced, all within a framework of much more stringent financial control.

Social obligations

However, it is not equitable to base a judgment of the profit or loss figures of a nationalised industry only on grounds of efficiency, because most of the nationalised industries have to fulfil certain *social obligations*. For instance, the Post Office is obliged to maintain and operate a postal delivery service to every mainland UK address. In remote rural areas, this would not be commercially viable, but it provides a vital service for remote rural communities.

Marginal cost pricing

A related problem arises in the coal industry, where a number of uneconomic coal mines have been kept in operation for 'social' reasons. (These are often in areas of high unemployment and so a government might have a positive reason for keeping them open.) However, this inevitably raises the overall cost of producing coal and highlights an interesting *microeconomic* problem which applies to a number of the nationalised industries. The marginal cost of producing coal from mine to mine varies considerably. In the very modern efficient mines the marginal cost is low, while in the older uneconomic mines the marginal cost is high. This creates a dilemma for the industry's pricing policy, which for obvious reasons has to be based on *average* costs rather than *marginal* costs.

Pricing at marginal cost is in theory the best way to maximise consumer welfare and also to allocate scarce resources most efficiently. However, while it may be an ideal, marginal cost pricing can lead to an industry making enormous losses if there are high fixed costs to cover. In the following diagram, if price is fixed at P_1 = MC, then the shaded area equals the losses made by the firm. However, it is important to note that marginal cost pricing does not always produce losses.

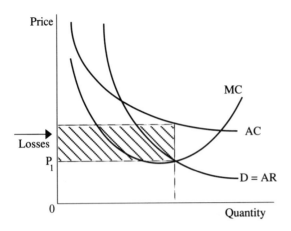

There is also another aspect to this particular problem. *Average cost pricing* has often in the past been used in nationalised industries because of the wide discrepancy between fixed and variable costs. For instance, *the marginal cost* to British Rail of transporting one extra passenger is virtually nil, and so marginal cost pricing would be totally unrealistic. However, the average cost is quite considerable due to the large amount of capital which has to be expended on rolling stock, track and so on, and may be more than the market could bear. Indeed, this also illustrates a major financing problem for British Rail and gives more weight to the practical need for nationalisation in certain areas of industry. British Rail experiences two periods of a relatively short duration every day when demand for its services is very high, that is, when people are travelling to and from work. For the rest of the day a very large proportion of its rolling stock and so on lies idle. There is very little that can be done about this, except operating a two-tier discriminating price policy where large discounts are offered to encourage people to travel during non-peak times. This cannot do much to alleviate the basic problem of very high fixed costs which confronts British Rail. When the rail network is returned to private ownership, there is concern that there may be a fall in facilities, because to maintain the current level and scope of services would be prohibitively expensive or non-viable.

It has been argued, however, that a deliberate policy initiated by the government of encouraging rail travel as opposed to road travel, both for passengers and freight, might prove beneficial not only to rail operators but also to traffic congestion, and so reduce the cost of road-building programmes. The calculations on which this argument is based are long and complex and outside the scope of this book, but they usually involve a statistical tool known as 'cost benefit analysis'. It attempts to evaluate not only the normal *monetary* costs of a project, but also the *social costs* and *benefits* which will flow from it. For instance, in the case of the encouragement of rail travel, an estimated monetary value would be given to items such as lower pollution levels, fewer road accidents, and so fewer days lost through hospitalisation and so on. It is a complicated and incomplete statistical tool at the present time, but it is being used more and more by the government in an attempt to evaluate the true costs to the community of any given investment project, whether it be the siting of a new airport, a road widening scheme, or the expansion of the railways. So far as the nationalised industries are concerned, it may help in the future to achieve a more accurate assessment and balance between the commercial aspects of their operations and their social obligations.

The government's privatisation policy

Privatisation – aims and achievements

One of the central pillars of the government's policy in revitalising the British economy has been its policy of returning state industries to the private sector. The privatisation programme continues to form a key element of the government's strategy for long-term economic growth, reinforcing the 'enterprise culture'.

The chief *aims* of privatisation are:

a *The reform of nationalised industries*. When the Conservatives came to power, the nationalised industries were costing the taxpayer £50m every week. They consistently performed less well than the private sector in terms of measures such as productivity and profitability. There were many reasons for this, but uppermost was the fact that these industries were cushioned from commercial forces by being able to fall back on government for financial support in difficult times. Furthermore, the nationalised industries were open to exploitation for political ends and were stifled by bureaucracy. Privatisation disciplines state industries by exposing them to market forces. The result is more efficient companies responsive to the needs of their customers.

b *Wider share ownership*. The number of adult shareholders in Britain has more than trebled since the Conservatives came to power. There are now about 9 million adult share owners, 20 per cent of the adult population. Since then, several major government share sales have taken place, all of which have increased that number. A more recent survey conducted by Dewe Rogerson concluded that there are now 9.4 million share owners. The government encourages the spread of share ownership, believing it to be a fair and constructive way of distributing wealth, as well as a means of enabling the public at large to gain a genuine stake in some of the nation's assets. The government also particularly encourages employee share ownership, and a feature of the privatisation programme has been the offering of incentives to employees of the privatised companies to take up shares. This policy has been successful: when British Gas was privatised, for example, 99.2 per cent of employees became shareholders, British Telecom 96 per cent, and British Airways 94 per cent.

c *Raising revenue.* Privatisation proceeds to date are over £23.5 billion. This money is used to reduce the burden of taxation on individuals and on industry, and to finance increased public spending on priority projects in a non-inflationary way. Furthermore, since privatisation acts to increase the profitability of industry, the government increases its long-term revenue by way of company taxation.

Sixteen major businesses have now been privatised, reducing the former state-owned sector by more than one-third. 655,000 employees have been transferred from the state to the private sector. Most of the privatised companies have improved their performance dramatically since they were sold. For example:

a *National Freight Corporation*: this previously state-owned company was privatised via an employee buy-out in 1982. At that time 84 per cent of the equity in the company was held by employees. This had fallen to 48.6 per cent by March 1991.

   Profitability in the company increased consistently up to 1990, partly due to employee ownership and participation, but also due to general economic recovery, and also to efficiency improvements.

   The company was floated on the stock exchange in 1989. At the time of flotation, the average employee shareholding of £600 in 1982 had grown to £60,000.

b *British Airways:* this was privatised in January 1987 via sale to the public. It had been turned around prior to privatisation, from a company which had been regarded as overmanned and inefficient. In the first years under private ownership, it increased operating profits each year. During and post the Gulf War, trading conditions were difficult, and many other airlines have made losses over the past few years. In contrast, BA's profits in 1992/93 were £200m.

Two million people received shares in BT, five million in British Gas. Although there has been some decline in the number of individual shareholdings, about three-quarters of investors retain their shares in BT and two-thirds in British Gas.

Competition policy

At the centre of the privatisation programme is the simple truth that market forces stimulate companies, encouraging them to operate as efficiently as possible. Usually, competition is the vehicle whereby this is achieved and much of the privatisation programme has been conducted with the objective of stimulating competition. Many of the smaller companies privatised by the government operate in a naturally competitive atmosphere where there is no reason that any one company should be state-run and hence protected from the forces of the free market.

Where privatisation has not been able to introduce serious competition, because the company forms a natural monopoly (ie gas), the government has not hesitated to introduce tough regulatory regimes which ensure that monopoly status is not abused and that customers benefit from the gains which result from privatisation.

A regulated private monopoly is still likely to be much more efficient than a nationalised one. British Telecom and British Gas, as the examples of the regulated monopoly, are discussed in detail in the next two sections.

British Telecom

British Telecom was privatised in 1984, following restructuring of the old Post Office to separate the postal functions from the telecommunications functions (via the British Telecommunications Act 1981). Prior to privatisation, British Telecom had been an inefficient monopoly with very poor levels of customer satisfaction, and a poor record for innovation both in products and processes. Lack of competition had provided no effective spur to modernisation. A limited degree of competition had been introduced in 1982 with the granting of a licence to Mercury (a subsidiary of Cable and Wireless) to provide a digital network linking 30 specified cities. Mercury was excluded from international business.

At the time of privatisation, the limited competition offered by Mercury had not impacted significantly on British Telecom, although the potential for future competition had caused some efficiency improvements.

In order to persuade Mercury to commit sufficient funds to become a fully-fledged public service provider, the government, BT and Mercury agreed the Fixed Links Duopoly policy in November 1983. This turned the industry into a duopoly, with further entry by new providers not to be allowed. The purpose of the government was to promote effective competition to BT.

As part of the privatisation, the government set up a regulatory body to oversee the telecommunications duopoly, OFTEL (Office of Telecommunications). The first Director of Telecommunications, Sir Bryan Carsberg, was successful in carving out a pivotal role in policy debates, and hence OFTEL had influence in excess of its regulatory powers.

Part of the role of OFTEL is to monitor prices, and ensure that BT does not make excessive profits (whilst allowing it to make a reasonable level of profits in order to encourage efficiency). A price cap was placed on prices, initially set at RPI–3 per cent and subsequently changed to RPI–6.25 per cent.

Another part of the role of OFTEL is to promote competition in the industry (via Mercury).

The third major facet of OFTEL's role is to monitor and deal with customers' complaints.

Mercury has recently experienced problems, and withdrawn all its public call box network, which had been providing effective competition to BT. It remains to be seen what effect this will have on the provision of public call box service by BT. This had improved considerably since the advent of Mercury call boxes.

Competition from Mercury, and from other equipment suppliers, has forced innovation and improvement in BT's equipment, such as telephones and answering machines. Competition has led to efficiency improvements. BT has recently announced redundancies as part of its efficiency drive; industry analysts believed that it was overstaffed.

A survey by the International Telecommunications Users Group shows that the UK has the lowest price for telephone calls of any of the main industrial nations (February 1995).

In an attempt to promote competition in the cable networks which are currently being laid in the UK (to lead possibly to the 'Information Super-Highway'), BT is currently prevented from entering this market.

British Gas

The British Gas Corporation became a private sector company in 1986. It was privatised as a complete entity, first, because it is neither sensible nor practical to have several companies' gas mains going down one street, and secondly, because to have split the company would have presented the customer with supply uncertainties from regional companies with no established record of service or experience.

British Gas is *not* a monopoly in the competitive energy market: it faces severe competition from other energy industries. Furthermore, the company does face competition at the margins under the Oil and Gas Enterprise Act 1982 and the Gas Act 1986 which allow for competition to develop in the gas supply system.

OFGAS, which, like OFTEL, is an independent regulatory body, has various statutory powers in the gas industry. These include the following:

a Ensuring that gas prices conform to a formula laid down on privatisation, which in turn ensures that the benefits of privatisation are passed directly on to the consumer. In the summer of 1988, British Gas cut its tariffs by 4.5 per cent after announcing record profits of over £1 billion. After going carefully through the accounts, OFGAS announced that it was satisfied that this price cut reflected correctly the drop in British Gas' costs.

b Protecting the interests of the consumer in the matter of continuity of supply and quality of service.

c Monitoring safety standards in the industry. These were improved by the 1986 Gas Act, for example, by reducing the maximum response time to *any* escape of gas from 24 to 12 hours.

d Enabling effective competition in the supply of large consumers.

The government intends to introduce limited competition in the domestic gas market in 1996. This will be expanded in 1997 with a view to the introduction of competition throughout the UK by the end of 1998. The domestic side of British Gas's business now accounts for only 15 per cent of the business. Legislation is currently being drafted to enable British Gas to dispose of its public supply arm (the part of the business which sells gas to domestic customers) if and when it wishes to do so. There is some speculation that British Gas may do this, in part at least due to the high profile nature of the rising tide of domestic consumer complaints. Legislation will have to ensure that any new suppliers of gas to domestic customers will need to share the burden of the 'universal service obligation' which currently falls on British Gas alone. This requires British Gas to supply anyone who requests supply.

New suppliers have already made substantial inroads in the supply of gas to industry. These suppliers believe that they may be able to undercut British Gas in the domestic market by as much as 10 per cent.

British Gas has recently caused controversy by announcing a 75 per cent pay rise for its chief executive Cedric Brown, in the same week as it announced a pay cut for its showroom staff. Large-scale redundancies are currently anticipated.

The future of privatisation

The current Conservative government is pressing ahead with its privatisation programme. One of the next on the list for privatisation is British Rail. This has now been reorganised, in anticipation of privatisation, into a number of separate operating units, which trade with each other: Railtrack owns all of the track, and charges others for the use of it; Inter-City runs long-haul services; Regional Railways operates the local services. This complex system (which is unique to the UK) has been developed in order to introduce elements of competition into the system. There has been some adverse comment on the complexity of the system, and also on environmental grounds. Some commentators argue that an integrated transport policy which encouraged use of the rail network, and discouraged use of the increasingly congested road system, would be beneficial for the country, and that a public sector rail system is more likely to achieve this.

Another target for privatisation is British Coal. This has recently been drastically trimmed, with a number of pits being closed (and some of these being reopened by the private sector). The most profitable pits remain in the public sector.

The government was also considering the privatisation of the Post Office. This has also occasioned adverse comment. There is concern that a privatised letter delivery service would not be willing to maintain a delivery service to every address as at present. There is also concern about the maintenance of all the services which post offices provide, and in particular about the future of rural post offices. The plans for the privatisation of the post office had to be abandoned following a backbench revolt by Conservative MPs.

Water privatisation

In 1989–90 the water authorities in England and Wales were transferred to the private sector. The water supply and sewerage functions of the water authorities, which account for 90 per cent of their business, have been privatised as separate plcs, but the regulatory functions have become the responsibility of the National Rivers Authority (NRA). The NRA is empowered to protect the environment, having control over water conservation and resource planning, pollution control, fisheries, land drainage, flood protection and navigation. There is no national 'water grid' as with electricity, although recent drought problems would suggest that it may be necessary. The privatisation of water caused a good deal of controversy. Many opponents of the scheme saw water as so important to life itself that private ownership was deemed immoral. Others pointed out that the legal ownership of water assets still rested with the local authorities who had relinquished control in 1974. Nevertheless, the privatisation was popular as a share issue. There has recently been widespread public concern over the sharp increases in the charges made to domestic customers. The water companies state that these are necessary to fund investment in the industry, to meet EU regulations. There has also been concern at the numbers of domestic cut-offs for non-payment.

Electricity privatisation
Before 31 March 1990 the responsibility for carrying out the functions of generation, transmission, distribution and supply of electricity in England and Wales rested principally with a number of public sector bodies.

Of these, the Central Electricity Generating Board (CEGB) produced most of the electricity generated in England and Wales. It also owned and operated the high-voltage transmission system, known as the National Grid. The 12 Area Electricity Boards distributed the electricity and sold it to customers within their own regional areas in England and Wales.

The Electricity Act 1989 paved the way for the substantial changes introduced within the electricity industry on 31 March 1990. The new industry structure is designed to encourage competition in the generation and supply of electricity and to regulate prices for activities where the scope for competition is limited, such as transmission and distribution.

Under the new structure, the CEGB's businesses have been transferred to four successor companies. Three of these – National Power plc, PowerGen plc and Nuclear Electric plc – are engaged predominantly in generation. The CEGB's coal, oil and gas powered stations have been divided between National Power and PowerGen which now compete with each other and with other generators in the generation of electricity. The CEGB's nuclear power stations have been transferred to Nuclear Electric which will remain in the public sector.

The National Grid is now owned and operated by The National Grid Company plc (NGC), the fourth successor company of the CEGB. NGC is itself owned through a holding company by the 12 Regional Electricity Companies. As well as operating the high-voltage transmission system, which remains a monopoly business, NGC has a central role in co-ordinating power stations so that the generation of electricity can be matched to demand.

The 12 Area Boards have been succeeded by 12 new Regional Electricity Companies. Each Regional Electricity Company at present has an effective monopoly in the distribution of electricity over the electric lines it owns. However, for part of their supply business, the companies now compete with others.

The structure of the industry in Scotland is very different from that which exists in England and Wales, in that Scotland has, historically, been served by two all-purpose electricity utilities. On 31 March 1990 Scottish Power plc and Scottish Hydro-Electric plc took over this structure, except that Scotland's nuclear power stations have been vested in a separate company, Scottish Nuclear Limited, which will remain in the public sector.

Changes in the structure of the industry in England and Wales, and the introduction of competition, have been accompanied by new commercial arrangements between the members of the electricity industry. In particular, a competitive wholesale market has been created for the sale of electricity by generating companies and its purchase by suppliers for onward sale to their customers. This replaces the old arrangements in England and Wales, under which the CEGB charged the Area Boards for the electricity it generated, which the Boards then sold on to their customers.

The industry is now subject to a new system of regulation overseen by the Office of Electricity Regulation (OFFER). Two important roles for OFFER are the promotion of competition in electricity generation and supply, and the protection of the interests of the consumer in the areas of transmission and distribution where natural monopolies remain.

The privatisation of the electricity industry has not been easy for the government. It had to withdraw the nuclear power sector from the sale and the timetable for privatisation had to be extended. Many would argue that the sale of electricity, the largest privatisation to date, was very complex, and that meant the final outcome was not ideal, with the assets being sold below their value. However, electricity was a popular privatisation with the small investor. Many small investors buy the shares in a new issue in order to 'stag' that issue; that is, they sell their new purchases quickly for short-term profit. Opponents to the sale of the electricity industry point out that shares in the regional distribution companies were offered at prices very generous to the small investor. This point has been made for all the privatisations in recent years. Thus, it is argued, the shareholder gains at the expense of the taxpayer. There has been much debate recently within the Labour Party as to whether or not to retain its traditional commitment to state ownership of public utilities such as water and electricity. The position is as yet unclear.

The arguments against privatisation
Although privatisation has been a popular policy with the share-buying public (largely because of the low issue price of shares) it still has its critics. Four successive Conservative election victories have made it impossible for opposition parties to consider large scale re-nationalisation as part of their policy but there is still concern about privatisation.

a   Despite the existence of OFTEL and OFGAS many believe that the public/social interest will be sacrificed for profit. Public-sector monopoly has been changed into private-sector monopoly.

b   Many people are concerned that vital 'strategic' industries are now no longer in the hands of the state. They once belonged to everyone, now they only belong to a few shareholders.

c   The revenue raised from selling off these industries is a 'once and for all' windfall, and will also mean the government or any future government having less control over the economy in general.

d Privatisation is meant to help develop a share-holding democracy, but many shares sold to employees/the public have been sold through the markets to the institutions (pension funds and insurance companies).

e There is some doubt as to whether the privatisation of the large 'monopoly' nationalised industries such as gas and telecommunications has produced the competition and efficiency which it is meant to.

f The privatisation of water led to arguments that the government did not own the water authorities in the first place and had no legal right to sell them, and that the provision of water to domestic customers has positive externalities (the total benefit exceeds the private benefit) by reducing the spread of disease.

Public and merit goods

Apart from the nationalised industries, the government is involved in the production of other goods and services. Nationalised industries are government operations which, like private firms, sell their output to consumers. They are generally very like large, privately owned operations, although there may be some important differences in pricing, output and investment policies. On the other hand, the provision of public and free goods is quite different from the nationalised industries in that the output is not sold to consumers. Lacking revenue from sales, the operation is financed from government funds raised from taxation or borrowing.

Public goods (collective consumption goods)

There are some goods and services which are desired by society which will not be provided by the market system. Public goods are characterised by non-exclusion and non-diminishability. This means individual members of the community can benefit from public goods (ie defence) without having to pay for them, and if an extra person benefits from, say, defence, this does not diminish the benefits available to others.

As an example, let us consider the situation of a private police force. The police are employed to provide a general protection for everyone. Their patrolling of the streets and availability in the event of any law and order crisis means that everyone is safer from threats to life or property. Suppose someone opposed to this particular police force refused to pay for their services. This person would still receive the general protection of a police presence in the community as long as somebody was prepared to employ the services of the police force. In the situation where consumers benefit from the service as long as someone else pays for it, no one would be prepared to pay – they would rather someone else did. The police force would then not be able to raise any revenue from selling their services and would not exist. No one would then have the benefit of general police protection. Other public goods are, for example, lighthouses, street lighting and cleaning, trees in cities, and national defence.

Should the service be provided or not? It should, as long as the total utility for the community exceeds the total cost of provision. Since no private firm will find that it pays to try to sell the services to individual consumers, the service must be paid for collectively.

In Britain the situation is always that the state acts as the firm, employing the resources with which to provide the service and using funds gathered from taxation or borrowing to cover the costs of provision. An alternative would be for the government to employ a private firm, paying them out of government funds.

Merit goods

It is part of the social policies of government to provide certain goods free. The aim is basically one of making sure that *certain goods and services are available regardless of ability to pay*. The unequal allocation of resources among individuals, and the resulting unequal distribution of the money income with which to buy goods and services, means that some individuals are unable to buy very much. There are certain goods and services which society wishes to see consumed by everyone. In Britain, these goods are education and medical treatment. Unlike public goods, these goods could be provided by the market system, but if that were so they would only be available to a few who could afford to pay.

The social argument is that, with a good education and good health, everyone has equal opportunities for earning the income with which to buy everything else. The goods and services may be provided free to everyone, or only to those whose incomes or other circumstances single them out as needing assistance.

The advantage of providing the service *free only to those in need* is obviously the reduction of the amount of government funds needed for providing the service. Anyone above a minimum level of real income would either be obliged to pay for the state service (providing a revenue and reducing the amount needed from government funds), or would have to buy the service from a separate, privately owned source (reducing the cost of providing the service).

However, the advantage of the system (generally adopted in Britain) of *free provision to everyone regardless of their income or circumstances* is that the same service is provided to the whole population.

Suppose education were provided free only to low-income groups, while everyone else had either to pay for the state education system or buy private education. The majority would probably choose the private system, since they are then likely to be able to buy the precise type of education that they want rather than having to accept the state model.

The public and private education standards would then diverge. The higher income groups, generally the principal source of taxation revenue, might then try to use political pressure in order to reduce the amount of funds going into the state education system, from which they derive no benefit. They would prefer to put the money into their own children's education in the private sector. The state education system might then be starved of funds and standards would deteriorate.

Two standards of education would then exist: a low standard for those with low incomes, thus reinforcing their disadvantage in society and the 'cycle of poverty' (low income parents producing disadvantaged children who will themselves be poor in adult life); and a high standard for those with high incomes, reinforcing their advantages. The inequality of society would be increased – the very problem that the 'welfare state' system was established to solve.

With a free state education available regardless of income, the high income group are less likely to choose private education. Standards in public education are then more likely to be maintained with the funds and political pressure of the higher income groups. An additional disadvantage of income-related benefits is the disincentive effect on effort if higher income simply results in fewer benefits in the form of free goods. This problem will be discussed in more detail in Chapter 14.

An obvious alternative to providing free goods and services is to give cash subsidies to the low income groups, so that they can buy these goods and services for themselves from private suppliers.

The advantage of cash subsidies to the poor is that they are then able to reflect their own preferences in the goods and services that they choose to buy. Their total utility will then be higher than if they were forced to consume free education or medical treatment for which their personal preference may be quite low.

However, at the cost of reducing the utility of the low income groups, the society that provides the funds might prefer to see the money being spent on education and medical care rather than on television sets or gambling. In terms of maximising the total utility of the whole population, the rational policy may be to reflect the preferences of tax payers, and not those of the people receiving subsidies.

Another problem with cash subsidies is that demand for goods will be increased without supply necessarily being increased sufficiently. Price increases would then eliminate the advantages of the subsidy. An example of this problem is in housing subsidies. The supply of housing is very inelastic, so it is generally accepted that cash subsidies paid to tenants or potential owner-occupiers will simply increase rents or house prices. No one (except landlords and house owners) benefits.

Housing policy

An example of state involvement in industry.

Housing – a necessary good

Houses, flats, and lodgings provide households with the essential (in Britain) shelter from the weather. They also provide people with a space in which to store their possessions, and serve an important function in providing us with privacy and a space which is our 'own territory'. Not all these services are essential to our survival, but they are regarded as basic requirements in developed economies.

(Note that throughout this section, the terms 'house', 'houses' and 'housing' will be used to refer to all houses, flats – anything that provides the housing services described above. The term 'household' will be used to indicate the consumers of housing. A household may be made up of a single adult, a couple or a larger group of adults (eg flat sharers), or a number of adults and children (eg the 'nuclear family').

Housing in a market economy

There are two basic ways in a market economy of obtaining the housing services described above.

Renting

The household rents housing owned by someone else. The owner of the property is the 'landlord'. He makes the housing available in return for rent. In a market economy, the rent that the landlord must be paid to make him willing to rent the property will depend on two factors. If he sold the property he would receive a cash payment of the current market price of the property. He could then deposit this cash in, for example, a bank deposit account and earn a regular interest payment. This interest payment is the *opportunity cost* of his letting the property to the household. In addition, the landlord will incur certain expenses as a result of owning the property, such as repairs and maintenance. The rent that must be paid to the landlord will be at least as much as the opportunity cost of the capital involved plus the costs of repairs and maintenance. If the rent is less than this, he will sell the property. (This is, of course, assuming that landlords are interested in maximising real income from money earned.)

An additional point is that landlords may expect in the future to sell the house for a capital gain (the difference between the price he paid for the house when he bought it and the price he gets when he sells it). The discounted value of any expected capital gain would then be added in as a benefit of letting, thus reducing the rent that landlords need to be paid for them to be willing to let.

In a competitive renting market, the rents paid would be close to this level, with landlords receiving only 'normal profits' from letting their houses.

The household renting the property is the 'tenant'. Households pay rent out of money income. The amount they are prepared to spend will depend on their preferences and their money income. (Housing is usually assumed to have a reasonably high positive income-elasticity of demand; that is, as consumers' incomes rise, they spend disproportionately more on housing, moving into larger, more central or more luxurious houses.)

The amount that households are prepared to pay will also reflect the prices of alternatives available – the rents on other houses and the costs of any alternative ways of obtaining housing services (see 'Owner-occupation' below).

We would expect that the market rent would be determined by demand and supply. The position of the demand and supply curves depends on the factors discussed above. The quantity demanded will increase at lower rents, with more households competing to obtain houses at these lower rents. The demand curve is therefore downward sloping. The number of houses available for rent will increase at higher rents, since the higher rents increase the return to landlords of letting houses. The supply curve is therefore upward sloping.

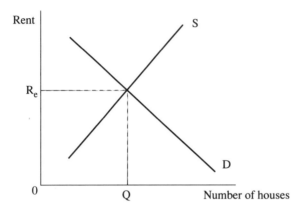

The contract between landlord and tenant may be short term or long term. For example, the landlord may agree to rent only from week to week or from month to month. At the beginning of each week (or month) a new contract is drawn up between landlord and tenant, and the new rent agreed. Alternatively, the contract may be long term – for a year, 5 years, etc. This may provide an example of market prices failing to respond to changing demand and supply conditions. Suppose demand generally has increased, so that market rents are rising. The landlord will naturally want to increase the rent but cannot until the existing contract expires. Only then will the rent reflect the increase in market demand.

This simple demand-and-supply analysis, with its resulting equilibrium rent, applies only for identical properties. The sub-market analysis used in Chapter 7 is relevant here. Obviously, superior properties earn higher rents. The higher rent will reflect the higher market value that the landlord could get by selling the property, and thus the higher opportunity costs. The higher rent must also reflect the higher value that households place on living in a superior property.

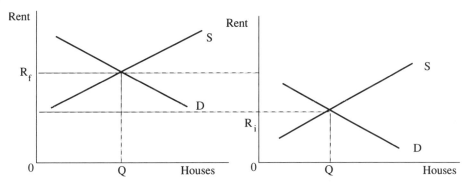

The higher rent on some properties will reflect a number of characteristics, as follows:

a The houses are larger.

b They are in better condition.

c They have more facilities, eg central heating, a garage.

d They have a larger or more attractive garden.

e They are in a more convenient location. (In London, this usually means near to an Underground or British Rail station and closer to the centre of London.)

f They are in a 'better' area. (In London, this usually means West London rather than East. This generally reflects the predominance of higher-income households in the area. Other factors will include being near to a park or the river, there being wider roads with trees, the absence of traffic, the quality of local shops, cinemas, etc.)

g The quality/usefulness of any furniture included in the amenities of the house. (Houses can be rented 'furnished' or 'unfurnished'.)

Owner-occupation

The household buys a house and lives in it. By paying the market price for the house, the household acquires the housing services listed above. In addition, the household acquires an asset which may be sold in the future. The discounted value of any expected capital gain should be added to the discounted value of the utility of the housing services during the years of ownership in estimating the price that households should pay for houses. The value of those housing services provided by the household for itself by its ownership of the house is referred to as '*imputed rent*'. This will obviously be related to the rent that tenants would be prepared to pay for renting the house from a landlord. (This 'imputed rent' is the basis of the local authority taxation discussed in Chapter 14.) The owner-occupying household has to pay any repair and maintenance costs for the house.

The value of the housing services provided by any house will depend on all the factors listed above. The market in owner-occupied housing is thus a series of sub-markets, just as the rented market is.

For any individual house, the number of people wishing to buy it will increase, the lower its price. The willingness of owners to sell will increase, the higher the price. The market equilibrium price will be where the demand is equal to the supply. Differences in equilibrium prices for any two houses will reflect differences in the characteristics of those houses, as listed above.

There will also be a connection between the rented and the owner-occupying sectors of the housing market Households will consider the owner-occupying and renting of housing as substitute goods. They will compare:

a The initial price they must pay for buying a house with the discounted value of housing services over the years of ownership, plus the discounted value of any expected gain when they sell the house, minus the discounted cost of all repair and maintenance expenditure over the years of ownership.

b The discounted value of the rent they expect to pay over the years if they rent a similar house from a landlord.

The higher the Net Present Value of owner-occupation, the lower the demand for renting from a landlord. The higher the NPV of renting, the lower the demand for similar houses for owner-occupation.

The supply side of the housing markets are also linked. The owners of property will compare the following:

a The discounted value of rents paid by tenants over the years of planned ownership.

b The price they would be paid if they sold the house to an owner-occupier.

The higher the value of discounted rents, the higher the price owner-occupiers must pay for the house. The higher the value of the house to owner-occupiers (reflected in the price they are prepared to pay), the greater the rent landlords will need to charge to the tenant if the landlord is to be willing to rent the property rather than sell it to owner-occupiers.

A final point about owner-occupiers is that few households have sufficient cash to pay the full price for the house. It is usual, therefore, for households to borrow money from financial institutions in order to pay the purchase price of a house. They repay this loan with regular partial repayments over the years of the loan, and in each year they pay an interest payment on the outstanding loan. The household may also be required to pay a deposit in cash at a percentage of the market price as a condition of the loan. Thus, the cost of owner-occupation becomes the sacrifice of annual interest and repayment plus the cost of the deposit (borrowing or sacrificed consumption opportunities in the past). We would therefore expect the demand for owner-occupation to increase the lower the interest rate on mortgages (loans for house purchase) and the lower the initial deposit required.

The aggregate supply of houses

Building firms will provide new houses in response to the demand for them. The higher the price offered by the purchasers (either owner-occupiers or landlords), the greater the supply that builders will produce in relation to the costs of land, labour and capital required to build houses. Profit-maximising builders will, of course, build the type of houses that consumers wish to buy. They will try to build the size, style and location of houses most demanded by consumers.

The aggregate supply of houses is mostly not of new but of existing houses. Houses are durable goods which can be resold to successive owner-occupiers or landlords.

Since most of the supply at any time is of existing houses, there is inevitably a rigidity in the housing market. The location and number of existing houses is fixed and cannot respond to change in demand conditions. Only new houses can respond to changing demand conditions, but the supply of land in any location for building houses is limited and the building of new houses takes a relatively long time. Short-term supply may therefore be completely inelastic, and even in the long run, in some locations, it may be very difficult to expand supply. Any increase in demand is, therefore, likely to lead to a sharp increase in house prices and rents.

The aggregate demand for houses

The demand for houses will be greater, the larger the population and the higher consumer incomes. There will then be more households seeking houses at any general price level.

An important point is that, even with a fixed population, the number of households seeking housing will increase as a result of higher average consumer incomes. Individuals want more space for themselves as their incomes rise, so they share existing housing units with fewer people. Children leave home sooner to find their own houses; young couples move straight into their own homes rather than spending their first married years with parents; adults sharing accommodation share with fewer people; and old people can afford to maintain their own homes rather than needing to move in with others.

The geographical distribution of housing demand will substantially depend on job availability and incomes in each area. If there are more jobs available and higher incomes offered in one area than in another, we would, ceteris paribus, expect greater housing demand there.

The aggregate housing market

The figures below show what happened to the aggregate demand and supply for houses during the 1960s and 1970s.

Housing stock and households	1968	1974	1980
Total housing stock at end of year ('000s)	18,670	20,100	21,510
Total number of households ('000s)	18,290	19,460	20,530
Crude surplus of housing over households (as % of housing stock)	2.0	3.2	4.6

These figures show an aggregate excess supply of houses. However, the location of jobs has changed more rapidly than the housing stock can respond. Many of these vacant houses will be in areas where people are not prepared to live, whatever the price and availability of houses, because there are no jobs there. Examples of such areas are Newcastle or the East End of London. The houses were built there in times of a much more buoyant local economy in these areas, and now are not required.

At the same time, the centres of economic activity have shifted to new areas where the existing supply of housing is insufficient and where little land is available for new building. There is currently great demand for housing in these areas because of higher incomes and greater job availability. House prices are therefore very high. (For the explanation of the geographical shift in economic activity, see Chapter 13.)

As at December 1991, there were 24 million dwellings in the UK, an increase of more than one-third since 1961. The annual change in the stock of dwellings decreased during this period from 250,000 during the 1960s, to a low point below 200,000 during the 1980s. This has now recovered to 213,000. (Source: *Social Trends 23*, 1993.)

The case for government intervention in the housing market

In Britain there is extensive government intervention in the housing market. The case for this intervention is as follows:

a   Basic housing facilities are regarded as *a necessity*. Certain households' incomes may be so low that they are unable to afford to buy (either by renting or owner-occupying) the level of housing services regarded by society as minimal, given the level of market rents/house prices. The government may then intervene to ensure that minimal housing services are available to these low-income households.

b The government may also use taxation and subsidies on housing as a way of redistributing income from higher- to lower-income households, thus achieving a more equal distribution of real income in society.

c Housing consumption may produce *externalities*. The condition of local housing influences the environment enjoyed by everyone in the area. If houses are well maintained, this improves the appearance of the area and may raise the value of properties owned by local owner-occupiers and landlords. Badly maintained housing has the opposite effect on the utilities of residents and on the value of properties. In addition, poor housing may be a contributory factor in the spread of disease. (This last was the initial reason for government intervention in the housing market at the end of the nineteenth century.)

d The government sees housing as a major contributor to the welfare of people in a way that may be underestimated by households. For example, children's performance at school may be inhibited by overcrowding at home; old people may become ill because they underestimate the dangers of living in inadequately heated, damp homes; the stress imposed on marriage by poor housing may be underestimated by the couples involved. Housing is thus a *merit good* for which the state preference exceeds that of individual consumers. The state, therefore, intervenes in the market to increase the consumption of housing.

e The government may wish to check the externalities associated with different land uses. For example, the spread of new house building over land which is currently open space will reduce the utility from that open space enjoyed by other consumers.

f Housing is a very complex good, and consumers may therefore be ignorant about the quality of the housing services that they buy. For example, a consumer might unknowingly buy a house that has been built with faulty electrical wiring or poor foundations.

g The amount of investment necessary to complete major housing projects successfully may be beyond the private sector. For example, private developers may realise that demolishing slums and rebuilding or starting new housing developments on greenfield sites may be profitable. However, these projects will only be successful if done on a large scale requiring enormous amounts of finance. In addition, the success of such a project is uncertain. Private landlords and owner-occupiers may not like the new development when it is completed. The developers may then make huge losses. Because of the amount of finance required and the uncertainty involved, private developers may fail to undertake such projects.

Government housing policies

a The availability of land for new house building is controlled (see Chapter 7) in order to check the externalities discussed above.

b Building regulations require that specific standards of building are followed in order to protect the consumers from poor-quality building.

One effect of these two policies has been an increase in the price of new houses, since land-use controls push up the price of building land and building regulations increase building costs.

Governments have in the past used rent controls to reduce the rents paid by tenants. Maximum rents are fixed, usually below the market equilibrium rent. This can bring rents within the reach of the lowest-income households, thus ensuring that they can have accommodation that they could not otherwise afford. Secondly, rent controls have been intended to achieve some re-distribution of income from rich to poor. Landlords (usually seen as higher income individuals) have less income because of the lower rents, while tenants (usually seen as lower income individuals) have increased real incomes as a result of the reduced rent they pay. The last of the many rent control Acts of this century was the Rent Act 1974 which imposed rent controls on furnished properties. In the following diagram, when rent controls limit rents to a maximum of P_c below the market equilibrium rent of P_e, landlords will be willing to rent only Q_s properties instead of Q_e. The number of properties available is thus reduced. There is an excess demand of $Q_s Q_d$. The rent Acts have usually included security-of-tenure provisions to try to control the loss of properties from the rented market. However, landlords have tended to sell as soon as tenants leave a property empty, and the security-of-tenure provisions have therefore made landlords even less willing to continue to let properties.

At the same time, lower rents increased the demand for rented properties. The result of the reduced supply and increased demand has been an excess demand for rented accommodation, reflected in the extreme difficulty in obtaining rented property on the London housing market.

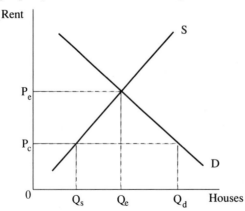

Landlords rationed the limited supply by letting to whom they chose (this is called allocation by seller's preferences). This was very disadvantageous to people from ethnic minorities. Additionally (as is always the case when there is a shortage) a black market developed where, by finding loopholes in the law or by simply ignoring its provisions, landlords let properties at market equilibrium rents.

The government has used various policies to reduce the costs of owner-occupation so that this form of tenure becomes available to more people. Building societies and banks provide the bulk of the finance for mortgages for house purchase. That part of the household's payments to the building society which are interest payments reduces the household's income tax liability. Mortgage tax relief is available on the first £30,000 on any mortgage (this has not been changed for some years).

The combination of rent controls and subsidies to owner-occupiers has caused many properties to be sold by landlords to owner-occupiers. Owner-occupiers, because of the subsidies they receive, have been able to offer higher prices for houses.

Local government is itself involved in building and converting homes for rent. After World War Two the 'council house' sector expanded greatly and formed the main alternative to owner occupation. The rents charged were historically low and subsidised.

The current government has made major changes to the council house sector, both directly and indirectly via its control of the local authorities. The 'Right to Buy' scheme has been very successful and over 1.4 million council homes have been sold to tenants at large discounts. Local authorities have not been permitted to use the receipts from sales of council houses to build more replacement council houses. The council house building programme has been severely cut back, in line with the government's belief that the private sector should provide rental housing, and the government should not be involved in this activity. At the same time, the Housing Associations have been encouraged with government assistance to provide more homes for rental.

Governments since the mid-1970s have given more legislative recognition and financial help to the voluntary housing movement. The housing associations specialise in building and renovating low-cost homes for low-income families. The Housing Corporation more than doubled its capital programme from £818m in 1989-90 to £1736m in 1992-3.

The government has tackled the problem of large areas of poor-quality housing through extensive slum clearance and rebuilding or renovation programmes organised by the local authorities. The properties built or renovated have then been let by the local authorities. There has been a significant swing in government policy from the 1950s and 1960s policy of demolishing poor-quality housing and then building usually high-rise blocks of flats, to the 1970s and 1980s policy of renovating the poor-quality houses where possible. This was largely a result of the objections of tenants to the quality of life in high-rise flats.

The New Town policy involved the purchase of greenfield sites for the building of housing, roads, shops and factories. This relieved the pressure on inner-city housing, and enabled people from depressed regions to find jobs and houses in one location.

Results of government intervention

These various government policies have had an enormous effect on the British housing system.

The private rented sector which housed the majority of households at the beginning of this century now houses less than 10 per cent of the households. The decline can be attributed to three factors related to government policy as follows:

a The series of Rent Acts, which have reduced the return to landlords from letting.

b The subsidies to owner-occupiers, which have both increased the preference of households for owner-occupation and increased the opportunity costs for landlords of continuing to let rather than selling to owner-occupiers.

c The availability of subsidised housing for rent from the local authorities.

The size of the public housing sector depends on government policy. There was a great expansion of local authority housing in the 1950s and 1960s (for example by 36 per cent in the 1960s), with slum clearance and new town programmes and high levels of government expenditure. By contrast, there was much less expansion in the 1970s and 1980s, and building has now virtually ceased with government expenditure cuts. Due to many people buying their own council homes, the public housing sector stock has fallen sharply.

The owner-occupied sector now houses the majority of households, with the number of new owner-occupying households in any year now largely determined by the interest rates and availability of funds for mortgages.

The following table shows the recent changes in tenure.

Housing stock by tenure (as % of total housing stock)	1968	1974	1980	1989	1990
Owner-occupied	48.6	52.6	55.2	66	68
Rented from local authority or new town	29.6	31.0	31.8	25	24
Rented from private owners and other tenures	21.7	16.4	13.0	9	8

(Source: *Social Trends 23*, 1993)

An important result of the significant and continuing decline of the private rented sector has been the reduction in the flexibility of the housing system. The private rented sector was the one principally used by new households and households moving into a new area (for example in search of work). Owner-occupation requires financial resources and/or the ability to obtain credit, which has been limited typically to higher-income, salaried workers. The waiting lists for local-authority accommodation has made that a difficult sector for new or moving households to enter. The decline of the private rented sector and the increasing dominance of owner-occupation and local-authority renting has greatly reduced the geographical mobility of the work-force. The massive difference in private-sector house prices between the South-East and the North has had the same effect.

Since access to owner-occupation or renting from a local authority is difficult, there remains a substantial problem of homeless households who are unable to gain access to either of these sectors. The voluntary housing groups (mentioned above) have consistently argued that there should be many more alternatives to these two dominant sectors.

The subsidies paid to owner-occupiers (in the form of tax relief on mortgages up to £30,000) and to local authority tenants (in the form of low rents) increase the real incomes of these households. One of the aims of housing policy is to redistribute income from rich to poor (see above). However, the actual subsidies paid out do not necessarily do this. Owner-occupiers are typically higher-income households. In fact the subsidy they receive, since it depends on marginal rates of income tax, tends to be greater the higher the income of the household. While many local authority tenants are low-income households, many are not, but receive the subsidies just the same. Thus, much of the government expenditure on housing subsidies goes to increase the real incomes of the already higher-income households.

Given these last two points, it is argued that the government intervention in the housing market has created the following three classes of households:

a Those who are lucky enough to have access to the subsidised owner-occupation and local authority-renting sectors.

b Those who are unable to get access to these sectors, and so are forced onto the declining and distorted private renting sector where they may have to pay high, black market rents.

c Those who are homeless – these are comprised of several groups of people: young single people who cannot obtain either private sector or public sector accommodation due to benefit entitlement rules; unemployed people who are unable to obtain private accommodation; families with children who have lost their homes; and women with children who have left their partners.

There are now record numbers of homeless people. There was an increase in Great Britain from 108,900 in 1986 to 160,100 in 1991 of households who were deemed to be in priority need. In addition to these figures, there are many thousands who are deemed not to be priority cases (mostly single people without children). It is mostly this category who are seen sleeping on the streets.

It has been argued that the problem with state provision of any goods at subsidised prices is that the suppliers (in this case, the local authorities) fail to respond to consumer preference. The local authorities have, for example, spent enormous sums of money building high-rise blocks of flats which they have then been forced to admit contribute to the level of crime, vandalism and general misery suffered by the inhabitants. Would private developers ever have built tower blocks and, if they had, would they have been able to persuade private households to pay realistic rents for living in them?

Conclusion

This section has been designed to show:

a The way in which a market operates.

b The arguments for government intervention in that market.

c The types of policies available to governments.

d The problems that may result from even the best-intentioned policies.

Helping markets to work better

The present government (1979-) believes in the creation of a flexible and adaptable market economy. In order to do this it has initiated a number of policies hopefully to create a deregulated enterprise economy with high growth. The thinking behind the policy is as follows:

Many of the government's measures have been designed to help the *labour market work better*, through, for example the following:

a Changes in the tax system to improve incentives.

b Changes in housing and pension arrangements to encourage mobility of labour.

c Legislation to make trades unions more responsible to their members, and more accountable for their actions.

d Improvements in education and training.

e Help for the unemployed.

Income tax rates have been cut. The basic rate came down from 33 per cent to 30 per cent in 1979, to 29 per cent in 1986 and to 27 per cent in 1987. The government has since reduced it to 25 per cent and also introduced a 20 per cent rate designed to help low income households. The top rate of income tax has been reduced from 83 per cent to 40 per cent, and the 15 per cent investment income surcharge has been abolished. The starting points for income tax are now nearly 22 per cent higher in real terms than in 1978–79, which means that well over $1\frac{1}{2}$ million people who would otherwise be paying income tax are not having to do so.

The *national insurance surcharge*, paid by employers on everyone working for them, was abolished in 1984.

The system of *national insurance* contributions was restructured in 1985. Lower rates of employers' and employees' contributions were introduced for the lower paid, financed in part by removing the upper limit on employers' contributions for the higher paid. This made it cheaper for employers to take on lower-paid workers, and allowed those workers to keep more of what they earned.

Arrangements for tax relief on *profit-related pay* (PRP), first proposed in the 1986 Budget, are now in place, and employers have been invited to register schemes for their workforces. PRP would give workers a more direct personal interest in the success of their firms, and safeguard employment by allowing some of their pay to fluctuate in line with market conditions. In registered schemes half of PRP will be free of income tax, up to a limit of £3,000 a year or 20 per cent of total pay, whichever is the less.

People who own their own homes usually find it easier to move to new jobs than people who are tied to subsidised rented accommodation. That is one reason why the government has *encouraged more people to own their own homes*, and 63 per cent of households now do so. The Housing Act 1980 gave public sector tenants the right to buy their homes, and over a million of them have exercised it. The rate of stamp duty on house purchases was halved to 1 per cent in 1984. The solicitors' near-monopoly on conveyancing was abolished in 1985. The Housing and Planning Act 1986 made it easier for public sector tenants to buy their flats, and for housing associations to provide opportunities for shared ownership. *The National Mobility Scheme* has helped 40,000 households to move between council houses.

Occupational pension arrangements, until 1985, made it difficult for people to change jobs without loss of pension. But pension schemes are now required to safeguard early leavers' pension rights. As of July 1988, employees now have the right to join a personal pension scheme instead of staying in their employer's scheme or fully in the state scheme. Personal pension schemes now have the same favourable tax treatment as for retirement annuities. In addition, people may now make additional voluntary contributions (AVCs), with tax relief, to schemes separate from their occupational pension schemes.

As a result of these legal changes, there has been a large growth in personal pension schemes. Unfortunately, many people were mis-advised by insurance company agents (mostly those working mainly or entirely on commission), and transferred from their employer's scheme to a personal one which is significantly worse in terms of benefits. This particularly applied to public sector workers.

As a result of much bad publicity, and the intervention of the Insurance Ombudsman, the insurance companies have compensated many of the affected people, and staff have been retrained, and the basis on which they are paid altered to reduce the incentive to give inappropriate advice.

Legislation in the sphere of trade union activity has: eliminated the closed shop, thus allowing individual workers the choice of joining a union or not; required pre-strike secret ballots, and cooling-off periods; removed the right to secondary picketing, and sympathetic strikes by workers not directly affected; and made mandatory secret postal ballots for the election of union executives. This plethora of legislation, together with the increasing propensity of employers to go to court in an attempt to claim damages against the union for losses suffered due to strike action, has resulted in a considerable reduction in union power. This has in turn resulted in a reduction in union membership, which has resulted in a further loss of power and influence.

The government are seeking to make *education and training systems* more adaptable and better able to prepare people for life and work in an advanced economy where technology is constantly changing. This includes the modernisation of occupational training and wider opportunities for adult training and retraining, as well as better preparation in schools and colleges. An essential element is that employers should recognise the importance of investing in the training of their work forces. The government believe that the *national curriculum* will lead to consistent raising of standards in schools.

Measures to improve vocational training include:

a expansion of the Technical and Vocational Educational Initiative, announced in a White Paper in 1986;

b City Technology Colleges with an emphasis on science, technology and understanding of business;

c a new kind of grant for teacher training to improve the supply of teachers in mathematics, science, and craft, design and technology;

d a programme (PICKUP) to help keep work-force skills up-to-date.

There are many training schemes to *help the unemployed* to get jobs (under the umbrella of employment training), for example:

a The *Employment Training* (ET) programme and, for young people aged 16–17, the Youth Training Scheme offer several benefits to small firms wishing to train young people or adults and able to deliver a good quality training programme. These include:

  i the chance to train and get to know people before making long-term commitments;

  ii access to people who can be trained to meet the firm's needs;

  iii the opportunity to develop a route for recruiting and training young people and unemployed adults as the number of school leavers falls.

However, only a quarter of those who leave the Employment Training Scheme move into full-time jobs afterwards.

b The Business Enterprise Programme offers both short courses and an open-learning package on basic business training for people starting their own businesses.

c Unemployed people who would like to start a business can take the Enterprise option in the Employment Training programme and receive a training allowance of £10–£12 a week more than their benefit entitlement.

d Open Learning Courses enable people to study at their own pace when business pressures permit. A wide variety of short and long courses is now available, covering the full range of business skills.

e Training Access Points (TAPs) are now available in many areas. You can telephone your local TAP, or use mobile TAPs or TAP information points in high-street locations, to find out about the full range of training opportunities available locally and nationally to suit your particular needs.

In March 1989 the government set up Training and Enterprise Councils (TECs) to manage training schemes and also to set targets to stimulate greater private sector investment and involvement in training.

The TECs which are organised geographically give an important role to local businessmen and community leaders in administering government training schemes such as Employment Training (ET). Many of the new jobs have been among people who work for themselves. After many years at around 1¾ million, the numbers of the *self-employed* are estimated to have risen by more than 40 per cent or 750,000 since 1979, to about 2¼ million. Apart from providing work for themselves, many of them create jobs for others, and often respond more quickly than larger employers to changing market conditions.

Many government measures have helped *small businesses*. For example:

a The small companies' rate of Corporation tax (42 per cent in 1979) has come down, and is now 25 per cent for profits above £150,000.

b The taxation of lifetime gifts has been abolished.

c The limit for capital gains tax retirement relief has been increased.

d Measures have been taken to relieve the burden on VAT; the registration threshold has been increased and is now amongst the highest in the EC; small businesses are now allowed to opt for cash accounting, which means that they need not account for VAT on their sales until they have been paid by their customers, which helps their cash flow and provides automatic relief for bad debts.

e The *Business Expansion Scheme* (BES), provides tax relief on individual investment in small unquoted companies. An investor who buys shares in certain unquoted companies can obtain tax relief on investment of up to £40,000.

f The *Small Firms Service* provides a free telephone enquiry service, and in-depth business counselling throughout Great Britain.

  i The enquiry service can provide basic information and put you in touch with sources of detailed advice on any business query.

ii The counselling service is provided by experienced businessmen and women. Appointments are arranged by the enquiry service. Counselling sessions are impartial and confidential, and can be arranged to take place at your business premises.

g The Loan Guarantee Scheme provides a government guarantee for loans by banks and financial institutions to firms unable to obtain conventional loans because they lack security or a track record. The government guarantees 70 per cent (85 per cent in certain inner city areas) of loans over two to seven years in return for a premium of 2.5 per cent on the guaranteed portion of the loan. Overall the interest rate is likely to be the same as the interest charged to small firms generally.

h Share buy back. Recent changes in the law have made it possible for small business owners to sell shares to outside investors and make an agreement with them that the company will buy back the shares after a certain time. This benefits small firms who want to raise capital but who do not want to part with equity permanently.

i The Enterprise Allowance Scheme helps unemployed people who want to set up their own business and have £1,000 available to invest. It pays them a weekly allowance of £40 for their first year, which helps to compensate for loss of benefit while the business gets under way.

The government have removed a large number of controls on financial markets, notably on foreign exchange transactions, dividends, hire purchase and bank lending. The abolition of the investment-income surcharge has removed a possible disincentive to saving.

Tax distortions favouring certain forms of investment have been removed (for example, abolition of tax relief for life insurance premiums and reform of the capital allowance system). The tax treatment of different types of financial institutions and transactions has been brought more into line (for example, the similar treatment of bank and building society interest).

Recently the building societies have been given new powers, allowing them to compete more effectively with banks and other financial enterprises. Far-reaching changes are taking place as financial markets adapt to meet intensifying international competition. Following an agreement with the government, the Stock Exchange has:

a abandoned fixed commissions;

b allowed outside ownership of members;

c removed the separation between broking and jobbing functions; and

d introduced new dealing systems for all types of stock.

Compared with some three million people in 1979, about nine million people *owned shares* at the beginning of 1987. Since then, several privatisation flotations have increased the number further. However, recent evidence seems to suggest that share ownership drops if there is a large gap between quite large privatisations.

Share ownership has been boosted by:

a privatisation;

b tax incentives for employee share schemes (up from 30 in 1979 to over 1,300 all-employee schemes now and over 2,000 discretionary schemes);

c Personal Equity Plans (PEPS).

Price controls were abolished in 1979. Competition policy has been strengthened, for example, through the operations of the Monopolies and Mergers Commission. Producers were made responsible for their own decisions and directly subject to the discipline of market forces. The government have continued to remove unnecessary regulation. Having transferred many enterprises from the public to the private sector, they are exposing those activities remaining publicly owned to market pressures as far as possible, for example, by encouraging, or in some cases requiring, the provision of services to be put out to public tender. The privatisation programme has transferred 16 major companies to the private sector, reducing the state sector by one-third.

The government wants to encourage efficient, flexible markets, capable of responding quickly and effectively to changing economic conditions. With a better performance on the supply side, they hope to have more growth and jobs without more inflation.

Questions for review

1 What are the main reasons why the government may choose to intervene in private sector industry?

2 What are the main forms which such intervention may take?

3 What is 'indicative planning'? Give some examples.

4 What are some of the potentially negative effects of government intervention in the private sector?

5 How have recent governments attempted to help small firms?

6 What are the 'nationalised industries'? Why have previous governments chosen to nationalise them?

7 What are the potential problems of nationalisation? What are the potential benefits?

8 What is 'privatisation'? What are/were the objectives of the privatisation programme?

9 How successful has this programme been in terms of meeting its objectives?

10 Give some examples of (alleged) problems resulting from the privatisation programme.

11 What are public goods? Give some examples.

12 What are merit goods? Give some examples.

13 Why have successive governments chosen to intervene in the market for rental housing? What forms has the intervention taken? What have been the effects?

14 In what way have the governments policies on rental housing been different from those of their predecessors?

Money and banking | 9

The development of money   249

The clearing banks   254

The Bank of England   262

Merchant banks   264

Discount houses   266

The development of money

Money and economics

Economic theory and practice with regard to money has two sides:

a *the micro side* – the basic functions of money and the various institutions which are necessary to fulfil those functions; and

b *the macro side* – the overall supply of money within an economy is a major variable in economic terms and it has far-reaching effects on other variables.

There is a considerable amount of overlap between the two sides and the discussion of each side cannot be separated from the other.

A means of exchange

'Money' is a one pence piece, or a fifty pence piece, or a pound coin. It is also a dollar or a franc or a Deutschmark. However, all these pieces of money are only outward signs of money – an adequate and useful definition of money must cover *what it is used for*. Money is used as a *means of exchange* or, in economic jargon, a *medium of exchange*. In fact, before the development of money, people in primitive societies used to 'barter'. They used to exchange goods. For instance, a man in need of food might offer to exchange an axe for a week's supply of food. However, there are obvious difficulties in this method of transacting business. First, it is not always easy to find someone who wants, say, cows in exchange for, say, clothes. There has to be what is called a '*double coincidence of wants*'. Second, even if two such people did meet, the goods are rarely *divisible*. If the rate of exchange is six pairs of trousers for one cow, then how do you 'buy' a pair of trousers?

Measure of value

Clearly, it is easier to transact business if there is a common unit in which to measure the *value* of goods. So money, in various forms, gradually came into existence as a *measure of value or unit of account*. Eventually 'precious' metals such as gold and silver became universally acceptable as the most effective basis for money. All money today is based on a common agreed standard for valuation purposes, whether it is pounds sterling or the French franc.

Characteristics of money

In the modern world, the principal characteristics of money are:

a it must be generally acceptable as a means of paying for goods or services; that is, an *acceptable medium of exchange*;

b it must be *durable* or *lasting* – it should not wear out or decay, which is why metals like gold and silver were chosen as the basis for money;

c the basic money 'unit' must be easily *divisible* into smaller units;

d money must also be *portable* for users.

Functions of money

The primary function of money is as a *medium of exchange*, but there are two subsidiary functions;

a as it is a medium of exchange, it also needs to be a *measure*, or *store, of value*: a pound coin remains a pound coin; and,

b it is a *standard for deferred payments*: as money is a store of value it can be used for making payments in the future at the same rate.

Kinds of money

It was noted above that the basis for the value of money was usually a precious metal such as gold and silver, but in the last century or so there have been a number of important modifications in this method of valuation. When coins were first minted, they always contained metal equal to their face value. In short, *gold* – rather than *money itself* – had a *value*. Such minting procedures worked for coins with a relatively low value, but it was not practicable when a coin with a high value was required. The way in which this problem was solved was the forerunner of the modern banknote.

During the seventeenth century, *goldsmiths* in England developed the practice of storing large quantities of gold for customers and, in return, giving the customers a 'document of title' to the gold. Those customers then exchanged those documents for goods, rather than exchanging the gold itself. It is important to realise that at that time all these documents of title or notes – were convertible into gold *on demand* – or that was the idea. Certain rogue goldsmiths quickly saw an opportunity for a quick profit, through issuing documents that were not convertible into gold. Money must be acceptable to everyone if it is to perform its prime function as a medium of exchange, and the rogue goldsmiths were bringing the system into disrepute. So, in 1844 the Bank Charter Act was passed and, from that date, only the Bank of England was authorised to issue new bank notes. (Naturally, the notes which were already in existence remained valid currency.) The Act also authorised the issue of a *fiduciary currency* (fiduciary from the Latin word for 'faith'). This currency is not 'fully backed' by gold. At the time, it only constituted a very small part of the total amount of money in circulation, but now almost the entire money supply is fiduciary. When *all* money is fiduciary, then the problem of 'convertibility' does not arise. Although the words 'I promise to pay the bearer on demand the sum of £5' are printed on banknotes today, it is not possible to walk into the Bank of England and ask for five pounds' worth of gold in exchange. A fiduciary issue of money is a practical proposition, providing the population has confidence in the currency.

This is naturally an oversimplification of the position, because, as will be noted later in this chapter and in subsequent chapters, the *real* value of the fiduciary currency in existence today is dependent on a variety of factors, including the general and relative economic standing of the country and the actual amount of money in circulation in relation to the total quantity of goods available.

Apart from the *fiduciary issue (ie cash)*, a new form of money has developed in the modern world. Bank accounts are now accepted by the vast majority of people as the equivalent of cash. Bank current accounts are operated through the cheque system. A person who holds an account simply writes an instruction (usually on a printed form) to the bank and signs it. This is known as a cheque. On receipt of this form, the bank will transfer the amount stated from the person's account to the account of the person receiving the money. The person paying the money is known as the *drawer* and the person receiving the money is known as the *payee*. The vast majority of money transactions in terms of the amounts transferred are made through the cheque system. However, in spite of this, so far as the law of the land is concerned, cheques are still not regarded as *'legal tender'*. In other words, a person can insist on being paid in *cash*, although this legal right is rarely enforced now that cheques are often 'backed' by a bank guarantee in the form of a banker's card. When certain conditions are met, cheques up to £50 will be paid by a bank, even if the person drawing the cheque defaults.

For very large amounts of money, the payee can also ask for a banker's draft, which is really a cheque drawn on the bank's own account. Naturally, a bank would not make out a banker's draft until it was certain that the money was available in its customer's account. In this way, payment is guaranteed. Finally, a payee can decide not to part with the goods which have to be paid for until the drawer's cheque has been *cleared*.

The clearing system

Clearing a cheque effectively means the payment of the amount stated on the cheque. No money as such changes hands – paper entries are made on the two accounts involved: the drawer's being reduced by the amount stated and the payee's account being credited with the amount.

Clearing a cheque used to be a complex process, but now with the widespread use of computers and mechanisation it is a relatively simple process, although it still takes time. A highly efficient, well-organised system for ensuring the easy transfer of large (and small) sums of money between people and companies on a day-to-day basis has been developed. Every day of the year many thousands of individual cheques are drawn on many thousands of individual accounts and the banks use four basic methods of handling these transactions:

a   *local branch clearing* – when both the drawer and the payee have accounts at the same branch, the transfer is naturally easy and immediate;

b   *head office clearing* – when both the drawer and the payee have accounts with the same bank, but at different branches it is naturally necessary to 'clear' the transfers centrally;

c *local clearing houses* – major towns will operate local clearing houses for cheques drawn on, and payable to, different branches in the same town; and

d *the London clearing house* – this is the main centre for clearing cheques for the country as a whole: each day the totals payable by one major bank to another are calculated and the difference between the amount payable and the amount receivable is settled by Bank A drawing a cheque on its balance with the Bank of England (which is the 'bankers' bank) and paying it into Bank B's account there.

Definitions of the money supply

Given the clearing system, it is obvious that much more money can be spent than there is 'cash' (notes and coins). Suppose we look at the London clearing house where inter-bank debts are settled by cash transfers between accounts at the Bank of England.

Suppose Bank A's account holders pay for goods and services bought from Bank B's account holders with cheques drawn on their accounts with Bank A. The total spent in one day is £1m. Bank A now owes Bank B £1m. In the same day, Bank B's account holders buy goods and services from Bank A's account holders worth £0.9m and pay for them with cheques drawn on their accounts with Bank B. Now a further £0.9m has been spent and Bank B owes Bank A £0.9m. The total amount of money spent is £1.9m but the banks only settle the *net* debt between them. In this example, only £0.1m is needed for Bank A to settle with Bank B. The 'cash' is transferred from one account to the other in the Bank of England. The ability to write cheques (holding a current account at a bank) is the ability to spend money, and this far exceeds the amount of 'cash' in the system.

The measurement of the amount of money in the system is, as a result, more complex. It should include cash, the ability to write cheques (current accounts with banks), but also perhaps the ability to withdraw cash from the banks or other financial institutions (deposit accounts, building societies' accounts, etc). It should perhaps include all those things normally regarded as assets which could be used as money under certain circumstances. For example, an individual *might* use a government bond in payment for a debt, if this was acceptable to the creditor.

These different types of 'money' vary in how liquid they are. Cash is very liquid, but cheques drawn on a current account backed by a bank guarantee card are also very liquid. Deposit accounts with banks and building societies vary in liquidity; they can be divided into 'sight' accounts (you are able to draw your money out on demand), and 'time' accounts (you have to give notice of withdrawal). Clearly, sight deposits are more liquid than time deposits. There are a number of official UK definitions of 'money' (known as the 'monetary aggregates'). These various definitions of money can be divided into 'narrow' money (which is very liquid) and 'broad' money (which is not very liquid). It should be emphasised that the monetary aggregates in use in the UK at any one time are by no means the only possible such aggregates. These have changed over the years, and will change again in the future, as more and more sophisticated forms of 'money' are invented and become accepted as 'money'.

The government and the Bank of England use and publish statistics on two main measures of money supply: M0 and M4.

M0 is a measure of so-called 'narrow money', whilst M4 is a 'broad money' aggregate.

M0	=	notes and coins in circulation
	+	cash in bank tills
	+	banks' operational balances with the Bank of England
M4	=	notes and coins in circulation
	+	all sterling deposits held by the non-bank, non-building society private sector with UK banks and building societies.
		(This measure of money supply recognises the recent changes in building society activities, such as cheque accounts.)

Details of the movements in these monetary aggregates can be found in *Financial Statistics*, a monthly publication of the Government Statistical Service.

No broad money targets have been published since 1986, but a monitoring range of 3–9 per cent per annum for M4 was announced in spring 1993. Experience with attempting to control and predict broad monetary aggregates prior to sterling's entry into the Exchange Rate Mechanism of the European Monetary System had not been very satisfactory. Not only were such aggregates unpredictable, they were also deemed to be in some ways inappropriate. They were all simple-sum aggregates which weighted each component equally. It is clear that the components, eg of M4, are not perfect substitutes: notes and coins bear no interest, whilst bank and building society deposits may do so, and the interest rates may be different. It was felt that it would be better to construct a monetary aggregate which attempted to better measure the transactions services of the different components by weighting them differentially.

Following sterling's exit from the ERM on Black Wednesday, 16 September 1992, attention turned again to targetting the growth of the money supply rather than the exchange-rate. The Divisia index (see following table) consists of the components of M4, but weighted to represent the transactions services of money.

		Interest rate
Divisia =	notes and coins	
	– personal sector	zero
	– corporate sector	zero
	non-interest bearing private sector bank deposits	
	– personal sector	zero
	– corporate sector	zero
	interest-bearing-bank private sector sight deposits	
	– personal sector	clearing bank instant access account rate (gross)
	– corporate sector	overnight London interbank deposit rate
	interest-bearing bank private sector time deposits	
	– private sector	clearing bank interest bearing personal account rate (gross)
	– corporate sector	three-month London interbank deposit rate minus 0.5%
	building society deposits	
	– private sector	building society savings account rate
	– corporate sector	three-month London interbank deposit rate

All of the above components are weighted by the appropriate prevailing interest rate.

Details of the movements of the Divisia index can be found in the *Bank of England Quarterly Bulletin*.

The clearing banks

Introduction

The mainstay of the banking system is the clearing banks. These are limited companies in the normal way, but they specialise in banking and associated activities. The banks which transact the majority of banking business today in the UK are Barclays, National Westminster, Midland, Lloyds, TSB and Girobank. They play a crucial role in the day-to-day financial and commercial activity of the economy as they form the main link in the credit-transfer facilities which are the backbone of trade and commerce in the world today.

The current market structure of retail banking in the UK is the result of a number of mergers and takeovers. These resulted partly from increased competition from foreign-based banks, and more recently from competition from the building societies.

There are two main types of structure common in the western world – the branch system as in the UK and the unit bank system as in the USA. The UK structure is highly concentrated in that there are only a limited number of banks with a large number of branches whilst in the USA there are many more separate banks (approximately 13,000).

Basic services provided

The clearing banks as well as accepting deposits from the general public provide a wide range of financial services:

a credit transfer through cheque accounts, banker's drafts, standing orders, direct debits, credit transfers, etc;

b overdraft and loan facilities;

c spreading financial commitments over a longer period than would otherwise be possible through 'budget planning' facilities;

d foreign exchange facilities;

e advice on taxation affairs and planning;

f advice on export markets, etc;

g executor and trustee services;

h security services;

i credit card facilities/cash dispenser services; and

j mortgages.

Recent developments

In the last few years the major banks and building societies have been in competition to a much greater degree. With banks offering mortgages and building societies offering current accounts, the general public is beginning to see little distinction between them. Also, with some banks opening on Saturdays and some building societies 'going public', the distinction may even disappear in the 1990s.

The essence of banking

One of the principal facets of any banking organisation is that it operates with other people's money, while its basic functions are to keep, transfer and lend that money in order to make a profit for its shareholders. There are, therefore, two important aspects of a bank's balance sheet to consider. First, is the summary of the value of the assets (ie the items of value that can be turned into cash), and second, is the summary of the value of liabilities (ie the responsibilities owed by the bank to the actual owners of the money that it is using). (It should be remembered by accountancy students that a balance sheet is a *summary of the assets and liabilities that are held by a business organisation at a given point in time*).

The following is a simplified balance sheet for a clearing bank.

Liabilities		*Assets*	
Shareholders' funds	£100	Cash and investments	£300
Deposits	£1,000	Loans	£800
	£1,100		£1,100

So far as the right-hand side of this hypothetical balance sheet is concerned, the bank does not lend all its money – it keeps some cash and easily realisable securities (notably government stock). This enables it to meet any withdrawals that may occur within a reasonable margin above the 'norm' for such withdrawals.

The function of the shareholders' capital (on the left-hand side) is to provide a cushion to protect the depositors should the bank suffer any losses or bad debts. For instance, in the example above, if the bank was unable to recover a £50 loan, then the value of the loans on the right-hand side would be written down by £50 and – in order to balance it – the shareholders' funds would also be written down by £50, thus leaving the depositors unaffected. If the 'bad debt' in question was in the region of £200 rather than £50, the bank would naturally be in serious trouble, but the vast majority of banks are prudent enough in their lending policies to limit their losses on their loan portfolios to no more than a tiny percentage of the total – perhaps only 1½ per cent per year on average.

The liabilities of a bank

A typical clearing bank has four principal liabilities:

a *Shareholders' funds*. A bank is no different from any other limited joint-stock company. The shareholders' funds represent the bank's capital and as it is permanent capital the bank is at liberty to use it for either short-term or long-term expenditure.

b *Customers' accounts*. The total of all customers' accounts, whether current, deposit, savings or otherwise, represent the major part of the money which a bank uses to transact its business. The volume of these accounts is, therefore, the main determinant of the scale of the bank's activities.

c *Reserves.* Any business organisation sets aside a proportion of annual profits to 'plough' back into the business and, similarly, banks build up reserves of undistributed profits. The bank is directly responsible to the existing shareholders for the way in which it uses such accumulated reserves.

d *Other liabilities.* Under this heading come such responsibilities as Bills of Exchange and other foreign trade debts that a bank often incurs on behalf of its customers. These are incurred because a foreign customer will usually accept the guarantee of a bank more readily than that of an individual company.

The assets of a bank

The assets of a typical clearing bank are:

a *Physical assets.* A bank's physical assets are very similar to any other company's physical assets; namely, such items as premises, equipment and so on.

b *Cash, etc.* At any particular time a bank will possess stocks of money in the form of banknotes and coins. In addition to the stocks of money that it holds in its tills and in its own vaults, the bank holds considerable sums of money at its own account at the Bank of England. A bank uses this account to settle its debts with other banks.

c *Special deposits.* As well as the ordinary deposit account that a bank has at the Bank of England, a clearing bank will, from time to time, be obliged to place extra money on deposit at the Bank of England. (The reasons for this are discussed below.)

d *Loans.* A bank makes its profits primarily from lending money to individuals and companies. In fact, this item comprises the most important part in terms of size of a bank's assets. A bank will try to keep a balance between very short-term lending, short-term lending and medium-term lending. As a rule a bank does not lend 'in the long term', except perhaps in the form of renewable overdrafts or renewable short-term loans. A proportion of a bank's lending falls due for repayment every day, so it is possible for a bank to adjust its lending policy in line with the prevailing economic and financial conditions.

The different types of bank lending can be listed in order of *liquidity*; that is, the speed with which the loan in question is likely to be repaid:

   i *Money at call* or short notice. This includes the loans made to the London Money Market and Discount Houses. This market borrows very large sums of money for very short periods: sometimes the amounts are repayable 'on demand' or overnight, but at most this money is lent for only two or three days.

   ii *Treasury Bills.* A substantial amount of money is lent direct to the government on the security of the 90-day bills issued by the Treasury.

   iii *Commercial Bills of Exchange.* The clearing banks play a major part in the financing of foreign trade and they often 'discount' commercial bills in preference to giving a customer a conventional overdraft.

    iv *Advances to customers.* This is usually the largest single item under this heading and includes both overdrafts and other loans to the bank's customers, both private and business.

    v *Trade investments.* Banks often own, or partly own, more specialised institutions such as finance houses or hire purchase companies, and they make money available to them.

e *Balances with other banks.* The transfer of sums of money is such a large operation nowadays it is inevitable that at any one time there will be many thousands of transfers in the course of being 'cleared'. Consequently, so far as a bank's balance sheet is concerned, the total amount of such balances and credits has to be included as an asset.

f *Other assets.* The miscellaneous liabilities of the previous paragraph must be balanced by the responsibility of customers in respect of such liabilities. However, as in all cases of bank liability, the bank's responsibility will always remain a *residual responsibility* – if the customer defaults then the bank must make payment itself.

The balance sheet summary

The items listed in (e) and (f) above are the principal items in the balance sheet of any clearing bank and it will be useful to summarise them:

Liabilities	=	*Assets*
Shareholders' funds		Physical assets
Customers' current and deposit accounts		Cash and ordinary balances at Bank of England
Reserves		Loans – inc money at call, Treasury bills
Other liabilities		Commercial bills, advances to customers and trade investments
		Balances with other banks and cheques in the course of collection
		Special deposits at Bank of England
		Other assets

The credit creation process

Until recently, few of the main banks gave interest on current accounts, and so there was much larger profit on any money that was – effectively – lent from current accounts. Recently, fierce competition from the building societies, some of which offer current accounts (cf Nationwide's Flexaccount), has forced the banks to offer interest on some current accounts.

It may seem surprising that a bank can lend money that is deposited in current accounts. However, even as early as the seventeenth century the goldsmiths who stored people's gold for them realised that, at any one time, only a small proportion of the total amount of gold that they held was actually required by its real owners. Hence, they began to lend out some of the gold to other people. It is a small step from there to realise that, in fact, it is perfectly possible for a bank to *create money*.

Suppose the bank knew from experience that only about 10 per cent of its cash holdings were in demand at any one time. It would naturally feel able to lend up to 90 per cent of its cash holdings knowing that it would not be 'caught' without the liquid funds to meet the demand for cash. So it can be seen that if a bank received another £100 in cash deposits it can, without danger, lend another £90 and only 'keep' £10 in cash. This 'extra' £90 then enters the banking system and is used to make further investments and purchases and so on. This process can only continue for a limited period as it is based on a 'geometrical progression' – at each point of 're-depositing' there must be a 10% 'cash leak', as each time the bank must keep 10 per cent of the 'new' deposit to meet the demand for cash. Eventually, of course, the increase in 'new deposits' will become too small to have any practical significance.

This can be illustrated more clearly perhaps by using a simplified balance sheet. If the bank has £1,000 of deposits, its balance sheet would be:

Liabilities		Assets	
Deposits	£1,000	Cash	£100
		Loans	£900
	£1,000		£1,000

This balance sheet is possible as the bank knows that it can lend up to 90 per cent of its total deposits. If a further deposit of £100 is made, the bank's balance sheet will initially be altered as follows:

Liabilities		Assets	
Deposits	£1,100	Cash	£200
		Loans	£900
	£1,100		£1,100

However, as the bank can lend up to 90 per cent of the new deposit, the balance sheet will change to:

Liabilities		Assets	
Deposits	£1,100	Cash	£110
		Loans	£990
	£1,100		£1,100

(For convenience, it is assumed that there is only one bank. However, this does not, by itself, affect the validity of the example as it could represent the whole banking system.)

The £90 that the bank lends will be spent on goods and services, and will eventually find its way back to the bank in the form of new deposits; and so a new position will arise:

Liabilities		Assets	
Deposits	£1,190	Cash	£200
		Loans	£990
	£1,190		£1,190

The process then begins again. £81 can be lent (90 per cent of £90) and so:

Liabilities		Assets	
Deposits	£1,190	Cash	£119
		Loans	£1,071
	£1,190		£1,190

This process can clearly continue, although the extra money injected into the system becomes smaller at each stage and will eventually become so small that it has no effect on the system as a whole.

Profitability versus liquidity

We saw above that the assets of the commercial banks can be listed in order of liquidity. Money-at-call is a very liquid asset but earns a very low rate of interest, while, moving down the list into the more illiquid assets, higher interest rates can be earned on these assets. For example, a very high rate of interest, by comparison, can be earned on advances to customers.

Thus, there is a trade-off between profitability and liquidity.

Profitability is important since profits are needed to satisfy the banks' shareholders. Liquidity is important since the banks cannot risk being unable to satisfy their customers' demands for cash. In the numerical example above, the bank needed to hold 10 per cent of any deposit in cash, a highly liquid form, to meet customers' demands for cash. If the bank allows its assets to become too liquid, it is safe from a liquidity crisis but is losing potential profits. If its assets become too illiquid, it will be making high profits but risking a liquidity crisis.

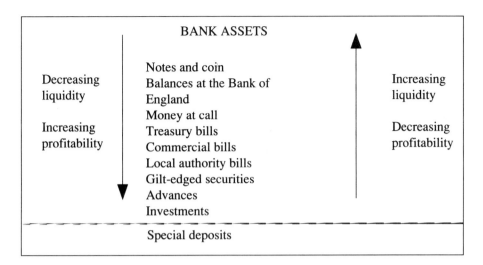

Special deposits do not fall into the above pattern because they are an illiquid asset for a bank but gain a low return.

Experienced bankers would naturally develop a 'rule of thumb' system for balancing the conflicting claims of liquidity and profitability. They would hold a range of assets of varying liquidity and profitability but always ensure that it could match, for example, 10 per cent of its liabilities with cash and an additional 5 per cent with assets that can be turned into cash within 7 days.

The money (or credit creation) multiplier

The existence of the liquidity ratio (the ratio of liquid assets and eligible liabilities) means that there may be a relationship between any change in the volume of reserve assets held by the commercial banks and an expansion of the availability of credit to the banks' customers. Suppose that the holding of liquid assets is increased by £1m while the banks are operating a liquidity ratio of, say, 12½ per cent. Through the process of credit creation discussed above, the banks will lend out this cash, receive it again as new deposits and re-lend it until its cash holdings have been expanded by £1m and its liabilities by £8m. In this example, the money multiplier is 8 where this money multiplier is calculated as 1/liquidity ratio and the liquidity ratio is 12½ per cent or ⅛.

The formula to be used is:

the change in bank lending = the money multiplier × the change in liquid assets

ie $£8m = \dfrac{1}{\frac{1}{8}} \times £1m$

Of course, it may be that the banks are more cautious than the government with regard to the liquidity ratio and prefer to operate a minimum liquidity ratio of 15 per cent. In this case, the money multiplier will be lower and the associated credit expansion will then be smaller in response to the same change in the banks' holdings of liquid assets.

Alternatively, the banks' ability to lend money and thus expand credit availability (and thus the money supply) may be dependent on the rate of interest they charge. If the cost of borrowing is high, potential borrowers may be discouraged and the banks will be unable to expand lending by the full amount indicated by the money multiplier.

The relationship between changes in bank lending (a very large part of the money supply, as discussed above) and changes in holdings of reserve assets is an important route by which the government can control the level of bank lending and therefore the money supply (discussed below).

The Bank of England

Central role

The clearing banks are profit-seeking organisations like other companies, the only difference being that their commodity or product is money itself. However, due to the crucial importance of money within any economy, it is usual for there to be a central governing body. The financial departments of the government, such as the Treasury, are naturally very involved in the economic and financial management of the country's affairs, but the Bank of England also plays an important role, particularly in the banking sector.

Functions of a central bank

The Bank of England is the *central bank* of the UK. A central bank is invariably owned by the government of the country concerned and it is, therefore, an instrument of the central government machine. Although all central banks have different structures and forms of organisation, they all perform the same basic functions:

a   controlling the note issue;

b   holding the reserves of the banking system;

c   administering the government's own credit transfers;

d   managing the National Debt and acting as the paying agent for the interest thereon;

e   acting as a general financial advisor to the government;

f   controlling the banking system in general;

g controlling or influencing the overall structure of interest rates; and

h often controlling the foreign exchange system, although in some instances this is administered by a separate Ministry of Finance.

The lender of last resort

The Bank of England performs a central function in guaranteeing the security of the British banking system. During the development of British banking in the eighteenth and early nineteenth century, there were a series of bank failures. The banks, as we have discussed above, would lend out money deposited with them in the pursuit of interest payments from these loans. They could not, therefore, necessarily meet a demand from all of their customers for all of their deposits at once. Additionally, banks can make unwise investments and could occasionally not be repaid the money owed to them. Particularly in times of economic uncertainty, a rumour would spread that a certain bank had lent its depositors' money to individuals or institutions that could not repay. All the depositors would then rush to the bank to get their deposits out before the bank ran out of money. The bank, unable to meet all these immediate demands for cash, would have to close its doors. Chaos would, therefore, be caused even when the bank was in reality sound and the rumours incorrect.

To avoid this type of crisis, the Bank of England guarantees the liquidity of the commercial banking sector and will meet any demands for immediate liquidity. These demands are usually made through the discount houses (discussed below) since these are the only institutions to have automatic access to the Bank of England.

History of Bank of England

The Bank of England (the 'Old Lady of Threadneedle Street') is the oldest and probably the most famous of all the central banks. It began to operate as a central bank in the sixteenth century and as general banking activity increased during the nineteenth century it tended to concentrate solely on central banking functions. The Bank Charter Act 1844 gave it an effective monopoly of new note issue and eventually it controlled the entire note issue in the country. (The Issue Department of the Bank has now developed as a separate entity from the Banking Department.) The Bank remained in private hands until 1946 when it was nationalised, although it had been closely associated with the Treasury for a considerable period prior to the actual act of nationalisation. The Treasury and Bank of England are the monetary authorities in the United Kingdom.

Structure

When the Bank was nationalised, executive authority was placed in the hands of the Court of the Bank which functions similarly to a Board of Directors. The Court consists of the Governor, the Deputy Governor, four executive directors, and twelve part-time directors who represent a broader economic viewpoint. In addition, the Court has an 'inner cabinet' – the Committee of the Treasury. This is the effective power base within the Bank.

A communications link

Over the years, the Bank has developed a very close working relationship with the Treasury and much government policy is developed in liaison with the Bank. Indeed, because of its close connections with the financial markets and commerce the Bank is able to act as a very effective communications link between the private and public sectors of the economy. (As implied by the titles, the *private* sector comprises all the companies and so on which are owned by private shareholders, while the *public* sector comprises all those industries or services which are owned by the State as well as all central government activities.) Businessmen and financiers use Bank of England channels to communicate to the government their own views on the economy and the feelings of both national and foreign banks. Conversely, the government can use the Bank to convey its own thoughts and wishes to the private sector. Sometimes this is achieved informally, but sometimes through official mechanisms such as interest rate control or credit control. In recent years there have been many calls for the Bank of England to operate independently of the Treasury. This would detach the Bank from direct government influences particularly of a political nature.

Merchant banks

Introduction

Merchant banks play a very important, yet specialised, role in the UK banking system. In recent years the work and activities of merchant banks has received increased publicity, partly because the scope of their activities has grown considerably. Indeed, in the eighteenth and nineteenth centuries, the name 'merchant bank' was only applied to very few exclusive banking partnerships, which were mostly controlled by individual families. However, such banks dealt in huge sums of money and wielded enormous financial power. This power is still there today, but, although some families still have close ties with such merchant banks as Hambros and Rothschilds, the family influence is waning. Many merchant banks are now large public companies – owned by ordinary shareholders – and they operate throughout the world, with branches in many major cities. Furthermore, these banks now employ many of the best brains in the world of finance and economics.

The origins

In the eighteenth and nineteenth centuries there was a rapid expansion in trade, both national and international, and a considerable amount of that trade was financed through *commercial bills of exchange*. A bill of exchange is effectively a guarantee to pay a specific amount of money at a definite time and place – say 30 days from the date of the bill. The firm or person who expects to receive payment will issue a bill which a person or business due to make that payment will sign – or, in legal jargon, accept. It was noted above that clearing banks often sign (or accept) bills on behalf of their customers because companies which are expecting payment are more likely to accept a bank's commitment to pay rather than an individual person's commitment. In the eighteenth and nineteenth centuries, before the widespread use of the clearing-bank system, a few select individual merchants of repute found themselves much in demand in the business of 'accepting' bills of exchange. The merchants concerned began offering the service of accepting bills on behalf of other firms and people. This was really only the same thing as guaranteeing those firms' debts. Inevitably, these merchants had to acquire a great deal of knowledge about the whole financial system – and particularly the firms on whose behalf they were accepting bills of exchange. It was a small step from this activity to the many activities in which merchant banks are occupied today. Gradually, the older merchant banks dropped their other commercial activities and concentrated solely on the provision of financial services to individual customers.

Services

Merchant banks in the twentieth century provide the whole spectrum of personal and commercial financial advice to their clients. They do not, however, act as bankers to the general public in the same way as the clearing banks do. They do admittedly take deposits from customers, but these are usually only from people (or firms) with very large amounts to deposit, and this is usually with a view to investment. The merchant banks' main activities are the provision of expert advice on foreign trade and exporting, advice on investment in government bonds and the shares of public companies, and advice on raising large amounts of capital for major investment projects by firms and businesses. A by-product of this service is naturally advice on take-over bids either by their clients or *for* their clients. Similarly, a merchant bank will often advise a client on the best investment strategy and, on occasions, will actually manage a client's investments for him.

Present position

During the past few years they have met with considerable competition, either directly from the clearing banks themselves or from associated subsidiaries of the clearing banks. In addition, of course, there has been aggressive competition from a number of American and Far Eastern banks.

Perhaps the greatest problem facing the merchant banks is one of size. They may be large in terms of many public companies, but they are still relatively small compared with the four major clearing banks and the giant American and Canadian banks. The largest (in terms of assets) is Hambros, but even this bank is less than one-fifth the size of Barclays. In spite of this difficulty, it is likely that merchant banks will continue to provide a useful and necessary service to the financial world. They are often more able to take risks which the clearing banks cannot take, and so they are much sought after by young entrepreneurs with projects which are not acceptable to the clearing banks. As a result, they are in an important and influential position. They can, and often do, provide the capital needed for exciting and new productive enterprises, which are vital if the economy is to expand and grow. The new air of competition in the banking sector has encouraged the merchant banks to be more aggressive in their approach to finance and, though this may not be approved of by the 'old school' of merchant bankers where 'clients came to you', it should, over the years, have a beneficial effect on the economy as a whole.

Discount houses

Their role

The discount houses which make up the London Money Market are institutions which are engaged in the discounting of bills of exchange. This includes both *commercial bills* and *Treasury bills*. (Discounting a bill means exactly what it says – the holder of a bill can 'sell' it to someone else at a discount off its face value and the buyer then collects the full proceeds when the bill matures.)

Originally, the discount houses – of which there are now only twelve in the London money market – were principally involved in the discounting of commercial bills of exchange, but with the wide acceptance of ordinary credit terms in the commercial world, the use of commercial bills of exchange is not so widespread. Instead, there has been an enormous growth in the number of Treasury bills issued by the government. This is partly because the government's role in the life of the nation has become more important, resulting in its own financing needs increasing substantially, and partly because the issue of government stock is a very useful method of controlling the money supply. The discount houses now play a vital role in the highly organised and efficient market in short- and very short-term finance. Indeed, they are effectively the 'go-between' between the government and the clearing banks.

The details

The clearing banks regard their 'money-at-call' with the London money market as a cash asset for liquid ratio purposes and it is this important fact which holds the key to the operation of the market. The discount houses borrow money on a very short-term basis from the clearing banks – this is 'money-at-call'. If this money is required by the banks they can recall it literally by picking up the telephone. The discount houses then lend this money on to the government through purchasing Treasury bills at the weekly government tender of such bills. In fact, the discount houses effectively 'bid' for the whole quantity of Treasury bills which is offered weekly by the government. Once the bills have been allocated, the discount houses nominally 'sit back' and wait for the bills to mature. Their profit is the difference between the rate of interest which they are paying for their borrowed money to the banks and the rate of discount which they have obtained on the bills. However, in reality, it is not that simple, as the discount houses are the middlemen in the government's open-market operations.

If the clearing banks require an increased level of liquidity for any reason, they are likely to ask for immediate repayment of some, or all, of the money-at-call with the discount houses. It is probable that the discount houses will not be able to meet such a call for cash from either their own cash reserves or from the cash available from currently maturing bills, so they will have to turn to the Bank of England and re-discount a number of their prime bills there. However, for the privilege of doing so, they will have to pay the base lending rate, which is effectively a penal rate as it is always higher than inter-market rates of interest. Inevitably, it immediately destroys the discount houses' level of profitability. To avoid this, the houses obviously have to repay the central bank's loan as quickly as possible.

Interrelation of whole financial system

It can be seen that the whole spectrum of interest rates and credit creation by the clearing banks is closely interrelated, and that the discount houses play an important central role, partly through the actions which are forced upon them by circumstances and partly through their assessment of the future movement of interest rates when they are 'bidding' for each week's tender of bills. There is a constant flow of very large amounts of money through the money market and, indeed, its very existence enables the system to work smoothly. The Treasury and the Bank of England are the *monetary authorities* acting to control the price and availability of money. With the creation of the European Single Market in 1992 there have been calls for a European Central Bank, a move which would obviously dilute the power of the Bank of England.

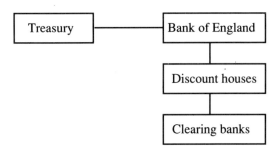

Questions for review

1. What is 'money'?
2. Why do we need money?
3. Explain the different forms which 'money' takes in the UK at present.
4. Why is more than one monetary aggregate needed?
5. Explain the role of clearing banks.
6. What are the functions of the Bank of England?
7. What are the discount houses? What is their role?
8. Explain:
    a   money at call;
    b   Treasury bills;
    c   merchant banks.
9. How do banks create money?

Inflation, money, interest rates and monetarism | 10

Inflation (see also Chapter 15)　271

Money demand　274

Money supply　277

Monetary equilibrium and the rate of interest　280

Monetarism　285

Inflation

Definition

In modern economies a central characteristic of money is that its value changes. In one year, a particular good costs £1 and three years later the same good costs £2. From microeconomics, we might conclude that changes in the demand and supply factors for this particular good are the explanation. But the usual situation is that the prices of all other goods are rising as well, by similar amounts. A better way of categorising the situation is, then, to say that the value or purchasing power of money is falling (ie each £ can be exchanged for less than it could before). Generally during a period of inflation, not just the price of goods and services rise, but also there is a rise in the prices of factors of production and therefore in earnings.

Inflation is defined as a general rise in prices and incomes or a fall in the value of money.

Measurement of inflation

One way of measuring inflation would be to look at every type of good, service and factor of production and calculate the average change in the price over a period. The general rate of inflation would then be x per cent over that period. Alternatively, inflation might be expressed as proceeding at a rate of y per cent per month/year. Thus we might say that the average increase in the prices/incomes in the economy was 80 per cent between 1977 and 1981 or that inflation has been proceeding at a rate of 15 per cent per year during that period. The prices of some goods, services and factors rise more rapidly than others. The average rate of inflation does not, therefore, give sufficiently precise information, particularly when observers are interested in the impact of inflation, where this will depend on the rate of change of particular prices. Various indices of inflation are therefore calculated to indicate the rate of price increases for particular groups of goods, services and factors. Thus, there is a house-price index, an index of industrial wages, of earnings in general, of building costs, of industrial costs, of industrial raw materials and so on.

The most frequently mentioned index is *the cost-of-living index*. In the UK this is called the Retail Price Index (RPI). The statisticians take a 'basket' of goods and services which represent the typical expenditure of the average household. The change in the price of this basket over a period is then calculated, given the rise in the price of all its items. The index is therefore a weighted average of the rise in the prices of the goods and services bought by households. Obviously, the items included and the weight given to them must be varied in line with changes in consumption patterns through time. For example, in 1950 relatively few families owned their own cars compared to the number that do in 1988. In 1950 the prices of cars, petrol, oil, and car-repair services would then make up only a small part of the cost of living index, while in 1988 they are quite important items. Some items drop out of consumer spending (eg washable nappies), and others come in (eg compact disc players). There are 1,000 weight units; for example, food has 167 and electricity 28.

The accuracy of the Retail Prices Index has been criticised by the House of Commons Public Accounts Committee. As the index is crucial in pay negotiations and in the indexation of social security benefits, errors can distort wage increases of workers or payments to the unemployed and pensioners. The members of the Committee identified several shortcomings in the calculation of the RPI. First, there was criticism of the use of the same geographical areas for compiling the 'shopping basket' for the last forty years. Secondly, there was the failure of the RPI to reflect differences between regions and the types of shop used. Thirdly, almost 30 per cent of goods chosen for the index become unavailable during the following twelve months.

The cost of living index is important because it represents the increase in the money expenditure of the average household if it buys the same goods and services as before. In order to maintain the same standard of living, households therefore need to spend more. As a result, the cost-of-living index becomes the basis for wage claims in negotiations between employer and employees. For example, if the expected rate of inflation as measured by the cost-of-living index is 2 per cent per week, wages need to go up by that amount if the standard of living is to be maintained.

Note that the *standard of living* is the ability to consume goods and services while the *cost of living* is the expenditure required to buy those goods and services.

Although the RPI is the measure of inflation which is most commonly quoted, there are other measures of inflation in use in the UK. The most important of these is the Producer Price Index, which consists of two elements: so-called 'factory gate prices' which measures the price of goods as they leave the producers, and the 'raw materials index' which measures the prices of raw materials used in production. The latter is particularly useful as a predictor of the rate of retail inflation several months ahead. For example: the recent failure of the important Brazilian coffee harvest has resulted in sharp rises in the price of coffee beans on the commodity exchanges; these rises will result in rises in the cost of instant coffee in the shops in the next few months. The producer price index would enable statisticians to estimate the amount of retail inflation which will result from the rise in the cost of coffee beans.

Real changes versus nominal changes

The fact that the value of money is falling during a period of inflation makes it difficult to identify important changes in relative prices and incomes. For example, suppose a writer is negotiating fees for an annual article that he has written for a paper for several years. The editor offers to increase the fee by 25 per cent. Whether the writer is pleased or disappointed with that offer depends on what has been happening to the prices of the goods and services that he will use that money to buy. If the prices of these goods have risen by 30 per cent since he last earned the fee, he will be disappointed. He will be able to buy 5 per cent less with his fee than he could in the previous year. On the other hand, if inflation has been only 20 per cent, he is 5 per cent better off as a result of the fee increase. In the first case, with inflation of 30 per cent, his *nominal income* increased by 25 per cent but his real income fell by 5 per cent. With inflation of 20 per cent, his nominal income increased by the same 25 per cent but his real income (or purchasing power) *rose* by 5 per cent.

Thus, the real increase in income = the nominal increase in income minus the rate of inflation.

It can be argued that an increase in real income helps to increase the *standard of living* of an individual. Similarly, a distinction is made between *nominal* and *real* increases in government expenditure, in taxation revenue, in the revenues, profits and costs of firms, and in the prices of goods and interest rates.

For example: the nominal interest rate minus the rate of inflation = the *real* interest rate; ie, if a saver received 12 per cent interest during a period of 5 per cent inflation, the real interest rate would be 7 per cent.

The effects of inflation

Inflation causes a number of problems in the economy which will generally be worse the greater the rate of inflation. In the 1920s in Germany there was what is called *hyperinflation,* where the rate of inflation became so rapid that the prices of goods were doubling in a few hours and wheel-barrows full of bank notes were needed to make normal purchases. Eventually the value of money was falling so rapidly that no one would accept it – its value would fall before they could spend it. Once money ceases to be acceptable it is no longer really money. Bank notes were replaced by cigarettes as the generally acceptable currency. The collapse of the currency pushed the German economy into a major crisis. People and government are, as a result, nervous of inflation, particularly where the rate of inflation is increasing.

Inflation, especially when the rate of inflation is fluctuating, makes using money more difficult. An important characteristic of money is that its value is certain. When its *value becomes uncertain* people become uncertain about the real value of the price being charged for a good or of the income being offered. They may be inhibited in buying goods or accepting offers of work.

Inflation may result in an *arbitrary redistribution of income*. Some groups have fixed money incomes (eg pensions, student grants) or incomes dependent on assets with a fixed money value (eg annuities and insurance policies). Inflation will mean that the real incomes of these people will fall. Other groups have their incomes rising at the same speed as or faster than the rate of inflation (eg members of strong trade unions). Their real incomes, therefore, maintain their value or rise.

Real interest rates tend to fall in times of inflation because nominal interest rates fail to rise sufficiently. For many years during the post-war inflationary period, the real interest rate has often been negative. As a result, savers and lenders of money tend to lose, while investors and borrowers of money gain. It is unlikely that this negative return on saving will discourage saving significantly. In the early 1970s when real interest rates became negative, saving actually increased. The low real-interest rates may certainly stimulate investment and consumer spending, boosting the economy. Firms generally tend to gain from inflation, because the price for which output can be sold has increased since inputs were bought. Profits are therefore increased. Rapid inflation may, however, create uncertainty, which *discourages investment.*

If the rate of inflation in Britain is faster than the rate in other economies, this means that the prices of British goods are rising more rapidly than those of our foreign competitors. British goods therefore become *less competitive* in domestic and export markets, and British industry may be faced with falling demand for its output. Up until recently Britain's above-average inflation rate in relation to our trading partners did much to damage our competitiveness.

The causes of inflation and the policies indicated are discussed in the rest of this chapter and also in Chapter 15.

Money demand

Keynes identified a number of reasons why people would want to hold money, rather than own assets which produce benefits (eg interest payments, utility from use) but are more difficult to use as mediums of exchange. The resulting identifications of the demand for money are the transactions demand, the precautionary demand and the speculative demand for money.

Transactions demand for money

People require money in order to buy goods and services. People spend more the higher their incomes, and spending in the economy will therefore be greater the higher the level of national income (aggregate income earned – see Chapter 11). We would therefore expect that higher levels of national income (measured in money) would lead to an increased demand for money for transactions purposes.

People do not just hold money for their transactions each day, returning to banks or other sources of cash for a new supply each morning. There are 'transaction costs' associated with many economic activities. For example, to withdraw money from an account in a building society, the individual must make the trip to the building society branch, spend time waiting in the queue and may have to pay a charge for this use of the society's services. People will, therefore, take out enough money in one day to meet their anticipated transactions for perhaps a week. We might, therefore, expect the demand for money to be related to the convenience of such services as building-society branches. If there were more branches, shorter queues and no charges, people might visit branches more often and hold less money at any time. The transactions demand for money would then be reduced.

The transactions demand for money may also depend on the rate of interest. Interest payments can be earned by not spending money but by leaving it in an account in some financial institution. Suppose interest rates were very high, some people would cut their expenditure, and thus their transactions demand for money, in order to leave money in an interest-earning account. The money spent by individuals and institutions may be borrowed, in which case interest must be paid on it. If interest rates rose, these individuals and institutions would try to reduce their borrowing, and thus their demand for money, in order to avoid these high interest charges. However, one interesting lesson of the attempts at monetary control in 1980 was that, when national income falls and interest rates are high, firms, in particular, have an *increased* demand for money, not a *reduced* demand as might be suggested by the theory of the determinants of monetary demand. As national income fell firms found their profit margins squeezed and they had insufficient revenue to meet their existing interest charges on their debts. Higher interest rates on those debts simply made the problem worse. Firms were forced to borrow more, not less.

Precautionary demand for money

People may choose to hold more money than they need for predictable transactions. There is always some uncertainty about future expenditure and people hold some extra money in case of unforeseen expenditures.

The determinants of the precautionary demand are similar to those of the transactions demand. Particularly, we might expect the precautionary demand to be inversely related to the rate of interest. The greater the interest earned on not holding money, the greater the risk people will be willing to take of running short of money because of unforeseen expenditure.

Speculative demand for money

Keynes identified the speculative demand for money as that part of money demand which is most closely related to the rate of interest. The simplest explanation is that the interest rate is the opportunity cost of holding money, so the speculative demand for money will be inversely related to the rate of interest. The second explanation relates the demand for money to the price of an alternative asset, government bonds. However, the analysis could be extended to include such assets as debentures bought from private companies.

The price at which bonds are traded is inversely related to the rate of interest on them. For example, suppose a bond with a face value of £100 yields an interest payment of 5 per cent per year, which means an interest payment of £5. Now, suppose the bond were sold for £50, the £5 interest payment represents an interest rate of 10 per cent on the price of the bond. If the price of the bond rose to £150, the 5 per cent interest payment represents an interest rate of only 3.3 per cent. Thus, the price of bonds bears an inverse and precise relationship with the interest rate earned on them.

Speculators will have a view of what is the 'normal' rate of interest to be earned on such assets as bonds, given prevailing economic circumstances. If the current rate is low compared to this expected rate, interest rates can be expected to rise, which means a fall in the price of bonds. Holders of bonds will sell, preferring to hold money. Conversely, if the interest rate is currently high compared to 'normal', it can be expected to fall. In this case, bond prices can be expected to rise, giving holders of bonds a capital gain. Speculators will, therefore, prefer to hold bonds rather than money and the speculative demand for money will be low. Thus, the speculative demand for money is inversely related to the rate of interest.

The total demand for money – liquidity preference

In the following diagram, T+P represents the transactions and precautionary demand for money combined. Its position depends on such factors as the level of national income and facilities for withdrawing money from banking institutions. Its slope shows some responsiveness to changes in interest rates. The speculative demand for money is shown by the curve S and is inversely related to the interest rate. The curve M_d shows the horizontal sum of these two curves and is the total demand for money.

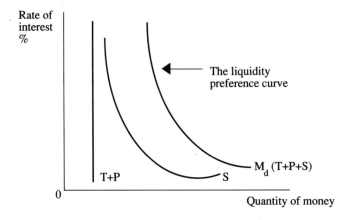

The following diagram shows the effect on this money demand schedule if there is an increase in national income which increases the transactions and precautionary demand for money and therefore the total demand for money at any interest rate.

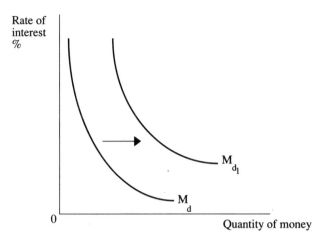

Money supply

Determination of money supply

The money supply was defined and the importance of bank lending as a part of money supply discussed above.

The ability of the banks to lend depends on their holding of liquid assets, and the reserve-assets ratio they operate. Where the liquid ratio is 10 per cent and the banks hold £10m of reserve assets, the level of lending by the banks will be £100m. (These relationships were discussed above.) Adjustments of the money supply will then tend to relate to these two variables, ie the holding of liquid assets by the commercial banks and the liquid-assets ratio that they operate.

Adjustments to the holdings of liquid assets

Suppose that the government wants to force the commercial banks to reduce their lending. Suppose that the commercial banks are currently holding a level of liquid assets which is just enough to meet the minimum liquid ratio required by the Bank of England, given their current level of lending. *Suppose* the liquid ratio is 12½ per cent:

	Holding of liquid assets	Level of lending (eligible liabilities)	Liquid ratio
a	Existing situation £10m	£80m	12½%
b	Government reduces reserve asset holding by £2m £8m	£80m	10% (below minimum requirement)
c	Banks reduce lending to restore reserve assets ratio £8m	£64m	12½%

Notice how a reduction in the liquid asset holding by £2m results in a much larger reduction in bank lending by £16m. The relationship between them is the money multiplier discussed above.

Similarly, the Bank of England can cause an increase in the level of bank lending by increasing the level of holdings of liquid assets in the commercial banks. An expansion of liquid assets by £1m will mean that, with a liquid asset ratio of 12½ per cent, the banks can expand their lending by £8m.

Open market operations

The Bank of England can reduce the holding of liquid assets in commercial banks by increasing its sales of government stock such as bonds. The bonds are bought by either the banks or their customers. The banks must pay the government for them in cash through their accounts with the Bank of England, which immediately reduces the balance in those accounts and thus the banks' holdings of liquid assets. If the banks' customers buy the bonds they pay for them with cheques drawn on their bank accounts, which means that the banks must pay the government in cash on behalf of their customers.

Open market operations can also be used to expand the money supply. If bond sales are reduced, the private banking sector is left with more cash, and this can be used as a basis for the expansion of lending.

Open market operations also have implications for the rate of interest. In order to sell an increased number of government bonds the government must offer to pay a higher reward on them in order to attract more buyers. The nominal interest payment on bonds will be higher and their price lower. Similarly, reduced bond sales will be rationed with lower nominal interest on them and higher prices. If the interest earned on government bonds changes we would expect this to affect interest rates elsewhere in the economy. A higher interest earned on government stock will attract funds from private investment. Private firms will have to offer higher interest in order to compete for funds. Similarly, lower interest on government stock will put more funds into the private investment market, so that firms find funds available at lower interest payments.

Funding

With a given need of the government for borrowed money, it can raise that money by selling long-term debt (bonds or gilts) or short-term debt (Treasury bills). If the government wants to reduce the money supply, government stock sales should be predominantly of long-term debt. The banks' holdings of government debt will then include more bonds and fewer Treasury bills. Since Treasury bills are liquid assets while most bonds are not, the banks' holding of liquid assets are reduced.

Governments can engage in 'over-funding' by selling more long-term debt than is necessary to cover the budget deficit. This will reduce the money supply. Similarly, the bank's holdings of liquid assets can be increased by selling an increased proportion of Treasury bills to them.

Special deposits

The Bank of England can require the banks to deposit some of their liquid assets in a special account in the Bank of England, where they no longer can be used as a basis for credit creation. This reduces their lending capability and the money supply. The special deposits will usually be fixed as a proportion of eligible liabilities.

Direct controls on bank lending

During 1981, the list of banks whose bills are eligible for rediscounting by the Bank of England (ie 'eligible' banks) was extended. Banks within this newly extended category have to undertake to maintain at all times not less than 4 per cent of their eligible liabilities as secured funds with the London Discount Houses, and a further 2 per cent as secured money on call with authorised gilt-edge jobbers and money brokers. Also, all banks must keep ½ per cent of their deposits in non-operational deposits at the Bank of England.

The Mandatory Liquid Asset Ratio is the term applied to the combined value of these two requirements, that is to say, 6½ per cent of eligible liabilities. All London clearing banks and major accepting houses are included in the list of eligible banks, which now accounts for about one hundred individual banks, and, because of this scope, the mandatory ratio guarantees an adequate liquidity reserve with the London money market.

The continuing importance of that market has thus been emphasised, despite the abolition of the reserve assets ratio in 1981. The money market is still used by the Bank of England by this means as an instrument of monetary policy. The alternative course of dealing directly with the major clearing banks has been rejected by the Bank of England, in the interests of avoiding an over-concentration of transactions which would substantially reduce the effect of market forces upon interest rates.

Changes in the money supply

It will have been noticed that the authorities are, in practice, concerned to control the rate at which the money supply is expanding rather than to stop it growing altogether. The price level in the economy has been rising persistently during the post-war period. The present government would like to see money supply grow by only as much as growth in the economy, thereby ensuring that growth in the money supply 'finances' the extra transactions in the economy and does not fuel inflation. The following graph shows the percentage change in the growth of money supply (M0) during the period May to November 1990. The government wishes to keep M0 within a specific target range of growth per year.

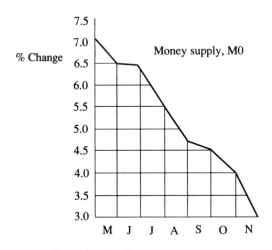

(Source: Bank of England)

Monetary equilibrium and the rate of interest

Monetary equilibrium

The liquidity preference schedule (see above) shows the aggregate demand for money. The money supply has been defined and its main determinants discussed above. We will assume that the money supply can be determined by government policy and is not responsive to changes in the rate of interest. This gives us the following diagram, where money demand will be equal to money supply at the interest rate r_e.

Inflation, money, interest rates and monetarism | 281

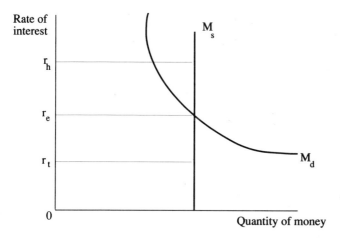

If the interest rate in the economy is too high (eg at r_h), the authorities wish to make more money available than the private sector want to take up at the existing interest rates. As the interest rate falls, more money will be taken up by borrowers and other holders of money. If the interest rate is too low (eg at r_t), the demand for money at that interest rate exceeds the supply that the authorities wish to make available. The shortage of funds will bid up the interest rate throughout the banking sector.

Effects of changes in monetary demand on equilibrium

Suppose the money demand increases because of increased income in the economy or an increase in the price level. Unless the money supply also expands, the interest rate will be forced up to ration the available money supply over the demand. If the money supply expands by the same amount to M_s^1, there is no change in the interest rate. The reverse effects, lower interest rate and/or reduced money supply, will follow a reduction in monetary demand.

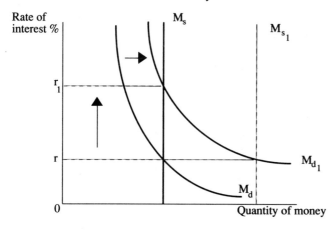

Effects of changes in the money supply on the rate of interest

If the authorities want to reduce the money supply, we can see the effect that this will have on monetary equilibrium and the rate of interest. In the following diagram, the money supply is reduced to Ms_1. The interest rate must rise to r_1 so that demand for money falls in line with the reduced supply.

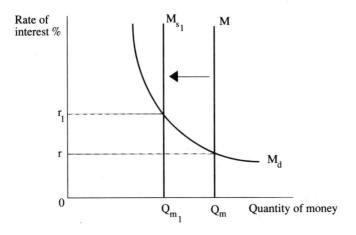

An increased supply of money will similarly be associated with lower interest rates and increased monetary demand.

The monetary equilibrium thus gives an indicator of what determines the interest rate in the economy. Given the level of monetary demand and the authorities decision on money supply, there is an equilibrium rate of interest. Indeed, considering the ways in which the authorities can expand or reduce the money supply, we can trace the effect on the interest rate.

Suppose, specifically, that the bank uses open-market operations to reduce the money supply. As discussed above, in order to sell more bonds the government must offer a higher return on them. This attracts funds away from the private sector, which must offer higher interest rates in order to compete for funds. Similarly, increasing money supply through open-market operations means lower interest rates (higher prices for bonds) to ration the smaller supply of bonds. As interest rates on government securities fall, so will interest rates elsewhere in the economy.

More generally a reduction in the ability of banks to lend, caused by any of the measures discussed above, will mean that banks must ration the funds that they have. They will discourage borrowing by putting up the interest rates on overdrafts and loans. If the authorities increase the ability of the banks to lend, they will increase their lending by reducing interest rates.

The rate of interest

The control of the Bank of England over short-term interest rates (base rates) is assured, for two main reasons. First, it offsets, at its own terms, shortages (or surpluses) of cash in the money markets via the discount houses; in this way, it can control the marginal cost of funds to the banking system. In theory, the bank is not expected to act as the lender of last resort to the banking system, yet in practice it does; it has to, for it cannot abdicate its responsibilities as the central bank!

Secondly, in its money-market operations, the bank buys and sells eligible commercial bills and Treasury bills in the discount market in four bands, according to the maturity of the bills. The bands where the bank's control is the strongest are bands one and two, ie banks in which bills have maturities of up to 14 days and one month respectively. Bands three and four include bills with longer maturities; in these bands the bank's direct influence is less strong. Changes in the bank's dealing rate in bands one and two are taken by the money markets to mean that the bank intends to bring about a change in the cost of marginal funds and therefore in the general level of short-term money-market rates. Clearly, if the bank makes short-term funds more expensive to the banking system, the banks in turn will charge more for overdrafts and short-term loans. Thus, despite the suspension (not abolition) of the Minimum Lending Rate in August 1981, the bank exerts the key influence on the level of short-term rates in the money markets. The interaction between the bill operations of the bank and market expectations is the main determinant of the level and structure of short-term rates in the UK, and it plays an important part in determining long-term rates in the money markets.

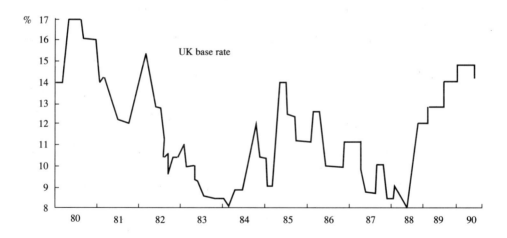

The importance of the rate of interest in the economy

The rate of interest is most important because it affects the level of borrowing in the economy. We discussedearlier how interest rates may be expected to affect the level of investment by private firms. Interest rates may also be an important influence on the level of spending by consumers. A large part of this spending is on borrowed money (eg bank overdrafts, hire-purchase arrangements) and will be discouraged by high interest rates and encouraged by low ones.

It may be that firms are unable to reduce their borrowing as a result of an increase in interest rates. For example, the only way that firms can reduce the borrowing required to cover the time gap between paying for factors of production and receiving payment for finished goods (ie the 'cash-flow' problem) is to reduce inputs and, therefore, output, revenue and ability to meet interest charges and repayments of existing debts. The increased interest rate may, therefore, increase firms' costs rather than reduce their borrowing.

Consumers may find themselves in a similar position with their outstanding debts. In this country 65 per cent of the householders own their own houses, and a large proportion will at any time be repaying the loan that enabled them to buy the house. Interest is charged each year on the outstanding debt. Suppose a householder borrowed £30,000 to buy a house and has already repaid £5,000 of this loan. His outstanding debt is £25,000. If interest rates in the economy rise, so do the rates payable on mortgages. Suppose the interest rate on the mortgage rises from 12 per cent to 15 per cent. The interest-payment outgoings of this householder will go up from £3,000 to £3,750. Not surprisingly, interest rate increases are very unpopular with a large proportion of the electorate.

Another influence of the interest rate is the effect on the amount of saving in the economy, and thus on the supply of loanable funds. However, the amount of saving is not particularly responsive to changes in the interest rate.

A more important factor is that, if interest rates are higher in this country compared to other industrial countries, holders of funds will be tempted to use them to buy British securities. This inflow of funds will, ceteris paribus, lead to an improvement on the balance of payments and a rise in the exchange rate, as well as an increase in the supply of loanable funds. The balance of payments/exchange rate effects are discussed in Chapters 17 and 18, but briefly the higher exchange rate leads to a drop in the competitiveness of British goods in foreign and domestic markets. As a result, the output and employment in British industry may soon be reduced. It should be noted that the only way that the authorities can 'neutralise' the inflow of funds so that it does not lead to higher interest rates, is to increase the supply of sterling by printing money (ie expanding the money supply). Similarly, low interest rates will cause funds to flow out of the country, reducing the supply of loanable funds and also pulling the exchange rate down, moving the balance of payments towards deficit.

The rate of interest as the price of money

The diagram which shows the intersection of the demand and supply-of-money curves arrives at a rate of interest 'equilibrium'. The 'price' of money can thus be called the rate of interest. If someone deposits money in a bank, the reward the saver receives for parting with liquidity is interest. This is the 'price' the bank has to pay the saver. If the saver deposits a large amount for a long period of time the bank will pay him/her a higher price for parting with liquidity (ie a higher rate of interest), hence the high rate of interest given to savers who deposit money in 'limited access' savings accounts. By the same token the banks' 'price' for loans/overdrafts is the rate of interest they charge to borrowers. In all cases the real price of borrowing is the nominal interest rate (ie the inflation rate).

Monetarism

The importance of money supply in the economy

An essential feature of monetarism is the so-called 'Quantity Theory of Money'. Monetarists regard the money supply as the main determinant of the price level in the economy. An 'excessive' expansion of the money supply will lead to inflation. Inflation can be checked by suitable adjustments to the money supply. Those who advocate monetarist policies may also argue that the money supply has no long-term impact on the level of employment and output in the economy. This view is by no means uncontroversial. This school of thought in economics did, however, have a profound influence on government policy during the early years of the Thatcher administration.

Quantity theory

An essential feature of monetarism is the so-called 'Quantity Theory of Money', and Fisher's 'equation of exchange' is the simplest version of it. This equation is:

$$MV = PT$$

where M is the supply of stock of money; V is the velocity of circulation (or rate at which this money stock is spent and re-spent); T is the number of transactions; and P is the average price of these transactions.

Thus, an increase in the money stock, unless balanced by a reduction in the velocity of circulation, will lead to an increase in the volume of transactions and/or the price level. A fall in the money supply will have the opposite effect.

Monetarists will argue that changes in the money supply will not cause any change in either the velocity of circulation or the number of transactions. Thus, any change in the money supply will lead to a proportionate adjustment of the price level. If the money stock rises by 10 per cent, so will the price level. If the money supply increases at a rate of 15 per cent per year, the annual rate of inflation will also be 15 per cent. The way to bring the rate of inflation down to 10 per cent is to reduce the rate of growth of the money supply to this level.

Suppose there is a weekly market in an isolated town. There are always 100 units of goods for sale, and the inhabitants of the town have £100 in total to spend which they always spend at the market. The price per unit of the goods is therefore

£1. Now suppose that, for some reason, the inhabitants of the town have £200 to spend this week. They go along to the market with their £200 but only the same stock of 100 units of goods are available. Their attempts to spend the extra money push up the prices of the goods to £2 per unit. The way to get prices back to the previous level is to reduce the amount of money available to the inhabitants of the town.

We should examine the assumptions made in this story: first, it is assumed that the inhabitants want to spend the whole of their windfall money gain of £100 immediately. They might alternatively decide to save it. Suppose they save £80 of it. The extra money coming on to the market is then only £20 and the price level will only rise to £1.20. Thus, a fall in the velocity of circulation has counteracted the impact of the increased money supply.

Secondly, it is also assumed that there are no extra goods available to meet the increased expenditure of the market's customers. Suppose that the stall-holders had anticipated the increased expenditure by stocking twice as many goods as usual. There will then be 200 units of goods available, to meet the expenditure of £200, and the price level will stay at £1 per unit. Thus, an increase in the volume of transactions has checked the impact of the increased supply on the price level.

The monetarist interpretation of the quantity theory of money therefore depends on there being no change in velocity of circulation or in the volume of transactions as a result of some change in the money supply. Critics of monetarist arguments believe that monetary changes may be met by changes in velocity or transactions (output).

The velocity of circulation is reasonably stable most of the time and has been rising slowly during the post-war era. However, it has responded sharply on the occasion of big changes in money supply. For example, during the rapid monetary expansion which followed the introduction of competition and credit control in 1971, the velocity of circulation fell by 25 per cent. During the period of controls on the money supply in the late 1970s, the velocity speeded up by 49 per cent. We can see how this might happen. Because of the monetary controls, interest rates were high. Any business that had borrowed money to finance the cash-flow problem would demand the rapid payment of all trade debts in order to minimise the borrowing and interest payments, thus speeding up the velocity of circulation. Similarly, employees would demand rapid payment of bonuses, expenses, and so on. Looking at the liquidity preference schedule, we know that money holdings will fall when interest rates are high, which means that the velocity speeds up.

Changes in the volume of transactions (ie the level of output and employment in the economy) in response to changes in money supply are a more worrying argument against monetarism. Critics of monetarism argue that an expanding money supply will stimulate the economy, so that output and employment increase. This will be true as long as the expansion of the money supply is not too rapid and as long as there are suitable spare resources in the economy to produce this extra output. If output and employment are responsive to changes in money supply, the price level need not change. (Most economists agree that where expansions of the money supply are very rapid or where there are no suitable unemployed resources available, an expanding money supply will lead to inflation.)

What happens when the money supply is reduced is also controversial. Critics of monetarism argue that controls on the money supply will lead to a fall in output and employment, rather than a fall in the price level alone. The high interest rates that will be part of the tight money policy lead to less investment and less spending by consumers as the cost of credit rises.

Thus, the debate over monetarism centres on the responsiveness of velocity of circulation and the volume of transactions to changes in money supply. Monetarists believe that controlling the money supply is the way to check inflation. Their critics believe, in turn, that if there is any effect at all, it will be to reduce the volume of transactions, causing falling output and rising unemployment.

An alternative criticism of the monetarist school is that the equation of exchange is a tautology with no predictive power. It simply states that the amount of money spent (MV) is exactly the same as the amount of money received in payment for goods and services (PT). Since these would be the alternative ways of measuring expenditure it is no surprise that they are always identical.

The monetarist answer to this challenge has been that the theory is predictive and therefore useful. It is sufficient to argue that there has, in fact, been a predictable relationship between the rate of expansion of the money supply and the rate of inflation in the economy. It is also true, according to the writings of Milton Friedman (the great exponent of this type of economic theory), that reductions in the rate of growth of money supply have resulted, in Japan for example, in a subsequent reduction in the rate of inflation.

The lag between the monetary adjustment and the subsequent reduction in the rate of inflation is said to be 18 months to two years. The following table, covering data going back several years, does show some correlation in this respect. Ironically, £M3 is no longer regarded as a reliable monetary aggregate by the government, although some economists still support its accuracy and its effect on inflation.

The annual rate of change of the retail price index and the money supply (£M3) for the United Kingdom 1965-80

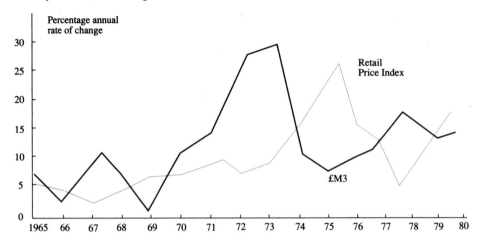

(Source: *Economic Trends*)

Target rates of growth of the money supply and the medium-term financial strategy (MTFS) (see also Chapter 14)

According to Friedman and other monetarist economists, the way to run a monetary policy is to look at the expected rate of inflation in the medium-term future. Money supply should grow less rapidly than the expected rate of inflation. The real money supply will then be falling.

The target rates of growth should be announced and should have a declining nominal rate of expansion through time. Thus, the rate of inflation would be pulled down to a lower and lower rate with each year of the monetary policy. Ideally, money supply growth should be in line with economic growth in the economy.

When the new Conservative administration came to power in 1979, it expressed its thinking on monetary matters in the Green Paper on Monetary Control (1980). Deregulation and monetary targeting figured prominently in this context, and were undoubtedly inspired by the then fashionable monetarism. 'The government believes that its monetary policy can best be formulated if it sets targets for the growth of one of the aggregates against which progress can be assessed. This gives the clearest guidance to those concerned in both financial markets and domestic industry on which to assess the direction of government policy and to formulate expectations.'

When MTFS was actually brought into operation (HM Treasury, 1980), its basic principles might well have been taken from a new macroeconomics textbook. Demand management was rejected. Support was given to supply-side management. Emphasis was placed on creating a climate of stability for the private sector to grow. This was to be achieved by monetary policy conceived as the principal anti-inflationary weapon. The policy was to be based upon targeting of one monetary aggregate (sterling M3-£M3), which was seen as a clear signal of intention and as such was to influence expectations. The instruments of monetary control were to be interest rates and fiscal policy. The latter, and in particular the PSBR control, was to be subordinated to the requirements of monetary policy and of anti-inflationary strategy, and not used as an independent means of demand management.

The table below shows clearly the implementation of the 'gradualist approach', providing, rather mechanically, for one per cent per year drop in targets or, in later years, in 'illustrative ranges'. Target ranges were raised in line with past overshooting or aggregates abandoned altogether. When £M3 overshot its target range, other aggregates were experimented with, including M0.

When, in 1984, the Chancellor introduced M0 as a target aggregate, economists were surprised, mainly because its largest constituent is currency and because of doubts in the existence of any causal connection between M0 and nominal income. The relatively low growth rate of M0 is essentially due to the fact that the holding of other assets, and especially interest-bearing deposits, has been preferred to the holding of currency. The elevation of M0 to the status of the only target in 1987 happened in spite of a conclusion by the Treasury and Civil Service Committee (TCSC, 1986, p7) that 'we have not been convinced that M0 is an efficient index of monetary conditions'.

		% Growth of M0*		
1989–90	1990–91		1991–92	1992–93
6	1 – 5		0 – 4	0 – 4

Per cent changes on previous financial year

Following target misses between 1980 and 1982, official statements on monetary policy became increasingly vague, claiming that all relevant indicators are used in the assessment of monetary conditions and not solely the targeted aggregates. In this context, more stress has been placed on exchange rates, reflecting the increasing openness of the international economy. Although the authorities have denied that there has ever been an exchange-rate target, interest rates have increasingly been adjusted in response to exchange-rate movements rather than in pursuit of money targets. Indeed, in 1986 economic policy in general began to depart from the main guidelines of MTFS. TCSC concluded that 'it is now clear that in respect of the key factors of public expenditure control, reduction in the money supply, and the use of interest rates and exchange rates there has been a substantial change in policy.'

But it is in monetary policy that confusion continued to be the greatest. While the Chancellor extolled the virtues of the well-behaved M0, the Governor of the Bank of England was, in his 1986 Mansion House speech, concerned about the 'overhanging glacier' of liquidity indicated by rising high-level aggregates.

Official explanations of the simultaneous occurrence of overshot £M3 and lower inflation rates starkly contrasted with confident pronouncements of 1980. The Chancellor, while confirming that monetary policy lay at the heart of MTFS, claimed that 'There has been this general tendency for broad money to grow very rapidly and yet, and this is the important thing, inflation has come down and come down very markedly and this is the proof of the pudding.' While controlling M0 the government has allowed private sector consumer credit to dramatically expand. Is monetarism now abandoned? The present government has managed a tight fiscal policy, but a loose monetary policy.

In spite of some very severe difficulties with monetary target practice in the UK and elsewhere, governments in the West remain faithful to the basic concept of targeting monetary quantities as a way of 'providing a stable monetary climate for economic growth'. The Bank for International Settlements – BIS (1986A P 117) – confirmed that 'Control over the money aggregates in the largest countries still seems to be the best safeguard against the revival of domestic inflation.' However, with the possibility of increased monetary integration in the European Union, member states may well be less able to pursue an independent monetary policy.

The independence of the banking sector

The commercial banking sector consists of privately owned and profit-making institutions. In return for the guarantee of 'lender of last resort' facilities from the Bank of England, they comply with the authorities' regulations and are vulnerable to 'moral persuasion' arguments. However, banking is extremely complex and adjusts its institutional arrangements rapidly to changes in market circumstances. If adjustments can be made which allow the banks to avoid the controls set by the authorities without directly violating the regulations, the banks will make those arrangements. So in 1979–80 they used the absence of exchange controls and the system of control's focus only on domestic lending to expand their lending in other ways. They did, of course, know that this strategy was against the wishes of the authorities.

The oligopolistic structure and behaviour of the commercial banking sector, the importance of the supply of bank funds for investment in the economy and the difficulty of running a successful control of money supply with a privately owned banking sector may eventually result in the nationalisation of the banks.

Money supply as a function of money demand

Many economists argue that the money stock is not determined by the money-supply strategy of the authorities but by monetary demand.

Suppose that, at a fixed interest rate, money demand exceeds the authorities' planned money supply. The banks will become short of liquidity as they try to meet the demand on their funds. As their reserve-assets ratio gets too close to or below the required minimum, they, through the discount houses, have the *right* to demand extra liquidity from the Bank of England as the 'lender of last resort'.

During 1980 the authorities operated a tight money policy and the banks became short of liquidity. The banking sector appealed to the Bank of England and, in the first eight months of 1980, all outstanding deposits held by the Bank (about £1,000m) were returned to the banks, and, in addition, about £1,500m of securities were re-discounted by the Bank. The huge expansion in the banks' lending ability enabled them to meet their customers' demands. Thus, it might be argued that money supply is perfectly elastic at any fixed interest rate. In the following diagram, money supply will expand to meet money demand at the fixed interest rate r.

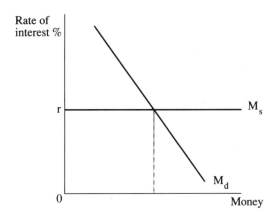

Thus, it appears that the focus of monetary policy should be on the interest rate rather than on the money supply. Only by raising the interest rate to reduce money demand can money supply be reduced.

There are a number of problems with raising interest rates. The interest elasticity of the demand for money may, under certain circumstances, be very low. In 1980-81, the problems with high interest rates appeared to be that industry needed to borrow more, not less, money in order to cover the higher interest charges in a situation of contracting demand for their output. If money demand is very interest inelastic, very high interest rates may be necessary to achieve a sufficient reduction in money demand to meet the money-supply targets. In the following diagram, the planned money supply reduction is from M_s to M_{s1}. With an elastic money demand schedule such as M_d, interest rate increases from r to r_1 are sufficient to achieve the appropriate reduction in money demand. If the money demand is interest inelastic as M_{d1} is, interest rates would have to rise to r_2 to achieve the necessary reduction in money demand.

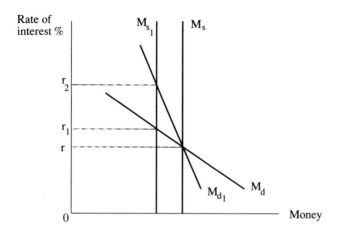

As discussed above, very high interest rates may produce very serious consequences for the output and employment level of the economy and for the standard of living. It may therefore be true that a really effective monetary policy would have unacceptably high economic costs in terms of output and employment.

Questions for review

1. What is 'inflation'?
2. How is inflation measured in the UK?
3. Why do people want to hold money?
4. What is 'liquidity preference'?
5. How can the government reduce the money supply? Why may they wish to do so?
6. How may the government control bank lending?
7. How does the rate of interest affect the demand for money?
8. Explain the Quantity Theory of Money.

National income analysis | 11

Circular flow of income   295

Determination of national income   304

Circular flow of income

Interlocking network

A modern economy such as the UK's consists of a vast interlocking network of relationships. No individual is self-sufficient. Indeed, it would be impossible to be a modern version of Robinson Crusoe unless one's tastes were exceptionally primitive and one only expected to satisfy very basic needs. Every job, every good and service produced, and the total level of saving and investment are dependent upon the activities of literally millions of other people.

The most important aspect of this interdependence is the relationship between *total production, total income and total spending for the economy as a whole*. This relationship can be described in very simple terms. In order to produce the goods and services which go to make up the total production of the economy, firms and businesses have to hire workers, acquire machinery and materials and organise them into productive units. Production, therefore, involves the payment of wages and salaries, the payment of interest and dividends, and an element of 'profit' for the entrepreneur. These various payments become *income* in the hands of the recipients and they then use this income to buy goods and services from producers. So, *production creates income, while income purchases the output of that production*. In other words, each and every person performs a dual role in the economy. In their capacity as workers or investors, they receive an income from firms and businesses and in their capacity as consumers, they spend that income by buying goods and services from firms and businesses. At the same time, firms and businesses are receiving income by selling those goods and services and this enables them to pay out wages, salaries and interest.

Four interrelated flows

There are four interrelated flows. Goods and services flow from firms to purchasers, while money flows from purchasers to firms; there is, meanwhile, a flow of services from individuals to firms, and a return flow of payment for these services from firms to individuals. In short, *production creates income, income creates spending and spending leads to production*, but there is no beginning or end. It really is a *circular flow* from one point to another and back again. No one can say whether the chicken or egg comes first – and no one can say which item in the *circular flow of income* within an economy comes first.

The four interrelated flows of national income

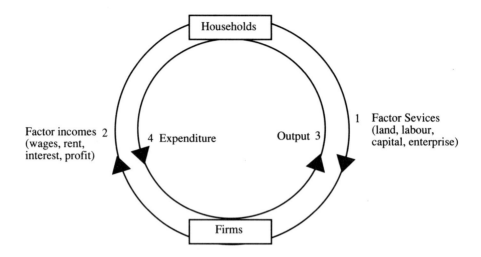

This diagram explains what happens in any economy, providing that all the income received by households is actually spent on goods and services. If this is the case, the receipts of firms will cover their costs and they will be content to continue the production process; and so the circular flow of production/income/purchases/production will carry on unimpeded ad infinitum. However, this does not automatically happen and, in simple terms, the major concern of macroeconomic theory (and the government's economic policy) is to discover why, more often than not, the flows shown in the diagram are not equal and what can be done to make them equal.

The only way in which economists can begin to study this problem is to isolate each variable. This will illustrate how each one fits into the overall economic model and so enable the economist to formulate theories (and later policies) about how the original model can be brought back into equilibrium.

Three basic assumptions

In the diagram above the circular flow of income was effectively in *equilibrium*. For this to be so, three basic assumptions must apply:

a households spend *all* their incomes on the purchase of the goods and services produced by firms;

b those firms keep their production levels exactly equal to their sales levels (ie firms do not build up any stocks of unsold goods); and

c the firms pay out to households all the money which they receive from their sales in the form of wages, salaries, interest or profit.

It follows from these assumptions that all the money which is paid out to households by firms eventually comes back to the firms when the households spend their incomes. Conversely, all the money which the firms receive from households is paid out to households in the form of wages, salaries, interest and profit.

This circular flow of income, once begun, will continue at the same level forever – whatever numerical value is put on the flows.

Withdrawals and injections

When the circular flow of income is in equilibrium – or, more precisely, in *neutral equilibrium* – the *flow of payments between firms and households continues indefinitely*, and nothing is ever taken away from the flow or added to it. However, this rarely happens. In fact, there are a number of *withdrawals* and additions (or, *injections*), ie from and into the flow.

In general terms, a *withdrawal* is *any income which is not passed on in the circular flow*. If households earn income, but do not spend it all on goods and services, then the amount which is not spent is a withdrawal from the circular flow. Similarly, if firms receive income from the sale of goods and services, but do not spend it on obtaining further factors of production and do not pass it on in profits, then they have withdrawn it from the circular flow.

In general terms, an *injection* is an *addition to the income of firms and households which does not arise from the spending of one or the other*. So, if firms borrow money from the banking system to pay households for factors of production over and above those which they would normally pay for, then an addition to the circular flow has occurred. Household income has not increased because they are buying more goods from firms, but because firms are borrowing money from outside the circular flow to hire additional factors of production.

The diagram above can be simplified and amended to show both injections to and withdrawals from the circular flow.

Injections to and withdrawals from the circular flow

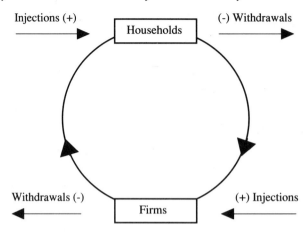

The withdrawals in the top-right hand corner represent any income received by households which they do not pass back to firms, while those in the bottom left-hand corner represent any income received by firms which they do not pass back to households. Conversely, injections create income for households – top left-hand corner – which does not arise from the spending of firms, or creates income for firms – bottom right-hand corner – which does not arise from the spending of households.

Effect of withdrawals and injections

Any *injections* into the circular flow will tend to *increase* the flow, while *withdrawals will decrease* the circular flow. The flow of income will increase or decrease according to whether the total volume of injections exceeds or falls short of the total volume of withdrawals. If more is being withdrawn than injected, the flow will decrease, whereas if more is injected than withdrawn, the flow will increase. Only if the two extra flows of withdrawals and injections are exactly equal to each other, will the overall flow of income around the circuit remain unchanged over time.

Savings

Every withdrawal and injection needs to be studied in detail and this can be done by building onto a simplified version of the diagram on page 296:

Equilibrium circular flow

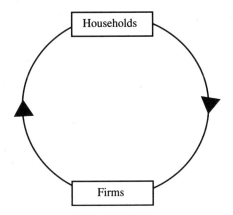

A very important withdrawal is when households do not spend all their income. To the economist, *not spending* on goods and services (or, *consumption*) is the same as *saving*. It may not be conscious saving as such, but as far as the model is concerned, it has the same effect: there is a withdrawal from the flow. In the same way as households can make a withdrawal from the flow by not spending all their income, firms can also make a withdrawal by not spending all their income on new factors of production or by not distributing all their profits.

Savings withdrawals

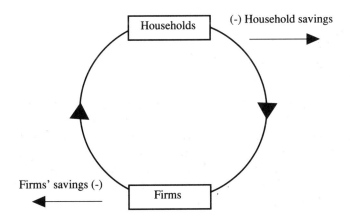

The arrows *out* of the model, together with a *minus* sign, illustrate household savings and firms' savings.

Investment

Investment can be defined as any expenditure on goods which are *not* for current consumption. The principal forms of investment are increases in the level of stocks (or inventories) and any expenditure by firms on *capital goods*, such as plant and equipment. The money for this investment is obtained from a variety of sources, such as borrowings from the banking system, from non-distributed profits (that is, past savings by firms) and from the savings of households. It is obvious, therefore, that much of the investment which is done is based on the money which has been withdrawn from the flow through household and corporate saving. However, it is important not to assume that savings necessarily equal investment in the short-term. Indeed, just because household A *saves* £100 during January, does not mean that firm B will want to invest £100 in February. So, it is preferable, so far as the model is concerned, to regard investment as an *injection* into the flow through firms. This can be shown by the addition of an *inward arrow* in the firms' sector, together with a plus sign.

Investment injections

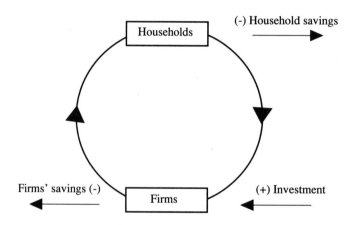

Investment expenditure represents an addition to the flow, because it creates *income* for households which does not arise directly out of the *expenditure* of households, as the goods are sold to other firms and not to households. If, for example, firms spend some of their own accumulated savings in order to build new plants, the incomes of households will rise even though there has not been an increase in the spending of households, because the income of the employees of the firms producing the new plants will rise.

Trade

The circular flow model was drawn originally on the assumption that it only related to the *national economy*, but a country cannot survive today without trading with other countries. International trade inevitably has significant effects on the flow of income within the national economy. Households may spend part of their incomes on goods produced in other countries, while firms may sell some of their goods and services to households in other countries. When households buy foreign goods, the country has to *import* them, while when firms sell goods abroad the country has to *export* them. *Imports* naturally constitute a *withdrawal* from the flow, because the money spent on them leaves the national economy and enters the flow of the countries where the imports come from. As a result, there will be less money passing to national firms and so, ultimately, they will hire fewer factors of production causing the flow in this country to decrease.

On the other hand, when goods or services are exported abroad, there will be an injection into the flow. Money from foreign countries is being paid to firms in this country and so the income of firms (and households) will increase. Obviously, there will be a *net* figure from these two items – if exports exceed imports, then there will be a net injection into the flow – but it is more convenient to add the *gross* figures to the diagram:

Import withdrawals and export injections

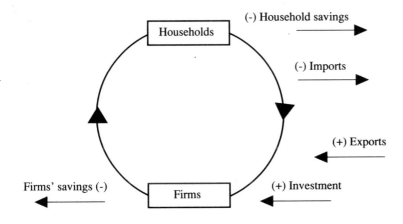

Taxes

The impact of government activity on the circular flow model is very significant. A government has certain tasks to perform such as defending the country, providing roads and health services, etc. In order to provide such services, it has to raise money to pay for the labour, the buildings and so on. It does this through a complicated system of taxation. Taxes *withdraw* money from the flow in just the same way as savings and imports do – the money involved does not pass round the model to firms in the normal way. If the government taxes firms, then part of the money received by firms is not available to be passed on to households. Similarly, if the government taxes households – either directly through taxes on their incomes or indirectly through taxes on the goods which they buy – then the money is not passed back to firms. Some of the money which is withdrawn may find its way back into the flow through the government's own expenditure, but it is preferable to regard *all* taxes as a withdrawal.

Government expenditure

Government expenditure is rather more complicated than the other injections and it must be divided into three distinct sub-headings. There are those expenditures related to the business-type enterprises, and these are really no different from the productive role of ordinary firms. The government owns and runs some industries within the economy – known as *nationalised industries* – and they purchase factors of production from households in the normal way and then sell their production to households. Most models of the circular flow of income therefore include this part of government activity in the firm sector.

The second sub-heading of government activity concerns all the goods and services which the government provides free of charge. In the UK this includes education, health, roads, defence and so on. All these activities use up various factors of production and these have to be hired by the government. The provision of these 'free services' provides a massive injection of income into both the household and the firms' sectors of the model, because doctors, nurses, teachers and army personnel are all individuals who receive wages and salaries for their services, while firms sell hospital beds, school desks and armoured cars to the government, receiving income in return. So, the government is responsible through its own expenditure for two injections into our model.

Thirdly, a significant proportion of government expenditure is not concerned with paying money out in return for either goods or factors of production. It is simply transferring money from one person to another through a complicated system of national insurance and welfare payments. For instance, when a person is unemployed he is entitled to certain benefits from the State. Similarly, handicapped or poor people receive State benefits of one kind or another, as do elderly retired people. Such payments are collectively known as *transfer payments* because they transfer money from one section of the community to another. As these expenditures do not directly increase the total output of the economy, they are usually excluded from the model.

The complete model

Government withdrawals and injections (complete model)

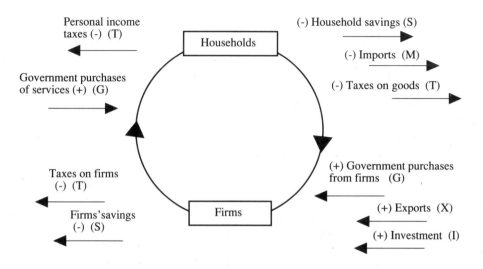

The relevant government withdrawals under three separate arrows – personal income taxes, taxes on firms and indirect taxes on the sale of goods and services – have now been added and there are two injections to cover government expenditure – the purchase of factors of production from households and the purchase of goods and services from firms. Thus withdrawals W = S + T + M, and injections J = X + G + I. An economy is in equilibrium when J = W although this does not necessarily mean full employment equilibrium.

Relationship between withdrawals and injections

Withdrawals and injections tend to come in pairs – savings and investment, imports and exports, taxes and government expenditure. If each withdrawal equalled each injection there would be very little to worry about. The circular flow of income would proceed uninterrupted forever and forever. There would be no decrease in national income and no increase and no wild fluctuations in economic activity. In fact, the economist would be out of a job! Unfortunately, this is not the case. There are continual ups and downs in economic activity – or, as the economist calls them, *booms* and *slumps*. For a few years, the general level of economic activity rises, everyone's income rises and everyone is very happy and prosperous, but then, suddenly, the situation reverses itself. Economic activity declines, incomes fall and everyone becomes depressed and poorer. The basic reasons for the decline might be found in the increase in numerical value of one or other of the withdrawals from the flow and it might be possible to follow the decline right through the model and find the turning point where a fresh injection caused the flow to increase once more. However, such an exercise would not help to keep the model in equilibrium in either the short or the long term. It is much more complicated than that. Each and every withdrawal and injection is totally independent of any other one, and even if one was controlled, or maybe even two, there are quite a few others which could be fluctuating wildly.

The problems of macro economics

The problems facing both the economist and the politician when they try to regulate the national economy, should now be obvious. Why does the overall flow of output and income fluctuate so much, sometimes falling well below the country's productive capacity, and sometimes racing ahead so fast that it strains against the limits of all the available resources in the country? What are the factors and determinants of a consistent and steady growth in productive capacity and what are the social and economic costs of such growth? Can they be avoided without detracting from the growth itself? These are the problems of macroeconomics, but before examining these it is necessary to understand how the national income (or national product) is made up and calculated as this will provide an effective measure of how the national economy is performing and what, if any, changes in economic policy might help to alleviate its problem.

Determination of national income

The background

Although adequate and reliable measures of national income and output are basic to any study of macroeconomics, it was not until the 1930s that any such measures were actually produced. This was partly because comprehensive and reliable statistics were a rare commodity, but the main reason was to be found in economists themselves. They were just not very interested. Up until the 1930s, most economists were concerned with the operation of the price mechanism and the allocation of resources, (ie they were interested in *microeconomics*). However, the 1930s forced economists to consider the overall level of economic activity as a priority. Throughout America and Europe there was mass unemployment and a very low level of economic and industrial activity. People were clamouring for solutions, and so economists abandoned their theoretical models of microeconomics and turned to the problems confronting the majority of countries in the Western World. However, in order to pursue such an analysis they needed data and statistics about the level of national income and output.

GNP and GNI

National income is now measured annually and the detailed figures are published by the Central Statistical Office in a book entitled *National Income and Expenditure*, which is usually referred to as the *Blue Book*.

The most comprehensive measure of the national output is called the *gross national product*. This is usually abbreviated to *GNP* and is represented by the *right-hand side of the loop* in the diagrams above. In short, GNP is the *value of all goods and services produced annually in a nation*. The other half of the circular flow diagram shows the flow of *gross national income* (or *GNI*) which is the *sum of all the incomes earned in the production of GNP, including wages, salaries, rent, interest and profit*. GNI *always equals* GNP because the left-hand loop of the original circular flow model equals the right-hand loop.

Calculation of GNP

It is all very well stating that GNP equals GNI *because* the diagram shows this, but that is only a theoretical model. It is necessary to see how to calculate each of these figures in the real world. First, it must be recognised that, although they each give the same answer when they are calculated, they are conceptually different to the statistician because they approach the problem from different ends. GNP is concerned with *output* while GNI is concerned with *income*, or *earnings*. GNP is calculated by adding together the value of the products of all the industrial, commercial and agricultural outputs in the country (ie all the *final* output values within the economy). The word 'final' is of the utmost importance.

Product	Sales		Value Added
Seed and fertiliser	5 pence		5 pence
Farmer	9 pence		4 pence
Milling industry	12 pence		3 pence
Baker	<u>15 pence</u>		<u>3 pence</u>
	41 pence	Sale price	15 pence

The table illustrates it is important only to add up *final* output when calculating GNP. The final value of bread in the shops is 15p a loaf, but in the process of getting the bread into the shop many other products were sold to the various people involved in the production of the bread. The economy has, as such, only produced 15p worth of bread *in total*, not 41p. So GNP only includes *final output values* for each production process. However, it should not be assumed that the entire output of, say, the seed and fertiliser industry is included in the output of other industries. If an individual buys some seed or fertiliser for use in their garden, then *that* value is included in GNP statistics because it is, in fact, a *final output*.

When the final output-value figures for all the production in the country are added together a figure for *Gross Domestic Product* (or *GDP*) is achieved. This indicates the value of what the country is apparently producing, but as was noted in the circular flow model, the country often has to import raw materials from abroad as well as exporting some finished goods to other countries. In order to get a truer picture of the real output of the country these transactions must be taken into account. The *net* balance from *all* the country's overseas transactions must either be added to or subtracted from this figure to give a reasonably accurate figure for the country's *gross national product*. (There should also be a minor adjustment for the level of stocks and their value, but this aspect can be ignored for the time being.) As the calculation implies, this method of arriving at GNP is usually referred to as the *output method*.

Calculation of GNI

The other method of arriving at GNP totals through the calculation of GNI is naturally called the '*income method*'. Every time a good or service is produced, someone somewhere will receive an income as a result, whether it be in the form of wages, interest or profit. If all the personal incomes received during the year are added together, a reasonable approximation to GDP should be obtained, although an adjustment is necessary for the net balance of foreign transactions in order to arrive at GNP as such. The main sources of income which have to be added together are income from employment or self-employment, the trading profits of companies and public corporations and rent. This figure will be approximately the same as the figure reached through the output method, allowing for statistical and other errors. The *incomes* which are generated in producing the loaf of bread above will automatically equal the *value* of the bread. This must be so even if the costs of producing the bread rose above the market value of 15p, because losses (ie *negative* profits) are the balancing item.

'At factor cost'

This also illustrates another important aspect of the GNP (and GNI) figures as they are calculated by either the income or output method. They are based on the costs of factors of production. In other words, they represent the *true value* of the country's output and income. This is why in publications such as the Blue Book, figures are usually referred to as GNP '*at factor cost*'.

Expenditure method

There is, however, another method of arriving at GNP, but it usually gives a slightly different result because it calculates GNP *at market prices*. It is known as the *expenditure method*. Incomes are earned because money has been spent on goods and services which are produced by the income receivers. It is possible, therefore, to add together all the expenditure made by consumers throughout the year as well as the net expenditure of the government to arrive at the total value of goods and services produced during the year. However, any capital expenditure made by firms during the year must also be included, so the gross level of fixed capital formation during the year and the value of the physical increase (or decrease) in both stocks and work-in-progress must be added to this figure. This last item allows for the market value of goods which have been produced but not sold.

National income analysis

The expenditure method can, however, give a very different answer to the other two methods, because indirect taxes and subsidies mean that goods and services are sold at different prices compared to their *true factor cost*. If a good is taxed before it is sold, then the cost to the consumer is *greater* than its value to the economy, while if a good receives a subsidy, then its cost to the consumer is *less* than its cost to the economy. So, in order to change *GNP at market prices* into *GNP at factor cost* the value of indirect taxes has to be subtracted and the value of subsidies added.

'Real' changes in GNP

If any meaningful policy decisions regarding the management of the country's economy are to be made the *real* change in GNP from year to year must be calculated.

If the general level of prices is rising quite rapidly as a result of inflation, the GNP statistics can be distorted considerably from one year to the next, because the *money value* of GNP might rise significantly while the actual level of *real output* might not change very much. For instance, one year the economy might produce 500,000 washing machines at a cost of £100 each leading to a figure in the GNP statistics of £50 million. The next year might see a 10 per cent inflation rate and so the same machine would cost £110 in year 2. Now, if the same number of washing machines were produced in year 2 the new figure in the GNP statistics would be £55 million. At first glance, the uninitiated would immediately assume that GNP in year 2 had increased by 10 per cent – from £50 million to £55 million – but in fact, GNP will not have changed. The country is still only producing 500,000 washing machines. Clearly, an allowance has to be made for this in GNP calculations, so that any increase reflects only the *rise in output* and *not the rise in prices*. However, sometimes there can be a *real* rise in price when the costs of production alter due to changes in supply or demand, so it is important not to confuse a *real* change in price, with a *money* change.

Deflated GNP

The way in which adjustments are made for inflationary changes in prices is conceptually very simple, although it is not so easy to put into practice. Each year the value of each kind of output is expressed in terms of the prices which prevailed in a given base year. An index of 100 is usually given to the base year. Each year after the base year, GNP is effectively measured in terms of the currency (or money) value prevailing at that time. This ensures that only changes in *real* output cause the index to change. (In economist's language, GNP is measured in terms of *constant pounds sterling* year after year after year. For this reason, in every year after the base year, a constant pounds sterling GNP figure is often referred to as 'Deflated GNP' – the monetary value is *deflated* to counter-balance the rate of *inflation*.) Despite the statistical difficulties in deflating GNP from year to year, the figures which are now produced do provide a first approximation to changes in *real output*.

Items excluded from GNP statistics

In the output method of calculating GNP there is a difficulty in deciding the correct treatment for any 'personal' activities such as growing one's own vegetables in the garden or building one's own garden shed. These are not included in GNP figures although any goods which are bought in the process of doing these activities, such as fertilisers and seeds or wood and nails, would automatically be included. In short, only items which are *sold in the market place* are included in GNP – personal hobbies or whatever are not included. However, this can lead to some anomalies so far as final GNP statistics are concerned. For example, the person who builds his own garden shed will not enter the statistics – his 'labour' is free and so will not be included. (The materials he uses, on the other hand, will be included because he has to buy them *in the market place*.) Conversely, if the person is not able to build his own shed either through lack of time or ability, and instead hires a builder to do the job, then the cost of building the shed *does* enter into the GNP statistics because it now takes on an *economic* nature. In this instance, not only the materials are included as before, but the labour and profit elements are also included. Similarly, a domestic help who cleans the house is included in GNP statistics whereas the 'unpaid' housewife who probably works harder than a paid help is not included. In fact, some research indicated that the work of a normal housewife was 'worth' at least £150 a week, and yet that £150 never appears as part of GNP. (Many years ago, one eminent economist pointed out cynically that if a man married his housekeeper he would end up reducing national income!!)

The 'quality of life'

Another problem with the statistics produced for GNP purposes is that they are not a useful guide to the *quality* of life. The statistics measure changes in the level of *real* output with the implication that if the level of GNP rises the country as a whole is better off. Some economists – and many more individuals – are beginning to doubt this. A modern industrial society such as the UK may experience a rising level of GNP as output increases, but GNP statistics are not designed to measure the costs which are incurred as a result. Many industrial processes cause considerable damage to the environment: air pollution, river pollution, health damage and so on are all what one economist called the *costs of economic growth*. Indeed, it is argued in some quarters that such 'costs' should be subtracted from GNP figures in an attempt to measure the real 'quality' of life, and the real growth in 'economic welfare' in its broadest possible sense.

Net national product

Net national product is derived directly from the *output method* of calculating GNP and is a measure of the *net value of total output*. Every year a certain proportion of the *capital stock* of the country is used up in the production process – machines and equipment wear out over a period of time, or, in an accountant's language, *depreciate*. So, every year the country has used up, and should replace, that part of its capital stock which has 'worn out' if it intends to at least maintain its output levels. As a result, it is useful to obtain a *net* measure of the total output which is available for current consumption, government purchases and additions to the capital stock. To obtain this figure, an amount for capital depreciation should be deducted from the GNP figure. Capital depreciation is sometimes referred to as '*capital consumption*'. So, in short, the *net national product* or, NNP is the gross national product *minus* capital consumption.

Personal income

Another very common figure in economic publications is that for personal income. This is derived from the income method of calculating GNP and is the *total income which is received by households from all sources before any personal taxes are paid*. So, any retained company profits and any taxes which companies pay on their total profits are deducted. (Particular note should be taken of the fact that total company profits after tax are not deducted because those profits which are distributed become the income of households.)

After these deductions have been made a further adjustment has to be made in respect of any transfer payments. Naturally, they *increase* personal incomes in some cases, while *decreasing* it in others. A proportion of the total revenue needed for these payments is met through direct taxation on individuals, but a significant proportion is raised through the '*national insurance system*'. Each employed person in the UK is required to pay a given percentage of his wages into the national insurance fund every week or month and this money is then used for paying the various benefits. As transfer payments do not represent an addition to total output, they are not included in the original calculations for GNI, so in order to calculate *personal income* it is necessary to add a balancing figure to the original GNI figure. This balancing figure is found by first deducting the total contributions made by individuals to the national insurance system and then adding back the amount received in benefits of one kind or another. This final figure gives an accurate guide to personal income: personal income is gross national income *minus* retained company profits *minus* company taxation on gross profits *plus* a balancing item for transfer payments. (This balancing item could, of course, be negative in certain circumstances.)

Disposable personal income

An extension of the concept of personal income which is very important in relation to consumption (which will be examined later) is *disposable personal income*. This is the *income which households have available to spend,* or, if they wish, *to save*, so it is that income which households have available after meeting all their *personal taxes*.

Illustrative tables

Finally, it will be useful to illustrate the three basic methods of calculating GNP (or, GNI) – the *output method*, the *income method* and the *expenditure method*. On the following pages a typical set of GNP statistics has been reproduced and these should be studied in connection with the text in this section. There are one or two additional items which have not been covered. In both the output and the income methods there is a figure for 'residual error'. This figure represents an allowance for errors and omissions in the original statistics as many returns are incorrectly completed and so on. In the output method table, there is an item called 'ownership of dwellings'. This figure not only includes the rent paid by tenants to their landlords, but also an estimate of the rental value of houses which are owned by their occupiers. In effect, the owner-occupier is treated as if he were a landlord renting the property to himself. (This estimate is essential otherwise the figures would be distorted. In the UK today, over 68 per cent of the population live in 'owner-occupied' houses and it would be inconsistent if the statistics included only those people who actually pay rent.) Finally, in each table there is a figure for capital consumption depreciation during the year. Each method provides the final figure for the country's national income.

The three methods of calculating GNP using typical (not actual) figures, are as follows:

Output Method	£s millions
Agriculture, forestry & fishing	3,500
Mining & quarrying	3,000
Manufacturing	29,000
Construction	3,200
Gas, electricity & water	3,000
Transport & communication	5,500
Distributive trades	6,700
Insurance, banking & finance	3,000
Ownership of dwellings	4,500
Public administration & defence	6,000
Public health and educational services	5,500
Other services	4,000
	76,900
Less: Stock appreciation -	-3,000
Residual error	-200
GDP at factor cost	73,700
Net property income from abroad	+1,000
GNP at factor cost	74,700
Less: Capital consumption (depreciation)	-6,200
NATIONAL INCOME	68,500

Income Method	*£s millions*
Income from employment	63,000
Income from self-employment	4,500
Gross trading profits of companies	4,000
Gross trading surpluses of public corporations	1,000
Gross profits of other public enterprises	400
Rent	+4,000
Total domestic income (before providing for depreciation and stock appreciation)	76,900
Less: Stock appreciation	-3,000
Residual error	-200
GDP at factor cost	73,700
Net property income from abroad	+1,000
GNP at factor cost	74,700
Less: Capital consumption (depreciation)	-6,200
NATIONAL INCOME	68,500

The Expenditure Method:	*£s millions*
Consumers' expenditure 66,000	
Public current expenditure on goods and services	17,000
Gross domestic fixed capital formation	10,000
Value of physical increase in stocks and work-in-progress	+700
Total domestic expenditure at market prices	93,700
Exports & property income from abroad	+26,000
Subsidies	+2,000
Less: Imports and property income paid abroad	-27,000
Taxes on expenditure (ie VAT)	-20,000
GNP at factor cost	74,700
Less: Capital consumption (depreciation)	-6,200
NATIONAL INCOME	68,500

Thus the three methods of calculating National Income produce identical results.
National Income = National Expenditure = National Output

Questions for review

1 Explain the circular flow of income model.

2 What are 'withdrawals'? Give some examples.

3 What are 'injections'? Give some examples.

4 Explain the difference between savings and investment.

5 What is the difference between GNP and GDP?

6 What are the three methods used to calculate GDP? What difficulties are experienced in trying to do this?

7 Explain:

    a   factor cost;

    b   market prices.

8 How well do national income statistics reflect 'standard of living'?

The macroeconomic model | 12

The consumption function 315

The model 321

Keynesian reasoning 327

The multiplier 328

The accelerator 331

Inflationary and deflationary gaps 333

The consumption function

Actual versus potential output

The previous chapter was primarily concerned with the definition and measurement of *actual* income and output through the use of GNP statistics. However, just as important – if not more so – for the management of the economy, is the possible, or *potential*, level of GNP. *Potential output* is the output which *could* be produced if all the available factors of production within an economy were fully utilised. In fact, the general level of prosperity in a country can only really be judged by comparing *actual* GNP with *potential* GNP. If the users of the final output do not spend enough to purchase all the output of a fully employed economy, then *actual* output will decline below *potential* output.

Aggregate demand

It will be remembered from the study of microeconomics how the word 'demand' meant *effective demand*, or demand that is backed by the ability to pay. So far as the economy as a whole is concerned, the sum total of everyone's effective demand – including individuals, firms and the government – is referred to as the 'aggregate demand'. Consequently, the amount of output which all firms taken together can sell depends on the level of aggregate demand within the economy. If the aggregate demand for goods and services (which includes consumption, investment and government purchases) is not sufficient to absorb all the goods which are being produced, then firms will find their level of stocks rising rapidly. This will eventually lead them to reducing their output levels to a point which is roughly in line with the prevailing level of aggregate demand. In short, if aggregate demand is *less* than *potential* GNP, then *actual* GNP will also be less than potential GNP.

In the depths of the depression in the United States and Europe during the early 1930s, the level of productive capacity, or potential GNP, was almost the same as it had been in the more prosperous 1920s. The disastrous collapse in the level of production was not the result of a reduction in economic potential, but rather the result of a dramatic fall in the level of aggregate demand. The question for economists is why such situations arise. Why does the level of aggregate demand fluctuate so widely from year to year?

Later in the chapter a stylised model of the fluctuations in the economic fortunes of a country will be examined, but first it is necessary to examine why actual GNP can be so different from potential GNP. The problem for the economy is very simple, yet often missed by students who have learned the basic truth of GNP equalling GNI. The difficulty is that *aggregate demand does not always and inevitably equal gross national income. Aggregate demand can,* and does, *fluctuate in relation to income.* Consequently, the market for total output and the amount that firms are willing to produce can often be either more or less than potential output.

To discover why and how this can happen, the relationship between income and aggregate demand must be studied, or, more precisely, the relationship between aggregate demand and GNI, as well as how, in turn, this relationship determines the actual level of GNP.

Influences on consumption

First, it is necessary to study the relationship between consumption and income. In economic jargon, consumption is a *function* of income, because its level depends on income. The actual relation of consumption to income is called the *consumption function*. The consumption function is an aggregate phenomenon and can be shown graphically; this will illustrate the important connections between it and the overall national income.

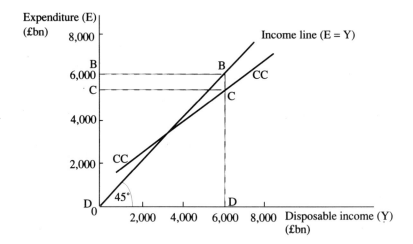

The line marked CC on the diagram represents the general relationship between consumption and income shown in the first two columns of the table on page 319.

The other line on the graph (labelled the *Income line*) enables the graph to be interpreted more easily. The line is drawn at an angle of 45° from the origin and, because the scales on each axis are identical, any point on the line must have an equal value on each axis. So, the Income Line represents a consumption function in which all the nation's disposable income is spent on consumption. At every level of income the nation has an average propensity to consume of 1. For instance, at point B on the graph the nation's income is £6,000bn while its consumption is also £6,000bn. The comparative point on the CC line to point B on the Income Line indicates that the distance CD represents the nation's actual consumption in accordance with the table (ie £5,650bn) while the distance BC represents the amount of the nation's income which is not spent – or rather, the amount that it saves (ie £350bn). In short, *the distance from the CC line to the horizontal axis measures the nation's level of consumption*, while *the distance from the CC line to the Income Line measures the nation's level of saving*. (When the CC line is *above* the Income Line the nation is consuming *more* than its disposable income, so it is dis-saving, or, to put it another way, its saving is *negative*. So, whenever the measurement between the CC line is a *downward* one this indicates dis-saving.) It is also possible to examine consumption and income relationships for an individual family as well as an entire nation. The economist just cannot take either an individual family or a country and *increase its income at will* to see how much it *actually* spends on consumption and how much it *actually* saves. He can only make intuitive guesses from the statistics which are available for different income bands, and assume that when an individual family experiences an income rise from, say, £4,000 to £5,000, its average propensity to consume (APC) and average propensity to save (APS) will change in the way indicated.

The factors which determine the relationship are naturally complex and, indeed, they vary from family to family, but there are a number of general guidelines. First and foremost, families probably regulate their expenditure (or, their consumption) in accordance with their lifestyle and their expected future income. In fact, certain assumptions regarding future income and expenditure are usually made fairly early on in life. These 'planned expenditures' will only be changed in response to unexpected income increases or reductions. Second, people most certainly base some of their consumption decisions on what they observe other people doing – or, in everyday language, people want to 'keep up with their next-door neighbours', or 'keep up with the Joneses'. Another relatively important factor in the modern world is the cost and the availability of credit. However, the really decisive factor is the level of *disposable income* available to the family, although three important points need to be made about disposable income. First, when its level rises, consumption may only rise slowly, as it may take time for the family to 'adjust' to the new income level. This concept was developed by Friedman with his 'permanent income' hypothesis. It was stated that people had both a short- and a long-run consumption function. They will only readjust consumption patterns to a change in income when they are sure a change in income is permanent. In the following diagram, C_s is the short-run consumption function and C_L the long-run one.

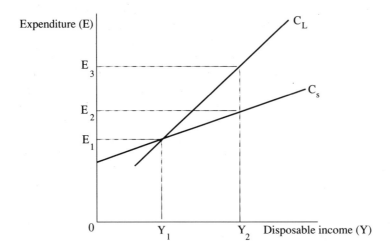

If an individual's income rises from Y_1 to Y_2 consumption will initially rise to E_2 but once the new income level has become 'permanent' consumption will rise to E_3 on the long-run consumption function (C_L).

Second, when disposable income rises, the higher income may be used initially for reducing the family's level of debt, and only when this has been done will a family contemplate increasing its consumption levels substantially. The third important point affects a *decline* in a disposable income. Consumption levels tend to be rather 'sticky downwards'. At first, people do not reduce their consumption by very much despite a fall in income; they try to maintain their consumption at the highest level possible, in the hope that the old income level will be regained.

One final point of interest. Many surveys have been undertaken over the years on consumption patterns at different levels of income, and one fact has stood out every time. When a family's income rises significantly in a short space of time, its consumption pattern is very different at the new level of income to the consumption pattern of families who have always had a high income. For instance, if income suddenly rises from, say, £3,000 a year to £50,000 a year, a person would probably spend, rather than save, much more of that £50,000 in the first few years than would a person who had been earning £50,000 regularly. However, this interesting point should not detract from the hypothesis that most people, and the community at large, have a fairly stable relationship over time between *consumption* and *saving*.

The propensity to consume

The consumption function as such describes what the famous economist Keynes called the *propensity to consume*. Keynes argued that a given increase in a family's disposable income would eventually lead to an increase in the family's level of consumption, but that – and this is the important point – the increase in consumption would not be the same as the *actual* money increase. When the family receives extra income it can either spend it or save it. The extent to which extra income is spent will depend on the family's propensity to consume. This is found by constructing a detailed table of how much a family would spend or save at various levels of income; but first one very important identity must be established. A family can only *spend* or *save* disposable income. So, a family's consumption added to its saving must equal its total disposable income. This still holds true if the family *spends* more than its disposable income – saving just becomes a *negative* figure.

The following table shows a family's disposable income and its level of consumption and saving at each income. However, for the economist, it is the fourth, fifth, sixth and seventh columns which are important.

Income, consumption and saving

Disposable income £s	Consumption expenditure £s	Saving £s	Average propensity to consume (APC)	Average propensity to save (APS)	Marginal propensity to consume (MPC)	Marginal propensity to save (MPS)
2,000	2,150	(-) 150	1.08	(-) 0.08		
3,000	3,100	(-) 100	1.03	(-) 0.03	0.95	0.05
4,000	4,000	0	1.00	0.00	0.90	0.10
5,000	4,850	150	0.97	0.03	0.85	0.15
6,000	5,650	350	0.94	0.06	0.80	0.20
7,000	6,380	620	0.91	0.09	0.73	0.27
8,000	7,050	950	0.88	0.12	0.67	0.33

From the above data the consumption function would be non-linear (curved) because the MPC is falling, and this is shown in the following diagram. A non-linear function will also produce a rising MPS.

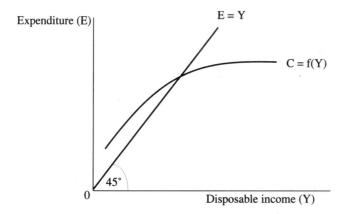

Average propensity to consume and save (APC/APS)

The fourth column – headed *average propensity to consume*, or *APC* – measures the *proportion of the family's income which is spent on consumption*. This is illustrated most clearly in the third *line* of the table, where all the family's disposable income is spent on consumption and so its APC (or average propensity to consume) is exactly 1. In the first two lines, where the family spends more on consumption than it receives, APC is *greater than 1*, but as the proportionate amount spent on consumption falls at higher levels of income APC is *less than 1*.

The converse of APC is naturally the family's *average propensity to save*, or APS and this is detailed in column five in the table. Just as APC measures the proportionate amount of income spent on *consumption*, APS (or average propensity to save) measures the proportionate amount of income *saved*. As it is based on the figures in the third column, it must inevitably be equal to the difference between the family's APC and 1. Just as the family's consumption added to the family's saving equals the family's disposable income, so its APC added to its APS must equal 1.

Marginal propensities to consume and save (MPC/MPS)

The sixth and seventh columns might seem unconnected with the rest of the figures in the table, but, as in microeconomic theory, 'marginal' always refers to the 'additional part' of whatever is being considered. So, the *marginal propensity to consume*, or MPC, which is detailed in the sixth column, is simply the *ratio of the change in consumption to the change in income*. Put another way, MPC refers to that part of any increase in income which is spent on consumption. So, when income increases from £2,000 to £3,000 the family spends .95 of the additional £1,000 (or, £950) on consumption.

The *marginal propensity to save* is the twin of the marginal propensity to consume. It indicates the *ratio of the change in saving to the change in income* and must, by definition, be *equal to 1 minus the marginal propensity to consume* (if there is a closed economy with no government).

Marginal propensities to tax and import (MPT and MPM)

If a government and international trade are introduced then increases in income can result in changes to taxation and imports. If a family's income increases by £1,000 and they spend £100 of the increase on imports and pay £200 in tax to the government, then the marginal propensity to import is 0.1 and the marginal propensity to tax is 0.2.

Thus the MPC + MPS + MPT + MPM = 1, and the MPS + MPT + MPM = the marginal propensity to withdraw (MPW).

The model

Introduction

The central problem for the economist is to determine the various relationships between production, income and spending. He has to consider not only the relationships within the personal sector of the economy; but also those within the business and government sectors. However, it will be easier to study the whole macroeconomic model if it is built up in parts.

Households

First, it will be assumed that there is only one variable 'sector' in the economy – households – so all decisions on consumption and saving are made by them and there is no business saving and no government purchases. (These will be added later.) Based on this simplifying assumption, all of the gross national income (GNI) will go into disposable income. The first step is to find the point at which the economy is in equilibrium (ie that point at which the circular flow of income just keeps on replenishing itself where net injections equals net withdrawals).

The consumption function for the country would probably be similar to this:

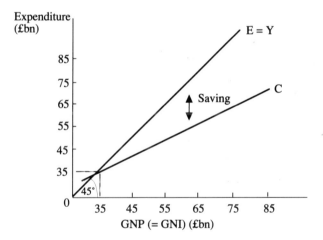

There is an element of *dis-saving* among the population until gross national income reaches approximately £35,000 million, whereas once GNI rises above that there is a greater and greater amount of saving. This is represented by the 'wedge-shape' between the income line and the C line.

Add investment

If the firms in the economy then decide to invest a total amount during the year of £8,000 million, and also that this amount will be invested regardless of the size of GNP, then this will result in a net injection of £8,000 million to the total level of consumption. This can be shown by adding a second line to the diagram to show a steady rate of investment whatever the level of GNP:

Steady rate of investment

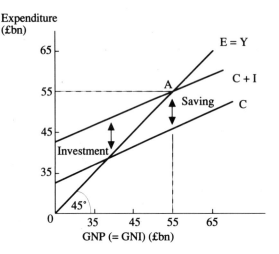

Point A is the equilibrium position. The total level of spending in the economy is now shown by the C + I line. In fact, using the previous terminology, this line represents the level of aggregate demand in the economy. The equilibrium point will now be where the level of aggregate demand just matches the level of GNP, or point A in the diagram, where GNI is approximately £55,000 million. At this point the level of saving by households exactly equals the required level of investment by firms – £10,000 million.

Excess demand or excess saving

The importance of the equilibrium position is best illustrated by describing what happens when the level of investment by firms is not matched by the level of household saving. For instance, if the level of GNP equalled £65,000 million rather than £55,000 million, then at that level of GNP, aggregate demand would only equal £61,000 million and there would be an excess of saving over investment of some £4,000 million:

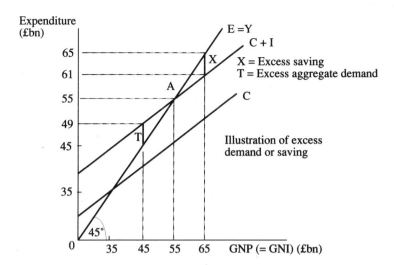

This diagram also shows the situation where GNP is only £45,000 million. In this case, aggregate demand would exceed GNP by £4,000 million and so there would be a shortage of funds for investment as a result. So, if at some particular level of GNP and GNI, saving tends to exceed investment, then the total level of spending (or aggregate demand) is too low to sustain that level of GNP and so *GNP will fall*. Conversely, if investment tends to exceed savings, then aggregate demand is too high for that particular level and so *GNP will rise*.

Two very important points arise from this analysis. When the circular flow of income is in equilibrium:

a aggregate demand always equals GNP; and

b savings always equal investment.

This can be put in terms of withdrawals and injections. In order for a particular level of GNP and GNI to be the equilibrium level, that part of GNI which is not spent on consumption (ie withdrawn) must be spent on something else, usually investment (ie injected).

Full employment GNP

However, the equilibrium level of GNP is not necessarily the same as the potential level of GNP. The decision to save is in the hands of households, while the decision to invest is in the hands of firms. It would be purely coincidental if these decisions happened to produce exact equality of saving and investment at the *full employment level of GNP*. This important qualification (to be developed later) shows how difficult it is to maintain the economy at the desired level of full employment. In a nutshell, it involves equating the saving by households in a *fully employed* economy with the investment decisions of firms operating in a *fully employed* economy.

Add firms' saving

Firms also *save* money, thus withdrawing it from the circular flow of income, and this now needs to be added to the model. As GNP or GNI increases, the profits of firms also tend to rise in normal circumstances by a fairly predictable amount. (Profits are, after all, closely related to the overall level of business activity and tend to be a constant percentage of turnover.) Some of the profits which firms make is paid to the owners (or shareholders), while the rest is retained in the business for its own use. So, for each level of GNI there must exist a corresponding level of saving by firms. At the same time, that part of the profits made by firms which flows into households' disposable income will be divided between extra consumption and extra saving depending on the consumption function.

An extra line can therefore be added to the consumption function to show this increase in household disposable income:

Effect of saving by firms

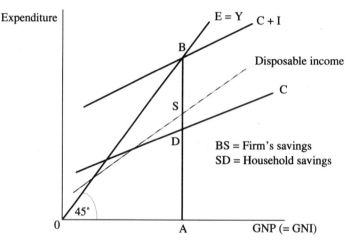

(For convenience, the numerical scales have now been omitted as it is the *principle* that matters.) The dotted line shows how disposable income rises as GNP rises, but the wedge-shaped gap between this line and the Income line shows how saving by firms rises by a considerably greater amount as GNP rises. It is also apparent that once GNP has risen above a relatively low level, all the increase in disposable income is saved by households as shown by the wedge shape between the original consumption function and the new dotted line.

The only major difference between this model and the previous one is that total saving now includes both the saving of households and the saving of firms. As there is more saving, a smaller part of GNI is spent on consumption, and so the overall level of investment must rise in order to match the increased saving if aggregate demand is to be equated with GNP. However, from the diagram, the following facts can be seen. At a level of GNP equal to OA (or AB) the level of saving by firms would be BS, while the level of disposable income for households would be SA, out of which AD would be consumed. In order to maintain the circular flow in equilibrium the level of investment must be equal to the level of saving by both firms and households – namely, BD.

Add government activity and trade

The model can be completed with the addition of the activities of the government. The economist Keynes believed that the government is in a crucial and vital position in the model and can help it to achieve equilibrium or cause it to get out of equilibrium.

It will be remembered that the government can withdraw money from the circular flow of income through the taxation system, but it can also inject money into it through its own purchases of goods and services. Tax revenues rise and fall as GNP varies, because they are based on the level of activity in the economy. This applies both to direct personal taxes and to those taxes which are levied on sales, and so on. So, as GNP increases, part of the additional GNI flows into the savings of firms, *part into government tax revenues,* and the rest into household disposable incomes. When taxes are added to the model, disposable income (and so, consumption) changes less when GNP changes than would be the case without any government taxes. Part of any rise in GNI is now taken out of the circular flow by increased taxes, and this inevitably leads to a smaller increase in disposable income (and, of course, consumption).

However, governments also spend money. Although taxes tend to lower the overall level of aggregate demand, government purchases of goods and services tend to increase it. So, this third component of aggregate demand must be added to the diagram:

Full macroeconomic model in equilibrium

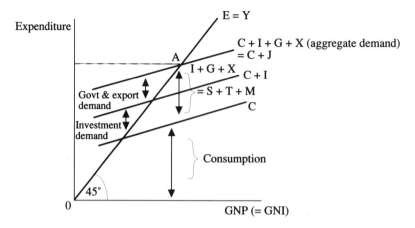

Point A is the equilibrium point.

Conclusions

The clear conclusion of the above completed model is that aggregate demand will equal total output, or GNP, when that part of income which is not spent – saving by firms and households as well as government taxes, excluding those related to transfer payments – is matched by the total level of investment and government purchases. This can be put here concisely, as indicated on the diagram itself. Aggregate demand will equal GNP when total saving plus taxes is equalled by investment plus government spending.

The national income equation

A very important economic question is related to the observation in the 'conclusion' above. If consumption plus investment plus government spending provides us with a final figure for aggregate demand within the economy (ignoring any complicating effects from trading with other countries), and if, when the circular flow of income is in equilibrium, aggregate demand equals GNP and GNI, then from these two basic facts it can be seen that, when the economy is in equilibrium (although not necessarily full-employment equilibrium) the *level of aggregate demand* will be the *same as the level of national income*. In other words:

National Income = Consumption plus Investment plus Government Purchases plus Exports minus Imports

$Y = C + I + G + (X - M)$

Some very important conclusions can be drawn from this equation. If there is a transfer of, say, £X million from consumption expenditure to government purchases, then the actual value of Y will not change, but if one of the three components of aggregate demand is increased for some reason while the other two remain constant, then there *will* be an increase in the value of Y, or national income. This is self-evident, but it has far-reaching implications for the formulation of economic policy.

Keynesian reasoning

Pre-Keynes

The first economist to study the problem of maintaining the economy in equilibrium through manipulating the circular flow of income was John Maynard Keynes in the 1920s and 1930s. Admittedly, other economists in earlier centuries had considered the problems of macroeconomic policy, but Keynes revolutionised economic thinking on the control of the economy. Prior to his work, most economists followed the work of a French economist, J B Say.

From the time of Say in the early nineteenth century, economists had believed that there could never be a shortage of purchasing power within an economy, because the circular flow of income ensured that just enough income would be created by the production process to take up all the output. However, they failed to realise that there are withdrawals from and injections into the system and that, if the withdrawals are greater than the injections, then there will be insufficient demand to take up all the output. Keynes saw how a reduction in expenditure by consumers would inevitably lead to a fall in the level of national income *unless* there was a parallel increase in either investment or government purchases.

The role of the government

Keynes recognised that the government was effectively in control of large areas of consumption and investment in its own right, and so should be able, if the need arose, to influence the general level of economic activity, either by increasing or decreasing its own expenditure. For instance, if there was a real danger of a fall in national income due to a decline in the level of consumption, Keynes argued that the government could compensate for this by increasing its own expenditure. However, although this is a simple procedure in theory, the practical application of it is not quite so easy. It is not just a matter of exactly counterbalancing any specific change in the level of consumer expenditure, because in practice the three main variables are interconnected. For example, if there is a sharp rise in the number of private motor cars on the road because of an increase in consumer expenditure on cars, then there will have to be an increase, rather than a decrease, in government spending, because the larger number of cars would require not only more road space, but also more police services, more hospitals, and so on.

The quantitative problem

There is also another difficulty. Suppose there is a fall in the level of consumer expenditure. This will result in a fall in the level of national income unless it is compensated for by a rise in one or other of the variables. So, if the level of investment spending does not rise, there must be a rise in government spending if national income is to be maintained. Keynes recognised this, and argued that the government should always seek to offset any change, either upwards or downwards, in one of the other variables by acting in the opposite manner itself.

The theory of this proposition is, undoubtedly, generally valid, but the difficulty arises in its application. The question for economists and the government alike was – and is – the precise quantitative extent of the action necessary to counterbalance any given change in either consumer spending or investment by firms. The reasons for this difficulty will become more apparent during the next two sections; both examine the Keynesian concept which he developed from the simple macro-economic model.

The multiplier

The simple process

If the government decide to spend £1,000 on redecorating some of its offices, an interesting and important process is started. The painters will receive extra income and the paint suppliers will also receive extra income. Indeed, by definition, it would appear that the extra income generated by £1,000 of extra spending will be £1,000, but that is not the end of the story. The recipients of the extra income will use it to satisfy some of their own unfulfilled wants. In short, they will spend the extra income, and by spending it they will create extra income for someone else. However, they will not spend all of the extra income. The exact amount they spend will depend on their propensity to consume, or, more precisely, on their *marginal* propensity to consume. After all, they are receiving *additional* income over and above what they were receiving already, so it is the *marginal* propensity to consume, rather than the *average* propensity, which is important.

If the *marginal* propensity to consume is two-thirds, then the recipients of the extra £1,000 of income will spend two-thirds of it, and save the rest of it (ie they will spend £666.67 on goods and services and they will *save* £333.33). The money which they spend becomes income for other people – and if their marginal propensity to consume is also two-thirds, then they, in turn, will spend two-thirds of their *extra* income and save one-third, and so the process goes on until the geometric progression runs itself out.

The secondary expansion

The original £1,000 of spending by the government is referred to as a *primary investment*, while the resulting extra spending round by round is called a *secondary expansion of consumption.* For the primary investment of £1,000 there would be a secondary expansion in consumption of £2,000 assuming an MPC of two-thirds. Put another way, the original investment of £1,000 would lead to an eventual increase in national income of £3,000 – the primary investment plus the secondary expansion of consumption (ie when the MPC is two-thirds, an initial investment of £X will lead to an eventual increase in national income of £3X).

The multiplier equation

Keynes recognised this process and he formalised it into an equation:

$$dY = k.dI$$

where dY represents the final total change in national income; k is the multiplier; and dI represents the original change in government spending or investment.

The *multiplier* is the number by which the original change in government spending or investment is multiplied in order to find the final total change in national income. The size of the multiplier depends on the value of the marginal propensity to consume plus its twin, the marginal propensity to save. When MPC is two-thirds MPS must be one-third and the multiplier is the *reciprocal* of MPS, or 3. In general, if the MPS is 1/X, then the multiplier will be X. This is for a closed economy with no trade.

$$K = \frac{1}{1-MPC} \quad \therefore \text{ If MPC} = 0.8, \text{ the multiplier is } \frac{1}{1-0.8} = \frac{1}{0.2} = \underline{5}$$

The effect of the multiplier concept

From the analysis of the macroeconomic model, it will be remembered that when there is a fall in the level of consumer expenditure, this will lead to a fall in national income, unless there is a compensatory increase in either investment or government spending. Suppose consumer expenditure fell by £1 million during the period of a year. If national income is to be maintained at its original level, then, assuming no increase in investment expenditure, the government will have to spend an amount necessary to replace the 'missing' £1 million. If the concept of the multiplier was ignored, it would appear that the government would need to spend £1 million, but in accordance with the argument in 'The secondary expansion' above a primary investment of £1 million will lead to a much larger increase in final national income. Indeed, if the marginal propensity to consume is 0.9 – leading to a marginal propensity to save of just 0.1 and a multiplier of 10 – the government would only need to spend a primary investment of £100,000 to replace the 'missing' £1 million of national income, because £100,000 multiplied by 10 gives £1 million.

The size of the multiplier in the UK

In fact, it is very unlikely that the multiplier in the UK is anywhere near this size. There are two principle reasons. First, the UK has a mildly progressive taxation system, so a higher percentage of any additional income is withdrawn from the circular flow of income and finds itself back in the hands of the government. Second, a significant proportion of the remainder will be saved – at least in the short-term – because most of the population's basic needs are already met. In short, there is a *low* marginal propensity to consume. Indeed, what little evidence there is, suggests that the multiplier in the UK is only about 2.

However, it is important to emphasise the practical difficulties of calculating the size of the multiplier with any degree of accuracy. Any given government spending programme will affect different sections of the population and, although there may be an overall marginal propensity to consume, there will be wide discrepancies between different sections. Furthermore, the multiplier concept assumes that the process continues uninterrupted, whereas, in reality, any one of the variables in the original national income equation can change at any time. In short, although the government may know the end result which it wishes to achieve, actually achieving it is a near impossibility.

Investment and consumption

The impact of the multiplier is not only confined to government purchases. A change in the level of investment spending will have a multiplier effect throughout the economy, as will a change in the level of consumption. So, to conclude, any *initial* (and *additional*) change in spending, by the government, by firms or by households, will tend to change the aggregate demand schedule and, through the *multiplier*, will lead to a change in the national income which is *larger than the initial change in spending*.

Basic assumptions

The multiplier concept as outlined above depends on two important assumptions. First, for the multiplier to be effective, it is necessary for there to be some unemployed factors of production within the economy, otherwise the primary investment will not be effective in increasing *real* income. If it simply raises prices rather than production, then *real* GNP will not rise. Second, the discussion so far has only referred to the *national* economy – in other words, the effects of trade have been ignored. In fact, many economists refer to the multiplier concept as described so far as the *investment multiplier*.

The trade multiplier

However, it is a relatively easy matter to extend the concept to include the effects of trade with other countries, if it is remembered how imports and exports affect the circular flow of income. *Imports* represent a *withdrawal* from the flow, while *exports* represent an *injection*. So, the original equation can be altered to allow for both exports and imports quite simply.

Obviously, the change in exports must be added and the change in imports subtracted, to find the *trade multiplier*.

$$dY = k.(dI + dE - dP)$$

where dY represents the final total change in national income; k is the multiplier; dI represents the original change in government spending or investment; dE represents the resultant change in exports; and dP represents the resultant change in imports.

Further difficulties

Although the concept itself is simple enough, the inclusion of foreign trade makes the practical application that much more difficult. The usual aim of additional government expenditure, or the encouragement of further investment spending, is to increase the level of aggregate demand within the economy and so reduce the level of unemployment, but the extra spending will be self-defeating if, by increasing aggregate demand, it increases the level of *imports* rather than the demand for *home-produced goods or exports*. The extra income created will not stay in the country. Instead, it finds its way into the pockets of people in other countries and so has no beneficial effect on the overall level of GNP or GNI. Indeed, the eventual effect will be even less beneficial to the country, because, if households spend their extra income on foreign goods, fewer goods will be produced in the UK and so incomes will be reduced still further. (The multiplier can, after all, work in reverse, multiplying the effects of a fall in demand.) Naturally, as exports have the opposite effect – bringing extra income into the country – any additional government spending should be directed towards encouraging exporting industries, particularly as the flow of extra income into the economy will, in itself, have a further beneficial effect as it will draw forth still more production.

It should be clear from this discussion that the government has to be very careful to ensure that any extra spending on its own part is directed towards benefiting the economy rather than increasing its problems.

The accelerator

The basis

Another important concept which is associated with the multiplier and the work of Keynes must be examined briefly at this point. It will be remembered from microeconomics that if there is an increase in the demand for a certain product, then the producers will try to increase their own levels of production to meet the demand. This increase in production will lead to an increase in the demand for the factors of production necessary to produce the good (ie the demand for a factor of production is a *derived demand*). Keynes maintained that the derived demand for capital goods in particular would be proportionately larger than the original increase in the demand for the finished product. This can be illustrated very easily.

An example

Suppose a factory can produce 10,000 ladders a year using 10 machines and that 1 machine is usually replaced each year. If the demand for ladders then rose by 10 per cent the demand for the machines to make those ladders would not rise by 10 per cent but by 100 per cent. The factory would still replace the machine it usually replaced each year, but, *in addition*, it would have to buy 1 extra machine in order to meet the demand for an extra 1,000 ladders. This is basically the concept behind the *accelerator principle*. An *initial increase in the demand for the finished product will eventually lead to a more than proportionate increase in the demand for capital goods*, or investment.

The accelerator in reverse

However, the accelerator principle can, and often does, work in reverse. If there is a decline in the demand for finished goods, then there will be a more than proportionate decline in the demand for capital goods, as there will be less need to replace machinery or to buy new machines. In the previous example, if the demand for ladders *decreased* by 10 per cent, then it is probable that the factory would not bother ordering the usual replacement machine, so the firm which produced that machine would be without any order at all! This type of situation occurred in the electricity generator industry in the UK during 1975 and 1976. Prior to this, the electricity supply industry – at the request of the government – had tended to 'over-order' new generators, and so, when the demand for electricity fell sharply during the period 1974 to 1976, the supply industry found itself with surplus capacity. As a result, it reduced its ordering of new generators to a very low level – leaving the generator supply industry with very little work and a large quantity of unemployed factors of production. This example shows very clearly how the capital goods industry can experience times of excessive demand when it builds up its own capacity, and then times of severely restricted demand when it has to shed many factors of production.

The size of the accelerator

As in the case of the multiplier there is also an equation which is used to determine the size of the accelerator. New investment (I) is said to be a multiple of the original change in the firm's income or sales level:

$$I = v(Y_t - (Y_t - 1))$$

where I is new investment; v is the accelerator coefficient; and $(Y_t - (Y_t - 1))$ is the rate of change in income or sales.

Effectively, the change in income or sales level (which, of course, is dependent on the change in the level of demand), is multiplied by the accelerator coefficient to give the new level of investment.

Limitations

However, the principle has its limitations. For instance, the presence of long time-lags makes it difficult to see the principle in practice. Most firms will utilise all their spare capacity first before they contemplate any further *new* investment. Indeed, very often the enterprising firm will be able to 'squeeze' even more production out of its existing capital goods simply by re-arranging its labour force and production schedules. The principle makes no allowance for this. Neither does it give any indication of the time-scale involved. Indeed, some capital goods take many years to produce. For instance, a new electricity generator plant takes as much as 5 to 10 years to plan and build, while a machine to make safety pins is a relatively simple affair. The principle also assumes that the necessary finance for the project is readily available, but any industrialist knows that this may be one of his main difficulties in securing a new capital good.

Perhaps the main weakness of the accelerator principle is that it does not adequately describe any *downturn* in economic activity. If it was carried to its logical conclusion, even a small downturn in activity would lead to a major economic disaster, because, once the demand for capital goods had slackened due to a fall in the demand for finished goods, there would be a 'snowball' effect. The multiplier in reverse would cause incomes to decline still further and this would lead to another 'accelerated' decline in investment spending. There would be no end to it. In fact, this does not happen in reality, because there is always some replacement investment going on in basic industries, and, more important, there is always a considerable amount of 'innovatory' investment in new products and so on. (This point will become clearer when the economic trade cycle of a typical western industrialised country is examined.)

Inflationary and deflationary gaps

Equilibrium is not necessarily 'good'

The concept of the multiplier and the accelerator enable the macroeconomic model to be developed further. The multiplier and the accelerator can both encourage the economy to expand quickly *and* exaggerate a depression (eg if investment is expanded by £1,000 then national income will grow by an amount equal to that £1,000 times the multiplier; but the converse also applies). It should, however, also be remembered that there is nothing particularly 'good' about the resulting equilibrium level in the model unless that equilibrium level is consistent with the full-employment level of national income. In short, if the resultant equilibrium level is in line with the potential GNP level then all is well, but if it is not then the situation can be improved.

Full employment GNP

The macroeconomic model can be drawn with the *potential*, or *full-employment* GNP level marked on the horizontal axis:

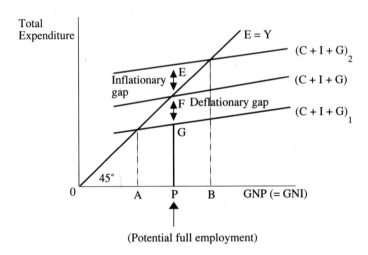

The middle C + I + G line shows the economy in equilibrium at the full-employment GNP level. All the variables are perfectly balanced – savings equal investment, taxes equal government spending, and so on – while all the factors of production in the economy are fully employed. However, as was noted earlier, such a position would be purely coincidental, as there is no reason *why* this should happen automatically. One of the other C + I + G lines is more likely. The bottom line – *marked with one dash on the diagram* – shows a position where there is a *deficiency* in aggregate demand *at the full- employment GNP level* (A). The economy would only be in equilibrium at a *lower* level of *actual* GNP, and many factors of production would be *unemployed*. The top line – marked with two dashes – shows a position where there is an *excess* aggregate demand *at the full-employment level of GNP,* and so more will be demanded than *can* be produced and prices will rise as a result (B).

The 'deflationary' gap

These two examples must be examined in detail, with particular reference to the multiplier. First, the bottom C + I + G line. The distance between this line and the 45° 'Income Line' represents a deficiency of demand. People are saving more than is wanted for investment or else the government is receiving more in taxes than it is spending. At the full-employment level this 'gap' is FG and is referred to as a *deflationary gap* because it leads to a fall in the level of GNP. For instance, if the 'gap' between saving and investment was £5,000 million, and the marginal propensity to consume was two-thirds, then the total national income would fall by £5,000 million *times* the multiplier of 3, or £15,000 million. Consequently, the size of the deflationary gap is increased considerably. In the diagram, total national income will fall from the full-employment level of 0P to the reduced level of 0A. A deflationary gap of this sort can only be eliminated by an increase in aggregate demand exactly equal to the original deficiency. So, an increase of £5,000 million spending by either the government or investment spending should, at least in theory, bring national income back to the full-employment level.

The 'inflationary' gap

The opposite situation is illustrated by the top C + I + G line. In this instance, the distance between the consumption function line and the 45° 'Income Line' at the full-employment level represents an excess aggregate demand. In the diagram, this is measured by the distance EF and is called an *inflationary gap*. Business cannot produce all the goods which are being demanded, and so prices will be 'bid up' and money will begin to lose its value. The operation of the multiplier would, in theory, raise the level of national income from 0P to 0B, but this rise in national income is not backed by production. In short, despite an apparent rise in the level of national income, there cannot be a *real* rise much beyond the full-employment level, because the capacity to produce more does not exist. So, when such an 'inflationary gap' rises, money GNP will rise because of 'paper' price-tag changes, but *real* GNP will not rise. Unfortunately, this upward movement in prices will continue for as long as there is an inflationary gap – higher 'paper' prices lead to higher 'paper' wages and so to an even higher aggregate demand.

The ever-increasing spiral can only be stopped by *reducing* the real level of demand. The most usual way of doing this is for the government to run a 'surplus' on its own account. In simple terms, the government will attempt to *raise* more revenue from taxes than it *spends*. This effectively takes money out of the circular flow, reducing the level of aggregate demand. Naturally, this reduction depends on the size of the multiplier, just as in the previous example.

Relevance to economic management

Although 'inflationary' and 'deflationary' gaps are a theoretical concept, because full-employment GNP is not often attainable, they do have a considerable relevance to the management of the economy. They help to explain just what happens when one sector of the economy alters its spending plans, and so sets off a chain reaction throughout the macroeconomic model via the multiplier concept. It is true, of course, that the 'real' world cannot be represented by simple diagrams, but it is important to understand the theory, so that the 'thinking' behind the economic policy decisions which are made by both the government and industry can be appreciated.

Questions for review

1. What does the term 'consumption function' mean?
2. Explain 'aggregate demand'.
3. What influences consumption?
4. Explain:
    a   APC;
    b   APS;
    c   MPC;
    d   MPS.
5. Explain:
    a   marginal propensity to tax;
    b   marginal propensity to import.
6. Explain the following equation:

    $Y = C + I + G + (X - M)$

7. Explain how the multiplier works.
8. Explain the 'accelerator'.
9. Explain:
    a   inflationary gap;
    b   deflationary gap.

The unemployment problem | 13

Unemployment 339

Cyclical unemployment 342

Structural unemployment 347

The natural rate of unemployment 359

Measures to help the long-term unemployed 361

Trends in employment 363

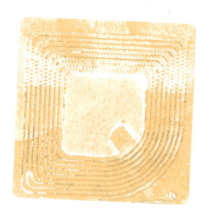

Unemployment

Definition and importance

The unemployment level at any time refers to the number of people who want to work and who, for one reason or another, are unable to find a job.

Economists are concerned about unemployment because it represents a waste of the labour resources of the economy. Given that the basic economic problem is that of reconciling unlimited wants to limited resources, it is obviously a serious failure for an economy to waste those resources by not using them. In economic terms, it is equally wasteful to have unused machines, buildings and land, but the unemployment of these resources does not have the same political and social costs.

The state provides cash benefits for the unemployed which are based on their previous incomes and on the domestic responsibilities of the wage-earner. Since 1965, a worker being made redundant also receives a lump-sum, tax-free payment which is related to his wage and length of period of employment. However, with the current high rates of unemployment, considerable evidence is emerging that unemployment puts a significant pressure on the individual and his/her family which appears to be a result of a loss of purpose, of structure to the day and of self-respect. The results are depression, alcoholism, domestic violence, lawlessness, even suicide.

Unemployment statistics

The quoted figures for unemployment in the press refer to a specific and exact calculation. For a person to count as unemployed he/she must be genuinely looking for work and entitled to receive benefit.

The official statistics may be quite inaccurate. The way in which this measure of unemployment (called 'the claimant count') is calculated has changed at least 30 times since 1979. The figures may underestimate the numbers of unemployed because:

a   Many people do not register as unemployed although they are out of work and seeking a job. There is a great incentive to register in order to gain the unemployment cash benefit. However, many people, most notably married women, cannot claim unemployment benefit and so have no incentive to register.

b   Some people feel that unemployment is a disgrace and are unwilling to admit to this by registering as unemployed in spite of the cash loss.

The official statistics may overestimate the numbers unemployed because:

a   A number of people may be drawing unemployment benefit while they are in fact working; the 'Black (or hidden) Economy' as it is often called.

b   A number of people may be unwilling to work even though they are registered as unemployed. Obviously their ability to do this must depend on some alternative sources of income or the fact that unemployment benefits provide an adequate income.

Since the early 1980s the unemployment statistics have only recorded those who are unemployed, actively seeking work, and entitled to claim benefit. This has led many to state that current figures are underestimated. The following graph shows the rate of claimant unemployment charted against the total workforce for the period 1986–94 (the workforce in the UK consists of the workforce in employment, plus the claimant count unemployed). From this graph can be clearly seen the higher level of unemployment at the beginning of the period, due to the aftermath of the recession of the early 80s. The chart also shows the decline in the total workforce in the early 90s, as the recession caused many 'discouraged workers' to drop out of the labour market. The numbers of unemployed rose again in the early 90s.

Workforce and workforce in employment, UK

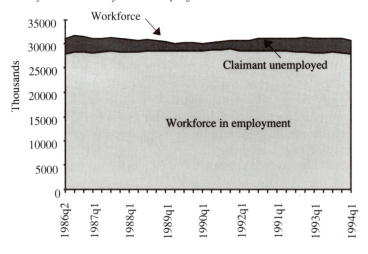

(Source: *Employment Gazette*, July 1994)

Clearly, the way in which unemployment is measured, who is included and who is excluded, affects the figures. Each national government has its own definition of unemployment, and they are all different. In order to facilitate international comparisons, the International Labour Organisation (ILO) definition of unemployment is widely used. This counts as unemployed everyone who has looked for work in the past four weeks and is available to start work in the next two weeks. For the European Union countries, these statistics are collected via the quarterly Labour Force Survey, which is carried out in every member country. For other OECD countries, standardised statistics are produced to enable comparisons to be made between countries. The following chart shows standardised (ie comparable) unemployment rates for various OECD countries in 1991.

International comparison of unemployment rates by country, 1991

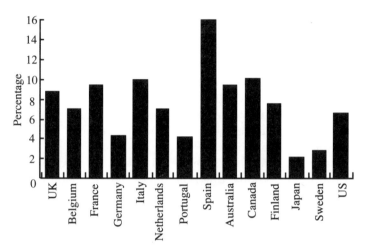

(Source: *Social Trends 23*, 1993, Table 4.23)

Explanations for unemployment

We have seen earlier that when aggregate demand in the economy is insufficient, the equilibrium level of income (output and employment) is below the 'full employment' level. There will then be unemployment. This type of unemployment, known as *cyclical unemployment*, is discussed below.

Even when the economy is at 'full employment' we would expect some people on any date to be unemployed. Economies are dynamic, constantly adjusting to changes in consumer preferences and in the availability of resources. Resources, including labour resources, must be reallocated in order to produce the necessary adjustment. At any time, therefore, there will be a number of people who are in the process of changing jobs. This is known as *frictional unemployment*. This type of unemployment must be regarded as normal although facilities such as 'job centres', where the unemployed and job vacancies can be swiftly matched up, will reduce the typical period spent 'between jobs' and thus the amount of frictional unemployment at any time.

Another largely unavoidable type of unemployment is *seasonal unemployment*, which occurs when the demand for labour is seasonal as in such industries as tourism and agriculture. The ideal solution to this problem is to have matching seasonal industries which can share the labour force.

A much more serious problem is *structural unemployment*, which is unemployment caused by a mismatch between the characteristics of the labour force and the characteristics of available jobs. The mismatch occurs because of changes in the relative demand and supply of labour. This problem is discussed below.

A new emphasis is being put on the so-called *natural rate of unemployment*, which is used by monetarists to explain their insistence that fiscal policies (manipulation of aggregate demand through adjustments of government expenditure and taxation) can do nothing to change the long-run unemployment situation, and therefore, that monetary policy with its impact on inflation should be the focus of government policy. This 'natural' level of unemployment is determined by structural factors (mentioned above) but also by the level of unemployment benefit and the level of trade union wage demands. It is discussed below.

Appropriate policy measures depend on identifying the precise problem. At any time the broad figures of the number registered as unemployed will include, perhaps, all types of unemployment listed above.

The people on the register who have been registered as unemployed for less than four weeks are indicative of frictional unemployment. What is regarded as much more serious is the number of people on the register who have been unemployed for more than a year (Long Term Unemployment). These people are indicative of structural unemployment. The length of the average period of unemployment tends to increase as the numbers of unemployed rise. This is indicative of cyclical unemployment. The Department of Employment adjusts unemployment figures for seasonal variation. The mismatch between vacancies and unemployment is often regional, ie the unemployed are in the wrong part of the country for the vacancies. Youth unemployment is often a big problem during times of recession, as firms operate 'last-in, first-out' policies. High unemployment rates amongst older workers (45+) are increasingly a problem, and such workers can find it extremely difficult to find employment.

Cyclical unemployment

Regular oscillation

There seems to have been a regular swing, or oscillation, between high and low levels of economic activity. Many economists have tried to formulate accurate theories which give specific time scales to the highs and lows, but it is all too easy to 'fit' the evidence to the theory. There is a great deal of evidence of swings in the economic cycle, but it is unlikely that *one* particular theory fully explains the swings which occur:

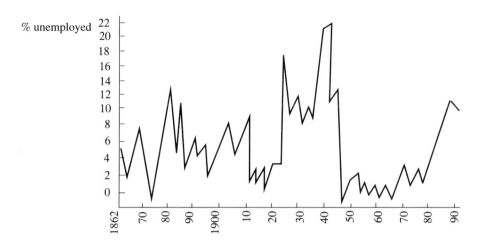

The cyclical fluctuations are immediately apparent. Indeed, during the nineteenth century the cycles seem to have been between 8 and 10 years in duration, while, since the end of World War II until the 1970s, unemployment fluctuated over a much narrower range. The post-war period has, initially, represented a substantial reduction in the average level of unemployment, with the 'swings' being shorter and less pronounced. The lower unemployment of the 1950s and 1960s was upset dramatically in the late 1970s!

A longer and more serious cycle, identified by economic historians (such as Kondratieff), is a 50-year cycle – 1880s, 1930s, 1980s. This has had renewed credibility in recent years. The above graph picks out the worst bouts of unemployment in the 1880s, 1930s and the 1980s.

Trade cycles

Cyclical fluctuations are the result of various economic and business forces. They may not be identical in every case but there are a number of common characteristics. In each fluctuation – or *trade cycle* – definite periods of low activity, or *depression*, can be distinguished which are followed by an upsurge in activity. This leads to a period of high activity or *boom*, which is eventually followed by a downturn, leading once again to a depression.

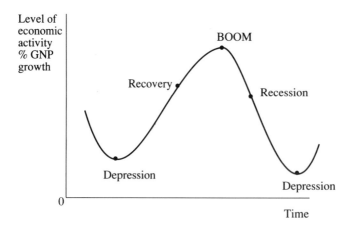

Scales have not been put on either axis – the graph and the following discussion are a stylised generalisation of a 'typical' trade cycle. They do not describe any *particular* cycle, but should illustrate the general pattern that was apparent in the first graph in this section.

A depression

A depression is characterised by a *high* level of unemployment and a *low* level of consumer demand in relation to the potential capacity of the economy (ie a depression is a time when actual GNP is well below *potential* GNP). This will lead to little, if any, pressure on prices and they will tend to drift lower or at least remain static. The low level of prices will mean that the level of profits will also be low. Inevitably, this will make entrepreneurs pessimistic about the future and it is unlikely that they will undertake much new investment. However, even in depressed economic times, some basic industries will still be in demand, relative to the rest of industry, and they will have to replace worn-out machinery eventually. In addition, there will also be someone who comes up with a new invention or idea and is either able to invest in it himself or persuade others to do so. These two factors will eventually set off a recovery in economic activity.

Recovery

Once the recovery has actually started, its pace will tend to quicken – old and obsolete machinery will be replaced and employment will start to rise as a result – while both the multiplier and the accelerator will encourage the process to 'feed on itself'. An upsurge in demand for machinery and equipment will cause employment in the capital goods industries to rise very quickly and the increased level of disposable income which comes from this employment will, through the multiplier, raise employment in the consumer durable industries. In short, as incomes rise, effective demand rises, and as effective demand rises, so do incomes.

Obviously, once this happens the entrepreneurs themselves change from being pessimistic to being optimistic and they will increase their own investment programmes in line with their optimism.

Boom

However, as the recovery gathers momentum, 'bottlenecks' will occur in many sections of the industry as all the existing unused capacity is taken up and as the capital goods industries, struggle to meet the revived demand for their products. Eventually, labour shortages will arise in key industries, and there may also be shortages of raw materials, as aggregate demand rises to the point where all the economy's resources are being stretched. (This is the 'boom' point in the diagram.) Once aggregate demand exceeds potential full-employment GNP, an 'inflationary gap' will appear and it is likely that prices will be pushed up without any parallel increase in output. Inflation has set in. Initially, many firms will not be unduly worried by their rising costs, because prices will also be rising and they can recoup their costs from their selling prices. However, the excess demand for investment funds will naturally raise the price of such funds, and, in an effort to pay the higher interest rates, entrepreneurs will raise prices still further. Higher prices will lead to higher wage demands and, because of the high level of demand for factors of production, such demands will probably be met. Higher wages lead to still higher costs, and so, higher prices – a vicious circle has set in, in earnest!

Recession

At the upper turning point of the cycle, it becomes increasingly difficult for firms to maintain their profit margins and activity will start to decline. (After all, *real* rises in output and income have a ceiling at the full-employment level and paper increases are eventually self-defeating.) Once entrepreneurs cut back on their investment programmes, a recession is inevitable. The reason is to be found in the accelerator principle. The demand for capital goods – machinery and equipment – will suddenly fall off and there will be considerable spare capacity in the capital goods industries. Employment, and therefore incomes, will fall, and again through the multiplier this will reverberate throughout the country. A falling level of aggregate demand must inevitably lead to a change of heart among the entrepreneurs, as they will once again become pessimistic, rather than optimistic, about the future. It is a sad fact of economic and business life that *expectations* of the future tend to be self-fulfilling. When spirits are high, business activity will be high, and this will encourage still further economic activity; but the reverse is also true. So, once the recession sets in, there will be a downward spiral to the *floor* of the depression. As the floor is reached, there will come again a lower turning point and the economy will revive.

Application of trade cycle theory in the modern world

Given the amount of government intervention in the level of activity in the modern world, it seems unlikely that the old cycles will persist. However, the characteristics of the 'depression', 'boom', and 'recession' stages of the cycle may still be relevant, since the national and world economy can be pushed into one of these movements by a shock to the system. For example, the oil crisis of the early and mid-1970s may have been such a shock, pushing the industrialised world into a major recession. The term 'cyclical unemployment' has a general applicability for any unemployment that can be attributed to deficient aggregate demand in the economy.

Policy for solving cyclical unemployment

In the following diagram, the level of aggregate demand is such that the resulting equilibrium level of national income (NYe) is below the 'full employment' level (FE). The way to solve this type of unemployment is to expand aggregate demand. This was the policy advocated by Keynes in the 1930s to deal with unemployment then. Either fiscal or monetary policy can be used. *Fiscal policy* involves increasing government expenditure and/or reducing taxation. The extra expenditure in the public and/or private sectors of the economy will stimulate production and employment, setting off a multiplier process (ie reflation). At the same time or as an alternative, the government can run an expansionary *monetary policy* to increase aggregate demand. More money available and lower interest rates will encourage borrowing and expenditure by firms and consumers. This will again set off an expansionary multiplier process. This type of policy was discredited by monetarist theorists in the 1980s because they felt that these 'reflationary' policies increased money supply or raised interest rates. Budget deficits which are associated with 'reflation' involve large-scale government borrowing. If the government borrows from the banking sector it will increase the money supply (and possibly inflation through the MV = PT formula). Alternatively, to persuade institutions such as pension funds and insurance companies to lend to the government, high interest rates must be offered.

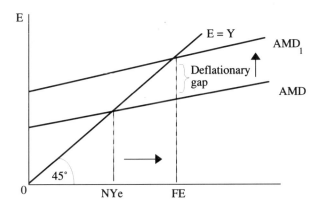

Structural unemployment

Definition

Structural unemployment exists wherever there is a mismatch between the characteristics of the unemployed workforce and the jobs available. Thus, the economy may be at 'full employment' with a large number of people unemployed and an equal number of job vacancies, but no possibility of matching people to jobs. The mismatch occurs because of changing economic circumstances.

As the economy adjusts to changes of demand and supply conditions in the domestic and world markets, some industries decline or close down while others expand. Unfortunately, people's working lives are so long (50 years for example) that the career they start with at 16 or so may no longer exist before they have completed their working life. This may mean that the skills and work experience acquired become irrelevant and the individual has no skills suitable for the jobs that are now available.

An additional problem is that industries are often concentrated geographically, so that when one declines, this removes the jobs in an area. New industries are expanding but in different regions. There is then a mismatch between the location of the workforce and the location of available jobs, which may be in addition to the mismatch of skills and experience. This specifically geographical problem is called *regional unemployment*.

A slightly different problem is what is called *technological unemployment*. Here, unemployment is created, not by the decline of an industry, but by a technological innovation which replaces the workforce with machines or which changes the type of workforce needed. For example, the development of computers has produced computer typesetters in the newspaper and publishing industry. These machines greatly reduce the number of human typesetters required, so a large number of skilled jobs have been lost. The smaller workforce needed to operate the new machines must have new skills. This is by no means a new problem. The Luddites protested violently about the introduction of new machines in the textile industry in the eighteenth century because of the job losses involved.

In 1983 the Institute for Employment Research, based at the University of Warwick, published the results of a programme of macroeconomic simulations aimed at establishing a relationship between increased automation and the resulting changes in overall employment levels. The model used assumed that sufficient investments were available to provide a standard of microelectronic technology which would give a rate of productivity growth one per cent higher than that of the UK's competitors.

The somewhat surprising answer was that, under these circumstances, more jobs would be created than would be lost. The gains would, of course, be in the fields of computer technology, software and systems analysis, whereas the losses would affect the engineering industry in particular – machine operators, welders, assembly operators, and so on.

Although experience of the mobility of labour does not augur well for displaced individuals benefiting from the new jobs created, the time-scale for such a degree of technological advancement provides an opportunity for the rising generation of the workforce to adapt to the changing environment, while many of the job losses will be absorbed by natural wastage.

The results of this research are therefore cautiously optimistic, and productivity would obviously be raised very considerably with no adverse net effect upon employment levels.

Mobility of the workforce (education and training)

The theoretical solution to the general problem of structural unemployment is to increase the mobility of the workforce in terms of skills and location. Even during periods of high unemployment employers experience difficulties in recruiting certain categories of skilled labour. The level of vacancies found in the UK, despite unemployment, is shown in the following graph.

Claimant unemployment and unfilled vacancies, UK, 1990 to 1993

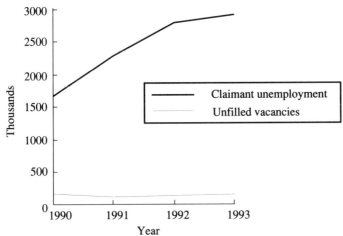

(Source: *Employment Gazette*, July 1994. NB: only about one-third of vacancies are notified to Job Centres.)

The skill mobility of the workforce can be increased by a number of policy measures which, if successful, will enable people to move from one job to another even when the skills required are changing rapidly. There are a number of ways in which the government might wish to change the provision of training in the economy. The present government believes in an efficient labour force to improve the 'supply side' of the economy:

a They may wish to increase the amount of training, since this reduces unemployment (reducing the waste of economic resources) and provides firms with a suitable labour supply (increasing industrial efficiency).

b The government may wish to redistribute the costs of training. Firms may minimise their own training costs by using workers trained by other firms. Since those firms then have to train a surplus, they may be discouraged and reduce their training programme. To check the potential inequity and subsequent drop in training, the government may step in to organise the industry's training programme.

c The government may feel that existing training is inefficient and may then distribute information about training techniques or set up central training facilities for the industry.

There have been a number of policy measures in recent years to meet the need for government intervention in education and industrial training.

The Technical and Vocational Education Initiative (TVEI) is introducing more technical education into the school syllabus at an average cost of £90 million per annum. The scheme went nationwide in autumn 1987, bringing courses for 14-18 year-olds more closely in line with employers' needs.

The Youth Training Scheme (YTS) was first launched in 1983, offering the same sort of vocational training to our young people as has been available in most of our competitor nations for many years. It began as a one-year scheme and was extended to two years on 1 April 1986; then on 28 January 1987 Lord Young extended it further by offering a YTS place to every unemployed 17-year-old school-leaver. This means that there is now a guaranteed place – for every 16- and 17-year-old who wants one – of training leading to a recognised vocational qualification. The scheme combines both on- and off-the-job training, paying trainees £28.50 per week in their first year, and £35 in their second year. Over one million entrants joined the one-year YTS, of whom two-thirds went into jobs or into further education and training.

Employment training (ET) was introduced in 1988. Anyone over 18 who has been unemployed for at least six months is eligible. Trainees receive six months' training and are paid a small amount in addition to their normal benefits.

Regional problem

Regional disparities in unemployment levels and the availability of job opportunities are the product of economic change over the last 200 years. In the nineteenth century, the bulk of industrial output, of exports and of employment, was concentrated in very few industries – coal mining, metal manufacture and engineering (including ship-building) and textiles (cotton and wool). These dominant industries, in the interests of profit, chose the locations which were ideal for them.

A major factor was the availability of coal which provided the power to drive machines but which is difficult and costly to transport. Hence, nineteenth-century industry picked locations near coalfields in South Wales, North Wales, North-East and North-West England and South-East Scotland.

Most of the output was exported or, like the cotton industry, required imported raw materials. The ideal locations from a transport point of view was on the coast near a port or on one of the great navigable rivers – the Clyde, the Mersey, the Tyne. Once these locations had been selected by an industry, any new firm would find certain *external economies of scale* available in those areas and would add to the concentration of that industry in that location to take advantage of these external benefits. For example, once the cotton industry was established in and around Manchester, that area provided enormous advantage for any cotton firm. The Cotton Exchange in Manchester became the world centre for dealing in raw materials and finished goods. The local workforce were skilled and accustomed to the shift-working necessary for a highly mechanised industry.

These industries have declined under the pressure of new foreign competitors, new products (oil, synthetic fibres) and decreasing efficiency in British industry (complacency on the part of management, labour problems of strikes and inefficient industrial practices).

They have been replaced by the much more diverse expanding industries of the twentieth century – electronics, pharmaceuticals, chemicals, paint, rubber, motor vehicles, aircraft, retailing, catering, education and government services. These industries focus much more on the domestic market and, since Britain joined the EU, on the European market. To minimise transport costs and maximise communication links to the market for selling and servicing, twentieth century industries chose locations near the centres of the internal transport system (London and the Midlands) and in the South-East of England. Industry was free to move away from the coalfields because of the increasing use of electricity (available everywhere) and oil (easily transported) as the source of power in industry. External economies again applied. It was cities like Birmingham and, most conspicuously, London which provided all the services required by modern industry.

Thus, while industry declined (and continues to decline) in the old industrial areas, new jobs were created in the expanding industries, but these were in different locations. As a result, there are substantial differences in the rates of unemployment in different regions which persist when the economy is in a boom or a slump. One estimate shows that during the 1920s unemployment in London and the South-East was between 5 and 6 per cent, rising to 15 per cent in 1932-3. In Scotland and Wales, Northern Ireland and Northern England, unemployment rates were between 12 and 15 per cent in the 1920s and rose to between 25 and 35 per cent in 1932. The regions also showed substantial differences in average income per head and in the average standard of living.

The high unemployment rates of the old industrial regions is a waste of labour resources. There are also unused and wasted capital resources in those areas – houses, factory buildings, railways, roads, docks. The other side of the regional problem is the increasing congestion of London and the South-East. As labour migrated to these areas in search of jobs and industries expanded there, space became short, pollution increased and the transport network became congested.

Justification for government intervention

An entirely market approach would argue that government intervention in the location of the workforce or of industry is unwarranted and damaging.

a Labour will migrate to the areas where there are job opportunities and higher wages until the differentials between regions disappear. If it does not do so, this implies that there are other advantages of the high unemployment regions which make up for the lower incomes and fewer job opportunities. Government intervention would then reduce utility.

b Firms will make their location on the basis of cost-minimising/benefit-maximising and this will therefore be the most efficient location. The depressed regions will become attractive to firms as unemployment pulls down wage rates and rents. Firms will relocate until the most efficient location pattern is established. Any interference with this pattern will reduce efficiency.

However, there are many arguments which can be used to dispute the optimality of the market in determining the location of industry and the labour force. First, there may be rigidities which make it impossible for families to move to more prosperous regions in search of jobs and higher incomes. The most important of these is the rehousing problem. Rent control has almost eliminated the supply of rented accommodation in the prosperous regions. Security of tenure for existing tenants makes people reluctant to move in search of jobs since this means giving up this security. Local authority tenants are similarly restricted. If they give up their council house in one region there is no guarantee they will get another elsewhere. This is particularly true for any family wanting to move to an area where job opportunities exist, since the competition for housing is greater there. House owners are no better placed. The differences in income and job opportunities between regions means that there is a big difference in house prices. A family living in Newcastle may get only £26,000 from selling the family house but will need £55,000 to buy even a flat near London.

Secondly, the institutional determination of wage rates through national trade-union negotiations, and the payment of unemployment pay and social security benefits at nationally consistent rates, mean that lower wages do not necessarily reflect the higher unemployment levels of the region. The labour force may not necessarily relocate since there are no higher wages to attract them and the depressed regions offer no labour cost advantages to firms choosing that location.

Thirdly, the location decisions made by the labour force and firms will reflect only private costs and benefits. There may be *externalities* associated with these location decisions. For example, when another family moves to London in search of work, they increase the congestion of the city, adding to the congestion on the transport system and to the housing crisis in the city, and imposing an external cost on the existing residents. A firm choosing to locate in London may similarly impose costs on other firms by competing for the workforce and raising transport costs by increasing the congestion on roads. When a family leaves the depressed region, they reduce the population of the region, and since the people who move are typically the most skilled and enterprising, they reduce the attractiveness of the workforce for any firm considering that location. When a firm chooses to locate in a depressed region, its local presence may reduce the costs of other firms in the region by supplying components with reduced transport costs.

The existence of these externalities means that the government may be justified in influencing location decisions in the interests of maximising social benefits and minimising social costs.

First, firms incur *search costs* in considering alternative locations. It costs time and money to amass information on the costs and benefits associated with every possible site. This is the only way the firm will be able to make the optimal location decision. To avoid these costs firms will only look at some locations, and there is thus no reason to assume that the choice will be optimally efficient. It is therefore not necessarily inefficient for the government to encourage or force firms to choose some alternative location.

Secondly, left to itself, the market may produce increased differentials between regions rather than reduced ones. The most prosperous regions provide the best market for goods, while the depressed regions provide the worst market. This in itself makes the more prosperous region more attractive. The firm locating there, by paying rent and employing labour, increases the prosperity of the area and, in turn, its attractiveness to other firms. As families leave the depressed regions they reduce the expenditure in that region, making local firms less profitable and ultimately causing more job losses. These *regional multipliers* mean that the market cannot be expected to produce more equal employment rates and job opportunities between regions.

Thirdly, even if the solution is left to the market, the process of restoring equality between regions may take a very long time. Firms do not relocate very often. There are personal costs associated with unemployment which suggest that a speedy solution is desirable.

Regional policy

The purpose of regional policy is to help reduce the disparities in regional employment opportunities and incomes. The UK has pursued a regional policy since 1934, but the following data show that it has had a limited effect.

	UK unemployment May 1994	Average gross weekly earnings – men April 1992 £
South East	9.2%	391.9
Greater London	10.9%	434.4
East Anglia	7.3%	321.4
South West	8.4%	315.2
West Midlands	9.6%	312.1
East Midlands	8.9%	306.1
Yorkshire and Humberside	9.6%	307.5
North West	9.8%	320.1
North	11.3%	314.3
Wales	9.5%	299.2
Scotland	9.3%	324.6
Northern Ireland	12.8%	298.2

(Source: *Employment Gazette*, July 1994; *Regional Trends 28*, 1993)

In a report entitled *Regional Industrial Incentives*, the all-party House of Commons Public Accounts Committee agreed that there were serious 'questions about the cost-effectiveness of the assistance' (HC 378, 11 June 1984). It is interesting to note that a region-by-region analysis shows a tendency for areas with older industrial structures to have higher rates of unemployment and lower levels of income per head. But this disguises changes which are taking place at the local level. Over the last 20 years we have seen a shift of population and wealth from the larger cities to the country and the smaller towns and cities. Towns such as Macclesfield, Kendal and Penrith in the north have benefited from this, as well as southern towns like Newbury and Didcot. Such locations are semi-rural and are able to offer residents a higher quality of life. They have no history of heavy manufacturing and, as such, they are ideally suited as sites for the newer industries, such as computer software design, financial services and distribution. As the Department of Trade and Industry's own analysis of regional development put it:

> 'The urban-rural shift in manufacturing change has occurred in all parts of Britain and indeed across Europe and the USA ... In every region in Britain small towns and rural areas have fared better than larger settlements, an indication of the persuasiveness of the forces at work.' (*Regional Industrial Policy*, 1983)

Unemployment figures by sub-region show that even within the most prosperous areas of the country there are pockets of high unemployment, just as the less affluent regions contain areas of great prosperity. The crucial distinction is therefore not between a rich south and a poor north, but rather between those parts of the country that have been well placed to take advantage of the new growth industries and those that have been less quick to adapt.

The wide variation in unemployment rates within regions confirms this view and suggests that the problems of structural economic adjustment tend to be highly localised (see following table).

It has been estimated that regional policy created 500,000 jobs up to the mid-1980s, but at the very high cost of nearly £20 billion (at 1982 prices), or £35,000 per net new job. For example, policy based on an automatic entitlement to grants for capital expenditure tended to be biased towards projects that created few jobs. In one project alone, £100 million of taxpayers' money was spent on the oil terminal at Sullom Voe in the Shetland Islands, which created only about 800 jobs – and the project would almost certainly have gone ahead without financial support.

UK regional policy remained broadly unchanged over the 1970s, but underwent substantial revisions. These revisions have been numerous and have included a drastic reshaping of the assisted-areas map, the abolition of automatic capital grants, and the introduction and subsequent scrapping of an employment-based marginal subsidy. There has also been a shift in the emphasis of policy away from the subsidisation of relocation projects, which formed the basis for earlier regional policy efforts, towards indigenous development and employment creation through efficiency effects within firms. An important objective of these revisions has been to improve the employment effectiveness of policy. To this end, the 1980s have seen a movement away from the blanket subsidisation of manufacturing investment towards a discretionary system under which firms have to demonstrate a proof of need and an employment effect at reasonable cost. The government was also keen to see control of public spending.

Regional Unemployment Rates by districts, April 1991

Region	District with highest % unemployed		District with lowest % unemployed	
North	Hartlepool	18.8%	South Lakeland	4.5%
Yorkshire & Humberside	Kingston upon Hull	17.6%	Craven	4.9%
East Midlands	Nottingham	16.6%	Harborough	5.1%
East Anglia	Great Yarmouth	13.0%	South Cambridgeshire	4.4%
South East (excl Gtr London)	Thanet	12.5%	Dacorum	2.6%
South West	Penwith	14.2%	Isles of Scilly	0.0%
West Midlands	Wolverhampton	16.2%	Stratford on Avon	5.5%
North West	Knowlsley	25.4%	Ribble Valley	4.3%
Wales	Rhondda	18.3%	Radnorshire	6.4%
Scotland	Glasgow City	21.3%	Gordon	3.5%
Northern Ireland	Strabane	24.8%	North Down	7.7%
Greater London	Hackney	24.5%	City of Westminster	4.2%

(Source: *Regional Trends 28*, 1993, Table 15.4)

Revised policies

The changes announced in November 1984 sought to improve the effectiveness of regional policy by linking assistance more directly to job creation and by restricting the amount of grant going to large and/or capital intensive firms. To this end, the phasing-out of the Regional Development Grant (RDG) was announced, and a revised RDG scheme introduced. Under this revised scheme, grant assistance was calculated as the maximum of 15 per cent of eligible capital expenditure or £3,000 for each net new full-time job created, subject to certain conditions laid down by the European Community. To restrict the amount of capital grant payable, a grant-per-job limit of £10,000 was imposed on firms with more than 200 employees, and on capital grant amounts exceeding £75,000 in the case of other firms.

The 1984 revisions also tightened the operation of Regional Selective Assistance (RSA) with a stricter economic appraisal of projects and a more stringent grant-per-job limit placed on all offers of assistance. As part of this, transfers to the assisted areas from within the UK which did not create extra jobs were no longer eligible for assistance, representing a major departure from earlier regional policy efforts which sought specifically to encourage relocations. The assisted-areas map was redrawn with Special Development Areas abolished.

A further reform of regional policy was signalled in January 1988 under the Department of Trade and Industry's Enterprise Initiative. The intention of this was to improve policy effectiveness still further, by reducing the amount of assistance which was non-additional. Thus, the revised RDG scheme, which was essentially automatic in nature, was scrapped, and the negotiation of RSA tightened further in the case of large firms.

The 1988 reforms introduced several new measures – a standard capital grant in the form of a Regional Enterprise Grant became available towards investment at a rate of 15 per cent up to a maximum grant of £15,000, and a 50 per cent innovation grant up to a maximum of £25,000 was also introduced. However, these grants could be claimed once only by firms which had fewer than twenty-five employees and which were located in the Development Areas. Under the Business Development Initiative, firms with fewer than 500 employees could claim assistance towards external consultancy advice in the areas of marketing, design, quality, new manufacturing technologies, business planning, and financial and information systems.

As well as these changes to UK regional policy, the 1980s also saw revisions to European Community (EC) regional policy, with perhaps the most comprehensive reform occurring under the terms of the 1988 Single European Act, and it now seems that the European Union is set to have an increasing influence on the formulation of UK and other member states' regional policies. Under this reform, the EU is planning to target 80 per cent of the European Regional Development Fund (ERDF) – the principal instrument of EU regional policy – on essentially underdeveloped rural areas mainly in the south of the EU. In the UK, these areas comprise the Highlands and Islands, mid-Wales, Northern Ireland and parts of Devon and Cornwall, and so exclude most of the older industrial areas which are designated under UK regional policy.

Expenditure on regional policy assistance, 1970-90 (£ million 1980 prices)

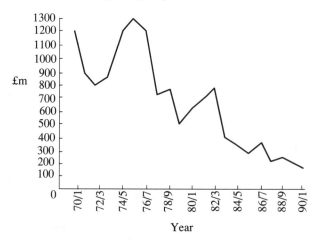

UDCs and Enterprise Zones

Many major towns and cities in the UK have become run down as industry has moved away to areas with more space and lower business rates. The decline in the housing stock of these areas has accelerated this process of 'urban decay'. In a wide-ranging policy, 'Action for Cities', the present government has attempted to reverse the decline. *Urban Development Corporations* have been set up and financed by the government to:

a assemble sites and reclaim and service large areas of derelict land;

b provide land for housing, industry, commerce and leisure;

c build roads, improve the environment, raise confidence;

d encourage private investment and jobs;

e ensure quick planning decisions; and

f give financial assistance to developers where necessary.

A number of *Enterprise Zones* have been set up to encourage development in run-down urban areas. Businesses which locate in these areas enjoy tax relief and much simpler planning processes. Many of these new initiatives listed above cannot as yet be fully judged. Critics have argued that policies for the cities have not directly created employment for local people, nor has the new housing always been in the price range of local lower-income families. Enterprise Zones have, additionally, been criticised for attracting businesses, such as warehousing, which create few new jobs.

Other financial help

British Coal Enterprise Ltd provides help to any business which is thinking of expanding, diversifying, locating or setting up in a coal-mining area. The assistance can include low-interest loans, help in obtaining suitable premises, and retraining for redundant British Coal employees.

British Steel Industry Ltd helps businesses to start up, expand or relocate in traditional steel areas. The assistance includes loan finance for projects, training in business skills and, in certain areas, managed workshops.

Unemployment – the eventual answer?

In recent years, prognoses of the unemployment situation worldwide have become more pessimistic. There no longer seems to be any possibility of a rapid return to anything near full employment. While the wants of even developed Western economies remain vast, the ultimate fulfillment (or partial fulfillment, since total satisfaction is impossible) of these wants is far more likely to be achieved by technological advancement and the increased productivity resulting from it, than by an increased demand for labour in general.

Because of these prognoses, more attention has recently been given to the redistribution of labour likely to be demanded among those able to supply it. Such an idea has often been mooted, but any really effective moves towards this end seems to have been frustrated.

It has been pointed out that any one of the following events would in theory at least reduce the present level of unemployment in the UK by about one-tenth:

a An average extension of the schooling/further education/training period of nine months.

b An extra three working days' holiday per year for everyone.

c A reduction in the normal retirement age of one year.

d A reduction in the average working week of 30 minutes.

Even if it were practical, it is not, of course, suggested that, if all four events were to be realised, there would be an immediate fall in unemployment by four-tenths! But this illustration does show that comparatively small adjustments to our accepted pattern of a working life can more equitably distribute the volume of labour necessarily demanded by industry.

If it is to be attained, this redistribution would certainly involve all the four factors already mentioned, plus perhaps such innovations as sabbatical periods (possibly restricted to managerial levels) as a general rule, and the wider application of day-release schemes for the younger members of the workforce.

Unfortunately, the implementation of any such policy would be at a price. This price would be a marked reduction in the rate at which the living standards of those fortunate enough to remain in work may rise; possibly even a standstill in real incomes over a period. For this reason, it does not seem to be attracting the enthusiastic support of three influential groups within the economy:

a The trade union movement: by definition, they have a prime responsibility to their members, who are all currently employed, and, while paying lip service to those who are not so fortunate, are more concerned with the plight of those who may *become* unemployed.

b The employers: where any reduction of the working year per person is involved, their costs are bound to increase. The employment of more people to perform the same work (even though the labour volume remains constant) incurs the need for more welfare facilities such as rest rooms and toilets, and higher costs in processing the payroll. Longer annual holidays would impose an immediate cost, even if ameliorated by effective pay policies restricting future increases in labour costs.

c The government: the present administration, is probably more favourably disposed towards policies of this type but, even so, it must be seen politically as a hot potato.

The natural rate of unemployment

Definition

Monetarists identify a 'natural' or 'normal' level of unemployment which may be, for example, 5 per cent of the workforce. Monetarists believe that a Keynesian attempt to reduce unemployment by reflation will just cause higher inflation. The 'normal' or 'natural' rate of unemployment will only be reduced, according to monetarist theory, by improving the efficiency of markets, particularly the labour market.

Since inflation may itself create unemployment (higher prices = reduced competitiveness in foreign and domestic market = falling sales, output and employment), the policy is disastrous.

This 'natural' unemployment which is not susceptible to expansions of aggregate demand will include:

a frictional and seasonal unemployment;

b structural unemployment;

c the 'voluntarily' unemployed;

d unemployment caused by excessively high wages.

Frictional, seasonal and structural unemployment have been discussed in detail above.

'Voluntary' unemployment

An unemployed individual can draw unemployment pay and social security benefits, and may receive redundancy pay. Low-productivity workers may find that their probable income from working will, after tax is deducted, be less than the money income they will receive when unemployed. Unless there are substantial non-money benefits from working, the rational individual will *choose* to be unemployed.

Unemployment caused by excessive wage claims

A large proportion of wages in this country are determined by union negotiation. Suppose that labour is homogenous and one union negotiates the wage level for everyone. The aggregate demand for labour is reduced at higher wage levels. Firms substitute other factors for labour, and rising costs of production result in falling sales, output and employment.

If full employment is shown by the line Q_s, the wage level needs to be at W_e for full employment to result. If the trade union fixes the wage at W_t, only Q_d workers will be employed and Q_dQ_s will be unemployed.

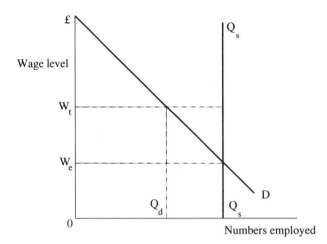

Note that this is largely contrary to the assumptions of the Keynesian multiplier working in a closed economy. This would argue that higher wages paid to workers because of trade union pressure result in increased expenditure by consumers and thus increased demand for labour. In the diagram above, this would mean that the demand for labour D would shift upwards to full employment and may be maintained at the higher wage level.

However, the British economy is not closed to foreign trade. A high proportion of the extra incomes will be spent on imports, and so will not generate increased demand for domestic labour. The rising costs of domestic labour because of higher wages makes British goods less competitive relative to foreign producers. As a result, sales of British goods on foreign and domestic markets fall, creating unemployment. (In the Income-Expenditure diagram, the increased income results in such a large increase in imports and such a large fall in exports that real aggregate demand shifts downwards.)

It is argued that the trade unions have damaged employment in other ways than just bidding wages up to uneconomic levels. An insistence on inefficient working practices (which in the short run appear to *protect* the jobs of union members) only result in reduced productivity and reduced competitiveness compared to other producers. The strikes used as a weapon to put pressure on firms permanently damage the credibility of British producers. There is substantial evidence to show that firms are often more interested in reliable delivery dates than in prices when placing orders for goods. If British industry has to delay delivery because of industrial disputes, the disappointed customers will place their orders elsewhere next time.

The present government (1979-) is clearly convinced that only when real industrial wages fall and union disruption of industry is limited will the demand for British labour start to increase and the 'natural' level of unemployment be reduced. Measures have been taken to make the labour and other factor markets more efficient. This is in line with the 'supply-side' economics of monetarism.

Measures to help the long-term unemployed

The present government have embarked on a number of policies to help the long-term unemployed and young people unable to get a foothold on the jobs ladder.

Restart

This was introduced nationwide on 1 July 1986 to offer direct help to the long-term unemployed. It was intended originally that everyone unemployed for over a year would be invited for an interview at their local Job Centre – where an assessment of personal employment needs would be made, so that these needs could be matched with the growing number of opportunities for employment and training.

The scheme was extended in April 1987 to cover all those who have been out of work for six months or longer, offering regular six-monthly interviews as long as the need persists. At a typical interview an unemployed person might be advised of a job vacancy; or encouraged to apply for the Enterprise Allowance Scheme, a place in a Job club or on one of the many training courses, including Restart.

The number of people who attended Restart interviews in the London and South-East during 1989 was 459,332. Of those 1.4 per cent went into employment, 3.2 per cent into Job clubs, 6.3 per cent onto Employment Training courses and 2.1 per cent onto other schemes. Restart counsellors are based in Job Centres across the country.

Job clubs

In October 1986 Lord Young announced a major expansion of this programme which was launched on a pilot basis in 1985-6, increasing the number of Job clubs to 1,000 by March 1987. Over 1,000 have now been established; and the government have made it clear that the programme will be expanded still further. Open to those unemployed for six months or more, Job clubs help people to help themselves back into a job: coaching in job-hunting techniques and motivation, free stationery, postage and telephones are all provided. Sixty per cent of those leaving Job clubs do so to take up a job.

The number of people who passed through Job clubs in London and the South-East in 1989 was 31,696. This programme has been extended to include specialist Job clubs. Thirty-six have been set up in the London and South-East region, to offer additional help to specific groups:

Young people (18–25)
Ex-offenders
Literacy/English as a second language
People with disabilities

The Jobstart Allowance

This helps the long-term unemployed to get back into the jobs market by offering a payment of £20 per week for the first six months of employment. Anyone unemployed for over a year is eligible – provided they take a job paying under £90 per week.

The Enterprise Allowance Scheme

This helps unemployed people who would like to become self-employed or start their own business, by providing £40 per week for the first year whilst the business is established. To qualify for the scheme entrants must be receiving unemployment or income support and also have at least £1,000 available to invest in the business. Over 250,000 people in total had benefited by April 1987. In January 1987 Lord Young announced that the scheme would be expanded to 110,000 places per annum by April 1988.

The Travel to Interview Scheme

This provides financial assistance for unemployed job seekers who need to travel to a job interview. The jobseeker's interview must be outside the normal travelling distance for the area.

Job Share

This was launched in April 1987 to replace the Job Splitting Scheme which gave financial support to employers who provide more part-time opportunities for unemployed people or for those leaving schemes. £1,000 is on offer to employers who are willing either to split an existing full-time job, combine regular overtime hours into a new part-time job, or provide two new part-time jobs as a way of offering more flexible working arrangements.

Employment Training (ET)

ET was introduced in September 1988, replacing the New Job Training scheme, Community Programme, Training for Enterprise, Wider Opportunities Training, and a variety of other programmes. The average length of stay on ET is six months, presently the maximum is twelve months. ET is designed to meet the needs of the individual. Anyone over the age of 18, continuously unemployed and available for work for six months or over is eligible. There are some exceptions to the six-month unemployment rule:

- People with disabilities
- Returners to the labour market
- Ex-regulars
- Ex-offenders

People whose first language is not English
People entering Enterprise Training (BEP)
Those entering training in a skills-shortage area

Participants who are in receipt of benefit upon entering ET will continue to receive their usual benefits and an additional £10 per week. There is help available for special clothing, tools and fares over £5 per week.

The measures taken by the present government to reduce the natural rate of unemployment were covered in Chapter 8.

Trends in employment

As the table following shows, employment in Britain has fallen over the last fifteen years. The major job losses have been in manufacturing but employment in the service sector has been increasing.

Employment in the UK (thousands with % of total shown in brackets)

	1981	1986	1991
Total numbers in employment	21386	20886	21719
Services	13142	13954	15457
	(61.45%)	(66.81%)	(71.17%)
Manufacturing	6099	5122	4599
	(28.52%)	(24.52%)	(21.18%)

(Source: *Employment Gazette*, July 1994, Table 1.2)

At the same time, the UK has one of the highest proportions of people in work amongst the major industrialised nations, being far above the European average. Some would argue that the UK's high activity rate in the labour market is a consequence of being a low-wage economy. Also, with large amounts of the nation's wealth tied up in housing, high mortgage repayments place a heavy burden on households. This often compels both husband and wife to work full time. The table below shows the UK to have a high activity rate compared with other nations in the EU.

Comparative Economic Activity Rates, by sex, 1989 percentage of total population

	Total	Male	Female
United Kingdom	50.9	59.5	42.6
European Union	44.9	55.6	34.9
Belgium	39.6	49.7	30.0
Denmark	56.1	61.8	50.6
Germany	47.9	59.9	36.7
Greece	40.7	53.0	29.2
Spain	38.0	51.0	25.6
France	44.7	52.1	25.6
Ireland	37.9	50.5	25.1
Italy	41.4	54.1	30.0
Luxembourg	42.4	56.1	28.7
Netherlands	45.6	56.8	34.7
Portugal	46.9	56.4	38.3
USA	51.2	55.4	44.6
Japan	51.1	60.2	39.8

(Source: *Europe in Figures*, Eurostat 1992)

Questions for review

1 What is 'unemployment'?

2 How is unemployment measured in the UK?

3 How is unemployment measured for the purpose of international comparisons?

4 Why is unemployment an economic problem as well as a personal problem?

5 Why does unemployment exist?

6 How may governments reduce the level of unemployment?

7 Discuss the regional dimensions of unemployment in the UK.

8 What economic justification is there for government intervention to reduce unemployment?

9 Explain the 'natural rate of unemployment'.

Public finance | 14

The budget 367

Taxation 368

Public expenditure 379

The budget

The political background

Before a government can *spend* any money it has to *raise* it, if it has no money of its own. The government can *borrow* money by issuing Treasury Bills or gilt-edged stock, but it gains its own *'income'* through the taxation system. The annual budget statement is the formal basis of the government's proposals for raising funds through the taxation system in the coming year. The Chancellor of the Exchequer, who is the chief financial minister in the Government, delivers this speech to Parliament during March or April. It is believed in the UK that there should not be any taxation without representation and so the people's representatives in Parliament must approve any tax changes before they become effective. Indeed, if the budget as a whole is rejected by Parliament then the government of the day has to resign because it would not have the funds necessary to continue in office. However, this is a rare event – although Parliament may change one or two of the government's proposals, it usually approves the overall budget proposals, due to the effectiveness of the party political system.

A balanced budget

During the nineteenth century and very recently it was believed that, whatever else the government did, it had to *balance its budget* – that is it had to keep its spending in line with its revenue. The government became closely involved with the economic management of the country. However, between the 1930s and 1970s the government was *expected* to manipulate its own spending and revenue-raising programmes in order to encourage full employment and stable prices. This was in line with Keynesian demand management policies. As a result, the budget was a *major tool of economic policy*. It was not only concerned with the immediate year ahead: just as firms tend to plan their financial strategies for a few years at a time, so the government, through its budgetary controls, tried to foresee the likely overall economic development of the country in the years ahead, and planned accordingly.

The budget itself is primarily concerned with the relationship between the total supply of goods and services within the economy and the total level of effective (or aggregate) demand, and so it is used to manage the level of aggregate demand. By raising taxes, a budget can close the 'inflationary gap' and by lowering taxes it can close the 'deflationary gap', assuming, of course, that the government's spending plans remain the same. More recently the idea of the balanced budget is back in favour. The unpopularity of 'demand side' Keynesian theory has been replaced by the 'supply side' monetarist theory.

Concerned with real resources

Finally, it must not be forgotten that, although the government wants money to pay for its spending, what it really wants is to build a hospital or maintain an army; that is, *real economic resources*. It needs a proportion of the country's land, labour and capital. So, in deciding how to tax themselves, the people are really deciding how resources which are needed for 'community needs' shall be taken from all the various families and firms and become available for 'public' goods and services. Consequently, the government's taxation – or *fiscal policy* – is not only a method of stabilising the economy and maintaining aggregate demand roughly in line with potential GNP, it is also concerned with the actual size of the government – or public – sector. The election in 1979 of the first Thatcher administration brought a commitment to reduce the size of the public sector as a percentage of GNP. This was in line with their monetarist belief that in many cases resources are more efficiently utilised in the private sector.

Taxation

The purpose of taxation

The main purposes of taxation and the manner in which they are achieved can be summarised as follows. Taxation could be used as follows:

a to provide community services such as defence, law and order and other public services, (part of these costs are met out of the rates levied by local authorities);

b to redistribute income by adopting a progressive system of taxation so that the burden of taxation rises with higher incomes;

c to redistribute wealth by means of capital gains taxes and inheritance tax;

d to maintain a high and stable level of employment by reducing taxation in times of depression or conversely increasing taxation in times of labour shortage;

e to check inflation by increasing taxes in order to reduce the purchasing power of the community;

f to maintain a sound balance of payments by increasing taxes to reduce home consumption of imports;

g to reduce imports (ie tariffs) by imposing taxes on foreign goods; and

h to deter consumption by imposing taxes on goods with health dangers, such as cigarettes.

A 'good' taxation system

The basic requirements of a good system of taxation are:

a *certainty* – no doubt as to the amount payable;

b *equity* – charged according to ability of taxpayer to pay;

c *economy* – not expensive to collect;

d *convenience* – as to manner and time of payment;

e *effectiveness* – meeting the government's expenditure requirements and policy goals;

f *flexibility* – easily altered to meet changing requirements; and

g *no adverse effects* – minimal effect on personal savings and hours worked.

Many of the above points were described in Adam Smith's works and became known as the 'Canons of Taxation'.

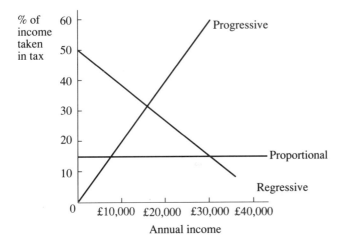

The above diagram shows how taxes can affect people on different income levels. A *progressive tax* on incomes, for example, would take a bigger percentage (proportion) of the incomes of high earners. It would therefore reduce income inequalities after tax. A *regressive tax* would do the opposite and widen the gap between rich and poor. A *proportional tax* takes the same percentage from everyone whatever their income. However, it can be argued that, say, 15 per cent from a low-income earner is a bigger relative loss than 15 per cent from a high-income earner.

Direct and indirect taxes

So far as the central government is concerned, there are two basic types of tax: *direct* and *indirect*.

Direct taxation affects the individual or the company solely on the *basis of the amount of income received* during a period or the *capital owned or acquired*. The most important forms of direct taxation are *income tax*, *capital gains tax*, *inheritance tax* and *corporation tax*. (Each of these will be examined in detail later in this chapter.)

Indirect taxation includes *value added tax*, *excise duty* and *stamp duty* and is levied on a person's *outlay* (expenditure) rather than on his *income*. The taxes are paid indirectly through the purchase price of a good or service and they are collected by the person selling the item. He is then obliged to account for it to the appropriate government department. In the case of value added tax (VAT) the amount of tax is calculated as a percentage of total turnover. However, in the case of registered suppliers – and most suppliers are registered with the Customs and Excise Department – the amount of VAT *paid by them* in purchasing new materials, etc, can be deducted from the amount of VAT they *receive* from customers before any money is paid to the department. A very few basic goods and services are exempted from having to charge VAT but the vast majority of all business transactions in the UK are liable to VAT. VAT was introduced in 1973, replacing purchase tax. There have been a variety of rates since then, but from 1979 to 1991 there was a single rate of 15 per cent. Some goods and services are either exempt or zero-rated. However, in the 1991 budget VAT was raised to 17½ per cent to fund a £140-per-head reduction in the community charge (an extremely unpopular tax which had been introduced to replace the long-standing local rating system providing income for local authorities). In April 1994, VAT was extended to cover domestic fuel. The other principal form of indirect taxation – excise duty – is specifically directed at a limited range of goods, notably petrol, alcohol and tobacco, and is based on a fixed monetary amount per quantity. It is usually added *before* VAT and constitutes an additional heavy tax on the good in question.

The present government has tried to shift the balance of taxation towards indirect taxes. The reduction in direct tax rates is designed to increase incentives and initiatives. Direct taxes are collected by the Inland Revenue and indirect taxes by Customs and Excise.

Central Government Receipts

	1989/90	£ million 1993/94
Inland Revenue:		
Income tax	48801	58401
Corporation tax	21495	15020
Capital gains tax	1854	711
Inheritance tax	1232	1321
Stamp duties	2117	1738
Petroleum revenue tax	1050	362
Total Inland Revenue	76559	77549
Customs and Excise:		
Value Added tax	29483	39248
Car tax	1519	-4
Hydrocarbon oils	8728	12742
Tobacco	5035	6518
Alcohol	4437	5170
Betting and gaming	976	1094
Customs duties	1814	2009
Agricultural levies	129	160
Total Customs and Excise	52134	66909
Vehicle excise duties	2993	3655
Oil royalties	575	607
Gas levy	335	240
Other	35	41
Total taxes and royalties	3938	4543
Social security contributions	31020	36918
Interest and dividends	9879	9332
Other receipts	3783	18815
Total Central Government Receipts	141492	226541

(Source: *Financial Statistics*, June 1994, Table 2.1A/B/C/D/E)

The obvious advantage of direct taxation, according to the principles of a 'good' system, is that it is *equitable*. Within certain limits, it is designed to ensure that people pay according to their means. However, a highly progressive structure of direct taxation (ie the more a person earns, the more tax he pays) may well act as a *disincentive* both to hard work and saving. Very high rates of marginal taxation may persuade people it is not worth working as hard as they might. Similarly, the less income a person has after paying his direct taxation, the *less he is likely to save*. In addition, the UK system tends to be *expensive to run*. Although many people have their income tax deducted from their pay packets by their employers under the PAYE (or pay-as-you-earn) system, the myriad of allowances makes the original assessment relatively complicated. In addition, of course, those people who do not have their tax deducted at source have to have individual assessments issued by the Inland Revenue. Finally, the UK tax structure has made it difficult sometimes to determine precisely what income and capital is liable to which rates of tax.

Income tax

Income tax has historically been a progressive tax levied on most forms of income, both direct and indirect. A series of allowances is given against income tax to everyone in the country, based on their personal circumstances (for example, do they have dependent children? other dependent relatives?). These allowances are designed to introduce a degree of equity into the income tax structure: people with children need more income than do those without to maintain the same standard of living. In most budgets, these allowances are uprated to take account of inflation.

The present government has reduced income tax rates considerably, in line with their belief that high rates of income tax have a disincentive effect. Income tax now starts at 20 per cent of the first £2000 of taxable income. The basic rate of tax is now 25 per cent, with a top rate on higher incomes of 40 per cent. Taxable income is what is left after all allowances have been deducted. It is on the remaining income that taxes are paid. This explains why marginal and average rates of tax are different. The marginal tax rate is the amount of tax payable on the last £ earned, wheras the average rate of tax is the overall proportion of income taken in tax.

The following table shows the amount of income tax payable on different income levels. The figures in the average rate of tax column show clearly that income tax is now only mildly progressive.

Income tax payable: by income range, 1992–93

	United Kingdom					
	tax payable at lower rate 20%	tax payable at basic rate 25%	tax payable at excess over basic rate 40%			
	number of taxpayers (millions)	number of taxpayers (millions)	number of taxpayers (millions)	Total tax payable (£million)	Average rate of tax payable (%)	Average amount of tax payable (£)
Annual income						
£3445–£4999	2.2	0.0	0.0	300	3	140
£5000–£7499	3.9	2.3	0.0	1830	7	470
£7500–£9999	3.8	3.3	0.0	3550	11	930
£10000–£14999	6.2	6.2	0.0	9980	13	1600
£15000–£19999	3.8	3.8	0.0	10050	15	2650
£20000–£29999	3.2	3.2	0.1	13430	18	4220
£30000–£39999	0.9	0.9	0.8	6150	21	7110
£40000 and over	0.7	0.7	0.7	15300	29	20810
All ranges	24.8	20.4	1.7	60590	16	2440

(Source: *Social Trends* 23, 1993, Table 5.7)

Another of the reforms which the current government has introduced is Independent Taxation for married women. Previously, married women were obliged to tell their husbands full details of their incomes, in order for the husbands to fill out the joint income tax forms. This has long been deemed inequitable.

Inheritance tax

Capital taxation is an emotive, yet serious, topic in the latter half of the twentieth century. It has to be recognised that *income* in itself is not an adequate measure of a person's *real* taxable capacity. The *ownership* of *capital* and *wealth* whether they produce any income or not, inevitably adds to the resources of the taxpayer and so there is a strong argument for taxing this aspect. In this country, it is naturally the Labour party which has been the main driving force behind the movement towards the taxation of capital, although the Conservative party also recognises the need for a measure of capital taxation.

The first major tax on capital in the UK was *estate duty*. This was a steeply progressive tax on the whole estate of a deceased person, with minor reliefs and exemptions. The principle behind it was that people should not be able to 'pass on' to their children and relatives large amounts of 'inherited wealth'.

Estate duty was renamed capital transfer tax (CTT) in 1974 and, more recently, changed again to inheritance tax. The Conservative government from 1979 onwards sought to lower direct/capital taxes and also to reduce their steeply progressive nature. In an effort to reduce the tax burden on the creators of wealth CTT's top rate of 75 per cent was reduced to 60 per cent in 1984 for wealth passed on at death. For wealth passed on during lifetime the tax rate was reduced to 30 per cent. In 1986 CTT on lifetime gifts between individuals was abolished and the remaining tax on death renamed inheritance tax. Gifts made within seven years of death were to remain on a tapered charge.

In 1987 the threshold for paying inheritance tax was raised and the number of rates reduced from seven to four. In 1989 the threshold for paying inheritance tax was raised to £118,000 and a single 40 per cent rate applies. Since then the threshold has been indexed in successive budgets. The tax had thus become much simpler to understand, but much less progressive. It should be noted that this tax is not a wealth tax (a tax on the possession of wealth) but only a tax on the inheritance of wealth.

Capital gains tax (CGT)

Capital gains tax was introduced in the mid-1960s in an attempt to tax an important element of a person's economic resources. Prior to its introduction it was possible for a person to make a 'profit' on buying and selling capital assets without having to pay tax on that profit. This was regarded as inequitable. After all, by carefully arranging one's investments it might be possible to make large capital profits without receiving very much in the way of regular income.

These profits would not be subjected to tax and so the person would have a much higher real income than other people in the comparable 'income' bracket. Capital gains tax was introduced as a tax on the profits made by people when they sold or disposed of capital assets, such as stocks and shares. Certain small disposals were, and still are, exempt and a person's own home is outside the scope of the tax – although a second house will not necessarily be exempt if a profit is made on its sale. Unlike other taxes, the taxpayer is allowed to deduct any capital losses from his capital profits before paying the tax. In 1988 there was major reform of CGT. Capital gains were effectively treated as income for tax purposes as from 6 April 1988.

Gains on sales of shares or property, for example, will be taxed at the individual's marginal rate, either 25 per cent or 40 per cent under the new rules. The government also simplified the threshold system for CGT which currently stands at £5,800 for individuals, and £2,900 for trusts. The independent taxation of husbands and wives will mean there will be two CGT allowances in a married household, giving them tax-free gains of up to £11,600 between them. Perhaps the biggest change in CGT, as far as investors in shares and unit trusts are concerned, is the withdrawal of pre-1982 gains from the tax net.

Corporation tax

Levied on the profits of companies in the 1970s, corporation tax was 52 per cent. The tax caused concern because of the effect it had on the incentives for profit-making in companies. Since profit-maximising implies efficiency it may be that efficiency in industry is reduced as firms choose alternative sources of company utility – growth, market share, a 'quiet life', etc. Certainly figures of the share of company profits in GNP fell dramatically in the 1960s and 1970s. It should, however, be remembered that many other factors explained this decline, eg loss of competitiveness in the face of new suppliers in other countries, labour problems, etc.

An additional problem is that profits provide the principle source of finance for investment by firms. Since lower profits are left after company tax, the source of finance is reduced and, as a result, the rate of investment by firms may fall. This obviously had serious consequences for the economy.

The present government has therefore carried out a major reform of company taxation in recent years. In the 1984 Budget the government launched a radical reform of company taxation. The standard rate of corporation tax has come down progressively from 52 per cent to 33 per cent, and that for small companies from 42 per cent to 25 per cent. The UK rates of corporation tax are now lower than those of most of our major industrial competitors.

The purpose of this reform was twofold:

a to ensure that business and industry should not have to bear an excessive burden of taxation; and

b to ensure that, given any particular burden, it should fall in the way that does least damage to the nation's economic performance.

Reduction of the rates of tax was accompanied by changes in the system of capital allowances. These will discourage companies from undertaking investment for the sake of tax relief and encourage them to invest money where it will create profits and new jobs.

Corporate profitability has improved since the early 1980s. How much this is due to the new corporate tax structure is difficult to ascertain. Improvements in company profitability and productivity have occurred for other reasons.

Indirect taxes

The Conservatives entered office in 1979 committed to switching part of the burden of personal taxation from direct taxes to indirect taxes – from taxes on earning to taxes on spending. In his first budget, Sir Geoffrey Howe made a bold start. The rate of *value added tax* – which was formerly levied at 8 per cent and 12½ per cent – was raised to 15 per cent. In the 1991 budget VAT was raised to 17½ per cent to raise enough revenue to cut the community charge by £140 per head.

Approximately half of all items of expenditure have remained exempt or zero-rated under VAT since the tax was introduced in 1973. These have included most food, passenger travel, house prices and rents, and young children's clothing. Some additional taxation was introduced in the 1984 budget, when building extensions and alterations and hot take-away food were brought within the tax. VAT was extended to advertisements in newspapers, journals and periodicals in 1985. A number of items used by charities, handicapped people and welfare organisations have been relieved of VAT in recent years.

In recent years the registration threshold for VAT has been raised in line with prices; currently it stands at £45,000. Although some sections of the small business world would like to see a lower threshold as a way of ensuring fair competition (eg small building and decorating firms), others have pressed for a higher threshold.

As a general rule, the *excise duties* are indexed in each Budget – ie raised in line with inflation. However, chancellors use their discretion in departing from the rule where industrial or broader budgetary considerations apply. For example, in the 1991 budget excise duties on fuel and tobacco were raised by 15 per cent (above inflation) with duties on alcohol indexed.

Overall, the combined excise duties and VAT have risen faster than prices, both since 1979 and since 1983. The duty on tobacco was up 27 per cent in real terms in the first Parliament, having lagged behind prices generally under the Labour government. The duty on beer was 38 per cent up in real terms between 1979 and 1983 and a further 7½ per cent since then. Only duties on wine and spirits have fallen in real terms, and then only in the second Parliament. On wine this reflected the government's response to pressure from the EU; on spirits it reflected the government's wish to compensate the distilling industry for the abolition of stock relief, which had hit the whisky industry in particular.

In the 1989 budget the Chancellor announced a reduction of 4p a gallon in the duty on unleaded petrol; this tax differential would offset its higher production cost. By making unleaded petrol significantly cheaper, hopefully this will reduce negative externalities in the economy.

Indirect taxes are generally regressive in nature as people purchasing goods pay the same amount in tax irrespective of their income. Excise taxes are levied on goods which have a fairly inelastic demand, thus giving a predictable source of revenue. Ironically, with cigarettes the tax is designed to reduce consumption. However, if consumption did fall dramatically the loss of tax revenue would pose significant problems for the government.

The completion of the Single European Market in 1992 also poses potential problems for some excise duties. Since some forms of alcohol are much cheaper in France than in the UK, people can now travel to France and come back loaded down with (cheaper) beer and wine. This poses problems not only for UK retailers of beer and wine, but also for government revenue. This retail price differential is caused by differing tax rates. It could be eliminated by harmonisation of EU tax rates.

North Sea Oil Taxation

North Sea Oil Revenues	
	£ billion
1979–80	2.3
1980–81	3.7
1981–82	6.5
1982–83	7.8
1983–84	8.8
1984–85	12.0
1985–86	11.4
1986–87	4.8
1987–88	3.9
1988–89	2.1
1989–90	1.6
1990–91	1.5
1991–92	0.3
1992–93	0.6
1993–94	1.0

(Source: *Financial Statistics*, June 1994)

The revenues from the UK's North Sea oilfields are shown in the above table. These take the form of royalty payments and petroleum revenue tax (PRT). Of late the government has been giving greater allowances to oil companies in order to encourage them to develop the more marginal fields. It seems likely that tax revenues from North Sea oilfields peaked in the mid-1980s.

Fiscal drag

Any progressive income tax system creates anomalies during times of inflation. Indeed, many people argue that the fall in the purchasing power of money which occurs during inflation is in itself a form of taxation. Unless the level of allowances is raised in line with the rate of inflation and the actual rates of tax lowered, it is inevitable that more and more people will be drawn into the tax net at lower and lower levels of real income. In technical terms, people's *marginal rate of tax* exceeds their *average rate of tax* by a considerable amount. This phenomenon is called *fiscal drag*. In recent years the indexation of tax allowances and the cuts in tax rates have helped to prevent fiscal drag.

Fiscal drag does not only affect direct taxation – VAT also leads to fiscal drag because as money prices rise so does the yield from VAT, since it is based on a percentage of the selling price. In 1973/74, for instance, VAT yielded £275 million more than was expected, mainly as a result of inflation. In 1987/88 tax revenues were far in excess of government estimates.

Fiscal lag

An associated phenomenon is *fiscal lag*, but there is little that can be done about this. Many taxes including corporation tax and the income tax paid by self-employed people are paid to the Inland Revenue many months *after* they are actually earned. In times of inflation this clearly has the opposite effect to fiscal drag – the value of the payments to the Inland Revenue decreases in real terms. However, short of demanding estimated advance payments, which would not be equitable or fair, there is not much that can be done to minimise this problem for the authorities. In money terms, the size of these payments is relatively small compared to the size of ordinary income tax payments.

Conclusions and suggestions

The UK taxation system has changed enormously over the last decade or so, by the reduction in direct tax rates and the shift toward indirect taxation. It has also been simplified and has become far less progressive in nature, the idea being to increase incentives and to reduce the burden of government on companies and individuals. Despite the sharp reduction in direct tax rates in the 1980s, the overall tax burden has risen with most people paying an increased percentage of their income in tax by the end of the decade.

The top rate of income tax of 40 per cent is less than half the rate which ruled for nearly four decades after the 1939–45 war. It marks an extraordinary contrast with the 98 per cent top rate (if the old investment income surcharge is included) in 1979. It is lower than the top rate in most countries and comparable with that in North America if state and provincial income taxes are taken into account.

The rich also gain substantially at present from the recent reductions in inheritance tax. The tax saving on an estate of £2m is around £345,000. The whittling down of taxes on capital transfers has been a recurrent theme of budgets over the past nine years. Yet there are good economic reasons for taxing capital – whether property, land or financial wealth – quite heavily. As the Meade committee argued in 1978, capital (unlike labour) provides a source of income that is compatible with a life of leisure.

The ex-chancellor, Nigel Lawson, has noted that there is now no tax rate in the system higher than 40 per cent. He did not mention the 500,000-odd people left in the 'poverty trap', who face marginal rates of 70–90 per cent as a result of the withdrawal of means-tested social security benefits. Nor did he mention that up to 60 per cent of welfare recipients faced real cuts in benefits in April 1989 – a sobering contrast with the £4bn of tax cuts announced in the 1988 budget.

The changes led to a further redistribution of income from poor to rich, a trend that began in 1979 after half a century of progress towards greater equality. But the philosophy, as expressed in a *Financial Times* interview, is that 'you don't make the poor rich by making the rich poor'.

It must be uncertain whether the claimed efficiency gains from lower rates will offset the social costs of greater inequality. The Institute for Fiscal Studies has pointed out that there is little evidence either to refute or confirm the hypothesis that lower rates would improve economic performance. The economy has anyway grown quite robustly in recent years without significant cuts in tax rates for most taxpayers.

Public expenditure

Introduction

In 1822 a rough estimate put the *total* expenditure of the government at around £70 million and by 1900 it had only grown to £280 million. The First World War naturally increased the level and by 1920 it had risen to some £1,600 million which represented about 25 per cent of GNP at the time. There was a considerable growth in public expenditure after the Second World War, mainly as a result of the introduction of the National Health Service which provided free medical treatment to the whole population. Indeed, by 1950 public expenditure had reached £4,680 million or 39 per cent of GNP. The table below shows how it has grown since that date to a point where it represents 50 per cent of GNP in the mid-1970s. Since 1979 government policy has been to reduce public expenditure as a percentage of GDP.

A flourishing private sector is seen as more important than an expanding public sector. An 'enterprise economy' is a priority and 'supply side' economics is concerned with expanding the use of resources by the private sector. The government is still committed to 'rolling back the boundaries of the public sector'.

General government expenditure as a percentage of GDP

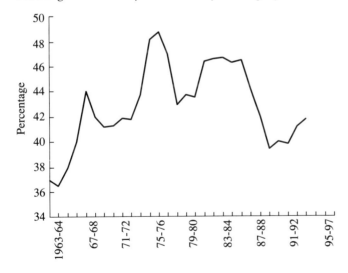

(Source: *Financial Statement and Budget Report 1992-3.*)

Shift in emphasis

The relative importance of different types of public expenditure has changed over the years as different priorities have arisen, partly out of necessity and partly from increased political and social awareness. In the 1970s pensions and social security benefits and services took a very considerable part of the public expenditure budget – around 30 per cent – while education was also a major item. In the 1990s these remain major items along with defence (see following table).

UK public spending 1991-95

	£ billion			
	1991/92 est outturn	1992/93 plans	1993/94 plans	1994/95 plans
Ministry of Defence	22.9	24.2	24.5	24.8
Foreign and Commonwealth Office	3.0	3.2	3.4	3.5
Ministry of Agriculture, Fisheries and Food	1.6	2.3	2.4	2.4
Trade and Industry	1.3	1.1	1.0	1.0
Energy	0.5	0.5	0.5	0.5
Department of Employment	3.2	3.5	3.5	3.5
Department of Transport	2.5	2.6	2.7	2.8
DOE: Housing	3.0	2.8	3.0	3.1
DOE: other environmental services	0.7	0.6	0.6	0.6
DOE: Local Government	0.3	0.3	0.2	0.2
Home Office (including Charity Commission)	2.2	2.2	2.4	2.5
Lord Chancellor's and Law Officers' Depts	1.7	1.8	1.8	1.9
Department of Education and Science	4.6	4.9	5.1	5.3
Office of Arts and Libraries	0.6	0.6	0.6	0.6
Dept of Health and Office of Population Censuses and Surveys	25.5	27.8	29.6	31.2
Department of Social Security	61.3	66.0	71.2	74.5
Scotland	5.4	5.8	6.1	6.3
Wales	2.4	2.7	2.9	3.0
Northern Ireland	6.2	6.7	7.1	7.4
Chancellor of the Exchequer's Dept	4.8	5.0	5.2	5.4
Cabinet Office, Privy Council Office and Parliament	0.4	0.5	0.5	0.5
European Communities	0.9	2.5	2.6	2.9
	155.4	167.5	176.8	184.0
Financing of public corporations other than nationalised industries	1.3	1.2	1.3	1.5
Central Government Expenditure	156.7	168.7	178.1	185.5

Central government support for local authorities	53.3	58.5	61.0	63.9
Financing requirements of nationalised industries	2.7	3.5	2.9	2.2
Reserve	-	4.0	8.0	12.0
Privatisation proceeds	-8.0	-8.0	-5.5	-5.5
Adjustment	0.3	-	-	-
Planning total	205.0	226.7	244.5	258.1
Local authority self-financed expenditure	10.5	8.5	9.0	9.0
Central government debt interest	16.7	16.5	17.5	18.5
Accounting adjustments	4.3	4.5	5.0	5.5
General government expenditures	236.5	256.2	276.0	291.1
General government expenditure (excl privatisation proceeds) as % of GDP	41.5	42	41.75	41.25

(Source: *Public Expenditure Analysis to 1994/5*, Cm 1920)

Every November the government publishes a *White Paper on Expenditure* which provides detailed estimates of its planned expenditure programme for the coming financial year, with projections for the following years as well. Very often these estimates are revised upwards, and the 'outturn' is quite different from 'plans'. Within the overall figures it is possible (and, indeed necessary) to distinguish three distinct areas of public expenditure, as each has a different effect on the government's management of the economy. The first two categories represent a use of *real* resources by the public sector. They are *current expenditure on goods and services* for public consumption and *investment by the public sector in capital*.

The former obviously includes the employment of teachers, doctors, army personnel and so on, while the latter includes public investment in schools, houses, power stations and so on. The third category of public expenditure is *transfer payments*, which, it will be remembered, are 'government payments for which no goods or services are received in return'. Their impact is very different from the impact of the other two categories. Although their cost is included in public expenditure figures and their size directly affects both the levels of national insurance and general taxation, the goods which are ultimately bought with the money form part of *personal* – and not *public* – consumption. Indeed, the government's finance department – called the *Treasury* – has taken to referring to this type of expenditure as the cost of *publicly financed private consumption*.

It must be remembered that transfer payments are redistributions of spending power from person to person – they are not claims on real resources as such and so do not take resources out of the private sector. In theory, it would be possible for public expenditure to *exceed* 100 per cent of gross national income, while most of the consumption and investment would actually be done by the private sector, because if the money raised through national insurance contributions and taxation was merely re-channelled back to (different) private hands, then the State would simply act as a clearing-house – it would not be using up resources on its own account.

Dangers of transfer payments

The dangers of large-scale transfer payments so far as the economist is concerned is that a fall in after-tax incomes coupled with a rise in transfer payments *may* lead to a distortion of the economy through their direct effects on incentives and the free market mechanism. The reason for the distortion can be stated quite simply – ignoring any *social* and *humane* reasons for an increase in transfer payments.

Many transfer payments are received on the basis of *need*, or rather, for *doing nothing*, while taxes are levied on those in employment who are *doing a job of work*. Some economists believe that the size of the so-called social wage, and in particular of unemployment benefits, has discouraged unemployed unskilled workers in the UK from actively seeking employment, and therefore may have made the unemployment problem worse rather than better. However, this view is by no means universally accepted.

The social wage

There is an important difference between straightforward *transfer payments* and the *social wage*. The social wage includes *all* transfer payments, but also includes public expenditure on education, housing, law and order and certain subsidies. In other words, it includes all those government activities which directly *lower* personal expenditure (eg individuals do not pay directly for their children's education but they gain considerable benefit from the education service). If transfer payments distort the supply of labour within the economy, subsidies, which are really a disguised form of transfer payment, distort the supply of goods and services. They effectively provide a false signal in the normal operation of the price mechanism, because by reducing the cost of a good, subsidies must increase the effective demand for that good. If economic resources are used to meet this excess demand, then fewer resources are available to meet the demand for those goods which have not been subsidised.

Expenditure and income of local authorities

A large part of total government expenditure is actually spent by the local authorities rather than by central government. It is, for example, local government that provides most education services, most government housing, social services, public lighting, street-cleaning and refuse collection, roads, police and fire services. How the money is spent depends partly on central legislation (for example, all local authorities must provide a free education for all children under 16); partly on instructions from the relevant department of state (the Department of the Environment takes responsibility for roads, planning and housing while the

Department of Health and Social Security takes responsibility for hospitals and social services), usually in the form of a White Paper; and partly on the decision of the local authority. The local authorities are elected by the local electorate on a range of specific policies for local government expenditure and are served by a local government civil service.

Until recently local authorities raised revenue from rates and revenue could be increased by raising the rate per £ or rateable value. Obviously, the local authorities with the greatest need to spend money (because they had the most poverty, poor housing, poor social conditions) tended to have the lowest rateable values (which depended on property values in the area) and ratepayers whose incomes were least able to stretch to pay a large rates bill. It was thus inevitable that these authorities needed subsidies from central government to supplement their rate income. Additionally, since a large part of local government expenditure is required by central government legislation and directives, it is only fair that central government should pay for this expenditure out of central government funds. About 70 per cent of local government expenditure is paid for by central government. The Rate Support Grant from central government was determined according to the rateable values of each local authority (with the authorities with the lowest rateable values getting the biggest subsidy) and the perceived need for local government expenditure in each authority's area. The local authorities supplemented their incomes from rates and from central government by borrowing.

In recent years local authority spending has been controlled in line with the public sector restraints. There have been limits put on both local authority borrowing and until recently the Rate Support Grant. Also increases in the rates were curtailed by 'rate-capping', and more recently by 'charge-capping'.

The rating system has now been replaced following a prolonged period of debate. The old system had a number of defects:

a business ratepayers provided nearly half the rate revenue but did not have a vote in local elections;

b only 18 million out of 35 million electors in England were liable to pay rates;

c rates took little account of people's use of services;

d rates also tended to be rather regressive.

The government introduced a reformed business rate (for shops, offices etc) and a replacement of the domestic rating system by the introduction of a *community charge* in 1990. Under this system, local authorities set the level of community charge which had to be paid by every adult resident of the area. The amount paid was the same for everyone, regardless of income (although there were rebates for students and those on some state benefits). Part of the purpose of levying the same charge on all was to ensure that people would think carefully before voting for high spending councils. Under the previous rating system, non-ratepayers were able to vote for high spending councils without fear of being required to pay for the services provided.

The community charge was very unpopular, causing many 'poll tax' protests throughout the country. It was a highly regressive tax, since it took no account of ability to pay. It also proved to be extremely difficult and expensive to collect, and courts throughout the UK became clogged with hundreds of cases of non-payment of community charge.

The government was forced to give in to public pressure, and raised the level of VAT to 17½ per cent in order to pay for a one-off reduction of £140 on everyone's community charge bill. (The actual bills had proved to be considerably higher than the government had estimated). Further protests forced the government to scrap the community charge system altogether, and a new 'council tax' was introduced. This abandoned the principle of the same charge for everyone, and returned to a system based on the value of residential property. Homes were assigned to one of a number of 'bands' depending on their value. Within each band, the level of tax was the same for each property. A 25 per cent reduction is granted for single occupancy. This has proved to be less unpopular than the community charge. Local authorities are still attempting to recover community charge arrears.

Local Authority Revenues

	England and Wales 1990/91 £ billion	% of total
Capital Income: Total	7725.3	11.67%
Loans	3067.5	4.6%
Government grants	1024.2	1.55%
Sales and other sources	3635.0	5.5%
Revenue Income: Total	58465.5	88.32%
Rates and community charges	21704.4	32.8%
Government grants	24163.0	36.5%
Other income incl rents/tolls/fees/interest	12598.1	19.03%
Total income	66190.8	

(Source: *Annual Abstract of Statistics 1994*, Tables 16.18/19/21/24)

Balancing income and expenditure of government

In very simple terms, taxation and national insurance contributions should finance public expenditure and transfer payments. In the nineteenth century a 'balanced budget' was the aim of all governments. Any shortfall between taxation and expenditure can be financed by government borrowing in the money market through the issue of Treasury Bills in the short term or gilt-edged stock in the longer term, but overall the budget should ultimately balance. However, as has already been noted, governments may try, as they did in the 1950s and 1960s, to influence the level of aggregate demand either upwards or downwards in an attempt to stimulate or depress the economy towards a full-employment level, and so they may deliberately plan an 'unbalanced budget'. The budget will be in *deficit* when the government wants to raise aggregate demand and it will be in *surplus* when it wants to *lower* aggregate demand.

Deficits arise

Unfortunately, the application of such theories is not quite so simple as it sounds. Ignoring the problems of obtaining precise estimates of the amount by which the government needs to stimulate or depress the economy, there is also the problem of equating the economy's overall needs with the government's own day-to-day spending requirements. Even if the management of the economy requires a sizeable government surplus, this does not mean it is possible to achieve one in the short term. For instance, many government spending programmes are long term and cannot be turned on or off at will. Similarly, transfer payments cannot always be stopped just because the demands of economic management say the government must run a surplus.

This problem will be examined in more detail in the next chapter on the management of the economy, but for the time being it need only be noted that the government accounts can be in a substantial *deficit* position (ie *the level of public expenditure exceeds the level of taxation*). In the early 1970s the government's deficit tended to be very large in relation to the size of GNP. However, the monetarist economics of the Thatcher administration demanded that the size of the budget deficit be reduced to zero. This was achieved in 1988, and a budget surplus continued until 1991 when the recession pushed government finances back into deficit again.

Deficit financing

A deficit is financed by borrowing from the public but, strictly speaking, short-term borrowing, in the form of Treasury Bills, is not used to finance such a deficit. Treasury Bills are designed to cover temporary differences between the level of receipts and the level of expenditure. The nature of taxation means that receipts tend to come in spasmodic bursts while the nature of expenditure is a continual flow. Inevitably, there will be times when expenditure is not covered by receipts during a given period of say, a month, and so the government issues a block of 90-day Treasury Bills to 'finance' the expenditure until taxation receipts 'catch-up'. In practice, of course, there is a continual process of renewing this type of short-term borrowing with a new issue of Bills replacing a maturing issue. The borrowing, which really finances an annual deficit in government expenditure, is the issue of gilt-edged stock or national savings schemes.

Terminology (the PSBR and MTFS)

In technical language, a government deficit is referred to as the *public sector borrowing requirement*, or the PSBR, because this is the amount it has to borrow in order to maintain its expenditure. There are two ways of measuring the PSBR, and until the latter half of the 1970s the UK was 'out-of-step' with most other industrialised nations. The first method (which was conventional UK practice) is to *include* not only the deficit in the *government's* expenditure programme, but also the borrowing which is done by the *nationalised industries*. The second method excludes the latter and this makes a difference to the figures. In order to avoid confusion, the smaller figure is sometimes referred to as the *General Government Borrowing Requirement*.

There has been an increasing policy emphasis on the size of the PSBR. When the government set its monetary targets for the medium term (see Chapter 10) it also announced targets for the PSBR. The reason for this is that borrowing by the government competes for funds in the money markets ('crowds out' the private sector) and will bid up interest rates. Thus, with any given private sector demand for money and the money supply, interest rates will be higher the higher the PSBR. Since high interest rates create a number of problems (see Chapter 10), the government might prefer to reduce the PSBR.

The PSBR can also cause an increase in the money supply if it is financed by selling Treasury Bills to the banking sector. Accordingly, the *medium-term financial strategy (MTFS)* has worked towards a zero PSBR from 1988 onwards. The commitment to lower monetary growth, and public spending as a smaller percentage of GDP, are also part of the present government's MTFS.

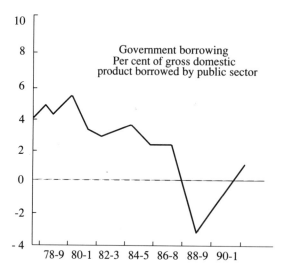

Government borrowing
Per cent of gross domestic product borrowed by public sector

The budget surplus of 1988–9 meant a repayment of the National Debt, lowering its burden on the economy. A lower level of public debt and the resultant lower servicing costs will lower the tax burden in future years. However, in 1991 the government found its finances running into deficit again. The recession of the early 1990s has meant falling tax revenues and rising government expenditure on benefits; these are the inevitable consequences of rising unemployment.

Public sector borrowing requirement

	£ billion	% share of GDP current market prices	
1989/90	-7.9	1.5%	Public Sector Debt Repayment
1990/91	-0.5	0.1%	(PSDR)
1991/92	13.9	2.4%	
1992/93	36.6	6.1%	
1993/94	45.9	N/A	

(Source: *National Income and Expenditure (Blue Book) 1993*, Table 1)

The National Debt

When the government has a deficit, the total level of government indebtedness rises, and conversely, as and when the government's account is in surplus, the level of debt is reduced. This total level of central government indebtedness is referred to as the *National Debt*. It is a long-term debt and has accumulated over the years, with new borrowing replacing maturing loans of one sort or another. Naturally, there have been times when the Debt has increased dramatically, notably during the two World Wars when vast amounts of borrowing were required to finance the war efforts. There was also a considerable increase in the total during the mid-1970s when there were enormous deficits in government expenditure. The National Debt relates only to the central government. Each part of the public sector (nationalised industries, local government and central government) has outstanding liabilities. The National Debt had been falling as a percentage of GDP during the late 1980s, due to Public Sector Debt Repayments (due to government budget surpluses). This position was reversed at the begining of the 1990s as the economy plunged once more into recession. The PSDR became once more a PSBR. In the financial year 91/92, the National Debt expressed as a percentage of GDP rose by 1.6 per cent to stand at 30.4 per cent.

Types of debt

a Funded debt arises from the permanent loans that the country is under no obligation to repay. Two examples of this are 2½ per cent Consols (Consolidated Stock) and 3½ per cent War Loan. People who hold this type of debt can realise their capital by selling the stock to someone else.

b Unfunded debt comprises those loans (gilt-edged securities) that fall due for repayment after a certain number of years, at which time they have to be either repaid in cash or renewed.

c The 'floating debt' should be treated separately from the other types of debt as it represents the government's accumulated short-term borrowing through:

   i   the issue of Treasury Bills; and
   ii day-to-day loans from the Bank of England (Ways and Means Advances).

Management of the debt

This is the responsibility of the Bank of England, although it is subject to certain policy instructions from the Treasury. Various parts of the debt (ie the unfunded debt) will be maturing at any given time and will have to be repaid. If it is not possible to repay the debt from surplus government revenue, the bank will have to re-finance the debt. Movements in the level of interest rates naturally affect the cost of borrowing and so the likely future trend of such rates is an important factor in the management of the debt.

Composition of UK public sector debt 1991

	£ billion
Central Government	
National Debt	190209
Sterling Debt	8270
Foreign Currency Debt	34646
Other liabilities:	
Net indebtedness to Banking Dept.	1245
Deposits with NSB ordinary account	1474
Accrued interest etc on National Savings	4311
Notes and coins in circulation	18720
Local Authorities	
Sterling debt	54148
Foreign currency debt	642
Public corporations	
Sterling debt	13252
Foreign currency debt	1160
Public sector debt held outside the public sector	194956
Sterling debt held by:	
Domestic private sector	163454
Overseas	21811
Foreign currency debt held by:	
Domestic private sector	916
Overseas	8775

(Source: *Annual Abstract of Statistics 1994*, Table 16.3)

The National Debt is the result of government borrowing over many years. When, in the late 1980s, the government's income exceeds expenditure, the surplus can be used to redeem debt or acquire financial assets. When borrowing, the government has to decide what kind of new debt to issue (or which financial assets to sell); and when repaying, which debts to redeem (or which financial assets to acquire). These decisions and, more generally, decisions about the management of the government's financial assets and liabilities can have important effects on the economy, and are guided by the government's funding policy.

How does the management of government debt affect the economy? Most obviously, when governments finance deficits by 'printing' an excessive quantity of money (notes and coin are a particular form of government debt) that leads to inflation. In order to defeat inflation, it is vital that funding policy supports monetary policy in maintaining steady downward pressure on inflation. On a different front, governments also seek, while avoiding inflationary financing, to manage their debts in a way that keeps the cost of servicing debt as low as possible.

Whether the government borrows 'long', in the form of gilt-edged securities, or 'short', in the form of 'Treasury Bills and other floating debt', depends on the relationship between current interest rates and expectations of future interest rates. For example, if interest rates are currently high and expected to fall, the government should borrow 'short', planning to refinance the loan at lower interest rates in the near future.

National Savings Securities are sold to the public directly and the government made a great effort to increase the proportion of debt financed in this way (to reduce its pressure on the financial system) by releasing index-linked National Savings securities. The public was naturally worried about the effect of inflation on the value of its savings and so took up this offer enthusiastically. The volume of externally held debt depends on the current interest rate on this debt compared to interest rates on similar debts elsewhere and on the expectations of likely exchange rate changes in the future.

Burden of the National Debt

It is necessary to differentiate between the 'money' burden and the 'real' burden:

a The money burden is determined by the sum that has to be set aside annually to meet the interest payments.

b The real burden is dependent upon the actual resources of the country that are used in providing both interest payments and repayment of the principle capital.

It should be clear that where any part of the National Debt is held by foreigners or people outside the UK, then the servicing of the debt will be a drain on the resources of the country. On the other hand, where the debt is held by people within the country, then the servicing of it represents merely a transfer of purchasing power from taxpayers to rentiers (holders of the debt); although it should not be forgotten that the servicing of the debt represents a high proportion of total government revenue, and therefore it can be argued that the resultant need for higher taxation acts as a disincentive to work and production.

Questions for review

1. What are the main purposes of taxation in the UK?
2. Explain the 'canons of taxation'.
3. Explain the following taxes (with examples):
    a. progressive taxation;
    b. regressive taxation;
    c. proportional taxation;
    d. indirect taxes;
    e. direct taxes.
4. What are the main sources of government revenue?
5. Why does the government need revenue?
6. Explain the PSBR.
7. Why does the government need to borrow?

Management of the economy | 15

The inflation problem   393

The Phillips curve   397

The inflation problem

The aim of governments

The main aim of governments is to manage the economy so as to ensure full employment, stable prices, a healthy balance of payments and substantial economic growth. This is perhaps the most serious and difficult problem which confronts economists, that is, how to ensure that both political and social demands are met. The present government has given greater priority to stable prices than full employment. These first two items can be examined in the broad context of monetary and fiscal policies as well as the other types of policy instruments which are open to a government. This chapter now discusses the overall management of the economy.

A warning

So far in this textbook, it has been possible to make fairly definitive statements about economic theories and ideas – if A, then B. However, in the area of economic management there are so many variables and so many indeterminate factors that it is impossible to make any definite predictions about the outcome of any particular policy decision. Admittedly, there are various schools of economic thought which maintain that any given policy would, if carried through effectively, solve all the problems facing an economy. Even if they were right, however, the chances of events all 'going their way' are remote. Indeed, it is not just a matter of deciding on the correct policy: what is wrong with the economy first needs to be analysed *correctly*, and, not surprisingly, that is open to many different interpretations.

An example

The extent and the causes of inflation are prime examples of the difficulties which economics students face when they examine different schools of thought. 'Inflation' has previously been defined as a *continual rise in prices which results in a fall in the purchasing power of money*, but, as a general definition, that does not give any indication of the *size* and *extent* of any inflationary problem. Before inflation can be cured the approximate size and cause of the problem has to be known so that the correct economic policies – whatever they are – can be applied in the correct dosage.

The various measures

The most usual measure of the current rate of inflation is based on the *retail price index*. This is a weighted index of all goods and services sold to the final customer. However, it is still difficult to choose the 'correct' measures even of this index. First, one could look at the change in the index over a one month period, but this could easily be affected by exceptional factors, such as a once-and-for-all reduction or increase in indirect taxes. Clearly, this would not give a fair measure of the general current rate. Secondly, one could look at the change over the preceding year and then project that rate of change into the current year, but there is very little evidence to suggest that this would be accurate. Circumstances change and it is unlikely that the rate of inflation would stay the same from year to year. So, a compromise formula is normally used. The change in the index in the preceding *three* months is taken and then projected forward for the coming year. However, even this figure can be misleading unless certain adjustments are made. One or two of the months taken could be exceptional and, in addition, different months of the year traditionally show different rates regardless of the underlying rate of inflation. This is particularly apparent in winter months when the price of food rises sharply. So, even with the three months' figures it is important to *annualise* the figures to take account of both ordinary and exceptional factors, such as changes in indirect taxation. It is also important to remember that the figures can only provide an indication of the *underlying trend* of inflation, rather than a definitive quantative value.

Demand pull inflation

One possible explanation for a general rise in prices and incomes is the existence of an inflationary gap between aggregate demand and maximum supply. As explained in Chapter 12, this inflationary gap may occur even when there is substantial unemployment. Indeed, government attempts to get unemployment below the 'natural' level through Keynesian expansionary policies may be creating the *inflationary gap*. The excess demand pulls prices up in the economy in exactly the same way as excess demand has this effect in an individual good or factor market. Firms have insufficient resources to produce the extra output required so prices of goods and services rise. The attempts by firms to acquire extra resources are unsuccessful since no spare resources exist of the right type, and so factor prices start to rise. There is, therefore, a general rise in prices and incomes in the economy, ie inflation.

Inflation caused by monetary expansion (monetary inflation)

According to monetarists, any expansion of the money supply which exceeds the rate of growth of real output will result in a rising price level after a two-year time lag (discussed in Chapter 10). It may be interesting to examine the differences between demand pull and monetary inflation. Do they seem the same but have different origins? Some evidence of a money supply time lag is seen in the following diagram:

Monetary base and inflation 12 month percentage changes

Cost push inflation

Prices of goods and factors may rise independently of demand or monetary conditions. If the price of a factor of production rises in excess of any increase in productivity, this will increase the costs of production of firms. In order to maintain their profits, firms will then increase their prices. We would then expect other owners of factors to demand higher money incomes in order to maintain their real incomes in the face of rising prices for goods and services. The two principle causes of cost push inflation are rising prices for imported raw materials and excessive wage demands from trade unions. From this a wage-price spiral develops with higher prices causing higher wage claims, which put up costs and then, consequently, prices.

Combination of factors

At any time, it is not at all clear exactly what is the cause of inflation. Several factors may be operating at once or in sequence. All that can be observed clearly is the process of inflation. The familiar picture is: inflation starts somewhere – prices rise; in order to preserve their real incomes all factors demand higher money incomes; this increases the cost of production; in order to preserve their profit margins, firms increase prices for goods and services; factors demand increased money incomes, and so on. Alternatively, the process may have started with rising factor incomes which lead to firms raising their prices in order to maintain profits; owners of factors demand higher money incomes, and the process goes on as before.

The process of inflation may itself generate inflationary pressures; first, if owners of factors expect inflation to continue they will demand incomes for the next year which are higher by the amount of the expected rate of inflation during that year. Any factor owners that want a *real* increase in income will demand an income increase which is greater than the expected rate of inflation. If they secure this income increase, the costs of production rise faster than the expected rate of inflation so the rate of inflation is higher than expected. The rate of inflation therefore tends to accelerate.

Secondly, domestic inflation, which is more rapid in the UK than the inflation rate in some other countries, will mean a loss in competitiveness for domestically produced goods in both the home and foreign markets. If fewer exports are sold and the home market buys more imports, the balance of trade moves towards deficit, putting pressure, ceteris paribus, on the exchange rate (see Chapters 17 and 18). When the exchange rate falls, exports become cheaper on foreign markets but imports become more expensive here. Since Britain's imports are largely of raw materials for industry and food, rising import prices result in higher costs of production and an increased cost of living. Higher prices for goods and demand for increased incomes will follow, ie more inflation.

Inflation in Britain (recent years)

The following table shows the rate of change in UK retail prices from 1985–90. The mid-1980s were a period of very low inflation. In the late 1980s the UK began to suffer from rising inflation again. In 1990 UK inflation hit the psychologically worrying level of 10 per cent ('double-digit inflation'). The recession of the early 90s has caused a return to very low inflation levels, due to very depressed consumer demand. The annual inflation rate fell to 1.6 per cent in 1993.

RPI and RPI excluding mortgage interest payments, percentage annual change, 1988 to 1992

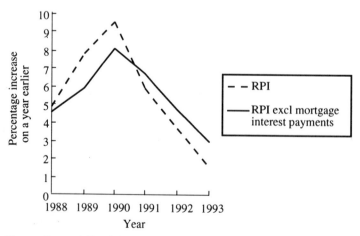

(Source: *Economic Trends*, June 1994, Table 3.1)

Management of the economy

International Inflation Comparisons (1993) (annual % change)

UK	1.6%
Germany	4.1%
France	2.1%
US	2.9%
Japan	1.3%

(Source: *Employment Gazette*, July 1994)

Earnings and prices: whole economy

In recent years UK inflation, as measured by the RPI, has been exceeded by the increase in wages as measured by the average earnings index (see following diagram). Thus those *in work* in the 1980s increased their real incomes and probably also their standard of living. However, by the early 1990s wages and inflation were running very close together.

Average earnings index and RPI index, 1988 to 1993

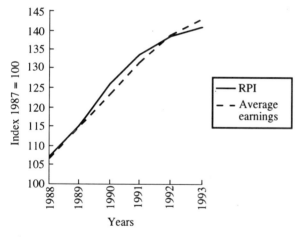

(Source: *Economic Trends*, June 1994)

The Phillips curve

Is there a connection between unemployment and inflation? Work published by Professor A W Phillips in 1958 seemed to show that there was historically a quite predictable relationship between the level of unemployment and the level of inflation. Between 1861 and 1966, the rate of unemployment in any year compared to the rate of inflation in that year fell into a reasonably predictable pattern with, for example, an unemployment rate of 1 per cent being associated with an inflation rate of 8.7 per cent, while an unemployment rate of 4 per cent was associated with an inflation rate of 0.5 per cent. The original Phillips curve is shown in the following graph.

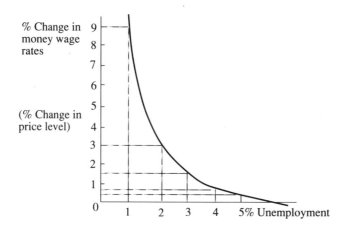

There thus appears to be a trade-off between inflation and unemployment, with lower inflation rates associated with higher levels of unemployment and the increase in the rate of inflation associated with any reduction in unemployment being greater the lower the existing level of unemployment. Thus the inflation cost of solving unemployment appears to be higher the lower the level of unemployment aimed for. Similarly, any government aiming to reduce inflation must expect higher increases in unemployment the lower the level of inflation aimed for.

There are a number of possible explanations for this relationship. Suppose that inflation is caused by demand pull pressures. Then, as aggregate demand rises in the economy, the inflationary pressures increase. This is particularly likely if we consider the true nature of the economy. At any time there are a number of industrial sectors, some of whom are expanding, others declining, and all at different rates. Any increase in demand will go more into some sectors than others, presumably more into the expanding rather than the contracting sectors. Now given that resources are relatively immobile, increasing demand will create inflation in the expanding sectors of the economy which are already short of resources, will create jobs in some intermediate sectors of the economy where there are some surplus resources, and will have little effect on unemployment in the declining sectors of the economy. As aggregate demand declines, this reduces inflationary pressures in some sectors while creating unemployment in others. Higher unemployment is an indicator of excess supply in the labour market.

Shifts in the Phillips curve

The relationship between inflation and unemployment changed substantially from the early 1970s. The following graph shows actual unemployment and inflation rates.

UK unemployment and inflation 1971 to 1993

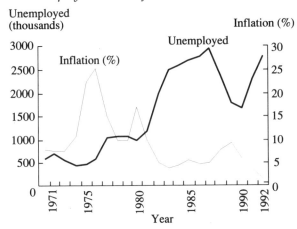

(Source: *Economic Trends*, June 1994)

Up to that period, unemployment tended to be high when inflation was low and vice versa, while both varied between 2 per cent and zero. After that, while there still seemed to be, some of the time, an inverse relationship between inflation and unemployment, the relationship was much more unreliable, and both were at much higher levels in the 1970s. The 1980s saw higher unemployment and lower inflation.

Therefore, there is evidence that the Phillips curve is shifting, as shown in the following diagram. A higher rate of inflation is now associated with any level of unemployment and a higher rate of unemployment with any rate of inflation.

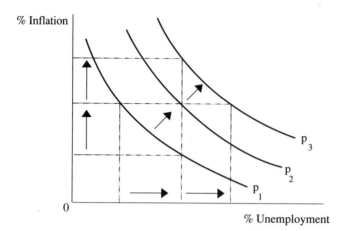

There are two explanations for this shift:

a There are external inflationary pressures, such as rising prices for imported goods or a declining exchange rate, which means that with a given internal situation there will be a higher level of inflation associated with any level of unemployment.

b 'Natural' unemployment has increased with increasing structural problems, such as higher unemployment and social security payments and trade unions pushing for wage increases in spite of possible unemployment effects. (See Chapter 13.) There is, therefore, a higher level of unemployment associated with any level of inflation.

Monetarist theory: unemployment and inflation and the Phillips curve

Inflation is induced if a government implements expansionary policies (Keynesian) because it considers that the level of unemployment at the natural rate is 'too high' and that the economy is not at 'full' employment. However, unemployment can be held below the natural rate only by an acceleration of monetary growth which creates the illusion of rising real wage rates and so induces the 'unemployed' to take jobs. According to monetarist theory, changes in the money supply feed straight through to the level of demand; in the short run this alters real output and employment, but in the longer run it changes only the price level. Hence, accelerating monetary growth leads to accelerating inflation.

In detail the argument goes as follows: let us suppose that unemployment is at the natural rate, U^* in the following diagram, that wage rates and prices are stable, the average real wage is constant, and the growth of the money supply is zero. For simplicity, we assume that productivity growth is zero so that wages and prices change in the same proportion. Assume that this stable situation has existed for some time and expectations, based on past experience, are that in the future the price level will be stable. The simple Phillips curve labelled pe = 0 (expected price change = 0) represents the trade-off between unemployment and inflation when workers anticipate stable prices. We are at point A in the diagram below. U^*, however, represents too high a rate of unemployment for the government which undertakes monetary expansion. The money supply is raised by 3 per cent, the demand for goods rises, employers anticipate higher prices for their products, and so the demand for labour rises. The demand for labour is now in excess of the supply and money wage rates begin to rise. Some of the unemployed interpret this as a rise in real wages – on the basis of past experience they expect that the price level will remain stable – hence they anticipate higher real wages, take jobs, and unemployment falls to U_1. We are now at point B. Unemployment has fallen but rising money wage rates raise costs and prices. With constant productivity, wage inflation of 3 per cent raises prices by 3 per cent; thus, real wages are again constant. Once this is perceived, unemployment will rise back to the natural rate (but now accompanied by 3 per cent inflation, point C), as the formerly unemployed, realising that they have not achieved higher real wages, once more move out of employment. The short run Phillips curve has shifted up to pe = 3, price expectations are now that there will be 3 per cent inflation. Only a rate of wage increases above this will reduce unemployment, because only the anticipation of rising real wages will keep unemployment below the natural rate. If the government wishes to avoid point C it has to increase monetary expansion above 3 per cent, to say 6 per cent. This induces money wage increases above the 3 per cent expected inflation rate and leads workers to anticipate rising real wages, which maintains unemployment at U_1. We are now at point D. Money wage rates and prices rise to a 6 per cent rate of increase; 6 per cent becomes the expected rate of inflation, the Phillips curve shifts up, and a money wage increase above 6 per cent is necessary to keep unemployment below the natural rate. Money supply growth and then inflation accelerate to 9 per cent. To keep unemployment below the natural rate, inflation must continue to accelerate. The long-run trade-off is between, not *the level of inflation* and *the level of unemployment*, but *the rate of change of the rate of inflation* and *the level of unemployment*. There is no long-run trade-off between wage inflation and unemployment, the long-run Phillips curve is vertical at U^*.

The acceleration of inflation will come to an end only when the government stops accelerating the growth of money and allows unemployment to rise to the natural rate. If, when monetary growth and inflation reached 24 per cent (point E), the government decided that the control of inflation should take precedence over the employment target and stopped the acceleration of monetary growth, then the acceleration of the rate of inflation would cease. Assume that the rate of growth of the money supply is held at a constant rate of 24 per cent, wage rates and prices rise at 24 per cent, real wage rates are constant, unemployment rises to U^*, the natural rate, and the actual and expected rates of inflation are equal. We have moved from point E to point F on the short Phillips curve ṗe = 24. This shows that raising employment to the natural rate by holding monetary growth at a constant rate merely stabilises inflation at a given rate, it does not reduce the inflation rate. Any *constant* rate of inflation is consistent with real wage-rate equilibrium and unemployment at the natural rate.

The monetarist model of the inflationary process

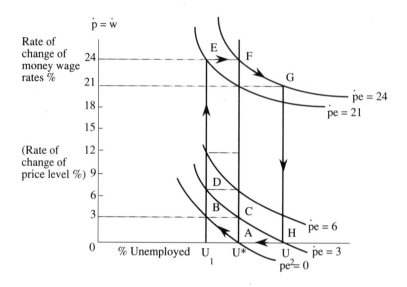

To reduce inflation, money supply growth has to be reduced below the rate of inflation, ie here below 24 per cent. The consequence of this, according to monetarist theory, is a fall in the demand for goods and deficient demand in the labour market. Now there is unemployment, and everyone willing to work at the going wage rate cannot find work. This causes downward pressure on real wages and so on the rate of wage inflation. If monetary growth is reduced to 21 per cent, wage inflation falls to 21 per cent, while workers anticipate, on the basis of recent experience, that price inflation will be 24 per cent, real wages are expected to fall and unemployment rises to U_2. We are at point G. The rate of price inflation comes down to 21 per cent. As long as unemployment is held at U_2 by a gradual reduction in the rate at which the money supply grows, then the inflation rate will fall, followed by a fall in the expected inflation rate; the short-run Phillips curve will shift downwards. Ultimately wage and price stability are achieved at point H. Money supply growth is now down to zero, the government need reduce it no further. Soon people come to anticipate the constant wage rates and prices which now exist, real wage rates are expected to be stable, and unemployment falls to U^*. We are now back at point A, government and people being wiser than they were before the journey (according to the monetarists).

Prices and incomes policy

Prices and incomes policies are a statutory or voluntary constraint on the increase in prices and incomes in the economy. The government imposes or secures from employees and firms an agreement that the rate of increase in prices and incomes will be checked.

For example, the government might legislate that there be *no* increases in prices or incomes for an indefinite period. This will, of course, immediately check the rate of inflation, with the great immediate advantage that this has been achieved without any drop in aggregate demand and employment.

However, a prices and incomes policy may not eliminate the inflationary pressures in the economy. Suppose inflation is being caused by an inflationary gap. Instead of the excess demand in the economy being eliminated by rising prices, prices will be held at a level below equilibrium. The excess demand will then have to be dealt with in some other way, such as rationing, which, however it is done, is likely to reduce consumer utility. Suppose, alternatively, that inflation is being caused by rising prices for factors of production – *cost push inflation*. The prices and incomes policy is unlikely to remove the cost pressures. If costs rise (most likely where these are the prices of imported raw materials) and firms are unable to increase their prices, profit margins will be squeezed. This may result in reduced investment and a fall in aggregate demand.

However, if inflation is caused by expectations of inflation, a firmly imposed prices and incomes policy will change these expectations and thus remove the inflationary pressure. If trade unions are assured that there will be no increase in the price of goods and services during the following year, there is no need for them to secure an increase in their money income in order to maintain their real income. If the inflationary pressures in the economy came from inflationary wage demands in anticipation of inflation, the inflationary pressure is removed by the prices and incomes policy.

It has, nevertheless, been argued that a prices and incomes policy removes all the *allocative flexibility of the price mechanism*. Suppose demand increases for a particular good because of a change in consumer preferences. Normally, without the control on prices, the price of the good would rise and this would encourage firms to put more resources into the production of this good. Similarly, factors of production are normally re-allocated from falling to rising priority production by changes in relative incomes. If incomes cannot change because of the incomes policy, this reallocation will not take place.

The trade unions dislike prices and incomes policies since they reduce their ability to use union monopoly power in labour markets to secure higher real incomes for their members. The government and firms may then be put under increasing pressure, with threat of strike action, to return to 'free collective bargaining'.

In order to deal with some of the problems created by a completely inflexible prices and incomes policy, the policies are usually made more flexible so that some price or income increases will be allowed. Where there have, for example, been substantial increases in the costs of imported raw materials, prices would be allowed to rise to check the squeeze on profit margins. Where there has been a rise in productivity, incomes are allowed to rise.

The problem with allowing some prices and incomes to rise is that some individuals begin to 'lose out' as a result of the prices and incomes policy. Suppose some prices are rising because of rising raw material prices, anyone whose money income does not rise will suffer a fall in their real income. Other individuals will appear to be doing better as their money incomes rise because of real (or apparent) increases in their productivity. The longer a prices and incomes policy lasts, the more unpopular it tends to become, as it increasingly causes a major reallocation of real income. In Britain, prices and incomes policies have always been abandoned after a certain period. For example, the latest effort at control of prices and incomes began in 1971 and ended in 1978. It was spread over a Conservative and Labour administration.

Disappointing evidence has been produced on *the long run efficacy of prices and incomes policies*. Given that they have to be abandoned eventually, a period of restraint on prices and incomes must be followed by a return to normal market conditions. The long-run efficacy of such policies must therefore depend on what happens *after* the policy has been abandoned. Evidence seems to show that, while incomes policies may check the rate of increase in money incomes during the period of the policy, as soon as the policy is relaxed the rate of increase in money incomes accelerates so rapidly that soon money incomes are at the level that might have been expected for the period in the absence of incomes policy.

Prices and incomes policies *cost* a great deal to administer. The wider the controls, the more effective, at least in the short run, the control on inflation, but the greater the administration cost. If the controls then produce no long-run advantage, one must ask whether the imposition of such policies are worthwhile given the cost and the long-run benefit.

It may also be true that prices and incomes policies can only be effective, even in the short run, when the economy is in a situation where a drop in the rate of inflation might be expected anyway. For example, the prices and incomes policy of 1971–8 was initially ineffective in checking the acceleration of inflation. The economy was at the time experiencing a boom (with high demand-pull inflationary pressures) and the money supply had increased enormously. The prices and incomes policy appeared to become effective in 1976–7 just when the economy was moving into a decline as a result of the disastrous effects on the world economy of the high increase in the price of oil. At the same time, the money supply was growing at a lower rate than the rate of inflation, so monetarists argue that the check in the rate of inflation can be attributed to the real drop in the money supply, and not to the much more divisive prices and incomes policy. If prices and incomes policies only work when aggregate demand or the real money supply are falling, there may be no need to use a prices and incomes policy at all. The claimed advantages of a prices and incomes policy is that it can check inflation without the 'movement down the Phillips curve' trade-off with unemployment. If domestic deflation is necessary to make a prices and incomes policy work, the policy loses its principle advantage over the alternatives.

Since 1979, wage, rent, price and dividend controls have been abandoned. The election that year of a government committed to non-intervention in the private sector meant free-market forces were allowed to return to factor markets. The Conservative government of 1979- believed that inflation was a result of excess money growth not 'wage push'; thus, controlling prices and incomes not only fails but also distorts the operation of the 'free' market. It should be noted that *defining* the money supply is a major problem for a government committed to solving inflation by monetarist measures. However, 1992 saw the introduction of a public sector pay freeze of 1.5 per cent maximum for the following 12 months, with future pay increases to be allowed for productivity increases only. Recently (February 1995) the Cabinet approved public sector pay increases as follows: 2.5–3.8 per cent for senior military officers, 2.5 per cent for the judiciary, 2.5 per cent for doctors, 2.5–2.9 per cent for the armed forces, and one per cent for nurses rising to 1.5–3 per cent with local pay agreements. The Treasury insisted that the rises will have to be paid for out of productivity savings. The government wishes to maintain its squeeze on public sector pay by forcing many workers to accept pay rises below the rate of inflation (in real terms a pay cut).

Conclusions – the problems of unemployment and inflation

Since the 1970s there has been a tendency for inflation and unemployment to occur together – what has been called 'slumpflation' or 'stagflation'. The difficulties of dealing with this problem led to the emergence of two schools of thought: monetarists and neo-Keynesians.

Monetarists see inflation as a monetary phenomenon caused by excessive growth in the money supply. Trying to deal with unemployment by 'reflation' causes an increase in money supply and only a temporary fall in the jobless total. Monetarists argue that a large percentage of the unemployment can be accounted for by the 'natural' level. The monetarists/neo-classical/'supply side' solution is to control monetary growth, reduce budget deficits by government, and carry out policies which will reduce the natural rate of unemployment (see Chapter 8). The result should be a more competitive economy which, with more efficient markets, can supply output more easily.

Neo-Keynesians would use some measure of reflation to deal with unemployment which should fall via the multiplier. Any inflation which may result would be controlled by a prices and incomes policy. If the increased level of activity in the economy led to a big increase in imports, import controls could be a possibility.

Monetarists argue that less intervention is better, which contrasts with the more interventionist Keynesian solutions. Many people doubt the effectiveness of *any* policy to deal with unemployment and inflation. It can be argued that economies take their own course, and government policies have only a marginal effect.

Questions for review

1 Explain the different causes of inflation.
2 What is the 'Phillips curve'?
3 What can be done about inflation?

International trade theory and the European Union | 16

Comparative advantage 409

The European Union 416

International competitiveness 426

Comparative advantage

The background to trade

It is virtually impossible for an individual to meet *all* his own needs and wants simply by the fruits of his own labour. He depends on others. If people specialise in whatever job they are good at and if an efficient system of the 'division of labour' is organised, then the country as a whole can produce much more than it could if everyone worked by himself for himself. The same reasoning applies to individual countries throughout the world – if they specialise in particular types of production and then exchange the goods which they produce freely between each country, the total output of the world will be maximised.

By specialisation and exchange the countries are able to acquire goods that would not otherwise be available to them (eg there are no diamonds mined in the UK yet they are able to obtain a supply of diamonds from mines elsewhere) and also to acquire goods at lower opportunity costs than would otherwise be possible.

An example

It can be shown that two countries can gain from mutual specialisation and exchange *as long as the opportunity costs of producing goods vary in the two countries*. For example, suppose there are two countries which can each produce the same two goods. The potential output per worker per year of producing these goods is shown below.

	Output (units) per worker per year	
	Good X	Good Y
Country A	400	200
Country B	150	100

Notice that country A is more efficient in the production of both goods. It has the *absolute advantage* (greater output per worker year) in the production of both goods.

There are still gains to be made for both countries by looking at *comparative advantages*. In country A the opportunity cost of using one worker to produce 200 units of good Y in one year is 400 units of good X. However, in country B, the opportunity cost of producing 200 units of good Y is lower, only 300 units of good X. Thus, country B has the comparative advantage (lower opportunity cost) in the production of good Y. Gains from trade are possible when the opportunity cost ratios are different. Country A is nearly three times better than B at producing good X, but only twice as good at producing good Y.

Country A has the comparative advantage in the production of good X since the opportunity cost of producing 400 units of good X in country A is 200 units of good Y, while the opportunity cost of producing only 300 units of good X in country B is 200 units of good Y. Thus, country A, while more efficient in the production of both goods, has a *greater* efficiency advantage in the production of good X, and country B is least efficient compared to country A in the production of good Y.

Now suppose that country B, following comparative advantage, shifts one worker from the production of good X to the production of good Y. It will lose 150 units of good X and gain 100 units of good Y. (Notice that the argument has nothing to do with the advantage of increasing the number of units produced in country B – after all, units of good X may be gold measured in tons while good Y is wheat measured in pounds.) Suppose it trades these extra units of Y with country A. If country A acquires 100 units of good Y, it can release some resources from the production of good X. With an extra 100 units of good Y, it can use half a worker-year to produce an extra 200 units of good X and still maintain its consumption of Y.

Have the two countries gained from this international specialisation, with A specialising in the production of X and B concentrating on the production of Y? Country B has reduced production of X by 150 units while increasing production of Y by 100 units. Country A has reduced production of Y by 100 units and increased production of X by 200 units. The two countries have together gained an extra 50 units of X while maintaining joint production of Y. They are therefore obviously jointly better off as a result of international specialisation.

Whether this international specialisation will or will not take place depends on whether *both* countries will separately gain from the specialisation. After all, both countries will only willingly trade if they *both* gain from the trade. This condition depends on *the prices at which the goods are traded*. In the example above, country A gains from the international specialisation and exchange as long as it does not need to pay as much as 200 units of X for 100 of Y (where 200:100 is its own opportunity cost of producing X). Country B only gains from trade as long as it is paid more than 150 units of X for 100 of Y (where 150:100 is its own opportunity cost of producing Y). Thus, both countries gain from trade as long as the price of 100 units of Y is more than 150 units of X and less than 200 units of X. Students should note that this proof of the possible advantage to be made from trade can be used wherever the opportunity costs of producing goods vary between two countries.

The argument above assumes that there are constant returns to scale since we assume, in the calculations, that the output per worker does not change as more resources are concentrated in one industry. In fact, there may be diminishing returns to scale (diseconomies of scale), in which case the output per worker will fall as the countries specialise and the advantage from specialisation will decline and eventually disappear. If, on the other hand, there are increasing returns to scale (economies of scale), the advantage of specialisation and exchange will increase as the countries become more specialised.

Comparative advantage theory

This example shows that specialisation within countries has a similar effect to specialisation within a labour force. By each country concentrating on the production of the good in which it has a *comparative* advantage, total production is increased, *but* – and this is important – such specialisation will only be of mutual benefit to all concerned if there is a free movement of goods between both countries. It is no use country A concentrating on the production of only one good if it cannot get the other good from country B.

However, assuming that there is free movement of goods between countries, the most important theory in international economics can be formulated. It is known as the *theory (or law) of comparative advantage,* and its principle is simple: *specialisation and trade will be mutually beneficial if each country specialises in the production of those goods in which it has a comparative advantage.* This theory holds true even where one country has an *absolute* advantage in the production of every good, providing that there are differences in the *relative* efficiencies of each line of production. (*Absolute* and *comparative* advantages must not be confused. A country may have an absolute advantage in the production of every good, but that does not necessarily mean that it will always have a comparative advantage.)

The encouragement of trade between countries on this basis must be beneficial to the world economy as a whole, and as output will be maximised in the most efficient manner, at the least cost. The theory is, in fact, sometimes called the *theory of comparative costs,* because it is concerned with the opportunity costs of different types of production. Indeed, the only time when specialisation will not be beneficial is when the opportunity costs are *exactly the same* in both countries – or when neither country has a comparative advantage.

Free trade movement

Furthermore, the national income of any country must be higher if it devotes its economic resources to those activities in which it has a comparative advantage. This is why the *Free Trade Movement* was started by Ricardo, the economist who first formulated the theory. He believed that any artificial impediments which were put in the way of trade between countries would inevitably lead to a fall in national income, and, so far as *economics* is concerned, this is almost indisputable. However, the argument takes little account of the 'political' and 'social' problems which might arise from its logical implementation. Free trade may help everyone everywhere a little, but impediments to free trade (or *protectionism*) help a few people a lot.

Free trade vs protectionism

The demands for full employment within an economy are very strong and they are encouraged by economists who point out that the country's national income will be higher if employment is bigger. This argument can be used to support the belief in free trade or it can be used to support the belief in protectionism, because the belief in free trade rests on *long-term* assumptions, while the belief in protectionism is concerned with the *short term*.

In the short term, it is logical for a government to be pressed into pursuing policies which are designed to expand the level of domestic employment, and one way of achieving this is to prevent too many goods coming into the country from outside, because this will encourage domestic production. Another way to expand domestic employment is to increase the level of exports. Both these policies encourage governments to place artificial depressants on imports and artificial stimulants on exports. In short, they are encouraged to adopt a 'protectionist' approach to trade, in order to increase domestic employment in the short term.

However, any protectionist policy will be self-defeating in the *long term*. One country's imports are another country's exports, and so, if country A places restrictions on the level of its *imports*, country B will experience a fall in its *exports*. This will have two effects in country B. First, its export earnings will be reduced. This will not only reduce its level of national income through the multiplier effect, but will also reduce its ability to import goods itself from country A. The next stage in the process will be for country B itself to impose import controls in an attempt to maintain its own domestic employment. Both countries will then be in a vicious circle. Each country will try to maintain its own employment levels at the expense of the other but, in doing so, each will suffer increasing unemployment in the long term. Increased unemployment is not the only adverse effect of import controls; import restrictions also lead to an inefficient allocation of the world's scarce economic resources.

These facts should encourage everyone to campaign for freer trade, but in a democratic country politicians are dependent on the electorate's favour. They may well believe fervently in free trade, but they also have to listen to the ordinary person's demands for a decent job at a decent wage – *now*. After all, if a person was out of a job or found his job threatened by fierce competition from a foreign company, his immediate reaction would be to demand protection from imports: an economic theory which may help the world in general in the long term is not likely to moderate political demands in the here and now! Furthermore, for free trade to benefit everyone, everywhere has to engage in it, and that involves a great deal of international co-operation.

Customs duties and import quotas

Protectionist policies take two main forms. A form of tax – known as a *customs duty* – can be levied on imports or a quantative restriction can be placed on the volume of imports. This is called an *import quota*; and once the specified volume has been reached, no more goods will be allowed into the country for the remainder of the period. Quotas can be fixed as a percentage share of the domestic market.

The primary purpose of protective customs duties is to restrict the demand for imports by raising their price in relation to similar home-produced goods. Another justification for the use of customs duties is their revenue-raising potential, since they are really only another form of indirect taxation. However, these two arguments are inconsistent with each other. If the duties are high enough to prevent many imported goods entering the country, then they will not raise much revenue and, if they are low enough to ensure a significant amount of revenue, they will not reduce imports! At the same time, of course, customs duties are *regressive*, and also encourage a *mis-allocation of resources* in the country which imposes them and in the world as a whole.

The use of *import quotas* is believed to be a more effective way of limiting imports. Import quotas do not have any regressive effects and they can also be used discriminately against goods from specific countries. (An added bonus is that they do not normally require parliamentary approval – they can be imposed on a Ministerial Order through delegated legislation.) However, they still do have undesirable long-term effects on both resource allocation and the level of world trade generally, because they tend to work against the free-trade principle.

In recent years a modification of the statutory quota system has found favour among many governments, partly because it avoids any direct breach of the various free-trade agreements which now govern the actions of most countries. Through the use of 'veiled threats and implications', a government can persuade other governments to impose 'voluntary' quotas on the volume of their exports to the country making those threats. The threats usually consist of public statements to the effect that if the volume of imports from specified countries is not reduced, then some direct restrictive action might be necessary. Naturally, any such threats have to be heeded, and so, rather than risk a compulsory and dramatic decrease in their own exports, the specified countries will often reduce their exports slightly on a voluntary basis. The Japanese are only permitted at present to export cars into the UK up to a level of 11 per cent of the domestic market.

The 'multi-fibre agreement' (MFA), one of the UK's principal import control measures, is designed to limit imports of textiles and clothing. When the MFA was first set up in 1974, the text of the agreement stated that it was intended to be a temporary measure.

The British textile industry employs over 400,000 people, equivalent to 2 per cent of the nation's workforce, and is widely spread throughout the country. The industry here, along with those of other Western countries, has undergone rapid change as new suppliers have penetrated our traditional markets. The MFA enables the government to impose discriminatory import quotas, in order to give British industry a breathing space in which to adjust. The UK textile industry has responded to the opportunity created by the MFA. During the first 11 months of 1985, textile exports rose 15 per cent compared with the same period in 1984. Exports of woollen and worsted fabrics to Japan – the UK's single biggest market for these products – rose by 26 per cent over the same period. Overall textile exports in 1985 totalled £1.3 billion.

In 1986 the UK government, along with its European Union partners, concluded negotiations on a new protocol which extended the Multi Fibre Agrement for a further five years. This provided for special treatment for the developing countries such as Bangladesh, which, under its bilateral agreement with the UK, had no quota restrictions. The protocol also stated that all participants should contribute to the liberalisation of trade. This constituted a clear signal that the UK government expects other countries to reduce their trade barriers to our exports.

The Multifibre Agreement has since been renewed again. This is in spite of the fact that it is a temporary arrangement designed to give the UK textile industry time to restructure and to concentrate on higher-value-added products. At present, almost 60 per cent of UK consumption by value is supplied by the UK textile industry. Of total imports, 20 per cent come from countries covered by the MFA, amounting to only 8 per cent of consumption.

Another variation of the import quota system which was used in the UK in the late 1960s was the *import deposit scheme*. A monetary deposit representing a proportion of the total value of the imports has to be placed with the authorities at the time of importation and this is only returned after a fairly long period – say, three or six months. The scheme was used in the hope that there would be a reduction in imports due to the financial penalty imposed. However, its effect was minimal in the UK, as those foreign companies which were affected usually provided the necessary temporary finance from their reserves, so the importing company was not penalised itself.

Embargoes

A country could put a total ban on the import of a particular type of good or on all the goods from a particular country. These actions are often for political reasons such as the UK's dispute with Rhodesia (Zimbabwe) and more recently its dispute with Argentina over the Falkland Islands. Sometimes embargoes are used to ban dangerous goods (ie drugs or flick knives).

Import substitution

Finally, it is possible to reduce the level of imports, by encouraging and helping those domestic firms which produce similar or identical goods to those which are being imported. This is known as *import substitution* and has been a popular policy in the UK in recent years, as it not only reduces the level of imports, but also develops the industrial base within the country. However, it is a very long-term policy and involves temporary subsidies and direct help to the industries concerned. Two types of industry usually receive such assistance.

First, the declining industries such as textiles and shipbuilding. Much of their problem lies in the fierce competition which they face from either low-cost imports or more modern and more efficient foreign companies. There may seem to be a strong argument for either the imposition of protective *tariffs* (the collective term for import restrictions) or direct subsidies, but a close examination of the *economic* arguments shows this to be a fallacy. If a country is at a comparative *dis*advantage in the production of a particular good, then it should discontinue the production of it in favour of a good in which it has a comparative *ad*vantage. There may, of course, be strong *political* and *social* arguments for helping declining industries which are situated in areas of high unemployment, but so far as the world's total economic resources are concerned, such help will lead to inefficient resource allocation. There can be little doubt that the resources at present tied up in such industries should – wherever possible – be released for use in other more efficient industries. Perhaps the best economic and social solution in the long term to this particular problem would be to reduce the level of protection and/or subsidy for such industries gradually, so that the necessary, but painful, transition can take place without too much personal hardship.

Another area where protection and/or subsidy is often used is the 'infant' industry. It is argued that there are some industries which *would* have a comparative advantage in a given country *if only* they had time to get started and reap the benefits of large-scale production and so on. They would then be in a position to reduce imports through the provision of competitive home-produced supplies as well as probably add to exports. However, if such industries have to face strong and established foreign competitors in their early days, they will probably have little chance of survival. As a result, many governments have been persuaded to provide both temporary protection and temporary direct help to new industries. Even from a world economic viewpoint, this type of protection has some justification. The problem is that once such protection has been provided, it is very difficult to discontinue it. Furthermore, there are innumerable instances of protection being given to the *wrong* industries – and such industries then become perpetual infants!

'Dumping'

There is one other area where some form of direct import controls might – in an imperfect world – be justified. In recent years there have been a number of instances of over-production of certain goods in various countries. The quantity produced just is not demanded, even through normal world market channels. As a result, a significant quantity has to be sold at a lower price, and this is often done in an 'export market'. Very simply, the goods of country X are sold in country Y at a lower price than they are in country X itself. This procedure is called *dumping*. Clearly, this is an example of 'unfair competition' and it may justify some form of protectionist policy on the part of the country which is receiving the 'dumped' goods. However, the actual practice of dumping is usually difficult to prove conclusively, due to different market conditions and so on.

In May 1986 the DTI re-established its Anti-Dumping Unit on a new basis, so that it could co-ordinate work on complaints about all forms of unfair practices in international trade. The new unit is called the Unfair Trade Unit. It collects information and advises industry on dumping – the sale of goods by foreign countries below their home market price – and on subsidised exports and unfair trade practices. The unit allows the DTI to respond quickly to complaints and helps in the preparation of particular cases for consideration by the European Commission.

Encouraging exports

In the UK in the past two decades, the threat of increased imports has been a very real one. There has, indeed, often been a higher level of imports than exports, a situation which cannot be allowed to continue indefinitely as it results in a net outflow of money from the country year after year. If the restriction of imports is self-defeating in the long term and against the best interests of the country, then clearly more has to be done to solve the problem through increased exports. After all, higher exports will pay for higher imports. Unfortunately, however, it is not easy to 'protect' or subsidise exports. Indeed, what little can be done has to be much more indirect. First and foremost, foreigners cannot be 'made' to buy goods just because a country wants to sell them. It is only possible to encourage them to do so because they 'need' them or because the goods are 'better' than the goods of other countries. The best government policy will, therefore, be one which encourages industry to produce the right goods at the right price at the right time. In fact, this really means making industry as efficient and as productive as possible. This can only be achieved through general 'growth-oriented' internal policies.

However, there is one specific area in the UK where a government policy has helped to subsidise certain exporting activities directly. It is a form of protectionism in reverse. Where a company in the UK has gained an export order, the government – through the *Export Credits Guarantee Department* – assists the company with the financing of the order. The ECGD provides guarantees to both companies and banks against the risks of default by overseas customers, within specified monetary and contractual limits. In recent years, the guarantees have been considerably improved with new forms of cover such as special insurance against steep rises in costs due to inflation. The services provided by the ECGD may encourage a higher level of exports than would otherwise be the case, but the quantative effect is inevitably limited, particularly as the level of aid is restricted for fear of retaliation by other foreign governments.

The European Union

The move towards freer trade

The first half of this century saw more and more tariffs being imposed throughout the developed world as every country tried to mitigate the worst effects of the worldwide depression of the 1920s and 1930s. However, after the Second World War it was realised that the process was self-defeating. There clearly had to be a general reduction in tariff levels if world trade was to increase significantly.

GATT

In 1947 the leading industrialised nations entered into a trading agreement which was designed to lower tariffs gradually. It was known as the *General Agreement on Tariffs and Trade* – or *GATT* for short – and had two main goals.

First, it aimed to prevent – or at least restrict – unilateral action by individual countries. It did this by producing an international code of conduct for trade which prohibited both import quotas and export subsidies. *Second*, the agreement aimed to reduce the level of the tariffs which already existed through a series of multilateral trade conferences. Although the GATT code of conduct has only been partially successful due to the lack of adequate enforcement procedures, the series of trade conferences has proved successful in gradually reducing tariff levels in the countries involved. The process received an added impetus in the early 1960s when the late President Kennedy instituted a new round of negotiations known as the 'Kennedy Round'. Under this series of negotiations, tariff reductions were agreed on a bilateral basis only, but then the reductions had to apply to similar trade with all other countries. As the members of GATT account for over 80 per cent of all world trade, it can be seen that this series of reductions must have had a significant effect on all tariff levels and so, in consequence, on the level of world trade. A similar series of negotiations in the 1970s (the Tokyo Round) produced less spectacular reductions in tariffs. During the late 1970s and early 1980s GATT was faced with the increased protectionism that often accompanies the onset of recession.

An eighth set of multilateral trade negotiations, the 'Uruguay Round', was launched at Punta del Este with a declaration by the trade ministers of the participating nations in September 1986. This declaration included two developments which are of particular note. For the first time, services will come within the remit of GATT. In the words of the Punta del Este declaration:

> 'Negotiations in this area shall aim to establish a multilateral framework of principles and rules for trade in services ... with a view to expansion of such trade under conditions of transparency and progressive liberalisation as a means of promoting economic growth.' (21 September 1986)

Second, it was agreed that government subsidies to, and tariffs on, agricultural trade needed to be examined. The demands of the US and other agricultural exporting countries threatened to provoke trade wars, effects of which would have damaged world trade as a whole. Such a threat was only lifted by the promise of international negotiations to reduce agricultural surpluses and dumping on world markets. Trade ministers agreed upon the urgent need

> 'to bring more discipline and predictability to world trade by correcting and preventing restrictions and distortions related to structural surpluses' (ibid).

Negotiations would also seek to increase discipline on the use of subsidies. The inclusion of agriculture within the GATT will add further pressure on the European Union to reform the Common Agricultural Policy. Unfortunately, the

Uruguay Round ended in acrimony, with the EU at odds with the USA over farm subsidies.

The real impetus

However, the real impetus towards freer international trade has come from the formation of various 'trading blocs' or 'economic communities' throughout the world. The most important of these was formed in 1957 by France, Italy, Germany, the Netherlands, Belgium and Luxembourg and is known colloquially as the *Common Market*. Its first official title was the *European Economic Community (EEC)*; however, that was shortened to the *European Community (EC)* in recognition of the moves towards social and political unity which are taking place within the Community, and this has now been changed to *European Union (EU)*. The EU from its inception was committed to forming a totally integrated economic unit with common external tariffs, in the belief that the free movement of goods between the member countries would be beneficial to all concerned. Although the erection of common external tariff barriers goes against the full principle of 'world' free trade, the EU countries negotiated a series of special agreements regarding reduced or concessionary tariffs with countries outside the EU.

The membership of the EU has now expanded to twelve full members – the six newer members being the UK, Denmark, Ireland, Greece, Spain and Portugal. The UK did not join the group originally partly because it had very special and unique trading links with the British Commonwealth. However, after an abortive attempt to join in the early 1960s, suitable transitional arrangements were made in the early 1970s and the UK joined with Denmark and Ireland in January 1973. (It should perhaps be noted here that after the original formation of the EU, those European countries which were not members formed themselves into the *European Free Trade Association* (EFTA). EFTA does not have a common external tariff nor plans to become an integrated economic unit, but it is committed to the reduction of tariffs between member countries. The EU is a *customs union* because it has developed a free trade area within a common external tariff. The EFTA is a *free trade area* but there is no common external tariff; so each member country fixes its own tariff levels with non-member countries. EFTA and the EU have now joined forces in an Association named the European Economic Area.

The purpose is to maintain and develop the existing trade and cooperation links between the EFTA countries (some of whom are now seeking to join the EU) and the European Union. The EFTA countries were concerned to ensure access for their goods and services to the EU market. The European Union was keen to ensure access for their goods and services to the high per capita GDP EFTA countries.

More than a free trade area

The original concept of the EU was for member countries to form themselves not only into an economic unit, but also a political grouping which could speak with a united and powerful voice in the world. It is, therefore, considerably more than a free trade area – or, at least, it will be if all the original ideals are fulfilled.

The principal motivation for the EU movement was the realisation that the barriers to trade in the modern world are not only tariffs. There are often institutional, fiscal and legal barriers as well. The aim, therefore, is to achieve common policies on all these matters as well. Such harmonisation requires an enormous amount of political will and determination, but moves have been made towards it. For instance, it was recognised that different indirect taxes in different countries were a barrier to the free passage of goods between countries and although actual rates of tax still vary, all members now operate a similar indirect taxation system based on the Value Added Tax. Common policies are also being evolved on a number of other important issues such as the control of monopolies, insurance, transport and energy. As these policies are developed, each member country will subordinate its own policies to the EU policy. It is also hoped to create a unified capital market so that the movement of capital between countries will be unrestricted. This should encourage the optimum allocation of resources between different uses in different countries. This unified capital market will go hand-in-hand with the creation (eventually) of a common currency. The EU is regarded as a single unit for economic purposes and so it is natural for it to attempt to formulate an overall policy for regional and economic development throughout all its members. The first steps have already been taken towards a common regional development policy – on a much grander scale than the UK's individual efforts, but based on similar principles.

The UK used its Presidency of the Council of Ministers in the second half of 1986 to hasten the completion of the *internal market* by the deadline the Community had set itself – the end of 1992. In particular the heads of government agreed to reach a settlement on public purchasing and standardisation in the field of information technology and telecommunications. A major boost to the aim of creating a genuine internal market in insurance was the European Court of Justice's ruling in December 1986 which outlawed a series of barriers to free trade in non-life insurance within the community. This should be of particular benefit to Britain's expanding insurance sector.

The creation of the single/internal market in 1992 has meant that goods are free to pass between EU countries. In addition to this, obstacles to the movement of capital have been abolished. In essence, this will mean the completion of the process begun in 1957. The gains of a unified internal market should be those resulting from the benefits of comparative advantage across the whole of the Community. The 1992 measures should bring bigger gains than the mere abolition of tariffs. All barriers to trade and to the free movement of labour and capital should disappear between EU members. However, a worrying aspect of the EU's common external tariff system is that good quality, good value goods from the Far East in particular are being penalised by duties. Consumer durables are particularly affected.

The benefits of EU membership

The UK joined the EU for a variety of reasons. The economic argument rested principally on the advantages of a large single market. The population of all the EU countries is around 345 million and access to such a large market should have provided an added stimulus to UK industry. In addition, all the other members are at an advanced stage of industrial development and their combined rate of economic growth has been much greater than the UK's in the past twenty years or so. This is undoubtedly due, in part, to the 'dynamising' effect which comes from the removal of barriers to trade as industry is forced to become more efficient in the face of direct competition from other countries. For instance, when the EU was formed, France was considered to have a very weak industrial sector and there were worries that it might not be able to withstand the fierce competition which would come from the industries of Germany, Holland and Belgium. In fact, the spirit of French industry was transformed and although France still has a very large agricultural sector, it is now also a formidable exporter of industrial goods in its own right.

The size of the EU also makes it a very attractive investment proposition for non-EU companies, in particular the large American multinationals. Before the UK became a member such investment would have bypassed it, but now it is hoped that at least some of this investment will be undertaken in the UK. (This is, of course, partially dependent on whether or not the relative rate of inflation in the UK remains in line with that prevailing on the mainland of Europe.)

Another contributory factor to the UK being more prepared to join the EU in the early 1970s, as compared with the 1950s, was the declining importance of its trade with the Commonwealth. Indeed, by this time, the developing nations of the Commonwealth were no longer so dependent on a free and ready access to the UK market. Furthermore, although the UK still benefited from the relatively cheap food which it obtained from countries such as Australia and New Zealand, industry itself in the UK was naturally gravitating towards Europe for its market rather than the far-flung reaches of the Commonwealth. (The Commonwealth countries now benefit from the associated links which they have with the EU.) Some 56 per cent of the UKs exports go to the other members of the European Union, whilst 53 per cent of our imports come from the EU. The UKs next largest market, North America, accounts for only 13 per cent of UK exports. Figures on the EU are shown below, with the UK's per capita GDP ranked eighth within the 12 member states.

EU Member country	Population (millions), 1990	GDP per capita (ECUs) (1989)
Denmark	5.1	18528
Germany (Fed Rep)	61.3	17421
Luxembourg	–	16907
France	56.1	15947
Belgium	9.8	13982
Netherlands	15.0	13684
Italy	57.1	13669
United Kingdom	57.2	13283
Spain	39.2	8924
Ireland	3.7	8760
Greece	10.0	4924
Portugal	10.3	4199
EU Average	–	13551

(Source: *Europe in Figures*, Eurostat, 1992; *Social Trends 23*, 1993)

The common agricultural policy

Farmers the world over have always had a powerful political and economic voice and the countries of Europe are no exception. Ironically, the very powerful farm lobby has resulted in an anomaly creeping into the European ideal. The market in agricultural products throughout Europe is very far from 'free' and the farming community is very heavily subsidised by the European Commission. (The European Commission is effectively the governing body of the EU on which all member countries are represented.) The immediate effect of the high level of subsidies which the farmers receive is that the economic resources of the EU are not allocated in the most efficient way.

However, the workings, effects and implications of the *Common Agricultural Policy* (CAP) are much more complicated and far-reaching than just a problem of resource allocation. This is probably best illustrated by comparing the CAP with the system of agricultural support which operated in the UK prior to it becoming a member of the EU.

Under the previous UK system, the market price for food was ostensibly free to move in accordance with world supply and demand conditions, but the farmer always received a guaranteed price for his product. Any 'shortfall' between the market price and the guaranteed price was made good by the government through either a direct subsidy or a 'deficiency payment'. (Such payments were financed out of ordinary taxation.) Under the EU system, the market price itself is guaranteed at a level which is fixed by the European Commission. This level is then protected by a series of import levies on any cheaper food which originates outside the EU's boundaries. At the same time, wherever necessary, the Commission subsidises the price of EU food exports to bring them down to the level of world prices. So, when the UK joined the EU it moved away from an essentially 'free market' in agricultural products which was open to normal economic forces to a system which involved 'managed markets' for the main products.

Under the EU system, whenever the world price of a particular product falls below the guaranteed price, the farmer is able to sell his product to an *intervention board* at the guaranteed price. This effectively means that the farmer will *always* be able to sell his product whatever happens to world demand conditions. The intervention board then stores the stock of produce which it acquires either till the world price rises or till it disposes of it at a lower price. The very large stocks of certain food – notably butter – which the intervention boards in each country have built up on certain occasions have led to the charge that the CAP has simply led to *over-production* and *under-supply* in many instances. Indeed, it appears that farmers are often encouraged by the guaranteed sale price to keep producing products for which there is little or no demand. Dried skimmed milk is the usual example given. So far as the consumer is concerned, he is often forced to pay prices for his food which are well above normal world prices. Indeed, it cannot be denied by even the most ardent EU supporter that the trebling in the price of butter in the UK between 1973 and 1977 was the direct result of the EU agricultural policy. However, at the same time, the CAP has not led to the anticipated sharp rise in the overall price of food nor has the UK been a major contributor to the agricultural fund, which is the fund from which the CAP is financed. The reasons for this reversal of expectations are extremely complex and they are due to a factor which is not directly connected to the CAP.

The main instruments of the common agricultural policy remain:

a Guaranteed minimum (intervention) prices, at which the community will buy from the market if internal prices are lower. Intervention prices apply to the main cereal crops, sugar, beef and milk products, and are fixed each year at levels which are generally higher than those ruling in world markets.

b Reference prices, which are used to determine the subsidies on EU exports, with respect to lower world market prices, and the levies on imports which protect EU farmers from foreign competition.

c Monetary compensatory payments, which equalise prices in agricultural trade among EU member states by making up the difference arising from variations in exchange rates.

d Subsidies to processed products, and complementary subventions which are granted to producers of tomatoes, olive oil, hard wheat and tobacco, so that consumption prices are kept lower.

In all, about 90 per cent of European agricultural products are now supported by intervention arrangements or other subsidies. Since the establishment of the Common Market, the CAP has certainly helped to raise production and sustain farmers' incomes, but in recent years large unforeseen surpluses of certain products, together with inflation and the consequent continuous, though moderating, rise in guaranteed prices, have brought the EC's agricultural policies to a state of crisis.

58.4 per cent of the European Union's budget is spent on the agricultural sector. Although this seems at first glance to be an extremely high proportion, given the relative importance of agriculture to the combined GNPs of the member states (2.6 per cent of EU GDP in 1989), this is in part at least due to the fact that it is in the agricultural sector that the EU has most taken over from the national economies. The agricultural sector is the only sector of the EU which has achieved integration in its policies. The CAP is the most sophisticated of EU policies.

Nevertheless, by the end of the 80s it was clear that reform of the CAP was long overdue. Under the CAP, the producer prices of the EUs main agricultural products are supported by intervention purchases and by levies on imports of products from non-EU countries. The intervention mechanism works to maintain producer prices at levels substantially above world levels. With 20.1 per cent of world agricultural imports, the EU is still the world's prime importer of agricultural produce. This should be set against a fall in the real price of agricultural products between 1965 and 1990 of almost 29 per cent.

Recent changes in the CAP have tended to cut back price support and increase aid paid directly to farmers. Reforms have included measures to tighten up on overproduction (to reduce/eliminate the persistent surpluses). Quotas for the production of some agricultural products have been introduced, and are considered by some farmers to be too rigorous, eg milk production/arable farming. These quotas have caused some hardship in UK farming, particularly amongst small farmers. At the same time, 'set-aside' has been introduced, a policy which pays farmers for leaving some fields untilled. While the purpose of this is also to reduce overproduction, it has caused some disquiet, particularly when large and wealthy landowners have benefited from it.

Milk quotas were first introduced in 1984, and amended in 1986. The cutback was then severe both in terms of milk quantities and in terms of dairy cows. Crop production accounts for 49 per cent of final agricultural output. In order to reduce surpluses, 'maximum Guaranteed quantities' have been introduced. In wine production, the emphasis now is on production of quality wines and the digging up of vines which produce inferior wine.

The Exchange Rate Mechanism (ERM)

The European Monetary System was set up in 1979. It was the second attempt at a currency system for the European Union. The purpose was to create a zone of monetary stability within Europe, to reduce transactions costs and uncertainties caused by floating exchange rates. There are three facets to the system: the European Monetary Cooperation Fund (which administers the system), the European Currency Unit (ECU), and the Exchange Rate Mechanism. All member countries participate in the EMS, and all of their currencies are represented in the composite artificial currency, the ECU. The ECU is a trade weighted basket of currencies, with each member country's currency weighted in relation to the importance of its economy. For example, the most heavily weighted currency is the Deutschmark, reflecting the dominance of the German economy within the EU. ECUs are used for all official transactions within the EU: the budget is denominated in ECUs, the CAP is denominated in ECUs. The ECU is increasingly being used also for private transactions. A composite currency is viewed as being less unpredictable than a single currency, and hence the use of ECUS reduces risk and uncertainty.

The Exchange Rate Mechanism is a system of fixed exchange rates. Each member currency of the ERM (not all EU member countries participate in the ERM) has an agreed central rate against the ECU. From these central rates are calculated each currency's central rate against each of the other currencies in the system. From these central rates are calculated each currencies permitted fluctuation band. Most currencies are permitted to fluctuate by +/- 2.25 per cent from their central rates. Some currencies are permitted a wider fluctuation band, +/- 6 per cent (as was sterling when the UK was a member).

Although it was not originally intended that the exchange rates within the system would be fixed and immutable, and some realignments have indeed taken place (eg 1987), realignments were frowned upon. Increasingly, as the EU moved towards closer integration of the economies, the ERM came to be viewed as the precursor to an eventual monetary union. Following the Maastricht Treaty, the intention was to move towards monetary union by stages: the first stage was to be the hardening of the exchange rate system, with wider band fluctuation currencies moving into the narrow band, and eventually to a totally fixed system by the end of this century. This timetable however is now very unlikely.

Sterling entered the ERM in October 1990, following a period of uncertainty during which differing views as to the efficacy of ERM membership were expressed by different members of the government.

Mrs Thatcher and her economic guru Sir Alan Walters were in favour of floating exchange rates, and did not wish to enter the ERM; the then Chancellor of the Exchequer, Nigel Lawson, was strongly in favour of ERM membership. He believed that it would be 'good discipline' for UK workers and employers, as they would realise that wage increases higher than productivity increases could not be afforded within a fixed exchange rate system. He believed that the ERM, being strongly anti-inflationary due to the Bundesbank's statutory duty to keep inflation down within Germany, would help to keep inflation in the UK down somewhere close to the low German level.

Sterling finally entered the ERM at a central rate of DM2.95 (this meant that you needed two Deutschmarks and 95 Pfennigs to buy one pound sterling). This was quite a high rate; in fact, many commentators believed that it was too high, and did not reflect the true strength of the UK economy. In order to maintain sterling within its agreed band, the UK government had to pursue a tight monetary policy, with relatively high interest rates in order to attract funds to

Britain. These interest rates had a bad effect on UK businesses, and the result was paid in UK jobs. At the time, the then Chancellor of the Exchequer, Norman Lamont, made his infamous remark that 'unemployment is a price worth paying' in order to keep inflation down.

During the summer of 1992, there was much uncertainty within the European currencies, partly caused by uncertainty as to the further process of European integration; the outcome of the French referendum on the Maastricht Treaty was in doubt, and the Danes voted against it. This placed a large question mark over the future direction of the European economies. There was heavy speculation against several currencies. This started with speculation against the Nordic currencies, which were then pegged to the ECU. Attention then switched to the lira and to sterling. There was very heavy speculation against these two currencies, and the central banks were obliged to use an unprecedented level of intervention in support of them. Eventually, on 16 September 1992, sterling was forced out of the ERM. The UK government withdrew it from the mechanism following a day of extreme turbulence, and allowed it to float down to its own level. The lira was also devalued at the same time, following great speculation against it. The peseta was devalued. Subsequently, there was also great speculation against the French franc, but with support from the Bundesbank this survived the speculation. There was also speculation against the Irish punt.

Following the withdrawal of the pound and the lira, the devaluation of the peseta, and the turbulence of the summer, it seemed as though the exchange rate mechanism itself would crumble. However, it has survived, with fewer currencies participating.

Following the withdrawal of sterling from the ERM, it was permitted to float downwards against the Deutschmark, the dollar and the yen. It is unlikely that sterling will rejoin the ERM in the foreseeable future.

Since leaving the ERM, it has been possible for the UK government to pursue a less tight monetary policy. During the UK's membership of the ERM, domestic policy was subordinated to the need to maintain the exchange rate. This loosening of monetary policy has facilitated the UK recovery. However, the Chancellor of the Exchequer, Kenneth Clarke, has recently raised interest rates in order to choke off potential inflation.

The future of monetary union is in doubt. At best, it may take place between a core of EU countries, including Germany and France, which meet the convergence criteria of the Maastricht Treaty. This raises the possibility of a 'two-speed' Europe, with some countries being more closely integrated than others.

The Maastricht Treaty also established the European Monetary Institute, set up in Frankfurt in 1994. This is part of the three-stage Delors plan for monetary union. The EMI is intended to coordinate monetary policy in the European Union. The next stage on from the EMI would be the establishment of a European Central Bank.

The EU in the world economy

With a high-income population of 345 million, the EU remains the largest import and export market in the world, second only to the USA in the size of its gross domestic product. The EU accounts for 21 per cent of total world trade, not including intra-EU trade, compared with 16 per cent for the USA and 9 per cent for Japan. The total GDP of the EU nations accounts for about a third of the total GDP of the industrialised world. The EU also accounts for just under a third of world trade in manufactured goods. The main trading partner of the EU is the USA, although the OPEC block of countries are more important collectively.

Over the years special relationships have been established with several groups of developing countries. The major benefits for these countries are free entry for their exports and technical/financial aid. Many of these agreements were negotiated at the Lomé Conventions. Most of the countries involved were ex-colonies of member countries.

The twelve member countries of the EU form a very powerful trading block in the world economy. With the completion of the Channel Tunnel and its opening to traffic this autumn 1994, and with the completion of the internal market and ever growing integration, the UK will benefit from much closer ties with mainland europe than has hitherto been the case.

What about the future of the EU? It is probable that the next enlargment of the EU will be to incorporate the EFTA countries, some of whom are keen to benefit from membership. Following that, on the distant horizon lies a possible opening up to the economies of Eastern Europe (although a very great deal of convergence will need to be achieved by these economies before they will be able to join the EU). Turkey has been an associate member since the 1950s, and may possibly eventually be allowed full membership.

International competitiveness

Introduction

International competitiveness will depend in part on the kind of factors reflected in the usual relative-price or cost-based measures of competitiveness (see below), but it will also depend on a host of less tangible factors.

Except in the case of homogeneous products (eg fuels, raw materials, some semi-manufactures) quality and design matter to purchasers, as well as price. For capital and other durable goods, delivery dates and after-sales service would be important; for non-durable goods and services it may be reliability and continuity of supply. Effective marketing may also have a significant influence on performance. The term 'non-price competitiveness' has been used to describe these other aspects of competition which, unlike relative prices and costs, are not readily quantified. It seems quite likely that non-price competitiveness is as important as price or cost competitiveness in determining overall performance, but the unquantifiable nature of non-price competitiveness makes this proposition virtually impossible to test. Moreover, favourable non-price competitiveness tends to be associated with favourable productivity growth.

Measures of price and cost competitiveness

The most widely used measures are the indices of relative unit labour costs, adjusted for exchange rates, compiled and published by the International Monetary Fund. By their nature, these indices give equal weight to movements in the exchange rate, earnings and productivity. This means that short-term movements in the indices, which are likely to be dominated by exchange rate changes, may often prove a misleading indicator of long-term trends in the underlying level of competitiveness which are likely to be influenced most of all by the trend in productivity.

The choice of labour costs, rather than total costs, mainly reflects the availability of suitable data and the difficulty of measuring capital costs. In practice, there are good reasons for believing that non-labour costs will vary much less between countries than labour costs, given the homogeneity and tradability of many raw materials. An important point to note is that the IMF measure of competitiveness (and indeed all the regularly published measures, both cost-based and price-based) relates to manufacturing industry only. The focus on manufacturing partly reflects the availability of data. However, manufactured goods are an important part of industrialised countries' trade. For the UK they account for about half of exports and imports, though only about a quarter of total output.

Changes in cost competitiveness

In practice, a change in cost competitiveness can come through a change in the exchange rate, a change in the growth of earnings relative to that abroad, or a change in the growth of productivity relative to that abroad. The different routes have implications for other aspects of the economy, especially for inflation and real incomes.

The first distinction to be made is between a change deriving from the exchange rate, and one deriving from domestic unit labour costs. A fall in the exchange rate improves cost-competitiveness, provided that domestic costs do not rise to offset it. But it does so at a higher level of prices than if the reduction in relative unit labour costs were the result of an initial fall in domestic costs. Thus, inflation is higher, at least temporarily, when the improvement results from a fall in the exchange rate rather than from a fall in domestic unit costs.

In both cases, real earnings have to fall relative to productivity if there is to be a sustained improvement in cost-competitiveness. In the first case this occurs because the rise in prices following the depreciation is not offset by a rise in nominal earnings. In the second case there is a fall in domestic costs without an offsetting rise in the exchange rate.

The second distinction to make is between different ways in which domestic unit labour costs might change. Since unit labour costs are the ratio of average hourly earnings to productivity (output per hour), a change can be brought about by movements in either earnings or productivity. Either route to lower unit costs will enable firms to compete better at home and abroad. Neither will in itself be inflationary. The difference between the two comes in their effects on living standards. Lower hourly earnings means lower living standards for those in employment, initially at least. With higher productivity, cost competitiveness can be improved without a lower level of real hourly earnings. Over a period of time, output will rise in both cases as exports and imports respond to the lower unit labour costs. Additional labour will be required to produce it, and total employment incomes may rise even when the improvement in cost competitiveness was initially brought about by lower hourly earnings or higher productivity. In the long run, higher productivity will support higher living standards for the community as a whole, and is therefore desirable in its own right.

Unit labour costs in manufacturing, % change on a year earlier

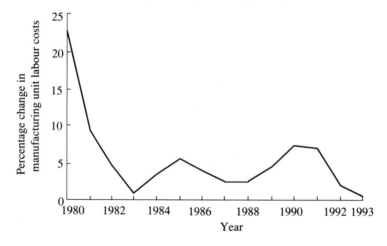

(Source: *Employment Gazette*, July 1994)

The table above shows the annual percentage change in unit wage costs during the 1980s and the begining of the 1990s.

Output per head in manufacturing rose by almost 5 per cent during 1986, and has risen by 3½ per cent a year on average since 1979. The 1980s' improvements in profitability and productivity helped the UK's competitive position in world markets. However, by the end of the decade the UK's unit labour costs in manufacturing were again rising faster than in other EC countries. ERM membership and high domestic inflation did not help UK competitiveness in overseas markets.

It can be argued that the UK has had an over-valued exchange rate in recent years, certainly during ERM membership. This has helped inflation through cheaper imports but has made exports more expensive. Decades of overmanning, restrictive practices, high inflation and poor management conspired to make UK manufacturing internationally uncompetitive. The improvements over the last few years have been from a position way behind many of its trading partners. The changes in the composition of the UK's trade will be examined in the next chapter.

Questions for review

1 Why do countries trade with each other?
2 Explain the difference between comparative advantage and absolute advantage.
3 If free trade is so beneficial, why do so many countries erect barriers to free trade?
4 What forms may such barriers to trade take?
5 What is the purpose of GATT?
6 What is the purpose of the European Union?
7 Explain the mechanisms of the CAP. What problems have been experienced with it? What recent measures have been taken to reform the CAP?
8 Explain the EMS.

The balance of payments | 17

The accounts 433

Methods of control 439

UK problems 441

The accounts

Introduction

The 'balance of payments' consists of the flows of imports and exports into and out of the country. The first aspect requiring attention is how the payments for these flows are recorded on a national basis. The balance of payments accounts are made up of various sections and in order that the significance of each section can be understood, the accounts will be built up in stages.

In the circular flow-of-income model, *imports* represented a *withdrawal* from the flow as money went *out* of the country, while *exports* were an injection as the reverse was true. In simple terms, it is these flows of money which are recorded in the first part of the balance of payments accounts, known as the *current account*. This is divided into two sections – the *visible* trade balance and the *invisible* trade balance.

Visible trade

The visible trade balance refers to all the transactions which a country makes as a result of buying and selling *physical goods*, such as food, raw materials and manufactured products overseas:

UK visible trade balance

Year	(1) Exports £ million	(2) Imports £ million	(3) = (1) – (2) Visible balance
1984	70265	75601	-5336
1985	77991	81336	-3345
1986	72627	82186	-9559
1987	79153	90735	-11582
1988	80346	101826	-21480
1989	92154	116837	-24683
1990	101718	120527	-18809
1991	101413	113697	-10284
1992	107047	120453	-13406
1993	120839	134519	-13680

(Source: *Economic Trends*, June 1994, Table 2.13)

Traditionally, the UK has had a deficit on visible trade and a surplus on invisible trade. During the last 25 years a visible trade surplus has only been achieved in 1971, 1980, 1981 and 1982. Since 1983 the UK has had a deficit on manufactured trade, and UK exports only account for 7 per cent of total world exports of manufactures. On the positive side, the UK's share of world trade in manufactures has stabilised after 20 years of decline.

The balance of a country's visible imports and exports (3rd column) is called the *balance of trade*. When exports exceed imports then the balance of trade is regarded as *favourable*, whereas when imports exceed imports it is *unfavourable*. (An unfavourable balance of trade is sometimes referred to as a *trade gap*.)

Terms of trade

A very important concept which is associated with the visible balance of payments is the *terms of trade*. This measures the *ratio of import prices to export prices*. When *import* prices rise while *export* prices remain unchanged, the terms of trade become *less favourable*, because it is necessary to sell a greater volume of exports in order to buy the same *volume* of imports. (It is important in this connection to distinguish carefully between the physical *volume* of imports and exports and their actual *monetary value*.) A movement in the terms of trade shows whether the relative trading position of a country compared with other countries is improving or deteriorating.

The terms of trade are calculated using the equation:

$$\frac{\text{Index of export prices}}{\text{Index of import prices}} \times \frac{100}{1}$$

The index starts from a base year when export and import prices are each given a value on the index = 100. The terms of trade in the base year would be = 100. If export prices grow faster than import prices the terms of trade will be greater than 100 and thus favourable. If import prices grow faster than export prices the result will be an unfavourable terms of trade.

If export prices rise 9 per cent from the base year level and import prices 12 per cent then the terms of trade will be:

$$\frac{109}{112} \times \frac{100}{1} = 97 \text{ (unfavourable movement)}$$

If on the other hand export prices rise 15 per cent and import prices 5 per cent then the terms of trade will be:

$$\frac{115}{105} \times \frac{100}{1} = 109 \text{ (favourable movement)}$$

However, the probable end result of a movement one way or the other may not always be quite as might be expected. Two simple examples will illustrate the potential pitfalls for the unwary observer.

The UK still relies on other countries for a significant proportion of its food and raw materials. The prices of these items tend to be very volatile as they are particularly dependent upon the overall state of world trade. During upturns in economic activity, there will usually be a sharp increase in the demand for raw materials, causing their prices to rise significantly. However, the prices of finished manufactured goods do not rise as quickly because the increase in raw material prices takes time to work its way through to the prices of finished goods. Inevitably, until the price of finished goods 'catches up', the terms of trade for a country such as the UK will deteriorate.

The second example is not quite so straightforward and illustrates how a movement in the terms of trade can be misinterpreted. During the mid-1970s the rate of inflation in the UK was generally much higher than the rate in its immediate trading partners. Differences in the relative rates of inflation will naturally have an effect on the terms of trade. Indeed, at certain times during this period the export prices of UK goods rose much faster than the prices of imported goods and so – on the surface – the terms of trade nominally improved for the UK. However, a rate of inflation which is substantially higher than the rate elsewhere must – in the long term – be harmful to a country's balance of payments. Although export *prices* may rise quickly, the actual level of export *earnings* may well fall because the rise in earnings per unit may be more than compensated for by a fall in total export *volumes*. So, a rise in export prices (ie an 'improvement' in the terms of trade) may not necessarily help a country's balance of payments, especially if the elasticity of demand for exports is relatively elastic.

Invisible trade

The current account of the balance of payments reflects the state of trade in visible items such as food, raw materials and manufactured goods, which have a physical existence, and 'invisibles' which cover a wide variety of transactions between UK residents in which no tangible item is directly involved. It is more difficult to collect information about 'invisibles' and, perhaps for this reason, they are less excitedly received than the popular monthly trade figures.

The balance on invisibles had traditionally made a large positive contribution to the UK's balance of payments. Invisibles have been in surplus since 1948, whilst the balance of visible trade has been favourable in just six years over this period – 1956, 1958, 1971, 1980, 1981 and 1982. However, since the late 1980s the invisibles surplus has been in decline. The invisibles surplus is no longer sufficient to outweigh the deficit on visible trade. The current balance has therefore been negative for the last eight years.

Services

These are the largest element of the UK's invisibles account, contributing nearly 60 per cent of total invisible earnings. Sea transport is the largest single element. Freight on UK exports and on trade between third countries, passenger fares and charter payments, together with payments for ships' stores, port charges and the wages of non-resident crew paid abroad, are all included in this category. North Sea oil had a substantial impact on credits and debits, with offsetting effects on the balance of earnings for shipping services.

In contrast, receipts from civil aviation, which include British airlines' overseas earnings and overseas airlines' payments in the United Kingdom, have risen sharply in recent years. So have passenger fares paid to overseas airlines by UK residents and expenditure abroad by British airlines. Payments on hotels, meals, entertainments, shoppings, etc, by foreign tourists visiting the UK are recorded in the Travel Account, as are payments by UK residents holidaying abroad. Financial services include the earnings abroad of Lloyd's, other insurers, banks, commodity traders and brokers. Since the 'Big Bang' the City of London's opportunities for earning foreign business have been greatly enhanced. 'Other' services include film and television royalties, earnings on construction work overseas and other consultancy work abroad. Government services have traditionally been in deficit because of the expense involving troops and embassies which are maintained abroad.

Interest, profits and dividends (IPD)
These are the returns on our overseas investments, banking flows and foreign investment in the United Kingdom. They now account for around 33 per cent of invisible earnings. These current account flows are directly related to entries in the capital account. For example, where a UK subsidiary overseas makes a profit which is reinvested in that subsidiary, the profit will be recorded as an IPD earning, while the investment is recorded as a capital outflow which increases the value of the UK's external assets. When the profit is not reinvested overseas, the balance of payments benefit will usually be received in the form of a dividend paid to the UK company by the overseas subsidiary. Interest on borrowing and lending abroad by the UK banks in foreign currency is recorded net (interest received less interest paid) to reflect the close links between banks' borrowing and lending, particularly on the interbank market where the gross sums involved can be large in relation to the net earnings.

Transfers
Much of the transfers part of the invisible accounts involves UK contributions to the EU (a debit), and receipts from the EU (a credit) such as regional aid. Bilateral overseas aid also appears in this section as a debit. Private transfers (gifts plus payments to charitable donations and to dependents overseas) account for a sizeable part of the section too. Transfers have always been in large deficit.

The current account

If the tables (for visible and invisible trade) are combined, the *current account of the balance of payments* is found.

UK Balance of Payments: Current account

Year	Visible trade		Invisibles	
	Exports £ million	Imports £ million	Balance	Current balance
1984	70265	75601	6818	1482
1985	77991	81336	5583	2238
1986	72627	82186	8688	-871
1987	79153	90735	6599	-4983
1988	80346	101826	4863	-16617
1989	92154	116837	2171	-22512
1990	101718	120527	541	-18268
1991	101413	113697	2632	-7652
1992	107047	120453	3439	-9967
1993	120839	134519	2753	-10670

(Source: *Economic Trends*, June 1994, Table 2.13)

Transactions section

Recently, there was a change introduced in the way in which the accounts for the balance of payments are presented. We have seen the demise of the 'currency flow' and the 'capital account'. *Assets* for the UK involve capital movements out of the country, and are therefore given a negative (-) sign. They also include additions to the reserves, ie funds taken out of the transactions account and stored up in the Bank of England Exchange Equalisation Account. Liabilities for the UK are funds which are owed, capital movements into the country, having been added to the transactions account with a positive (+) sign. The current account remains the same in its overall presentation.

Thus the old 'investment and other capital flows' section has disappeared, absorbed into the new transactions section, which now comprises all public and private movements of capital. Reserves are included under transactions in assets, largely because the use of reserves for balance of payments purposes has been much reduced and the old 'official financing' category has consequently lost much of its significance.

The new presentation is certainly simpler in that it emphasises the current balance which is the catalyst of the whole account, and downgrades the private investment flows which are always fickle and at the mercy of international arbitrageurs. All capital transactions, whether in the private sector or in the official domain, are put together, so that if we add the current balance to the net transactions and balancing item, the answer is zero – ie the balance of payments must always balance.

Investment *inflows of capital* (liabilities +) of a *long-term nature* (in factories, etc) are automatically of initial benefit to the balance of payments as well as creating employment. Long-term capital investment in the UK can also boost visible exports from this country. Ford, and more recently Nissan, are obvious examples of this. Governments have encouraged foreign investment, as it was hoped that additional benefits would include the advantages of more efficient foreign practices and management techniques. Despite the obvious benefits of encouraging investment in this country, there are a number of critics. They maintain that the net long-term benefit to the country and its balance of payments is probably less than is often thought, as any profits which are not re-invested in the business will usually be remitted back to the parent company overseas and so will represent a persistent outflow of funds year after year (negative (-) on the invisible account).

The second criticism has more foundation. A significant degree of economic sovereignty may be lost if large parts of UK industry are allowed to fall into foreign ownership or control. The economy may be at the mercy of large multinational companies which can switch production from plants in this country to other subsidiaries in other countries.

The question of long-term *capital outflows* (assets -) is more controversial. Capital flows out of the UK do provide interest profits and dividends on the invisible account as a (+). Income from the UK's huge investments overseas make an increasingly significant contribution to the UK balance of payments (in 1993 £2.7 billion). However, it can be argued that this money should have been invested in the UK to create jobs here. Additionally, it can be seen as immoral to invest in economies whose political regime is seen as authoritarian. However, it is not possible to make industrialists invest if they consider that an adequate return is not available.

Up to 1979 the UK had exchange controls to regulate overseas investment. It is argued that the controls placed UK companies at a disadvantage to companies in other countries when it came to exploiting investment opportunities overseas. Furthermore, UK industrialists argued that the restrictions limited the ability of companies which already had substantial investments overseas to develop them solely in line with their commercial judgment. However, any form of restriction on industrialists and entrepreneurs naturally brings forth criticism, and there is an element of 'special pleading' in all the arguments against investment controls. This is particularly true now that most companies make extensive use of the various international money markets and so effectively side-step the controls.

In line with the 'free market' approach of the government elected in 1979 under Mrs Thatcher, all exchange controls were scrapped. The UK was one of the few European countries still to have exchange controls, and their retention was seen as interfering with market forces in the capital markets.

In general terms, the economist should be in favour of the *free* movement of capital throughout the world as – other things being equal – this will help to ensure the optimum allocation of the world's economic resources. Long-term capital will, in theory, gravitate to those countries where the rate of return on capital is highest.

Under the present government, the UK became the world's second largest holder of overseas assets. At the end of 1986, the value of UK investment overseas was estimated to be over £100 billion, equivalent to 25 per cent of GDP. However, 1986 was a peak year, since when the value of UK assets abroad has fallen considerably. Part of the explanation for the large fluctuations in our overseas asset values was revaluation of Foreign Direct Investment (FDI) assets during a period of boom, fluctuations in exchange rates (for part of the 80s and early 90s sterling was significantly overvalued), and also (for portfolio investment) stock market booms and the stock market crash of 1987. The recession of the early 90s has resulted in revaluations downwards of UK overseas assets, both FDI and portfolio. (FDI means in this context UK multinationals investing in plant etc abroad; portfolio investment is investment by UK citizens, including pension and insurance funds, in securities of foreign based companies.)

Short-term capital flows of money between nations is very much related to the interest rates prevailing in certain financial centres. Money which moves from one country to another will move to places where interest rates are highest and there is a strong economy. For example, the early 1980s saw a lot of short-term capital flow into the UK. High short-term interest rates, the UK's North Sea oil, and the monetarist policies of the Thatcher government combined to make London an attractive financial centre. These speculative flows of 'hot money' can just as quickly move to other financial centres such as New York or Tokyo. These rather volatile flows of capital can often cause equally volatile movements of the exchange rate in the UK.

Methods of control

Introduction

A persistent balance of payments deficit naturally cannot be sustained for long periods as there must come a time when the country's official reserves of foreign exchange are exhausted. Similarly, other countries will not be prepared to continue to lend foreign exchange to the country if they can see no prospect of their loans being repaid from future balance of payments surpluses. So, a country must pursue economic policies which are designed to correct, and ultimately eliminate, a balance of payments deficit. Throughout the 1960s and 1970s, the UK has experienced deficits of varying sizes in most years and so its economic policies always had to take this problem into account. In the 1980s the benefits of North Sea oil made the balance of payments less of an economic issue or a problem. However, with income from North Sea Oil having peaked in the mid-80s the underlying problem has emerged once more.

Increasing exports

A balance of payments deficit effectively means that the country's imports are exceeding its exports and so any corrective policy should aim either to increase exports or to reduce imports. If the first option is pursued, the government can try to encourage exports through schemes such as the Export Credits Guarantee Scheme, but, as has already been noted, such schemes have a limited effect, as other countries cannot be 'made' to buy UK goods. The more usual method of increasing exports is to expand the level of national output in the hope that at least part of the expansion will find its way into exports. Again, the effect of this is likely to be limited as it is not possible to guarantee that the extra output will actually be exported. Furthermore, as any expansion of national output will inevitably lead to an increase in the level of national income, it is probable that imports will be increased as the extra income draws in more imported goods. Consequently, if any increase in exports arises from the expansion of national output, it may well be completely or partially offset by a rise in imports.

Decreasing imports

The dilemma just outlined naturally makes it very tempting to introduce a wide-ranging and stringent system of import controls instead. The problems associated with import controls have already been examined in some detail, but, in general terms, the imposition of import controls will probably not help the country in the long term as they will lead to retaliatory action from other countries. The Thatcher government's belief in free trade also meant import controls being frowned upon.

An alternative method of reducing the level of imports is to reduce the level of effective demand in the economy through fiscal and monetary policies. However, this will only be effective if the demand for imported goods is elastic and, unfortunately, in the UK many of its imports are 'necessities' such as food and raw materials. Despite this difficulty, it is still true that an effective deflationary policy will have some beneficial effects on the balance of payments deficit because the general price level will be reduced in relation to the price level prevailing in other countries. This will make the country's exports more competitive and so their volume should increase. Since the UK joined the EU in 1973, widespread use of import controls is not an easy policy option to adopt. There could be problems with our treaty obligations.

Devaluation

The effect of a change in relative prices between trading countries is very important in correcting a balance of payments deficit and a principal method of achieving the necessary relative change is through the *devaluation of the country's currency in terms of the currencies of other countries*. Although devaluation is really a topic for international finance, it is clearly very relevant to the correction of a balance of payments deficit. A simple example will illustrate both its importance and potential use. Suppose, for sake of argument, that before a devaluation, £1 could be exchanged for three American dollars. If complicating factors such as transport costs are ignored, this would mean that a UK good costing £1 could be sold in America for $3, while an American good costing $3 could be sold in the

UK for £1. If the pound is then 'devalued' against the dollar so that £1 could then be exchanged for only $2, then it is inevitable that the *relative* price of each good must change in the two markets. The UK good would still cost £1 in the home market, but it would now be much cheaper in the American market as it could be bought for just $2. Meanwhile, the American good would now cost £1.50 in the UK. In short, a devaluation of a country's currency makes its *exports* relatively *cheaper*, while its *imports* become relatively more *expensive*. So, the likely effect of a devaluation would be to *increase exports* and *reduce imports*.

However, the elasticities of demand for both exports and imports must also be considered, as a devaluation will clearly only be successful if both are *elastic*. If one or other has a relatively inelastic demand then the changes in relative prices will have little or no beneficial effect and, as has already been noted, unfortunately the demand is inelastic for many of the imports of the UK. There is also another complicating factor so far as the UK is concerned. Although the demand for UK exports may increase in the short term after a devaluation as they become relatively cheaper, their new-found 'competitive edge' may well be short-lived. It will be remembered that the cost of imports increases after a devaluation and so, inevitably, the cost of imported raw materials will increase, which will reflect eventually in the price of finished (exported) goods. Consequently, in the long-term, the benefits of a devaluation so far as the UK is concerned will probably be less marked than in the case of other countries. Indeed, the evidence of the two major devaluations of sterling since the Second World War (1949 and 1967) tends to bear this out, even when allowances are made for other factors.

A devaluation will only be really effective in the long term if it is accompanied by the appropriate *internal* economic policies. The government needs to restrain the level of aggregate demand and increase the ability of exporting industries to compete in overseas markets. Devaluation was associated with a policy of fixed exchange rates which prevailed in the UK before 1972.

UK problems

A persistent problem

The UK's balance of payments on current account has been creating problems during the whole of the post-war period. In the nineteenth century the UK had a strong industrial base which enabled it to sell sufficient manufactured goods (often using imported raw materials) to be able to buy the food and other raw materials needed by its huge industrial population and specialised industry. The UK's position as 'the workshop of the world' has been persistently eroded since then by the rise in new industrial competitors (ie Japan, Korea). They have competed in our traditional export markets, and have also competed for supplies of raw materials and food, pushing up their prices. Other problems have added to the UK's weakness. According to critics both at home and abroad, UK firms in the 1950s, 1960s and 1970s became complacent about innovation and marketing, and trade unions imposed rising real wages and unproductive working practices in industry so that labour productivity fell in relation to labour costs. As a result, UK goods had a diminishing share of both foreign and domestic markets, and the UK has been forced to pay higher prices for imported goods. This problem, of declining manufactured export sales while imports rise in volume and cost, has been a persistent feature of the balance of payments during this period. The following diagram shows the UK's share of world exports of manufactures falling, although this has stabilised recently.

Share of world export of manufactures, by country

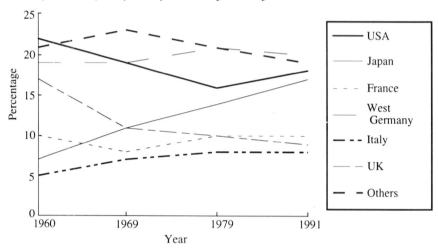

(Source: NIESR and OECD)

Up to 1972

During the post-war period, the previous great strength on the UK balance of payments, the invisible balance (which had until then been able to keep up with the increasing deficit on the balance of trade) became less strong as new financial centres set up in competition with the City. As a result, the current account of the balance of payments moved into growing deficits. Since the capital flows inevitably reflect the expectations about the future of the currency, the growing balance of payments deficit on the current account caused investors to move their funds out of the UK in expectation of a devaluation of the currency. (It should be remembered that the return on an investment in the UK for a foreign investor is any interest/dividends payments plus any capital gain on the £ between buying it for the purchase of the UK asset and selling it after the asset is disposed of.) The eventual devaluation of the £ in 1967, halted the speculation and also gave the usual price advantage to UK goods in foreign and domestic markets. The balance of payments as a result improved.

Figures for the visible balance, the invisible balance, the current account balance,

balance of long-term and other capital flows out, and the basic balance are shown in the following table. The annual average for selected periods is shown in £m.

	1956–60	1961–4	1965–7	1968–71
Visible balance	-94	-213	-281	-142
Invisible balance	+230	+182	+206	+627
Current account balance	+136	-31	-75	+484
Balance of long-term and other capital flows out	-130	-181	+498	+367
Basic balance	-53	-170	-212	+383

1972–77

1972–77 saw a major turn-round in the improvement indicated above. It is a useful period for indicating the vulnerability of the UK balance of payments to both internal and external changes. Internally, the problem was caused by the monetary expansion and consequent escalation in the rate of inflation. This increased the vulnerability of UK domestic and foreign markets to foreign competition, since the prices of all British goods rose faster than prices for the goods produced by most other countries.

At the same time, at the end of 1973, OPEC (The Organisation of Petroleum Exporting Countries) took the logical step for any cartel which jointly dominates the supply of a good whose elasticity of demand is low. They quadrupled the price of oil. This action, and subsequent price increases, put an immediate and lasting strain on the industrial countries and on the international financial system as a whole.

As a result, the visible trade balance went into an average annual deficit of £2,763m during the period 1972–77. Even by the end of 1974 the deficit wholly attributable to oil imports was £3,500m. The size of the oil imports problem became so great that it became usual to separate the balance of trade balance into two parts – the 'oil balance' and the 'non-oil balance'. In spite of the disasters reflected in the balance of trade, the balance of payments only moved into an average annual deficit of £214m during the 1972–77 period. The capital account had moved strongly into surplus as the OPEC countries put some of their new oil wealth into sterling assets and the development of the North Sea oilfields attracted foreign investment funds.

Of course, financing trade deficits with foreign borrowing is dangerous, in that interest payments on the debts put a cost on future balance of payments and, more seriously, the funds may be withdrawn in the future which creates an outflow on the balance of payments as big as the original inflow. In 1976, there was a huge outflow of long- and short-term capital.

1977-80

North Sea oil brought two main advantages to the British balance of payments:

a domestic production of oil reduced the need to import oil; and

b domestic produced oil could be exported.

The improvement is shown below:

UK Balance of payments	1976	1977	1978	1979
£m				
Trade in oil	-3,947	-2,771	-1,999	-779
Non-oil visible trade	+20	+492	+453	-2,625
Total visible trade	-3,927	-2,279	-1,546	-3,404
Invisible trade	+2,811	+1,995	+2,166	+1,541
Current account balance	-1,116	-284	+602	-1,863

While the oil problem on the balance of payments was solved it unfortunately contributed to the problems of the non-oil trade. The long-term competitive weakness of UK industry was accentuated by a strong exchange rate. The value of the £ was rising because of high domestic interest rates which attracted foreign funds. At the same time, the fact that the UK had oil stock gave foreign investors the expectation of a strong balance of payments and a strong exchange rate in the future. By 1982 the exchange rate was falling against the US dollar and continued to do so until 1985. In general this depreciation was not reflected in the pound's relationship with the European currencies.

After 1981

After 1980 the UK's current account remained in surplus until 1986. Deficits on the current account continued in 1987 and 1988. A number of factors have been involved in these changes. The UK has historically had a surplus in trade in manufactured goods, and a deficit in primary products. While the surplus in manufactured goods has tended to diminish, and in 1983 turned into a deficit, the deficit in fuels has moved into surplus as a result of the rise in North Sea oil output. Although this beneficial effect will ebb as North Sea oil output falls, oil revenues may not fall by the same proportion, as movements in the price of oil partly determine this. The miners' strike had an adverse impact on the current account, estimated to be in the order of £2.5bn in 1984 and £1.5bn in 1985. The invisible balance has for many years been in surplus, with the very large surplus on private invisibles outweighing the normal deficit on government invisibles. The beneficial effects of North Sea oil on the visible balance have been partly offset by the rising outflow of foreign oil company profits on the invisible balance.

During the 1983-86 period lower oil prices and high consumer spending contributed to the worsening position of the UK's current balance. In 1987 the UK's current account deficit was £2.5bn and in 1988 £14bn. For, although UK manufactured exports continued to grow at $9\frac{1}{2}$ per cent per year between 1983 and 1985 the surge in imports of manufactured goods weakened the current account. The appreciation of the exchange rate since the mid-1980s has not helped export prices either. The large outflows on the capital balance in the early 1980s contributed a further debit after exchange controls were scrapped in 1979.

Year	Capital balance
1980	-2,938
1981	-6,510
1982	-2,517
1983	-4,673
1984	-7,117
1985	-8,109
1986	-9,193

Although long-term capital investments are a debit item they yield future incomes on the invisible account. International trade is the life-blood of the nation: around 30 per cent of all that we produce is sold abroad. Although accounting for about 1 per cent of the world's population, the UK is the fifth largest trading nation. Some six million jobs depend on exports of goods and services. The possible future pattern of the UK's trading was outlined by the former Chancellor, Nigel Lawson, when he said:

> 'If it does turn out that we are relatively more efficient in world terms at producing services then our national interest lies in a surplus on services and a deficit on goods. The government's job is to create an economic framework and environment calculated to improve the performance of all industries, manufacturing and services alike.' (*Report of the House of Lords Select Committee on Overseas Trade*, Vol II, Session 1984-5, HL(238–II), p554)

In the late 1980s, exports grew but imports grew at the same rate or faster. During the period when sterling was in the ERM, its relatively high value hindered export growth (a high-valued exchange rate makes our goods and services less competitively priced).

During the recession of the early 1990s, the volume of imports plunged, whilst the volume of exports continued to rise, albeit more slowly than in the late 1980s. If we consider value rather than volume, then the picture is not very different. The following graph shows export and import value and volume indices for the period 1987–93.

Visible trade, volume and value, 1987 to 1993

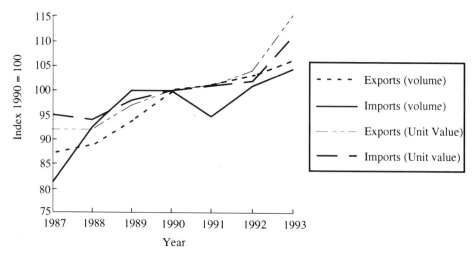

(Source: *Economic Trends*, Table 2.14)

Behind the overall shifts in exports and imports, Britain's surplus on its trade in oil has been decreasing during the 1990s. This may pose a problem for the balance of payments in the future. The fall in the price of oil in 1985-86 coincided with the levelling off of output from the North Sea, and this led to a decrease in the net oil contribution to the UK visible balance during the late 1980s. Whereas in the early 80s, the surplus on oil had helped to compensate for a non-oil deficit, this option will not be open to the UK in the future.

There is a debate amongst economists as to whether, with a floating exchange rate, the balance of payments is any longer a matter for concern. Samuel Brittan, writing in the *Financial Times*, suggests that the balance of payments is irrelevant as a guide to macroeconomic policy. The exchange rate will equilibrate the system, it is said, and interest rates can be adjusted appropriately. The experience with floating exchange rates following the collapse of the Bretton Woods system seems to indicate that this is not necessarily the whole truth. Another reason for considering the balance of payments as no longer a matter for concern is our membership of the European Union and the move towards monetary union. If we consider different regions within the UK, some regions have a trade deficit with other regions (eg the North East of England with the South East), but this is not a balance of payments problem within the UK. The same reasoning may be applied to the UK as part of the EU following monetary union. Against this view, one could argue that it is unlikely that the EU structural funds would be sufficient to counteract the problems caused by being a deficit region within the EU, or that the other members of the EU would countenance large outflows to the UK.

Looking to the future, prosperity for the UK will still depend on our ability to trade goods and services successfully. The UK is a very open economy, and trade is its life-blood. We can only trade successfully if our goods and services are competitive. Trade performance in home and overseas markets is of critical importance to our prosperity for the rest of the century.

Another cause for concern for the future lies in the narrowness of our manufacturing base, following the shake-outs of the past two recessions. Some economists believe that our manufacturing base is no longer sufficient to facilitate the strong growth rates which the UK has historically been capable of, once the recovery gathers momentum.

Questions for review

1. Explain the following terms:
   a. current account;
   b. capital account;
   c. visible trade;
   d. invisible trade;
   e. the 'trade gap';
   f. terms of trade.

2. Distinguish between a trade deficit and a budget deficit.

3. Why does the Balance of Payments always balance?

4. Outline the post-war UK record on the Balance of Payments. Why is there cause for concern?

International finance – the world economy | 18

Exchange rates 451

Recent exchange rate systems 458

The IMF 462

The Eurocurrency market 466

The problems of the Third World 466

The World Bank 468

Exchange rates

Need for exchange rates

One of the characteristics of money is that it is an acceptable medium for the exchange of goods and services. This characteristic is easily met when money is being used within the boundaries of one particular country, but the currency of one country is not usually acceptable as a medium of exchange in another country. A company in the UK cannot discharge its debt to a company in America in pounds sterling, because that company cannot pay its own debts in pounds – its creditors want dollars, as they are the accepted medium of exchange in America. So, the company in the UK will have to obtain dollars in order to pay its debts.

In previous analysis it was mentioned that money is a convenient means of measuring *the value of one good in terms of another*, as both could be given a monetary value. However, it is now necessary to value *one type* of money in terms of another *type* of money. In this case, pounds in terms of dollars. This is done through the *rate of exchange*. This rate effectively compares the value of one currency in terms of the other and it was originally based on a comparison of what each unit of each type of money could buy. In theory, international exchange rates should reflect the *purchasing power parity theory*. If £100 in the UK buys the same amount of goods and services that $200 buys in the USA, then, in theory, the exchange rate should be £1 = $2. However, this rarely occurs and the determination of exchange rates is much more complicated than that.

Foreign exchange and the balance of payments

Let us assume that the exchange rate is determined by market forces in the market in which countries exchange one currency for another in order to finance international trade. (We are therefore ignoring the problem of international capital movements and speculation in currencies.) In other words, the currency is said to be *'floating freely'* or *'floating cleanly'*.

The exchange rate of any currency is its price in terms of gold (£1 = x ounces of gold) or in terms of another currency (£1 = x US $) or in terms of a weighted average of a sample 'basket' of a group of currencies. In the following diagram, the price of £1 in $ is shown on the vertical axis.

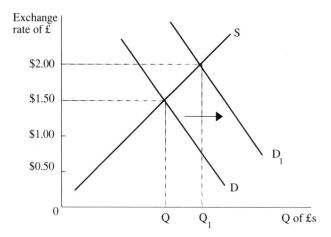

The *demand for the £* from current holders of dollars depends on their purchases of British goods and services. The lower the price of those goods and services in terms of dollars, the more goods they will want to buy and the more £s they will need with which to buy them. Thus, the demand for the £ is inversely related to its exchange rate.

Similarly, *the supply of the £* is positively related to the exchange rate. If the exchange rate of the £ is lower, imports appear more expensive since now more £s must be paid for any purchase whose price is fixed in dollars. If demand is relatively elastic, the amount spent on imports will be reduced and the supply of £s (or sterling) will be reduced. (It should be noted that the shape of the supply curve depends on the elasticity of demand for imports. If demand is relatively inelastic, the supply of £s will *increase* when the exchange rate of the £ falls.)

In the diagram above, the initial equilibrium exchange rate is at £1 = $1.50. Suppose that the demand for the £ increases for exogenous reasons. The production of North Sea oil and its sale on world markets starting in the mid-1970s had this effect on the demand for the £. The excess demand for the £ on the exchange markets will bid up the price of the £. British exports become more expensive for the holders of dollars and they buy less exports and less £s. At the same time, assuming that the demand for imports is relatively elastic, the amount spent on the now less expensive imports will be increased. The exchange rate rises to a new equilibrium of £1 = $2.00.

It should be noted that the equilibrium exchange rate of the £ implies an equilibrium quantity in the exchange market. The demand and supply sides of this market are the British *balance of payments*. Thus, equilibrium exchange rates imply equilibrium balance of payments, too. At the initial exchange rate £1 = $1.50 but, after the increase in demand, for $2, the balance of payments would be in surplus, more is being spent on British goods than the British are spending on imported goods. The rising exchange rate reduces the amount spent on British exports because of their higher prices. The expenditure on imports will increase (assuming demand for imports is sufficiently price elastic in response to a reduction in their price). Thus, as the exchange rate rises towards its new equilibrium, so the balance of payments is brought back to equilibrium.

Stable equilibrium and elasticity

Another important point is the significance of *the elasticity of demand for imports and exports* if this equilibrium is to be stable. Suppose that the higher exchange rate of the £ results in *less* being spent on imports after the reduction in the price (ie demand is relatively inelastic) so that the supply of the £ is reduced by the increase in the exchange rate of the £. Suppose also that the demand for exports is extremely inelastic. In these circumstances, a rise in the exchange rate of the £ will lead to an increase in the excess demand for the £ and further pressure for a rise in the exchange rate.

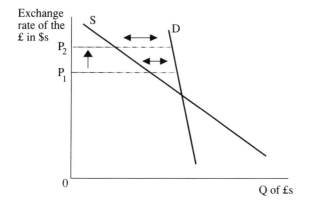

The Marshall-Lerner rule for exchange rates adjustments leading to a stable equilibrium is that the sum of the elasticities of demand for imports and exports should be greater than one. Only in these circumstances will an increase in the exchange rate lead to a reduction in the balance of payments surplus and a return of the exchange rates and the balance of payments to equilibrium. Similarly, under conditions of excess supply of the £ and balance of payments deficit, a fall in the value of the £ will only succeed in restoring equilibrium if the sum of the elasticities of demand for imports and exports is greater than one. If it is not, the falling £ will lead to bigger surpluses of the £ and further downward pressure on the currency.

Capital flows and speculation

Finally, we have so far ignored the capital flows and speculation in currencies which affect these markets.

Suppose that there is a balance of payments deficit and that the currency is currently over-valued. Anyone holding sterling assets will sell them immediately before they lose value. This increase in the supply of the £, when it was already in surplus on the currency markets, will lead to a larger drop in its exchange value than would otherwise occur. The balance of payments deficit will get bigger. Similarly, speculation in favour of a currency whose value is rising will boost its value further and the balance of payments surplus will increase.

The advantages of a system of floating exchange rates

A system of floating exchange rates allows the exchange rates to be determined by the forces described above. The factors determining the demand and supply of any currency are constantly changing as the world demand and supply of goods and services fluctuates because of technological changes, weather, war, changing preferences, etc. The advantage of a floating exchange rate system is that *the exchange rate will adjust automatically* through the market mechanism. Under the assumptions on elasticity discussed above, these exchange rate adjustments will lead to a new appropriate equilibrium exchange rate and will restore the balance of payments equilibrium. Thus, a system of floating exchange rates gives a flexible response to the volatile circumstances of the real world.

Since any imbalance on the balance of payments will be corrected by exchange rate adjustments, there is *no need for any policy action by government* to correct for this imbalance. Indeed, it is argued that floating exchange rates leave governments free to exercise internal economic policies of their choice.

The disadvantages of a system of floating exchange rates

As discussed above, the effectiveness of the floating exchange rate to deal with imbalance on the balance of payments depends on the elasticities of demand for imports and exports. Suppose that the demand for imports and exports is very *inelastic in the short run*. The falling exchange rate in response to balance of payments deficit will initially make the deficit larger. This is called the 'J-curve effect' (see following diagram). A reverse 'J-curve' is possible following a rapid appreciation of a currency.

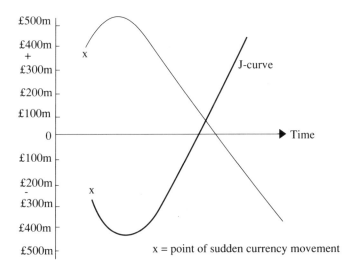

x = point of sudden currency movement

The falling exchange value of the £ makes imports more expensive which means that the cost of living and the costs of production will rise. This *inflation* will tend to reduce the competitiveness of British goods. The elasticity of demand and supply will tend to increase over time after the devaluation but, by that time, inflation caused by the devaluation will have wiped out the competitive advantage created by the devaluation. There is thus no reason why the falling exchange rate will reduce the balance of payments deficit even in the long run. Thus, the automatic correction for balance of payments deficit or surplus provided by a floating exchange rate may not work.

Secondly, the fluctuating exchange rate which will naturally result from constant changes in the factors influencing its value may *inhibit trade*. Traders may be unable to agree on future prices for goods and so may be unable to make contracts for trade taking place in the future. To some extent this problem can be solved by making use of *futures markets* when a contract to buy currency on some future date is made and the price is agreed now.

Fluctuations in exchange rates will be increased by *speculation*. For example, in the late 1970s, the £ might have been expected to rise in value because of the new and increasing sales of North Sea oil. However, inflation in Britain was more rapid than inflation in the economies of most of our trading partners, so British goods were becoming less competitive. In spite of this, the value of the £ rose dramatically against the dollar in 1980 and early 1981 in a way that was in part explained by large flows of short-term, speculative funds into Britain. The exchange rate then fell dramatically during the later part of 1981, even though oil revenues were increasing at this time. This, too, must, at least in part, be explained by the outflow of these speculative funds. Thus, if floating exchange rates fluctuate and fluctuations lead to problems for traders, speculation makes the problem worse.

Fixed exchange rates

An alternative to a floating exchange rate system is to have *fixed exchange rates*. In the diagram below, the exchange rate of the £ in terms of the dollar is fixed at £1 = $1.50. This may be the equilibrium exchange rate.

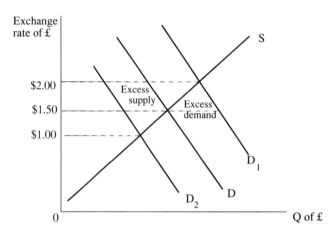

However, in a period of rapid economic change, it is likely that the equilibrium will shift up or down. Suppose that the equilibrium exchange rate rises £1 = $2.00 because of increased demand for currency due to the emergence of a balance of payments surplus. Instead of the exchange rate rising to the new equilibrium, other adjustments must be made to deal with *the excess demand for the £* at the fixed exchange rate £1 = $1.50. The Bank of England may increase the supply of sterling onto the exchange markets by using sterling to purchase foreign currency reserves. The use of sterling to do this increases *the money supply* with the associated effects discussed in Chapter 10.

Alternatively the government might use appropriate *monetary and fiscal policies* to adjust the demand and supply of sterling. For example, an expansionary monetary and fiscal policy will lead to more import buying (imports being income elastic) leading to an increased supply of sterling. Lower interest rates will reduce the return on sterling assets so that demand for them falls, reducing the demand for sterling.

Suppose instead that the demand for sterling has fallen so that the new equilibrium exchange rate is at £1 = $1.00 and there is a balance of payments deficit, the exchange rate is fixed at £1 = $1.50 and other steps must be taken to deal with the problem of *the excess supply of sterling* on the exchange markets and the balance of payments deficit.

The Bank may purchase sterling on the currency markets using its reserves of foreign currency. This will increase the demand for sterling. Alternatively, deflationary fiscal and monetary policies will reduce import buying and check any inflationary pressures which may have caused a loss of competitiveness. A high interest rate will attract foreign capital to buy British assets. By reducing the supply of sterling and increasing the demand for it, the equilibrium can be maintained at £1 = $1.50 and the balance of payments deficit will be eliminated.

Advantages of fixed exchange rates

The principle advantage of fixed exchange rates is *certainty* which encourages international trade. This system works best when there are *no long-term changes* in economic factors. The fixed exchange rate will deal with all *short-term fluctuation*, with the Bank of England buying or selling sterling, using and building up foreign currency reserves as it does so, to adjust for the short-term occurrences of balance of payments deficit and surplus.

Secondly, it is argued that fixed exchange rates force governments to deal with *internal problems* such as wage push inflation rather than relying on the floating exchange rate to solve their problems for them.

Disadvantages of a fixed exchange rate

The system of fixed exchange rates works as long as *the long-term equilibrium exchange rate is stable and equal to the fixed rate.* However, accelerating economic change world-wide has meant that long-term exchange rates are not stable. For example, Britain's lessening competitiveness on world markets is a long-term change which should mean that the value of the £ falls against other currencies on a long-term basis. This means that in a system of exchange rates the *balance of payments deficit* will, ceteris paribus, get bigger and bigger. The government will have to support the £ with purchases of it on the foreign exchange markets, using a diminishing stock of *foreign currency reserves.* Eventually the reserves will be exhausted. Other steps will need to be taken. *Deflationary fiscal and monetary policies* should correct the balance of payments deficit if they are firm enough – at the cost, however, of rising unemployment, falling output, company closures, and so on.

Alternatively, *the currency could be devalued.* A new, lower, fixed exchange rate will be chosen. If this is the equilibrium exchange rate, then the effect is much like that under a system of floating exchange rates. As long as the demands for exports and imports are sufficiently elastic, the lower exchange rate will eliminate the balance of payments deficit. However, if the elasticities are low and the higher import prices lead to *an inflationary spiral*, the deficit will be made bigger because of the devaluation. Further devaluations may be necessary with higher and higher rates of domestic inflation. This disastrous scenario may be exaggerated by *speculation* against the currency.

In a system of floating exchange rates, speculators may *win or lose*. The future value of the exchange rate will be uncertain. Those that guess correctly will win and will re-inforce any existing trends. Those that guess wrongly will lose and will counteract any existing trends.

However, under a system of fixed exchange rates, repeated balance of payments deficits will signal to all speculators that the currency will either be devalued or its value will be held by appropriate action from the Bank. Thus, those who sell sterling now will win if the £ is devalued *or* neither win nor lose if the £'s value is held. There is *no chance of losing*. Speculation will therefore be safer for the speculator and will all be against the £, putting further pressure on it. In these circumstances, the government may be forced to solve the balance of payments deficit by deflationary fiscal and monetary policies, with the associated consequences for the economy.

Recent exchange rate systems

The collapse of the Bretton Woods system

The Bretton Woods system which organised the international system of exchange rates in the post-war period collapsed in 1971/2 for the following reasons:

a The Bretton Woods system was fundamentally one of fixed exchange rates imposed on a world of increasingly rapid change where the experiences of different countries differed widely. For example, inflation rates became divergent between countries. The necessary devaluations and revaluations to restore realistic relative currency values were discouraged by the IMF.

b The dollar which was the central currency of the system became weakened by its role as a reserve currency and in 1971 the dollar was taken off the gold standard and devalued.

c Many countries found that the necessary deflationary policies needed to keep their currencies within the narrow zone of flexibility fixed by the system greatly constrained their macro-economic policy options. They wished to use the exchange rate as a discretionary policy instrument in the formulation of economic policy. For example, they might use devaluation to deal with the balance of payments deficit while aiming for higher economic growth to deal with long-term competitive weakness.

The 'dirty float'

Since 1972 the world currencies have been floating, but there has been a great deal of government intervention in the exchange markets to influence the market value of the currencies. In this sense, there is a 'dirty' rather than 'clean' (free market) float of the currencies.

There are two main ways used for influencing the market value of sterling:

a the Bank of England can buy or sell sterling on the foreign exchange markets so as to boost or reduce respectively the value of sterling;

b higher interest rates in Britain will attract foreign capital which will increase the demand for sterling and, ceteris paribus, raise its value on the currency markets. A lower interest rate has the opposite effect.

During 1988 there was a well-publicised disagreement between the then Prime Minister and the then Chancellor of the Exchequer over whether the government should engage in any intervention on the foreign exchange markets. The former wanted a 'clean' (free market) float whereas the Chancellor wanted to use interest rates to lower what he considered an over-valued exchange rate.

The intervention may be for one of two reasons:

a the intervention may be intended to *smooth out short-term fluctuations in the value of sterling* in the interests of certainty for international traders.

b the intervention may be intended to achieve some *unofficial target exchange rate*. The government may have an exchange rate policy because:

  i *a high exchange rate* tends to depress domestic inflation since it reduces the price of imports. It will also tend to depress the domestic economy as exports become less competitive on world markets. The depression of the domestic economy will check internal inflationary pressures such as trade union pressure on wages. However, the low level of demand in the domestic economy will lead to falling output, bankruptcies and rising unemployment. The purchases of sterling consistent with aiming for a higher exchange rate will tend to reduce the money supply which may be consistent with a 'tight money' policy for the economy. High interest rates will be consistent with this policy.

  ii *a low exchange rate* is inflationary since it makes imports more expensive. The demand for exports will increase which will result in an expansion of the domestic economy. There will be more internal inflationary pressures but there will also be rising output and reduced unemployment. The low interest rates and expanded money supply necessary to buy foreign currency reserves will also tend to be inflationary and expansionary.

The UK experience

The period since 1972 can be divided into six distinct periods: 1972–77, 1977–81, 1981–85, 1985–90, 1990–92, 1992–.

UK's Floating Pound

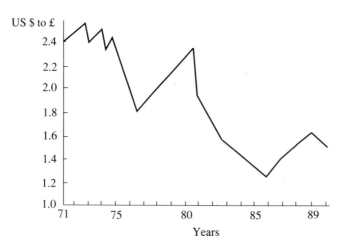

Before 1977, there were a number of factors which depressed the value of sterling. The long-term fall in competitiveness in Britian continued and inflation here was much more rapid than it was for most of our trading partners. 'Hot money' left the country in search of better returns and expectations elsewhere. The government twice tried to steady the decline of sterling, in 1975 and in 1976, unsuccessfully. The £ reached a low of £1 = $1.55 in 1976.

1977–81, 'hot money' poured into Britain because of the potential of North Sea oil which was itself beginning to boost export earnings and reduce expenditures on imported oil. Rates of interest here were rising and the dollar weakened. Again the government attempted to intervene to check the change in the market price of sterling. The government was hampered in any policy since it could not *control the money supply and print money* at the same time in order to sell sterling on foreign exchange markets. The £ rose to £1 = $2.40 in 1981 which represented a 60 per cent loss of competitiveness of British goods on world markets between 1979 and 1981. Not surprisingly, unemployment rose dramatically.

1981–85, the value of the £ began to fall largely because of high and rising rates of interest in North America. The dramatic fall in the value of sterling was accelerated by the miners' strike in the summer of 1984. It is important to remember that although the £ is usually quoted against the US dollar the sterling exchange rate index shows the £'s value against other major currencies.

1985–90 After 1986 the pound rose on the foreign exchange markets. The fierce debate on exchange rate policy in the mid-1980s centred around two issues. Should the £ be allowed to float freely in the spirit of Mrs Thatcher's 'you cannot buck the market' philosophy? Alternatively, should the £ be held down to keep inflation lower? By 1988 the pressure on the government to join the ERM of the EMS was a major problem for a Prime Minister unconvinced of the system. At the Madrid Summit of EU leaders in 1988 the UK government laid down conditions for joining the ERM. These were that UK inflation should be nearer the EU average and that other EU countries should scrap exchange controls and deregulate their financial markets. The UK finally joined the ERM in October 1990 (see Chapter 16) and in doing so returned to a fixed exchange rate system. The pound was fixed at 1.95 DM with a ± 6 per cent variation.

1990–92 In retrospect, it can be seen that this rate was too high. The government had opted for this rate quite deliberately, as they believed that the discipline of a high fixed exchange rate would help to squeeze inflation out of the system. Indeed, it was widely believed that one of the major benefits to the UK of joining the ERM would be that it would be anti-inflationary; due to the dominance of the Bundesbank in the system, and to their statutory obligation to keep inflation down, the member countries in the ERM had experienced converging inflation rates, that is, inflation rates being pulled down towards the low German rate.

But, as the high exchange rate made our exports uncompetitive, the cost was paid in jobs. Unemployment rose, and continued to rise until mid-93, when it almost reached three millions. The then Chancellor of the Exchequer, Norman Lamont, made the infamous remark that 'unemployment is a price worth paying' to squeeze inflation out of the system.

German interest rates were high, both in order to keep inflation at bay, and in order to attract funds for reunification. This meant that UK interest rates also had to be kept high. This made it very expensive for UK firms to borrow money. Again, the price was paid in UK jobs. The Bank of England was obliged to use large amounts of our foreign currency reserves in support of the pound, in order to hold it within its permitted band in the ERM.

There was much speculative pressure on the pound, and finally on Black Wednesday, 16 September 1992, following a day when the Bank of England had spent vast amounts of our foreign reserves in a vain attempt to maintain the value of the pound, sterling was forced out of the ERM.

At the same time that sterling was forced out, there was great speculative pressure on other member currencies. The lira was also forced out of the system, and the French franc survived only with German support. The whole fabric of the ERM began to crumble.

1992– The pound is no longer part of the ERM, and there is no indication that the pound will rejoin the ERM in the near future.

The débâcle with the ERM has put in jeopardy the proposed move towards a single currency for the EU. Clearly, a prerequisite for a single currency is fixed exchange rates.

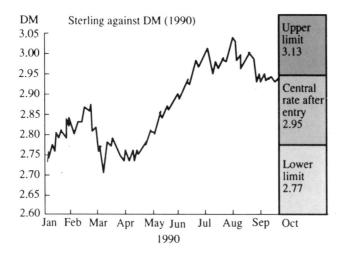

Sterling against DM (1990)

The IMF

A state of flux

The international monetary system has been in a state of flux in recent years and is likely to remain so for some time to come. Any general agreement on a widespread reform was difficult enough in the late 1960s, but the oil crisis of the 1970s complicated the procedure considerably. The differing interests and needs of the industrial countries, the oil exporting countries and the developing countries all have to be reconciled before any major and significant reform can take place. But why is a major reform necessary?

The gold standard

Originally the world's monetary system was based on the *gold standard* and individual currency values were tied closely to gold. This made the determination and control of exchange rates a very simple matter. If a £1 sovereign coin contained five times as much gold as a $1 piece, then the exchange rate was obviously $5 to £1. Even when paper currencies replaced minted coins, the process of determination was still basically the same, because those currencies were valued on the gold reserves held by the various countries. So, under the 'gold standard' a stable value was placed on all currencies through the operation of *fixed* rates of exchange. The gold standard was also, theoretically, the 'ideal method' for organising adjustments in the balance of payments. After all, if a country had a current account deficit, gold would have to be used to pay the debt. This would immediately reduce the money supply, as this supply was based on the country's reserves of gold. Inevitably, this would lead to deflation within the economy as a whole – prices would fall, exports would become more competitive and the balance of payments should improve quickly. However, this simple theory was not very acceptable in practice. Very few politicians could accept the stigma of increased unemployment and so counterbalancing policies were often implemented. Unfortunately, it proved impossible for countries nominally to accept the rules of one game and then play a different one.

However, there was an even greater problem with the ordinary operation of the gold standard. The overall price level in the world was dependent on adequate discoveries of gold, due to the relationship between the price level and the money supply within an economy. Unless the money supply keeps pace with the underlying increase in output, there will inevitably be a downward pressure on the price level and this is exactly what happened in the last part of the nineteenth century. World output was rising at around 5 per cent a year, while gold discoveries were few and far between. Something had to be done to maintain the potential level of economic activity and the answer was to move away from a rigid gold standard and economise on the use of gold. Gradually, countries issued more and more money which was not backed by their official reserves of gold (ie a greater percentage of the money in circulation was 'fiduciary'). Indeed, it quickly became usual practice to hold only about a quarter as much gold as there was money in circulation. However, this 'modified' gold standard where exchange rates were still fixed was far from ideal. The severe economic depression of the 1930s increased the strains between countries because there was a series of competitive devaluations as each country tried to pull itself out of the depression at the expense of other countries. The 'rules' of the gold standard were effectively being breached. It was clear, therefore, that a coherent system had to be devised urgently, either to replace the gold standard or to enforce it more rigorously on *all* countries.

Bretton Woods

The major countries of the world – except the Soviet Union – met in 1944 in an attempt to reach agreement on the necessary reforms. The agreement – known as the *Bretton Woods Agreement* – was designed to secure the theoretical advantages of the old gold standard without risking its disadvantages as well. In short, all exchange rates were supposed to be fixed in terms of gold through either the dollar or the pound, but as and when necessary there could – after the necessary consultation and agreement – be a realignment of rates. By ensuring that any realignment only occurred after international co-operation and agreement, it was believed that countries would not be forced to deflate severely in order to cure a serious balance of payments deficit.

The most important outcome of the Bretton Woods Agreement was the formation of the International Monetary Fund – the IMF. This body now has a membership of over 120 countries and it is recognised as a forum for international debate and monetary management.

Organisation

At its inception, each member country subscribed a 'quota' to finance the Fund. The size of the quota was determined by a country's GNP, its level of trade and its total monetary reserves. Seventy-five per cent of the quota was contributed in the country's own currency while the remainder was paid in gold. Any member of the IMF can draw up to 125 per cent of its quota in order to finance a balance of payments deficit. However, only 25 per cent can be withdrawn automatically – further drawings require the approval of the Board of Directors of the IMF. The Board will only give its approval if it considers that the country concerned is pursuing adequate internal economic policies. Furthermore, the money can only be borrowed for between 3 and 5 years as it is expected that a country's balance of payments will be back in surplus within that time.

The UK and the IMF

The UK has borrowed from the IMF in this way on a number of occasions in order to help it over the persistent difficulties which have arisen as a result of its balance of payments deficits.

The IMF is also able to provide medium-term finance to assist member countries which are in serious difficulty and it has provided such finance to the UK on two occasions in recent history. The IMF can only lend in this way by activating *its General Agreement to Borrow* from its major member countries. When this is done, these countries are able to make large amounts of money available to the IMF which it then on-lends to the borrowing country. However, in order to receive such a loan, the borrowing country will be required to embark on a series of complicated and detailed negotiations with an expert team from the IMF. The team has to be satisfied that the government of the country will pursue rigorous and strict economic and financial policies in the immediate future which are specifically designed to correct the underlying problems of the country's economy. In 1976 the UK borrowed $3,900 million in this way, but before the loan was granted the UK government had to sign a *Letter of Intent* to the IMF outlining both its policies and its economic targets over the period of the loan. Even then, the money was only made available in stages. If any of the prescribed targets had not been reached or if there had been a radical shift in policy, the IMF would have been able to withhold further instalments of the loan.

The IMF and devaluation

Under the Bretton Woods Agreement, an IMF member country was not supposed to devalue its currency except in very extreme circumstances, and then only on a once-and-for-all basis. There were three guidelines as to the circumstances in which a devaluation might be permitted:

a when a balance of payments deficit could not be 'reasonably' financed out of a country's ordinary reserves (ie there was thus a fundamental disequilibrium on the balance of payments);

b when it would be imprudent to borrow further large sums of money; or,

c when an attempt to correct a balance of payments deficit by internal economic measures would lead to an unacceptable increase in the level of unemployment.

Inevitably, the guidelines were too vague to be of much value in any given situation. For instance, the word 'reasonably' was not defined and so was open to various interpretations to suit member countries in difficulties. However, of even more importance was the fact that there was very little that the IMF could do if a country decided to act unilaterally and devalued its currency without prior consultation and agreement. (It should be noted in this context that the UK did consult its major trading partners in 1967 before the pound was devalued.)

Flaws and defects of Bretton Woods

The system devised at Bretton Woods had a number of flaws and defects which became more and more apparent during the 1960s. It was realised eventually that a system which relied almost exclusively on *fixed* exchange rates was unworkable in the long term. Exchange rates should reflect a country's relative trading strength compared to other countries, but there is no reason why such relationships should remain static and fixed over time. However, a system of fixed exchange rates implies that this is the case. Economies do change from year to year and from decade to decade. For instance, during the 1950s and 1960s the German economy became progressively stronger than the American economy, and so under a system of fixed exchange rates the German mark became progressively *undervalued* against the dollar. Eventually, this situation forced the upwards revaluation of the mark in 1969. (This was achieved by allowing the exchange rate of the mark to 'float' for a short period until a new equilibrium position was achieved.)

In short, the fundamental weakness of the Bretton Woods system was its insistence on building a *system of fixed exchange rates onto a world economic system which was in a constant state of flux and change.* However, there were other problems. Difficulties continued to arise as world output consistently outstripped new gold supplies. The only way in which sufficient world liquidity could be maintained was for the two major currencies – the dollar and the pound – to operate on a continual 'deficit' basis, but this was obviously self-defeating because the persistent deficits of the UK and America tended to undermine confidence in the two currencies and so put even more pressure on the whole insecure system. (This situation was particularly serious for the UK because its economy was fundamentally weak, anyway.) As is so often the case in economics, recognising that a problem exists and actually doing something about it often takes a considerable time. However, after some 10 years of discussion a small step was taken towards increasing world liquidity in 1970, although the dollar and the pound still remained under pressure.

Special drawing rights

World liquidity was increased by the introduction by the IMF of a new *international reserve asset* known as the *Special Drawing Right*, or *SDR*. SDRs were set up by the voting members of the IMF on the advice of its Director-General and were distributed to all member countries in direct proportion to their existing IMF quotas. SDRs are similar to official reserves and so can be used by individual countries to settle their everyday international debts. Originally, it was intended that just enough SDRs would be issued each year to maintain a steady growth in world liquidity, which would be roughly in line with the growth in world output. In the first three years, some $3,500 million worth of SDRs were created. However, the 1970s oil price explosion changed the entire world monetary situation, and so between then and 1977 no more SDRs were created in this way. It was considered that the substantial increase in liquidity which arose from the flow of 'oil money' around the world, combined with the large American balance of payments deficits, meant that there was no need for any further expansion of liquidity through the SDR mechanism.

The Eurocurrency market

The international money markets in the 1960s and 1970s have revolved around the *Eurocurrency market*. This market developed when large amounts of American dollars found their way into Europe after the Second World War, partly as a result of that country's direct aid to European countries for re-building programmes, etc, after the devastation of the war, but mainly because American investors were in search of better interest rates and the avoidance of the special credit restrictions which were operating at the time. What was then the *Eurodollar* market has now developed into the *Eurocurrency* market, as many other currencies operate outside their own national boundaries in response to the increase in international transactions.

This market provides an ideal method for companies (and countries) to borrow money on the international money markets: companies can obtain large amounts of capital at the most competitive interest rates available, while governments can utilise the market's facilities, partly for the purpose of raising capital, but mainly as a means of financing a balance of payments deficit.

The problems of the Third World

Outside the industrialised world it is often convenient to classify the rest of the world economy as the 'Third World' (or 'developing countries'). The OPEC countries should perhaps be seen as a separate entity because of their oil wealth. However, even within the remaining countries there is a massive difference between economies such as Ethiopia and, say, Brazil.

Indeed, there has been the creation of the status of 'newly industrialised country' for economies such as Taiwan, Korea and Brazil who are developing rapidly. For other countries though, the old problems of under-development remain. These problems vary in their gravity from one country to another; Bangladesh is more under-developed than Kenya, for example. It is difficult not to generalise about the difficulties of Third World nations. However, many developing countries suffer from some or all of the following difficulties in varying degrees:

a high levels of illiteracy;

b poor infrastructure/communications;

c high birth rates;

d shortages of skilled/managerial staff;

e corruption and inefficiency in government/administration;

f balance of payments/international debt problems;

g over-dependence of the economy on the export of primary products which are volatile in price;

h political/social instability;

i a lack of foreign exchange/inflation;

j poor development of irrigation/fertilising schemes in agriculture.

These problems divide the world almost North/South, with the northern hemisphere 'developed' and the southern hemisphere (with the exception of Australasia) 'developing'. Help to developing nations comes through direct aid from the industrialised world in the form of loans, gifts and technical advice (bilateral aid). The EU and agencies such as the World Bank (see below) channel aid from several countries to the developing world (multilateral aid). Despite these efforts the poorer countries of the world are still at a disadvantage in world trade, even though countries such as Taiwan and Korea have made major inroads into world manufacturing.

The large growth of population in these countries has given renewed credibility to the theories of Thomas Malthus, who predicted over a hundred years ago that the growth in population would outstrip the capability of a nation to provide resources to feed its people. The industrialisation of the UK proved this theory wrong here, but several countries in the Far East and South America do have a population problem, especially when one sees a high birth rate combined with a falling death rate. Indeed, it could be argued that many developing countries are populated beyond their optimum (highest output per head with given resources).

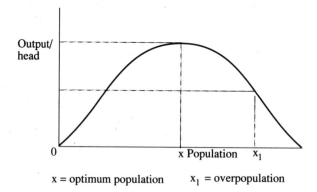

x = optimum population x_1 = overpopulation

Any point to the right of x is overpopulation.

The plight of the poorest nations such as Somalia, Bangladesh, Mozambique and Ethiopia has been highlighted by the famines and military crises of these countries. The spontaneous gifts to these countries from the people of the industrialised world via the relief agencies helped to cope with immediate problems. However, many developing countries need political stability, an improved infrastructure, better education, and training and advice on industrial and farming techniques.

The World Bank

The problems of the Third World would undoubtedly have been greater if the developed world had not already concentrated a considerable amount of help on assisting various under-developed countries with finance and investment programmes. Indeed, the UK itself has had an overseas aid programme for many years and, despite its own economic difficulties, it is still spending around £500 million a year in this area. (At the same time, of course, considerable sums are spent by the private sector in under-developed countries.)

However, the main need of the under-developed countries is very often the provision of 'social capital'. For private sector investment to bear fruit, a country needs roads, railways, irrigation systems, dams, health programmes and so on. All these items require vast amounts of capital, but they do not yield any positive return in terms of interest, profits and dividends. It is the type of expenditure which is normally undertaken by governments, but in the case of under-developed countries it is rare for the governments to have the necessary resources to undertake such programmes. Instead, they rely on outside assistance, either from individual countries such as the UK or America or from international organisations such as the United Nations, to provide direct assistance in the form of loan capital and industrial expertise.

One of the most important organisations in this connection is the *International Bank for Reconstruction and Development* (usually referred to as the *World Bank*). It was founded at the same time as the IMF in 1944 and is funded in a similar manner. The leading countries of the world subscribe towards the World Bank's capital stock in direct proportion to their own economic importance and size. The bank then uses this money to lend to poorer under-developed countries at favourable rates of interest for use on major capital projects which will assist the country's economic infrastructure (multilateral aid). The bank can also now raise money through the issue of its own bonds on the international money markets.

The bank has proved very successful in encouraging investment in the developing world, because it has enabled the developed world to 'spread' the risks of such investment more evenly. However, a scheme to provide the developing world with an increased share of world liquidity is also vitally important to future prosperity in that part of the world, particularly as some of the countries on the receiving end of World Bank loans regard them as a threat to their own economic sovereignty. It is, therefore, important to ensure that such feelings are minimised through the use of an automatic mechanism for the provision of medium- to long-term finance.

Questions for review

1 What is an 'exchange rate'? Why are exchange rates necessary?
2 What are the major factors which determine a country's exchange rate?
3 Consider the possible effects on a country's balance of payments of a depreciation in its foreign exchange rate.
4 Explain how the Bretton Woods exchange rate system worked. Why did it break down?
5 How does a system of freely floating exchange rates work? Why do Central Banks intervene to influence the price of currencies in floating systems?
6 Explain how the ERM works.
7 What does the International Monetary Fund do?
8 What does the World Bank do?

Economic growth | 19

Determinants of growth and production possibility frontiers   473

The benefits and costs of growth   482

Government action   483

De-industrialisation   485

Determinants of growth and production possibility frontiers

Introduction

Economic growth is defined as an increase in the productive capacity of the economy over time. It refers to an outward shift in the production possibility frontier. It is measured by the rate of change in real gross national product.

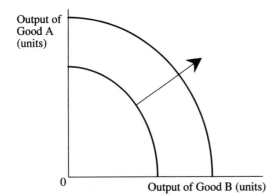

The productive capacity of the economy depends on the number of worker-hours worked and the productivity of those worker-hours. The productivity of labour is determined by factors such as the stock of capital equipment, the state of technical knowledge, the skill of workers and management and the supply of raw materials. The productive capacity of the economy determines potential supply while the national income accounts measure actual marketed supply.

Production possibility frontiers and technical efficiency

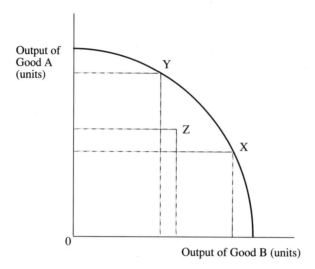

Notice that the production possibility frontier is concave to the origin. The economy has a stock of resources, some of which are more suitable for the production of A than of B and others are more suitable for the production of B rather than A. Suppose the economy is currently producing at output X, with a great deal of B being produced and relatively little of A. If it shifts its resources so that more of A is produced and less of B, moving along the production possibility frontier towards Y, it will, to begin with, be reallocating resources most suitable for the production of A into the production of A. Marginal productivity will therefore be high.

However, as resources continue to be reallocated from the production of B to the production of A, increasingly unsuitable resources will be used. The marginal productivity will therefore fall. Thus the sacrifice required of good B in order to produce more of good A increases as more A is produced. Similarly, if we had considered increasing the production of B, the *opportunity cost* of doing so in terms of the required sacrifice of A would rise as more B was produced. The production possibility curve is therefore concave to the origin unless all resources are perfect substitutes for each other (equally useful in the production of either good). In that case, the production possibility frontier would be a straight line.

Alternatively, we can imagine that there are some resources which are essential to the production of one of the goods (A) but in fixed supply. As more resources are allocated to the production of good B, the supply of these essential resources will become fully utilised. Output can then only be expanded by allocating X increasing amounts of variable inputs to this fixed input, in which case *the law of diminishing returns* begins to apply. Marginal productivity begins to fall, so opportunity costs begin to rise.

The production possibility curve shows all points which are *technically efficient*. Any point within the curve such as Z is technically inefficient. This is so because the resources of the economy could have been used to produce more of A while maintaining production of B (choosing a point such as Y) or could have produced more of B while maintaining production of A (choosing a point such as X) or more of both goods could be produced. Assuming that more goods mean more utility, it is a waste to produce less in absolute terms than is possible.

To give a numerical example, suppose the economy has 20 units of labour, 5 of land and 15 of capital. It would be technically inefficient to use them to produce a combination of 100 units of A and 100 units of B when the economy could, with greater efficiency, produce combinations of 150 of A with 100 of B or 100 of A with 150 of B.

Technical efficiency means that the economy is operating on the maximum range of output. Actual output may often be below this maximum. For example, if there are unemployed resources in the economy this may indicate that the economy is at a point within the production possibility frontier such as point Z. Similarly, if resources are employed but are operating less efficiently than could be possible, the economy will be operating within the production possibility frontier and will be technically inefficient.

There may be a conflict of priorities that limits technical efficiency. For example, suppose that the government puts a high priority on the redistribution of income to reduce the differences in standards of living between different groups in the society. A highly progressive system of taxation of incomes is thought to create disincentives which may mean that some of the population do not take jobs or take less productive jobs than they might have chosen or work less efficiently in their chosen job than they might. The priority of technical efficiency may therefore conflict with a policy of redistributing income. Similarly, if the government puts a high priority on checking inflation or on eliminating a balance of payments deficit, the cost of these policies may be a loss in technical efficiency.

Production possibility frontiers and economic efficiency

The economy must not aim just to be technically efficient. It should aim for *economic efficiency*. To be economically efficient, the economy must select the 'right' combination of goods as well as producing that combination efficiently. There is, for example, no point in producing at point Y with lots of A and little B if the consumers would have preferred to have the combination of goods indicated by point X with more B and less A. This alternative combination is also possible with the limited stock of resources. The 'right' combination depends on consumer preferences. Suppose that we could draw aggregate indifference curves very like the indifference curves used for individual preferences. This time the indifference curves express the sum of the preferences of all consumers. The economy wishes to reach the highest possible indifference curve in order to be economically efficient. With the map which follows, the economy should produce the combination shown by point T on the production possibility frontier. This gives a higher level of utility than points X and Y, which are technically efficient but on a lower indifference curve.

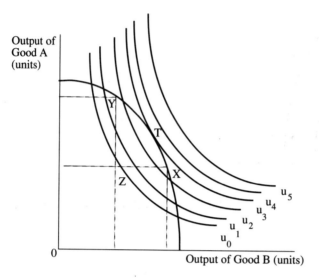

If the production possibility frontier represents the range of maximum output, economic growth means an outward shift of the production possibility frontier so that the maximum range increases. The economy can produce more of all goods than were possible before. In the following diagram the production possibility frontier shifts from PP to PP_1. The economy was previously at the economically efficient output of T. It can now produce more of good A while maintaining output of good B (by producing the output indicated by point S) *or* it can maintain output of A while increasing output of B (by choosing point R) *or* it can have more of both goods (by choosing any point on the curve between S and R).

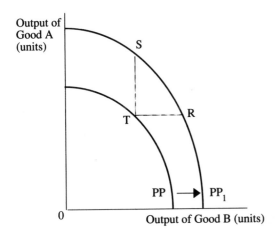

A higher indifference curve can now be reached so total utility has been increased.

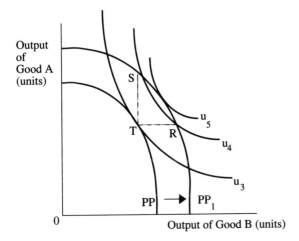

We should examine the factors which will cause the production possibility frontier to shift outwards giving the economy the potential for economic growth, and real increases in national income.

Quantity and quality

In practice, the production possibility maximum of an economy depends on both the quantity and *quality* of its factors of production and on the way in which they are combined in an effort to increase productive output. So far as labour is concerned – and in this particular discussion that includes managerial labour and enterprise – the size, age, distribution and general health of the population naturally affects a country's growth potential. However, probably of more importance is the educational standard of most of the workforce and the potential mobility of each and every unit of labour. If the general educational standard rises, then there should eventually be a rise in productive potential as people acquire better skills and so on. This is naturally a long-term policy. Of more immediate importance, particularly in the UK, would be a general move of the labour force away from the older industries such as textiles and coal-mining into the growth industries of the 1980s such as electronics and computers. This would raise national output rapidly and so raise the general standard of living.

It should be noted that economic growth entirely through increases in the size of the population does not cause an increase in the standard of living. The *standard of living* is increased when *real per capita national income* rises. If the population grows by the same percentage as the increase in real national income, per capita income is unchanged.

Economic growth may also be achieved by increases in the quality or quantity of land. Obviously major increases in the quantity of land available to an economy can only be achieved by treaty or conquest. More marginal changes in quantity and improvement in the quality of land can be achieved through investment such as drainage, irrigation, fertilisation. Investment in improving the quality of both labour and land inputs is thus an important factor in economic growth.

Technological change which can increase the productivity of the existing stock of resources is an important determinant of the rate of economic growth. Investment in research and development to produce technological developments is undertaken by private individuals and firms in the expectation of future rewards. A successful innovation can bring substantial monopoly profits to the innovator. The government may contribute to this process by expenditure on the education and training of those individuals who may be expected to produce successful innovations. As industry becomes increasingly technical, the level of education and training required of potential innovators rises. The state plays an important part in providing, through its own institutions and system of grants and subsidies, the necessary background. The state also directly pays for innovative research through its various research councils.

Capital accumulation

However, most economists tend to agree that the major determinant of economic growth potential is *the rate of capital accumulation*. Although the quantity and quality of a country's capital stock will undoubtedly influence the growth potential, what really matters is the *rate* of increase. It is necessary, therefore, to differentiate between *gross* and *net* investment. (*Gross* investment measures the total investment undertaken in any one year, while *net* investment measures only *new* investment.) The figures for both these types of investment are usually published by the government, but such figures should be approached with caution. The accurate measurement of the quantity (and, more importantly, the quality) of the capital stock is very difficult. Indeed, the figures produced by the government are based mainly on the tax returns submitted by firms and so tend to reflect 'allowable' depreciation rates rather than the actual capital stock in existence.

Differing growth rates

The recorded rate of growth may reflect a failure to achieve economic efficiency under current conditions and may also reflect a slow rate of expansion of that potential level of national income. An increase in the recorded rate of growth of national income may indicate either a movement out towards the existing production possibility frontier (by solving structural unemployment for example) and/or an outward shift of the production possibility frontier.

The quality of the capital stock is of overriding importance in determining the growth potential of an economy. In general terms, the newer the machinery the more efficient it will be, and so the greater its output as it will probably take advantage of the most up-to-date technology available. However, the difficulty of measuring the *quality* of a country's capital stock has not prevented some economists from making intuitive guesses as to why different countries have had significantly different growth rates in the years since the Second World War. They argue that those countries such as Japan and Germany which had to rebuild their capital stock virtually from scratch have had an automatic advantage over other countries because their capital stock has been that much more modern and, therefore, that much more efficient in terms of output. It is true that the performance of the UK economy has lagged behind the economies of Japan and Germany. It is worth noting, however, that the average rate of growth experienced by the UK in the past 20 years or so, of around 3 per cent a year, is well in excess of the rate of growth in the nineteenth century, which was only about 1½ per cent, although the fact remains that the UK's *relative* rate of growth compared with that of its immediate trading partners in the 1970s was very poor. During the 1980s, though, UK growth was above that of many trading partners.

Rates of growth of real GDP, international comparisons

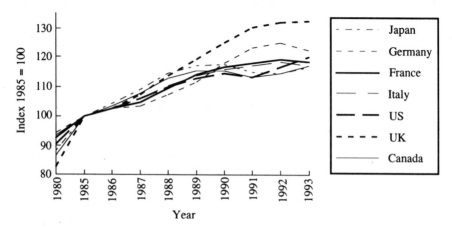

(Source: *Economic Trends*, June 1994, Table 1)

Consumption now or in the future?

We have seen that investment by the private sector or by the state is a central contributor to the rate of economic growth. The economy has a limited ability to produce goods and services, shown by the production possibility frontier. If it uses resources for the production of consumption goods, those resources cannot then be used for the production of investment goods. We might, therefore, express the production possibility curve in these terms.

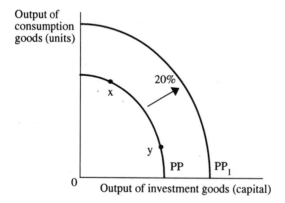

The economy can choose any point on the production possibility curve shown above. If it chooses point x the economy is opting for a high level of consumption but a low level of gross investment. Economic growth will therefore be slow, since only a small amount of investment is going on.

Alternatively, the economy could be operating at y with a very high level of gross investment while current consumption is low. The advantage of that choice is that a high rate of economic growth will be achieved. A second production possibility curve (PP_1) is shown which represents a 20 per cent increase in real national income. The choice now of an allocation of present resources between consumption and investment such as y will mean that the economy reaches this higher national income in, say, 4 years. If the economy instead opts for a high level of present consumption represented by point x, it will take, say, 10 years to reach that 20 per cent increase in national income.

There is, therefore, a *trade-off* between consumption now and economic growth which will generate the possibility of higher consumption levels in the future. In the diagram below, a high-present-consumption, low-present-investment strategy will produce the consumption path A below. The economy could alternatively choose a low-present-consumption, high-present-investment strategy which would produce the consumption path B.

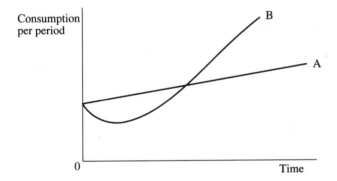

One of the reasons offered for the comparatively low rate of UK economic growth in the 1960s and 1970s is that the economy showed a high preference for consumption – both private consumption (consumer durables, food, alcohol) and state consumption (health and social services, defence, housing, transport facilities) – so little was left for investment. The UK economy might then be regarded as having followed the low growth path indicated by A, especially in the 1960s and 1970s.

However, despite these fairly exact observations about the probable determinants of economic growth, the economist is still unable to translate his observations into positive policy instruments. There are no examples of a government successfully intervening in a free market economy to raise the growth rate solely through its own policy measures. As quickly as possible examples are given – say, France in the 1950s and 1960s, where overall economic plans were devised – other examples can be quoted – such as Germany – where no such policies were implemented and yet the growth rates were similar. It would seem – and this is only a tentative suggestion which cannot be supported by empirical fact – that a major determinant of the potential growth rate within a country is the 'psychology' and the 'drive' of the population. The true 'entrepreneurial' spirit may indeed be the motivating force behind growth rates.

The benefits and costs of growth

The benefits

There are a number of benefits arising out of a rapid rate of growth. The most obvious is the overall improvement in the country's living standards – more people can afford more luxuries, without depriving other people of the basic necessities of life. At the same time, the country should be able to afford an improved level of national income. A side effect of an increased rate of growth is the greater freedom which it provides for the population to choose between different types of work, and even between leisure and work.

These 'benefits' are so important to a society such as that found in the western world – and, indeed, in most other parts of the world. The political appeal of higher economic growth rates (promised or real) is considerable. Unfortunately, the very politicians who encourage these aspirations among the majority of the people then have grave difficulties in formulating effective economic policies to fulfil them!

The costs

However, in a world where scarcity is the norm rather than the exception, almost nothing is 'free'. Growth – or higher output – can only be achieved by lower current consumption. So, the opportunity cost of growth is lower consumption than would otherwise be possible. There are other costs as well which individuals have to pay. If any economy is *growing*, it is also *changing*. Technical progress and innovation leave obsolete machines and jobs in their wake. A rapid rate of growth requires a rapid rate of adjustment, and this can cause a considerable amount of hardship and difficulty for those people who are directly affected by the adjustment. The decline in the number of unskilled jobs, which is usually a part of economic growth, makes the lot of the unskilled and untrained worker much harder. Similarly, over two or three decades, even the demand for certain skilled jobs might change dramatically. No matter how well equipped a person is at twenty-five, by the age of fifty he could be out of a job because his skills are no longer required. In short, however mobile the overall population is during a period of rapid economic growth, there will still be considerable *structural* unemployment. It is true, of course, that a growing economy is more able to support the people who are unemployed through increased social welfare benefits, but that in itself is no substitute for a productive job in most cases.

The costs of economic growth do not only affect individuals – there are often costs to the community as a whole. Indeed, there are many people who believe the relentless drive towards continued economic growth should be restricted. A growing industrialised economy tends to lay waste to vast areas of land and it uses up the limited resources of the world at a rapid rate. Raw materials and natural resources are often used indiscriminately with no thought for future generations. At the same time, a highly industrialised economy will usually pollute the atmosphere and the sea. All these are serious considerations against the drive for further economic growth. The *social costs* of any further expansion of output must be considered. The costs in human terms must always be considered. That does not only mean the quality of the environment in which we live, but also the quality of the work which we do; the monotony of much work today alienates the worker and may lead to increasing social unrest.

Government action

The government's role

An improvement in any country's rate of growth requires both an increase in the rate of new investment and an improvement in the overall level of labour productivity. How far should government be involved in achieving the four major economic objectives of growth, price stability, full employment and balance of payments equilibrium?

Policy clashes

Very often different policy decisions conflict. For instance, the policies used to reduce the rate of inflation or the balance of payments deficit often adversely affect the growth potential of the economy, because they are restrictive rather than expansionary. In short, it may be quite impossible to fulfil all the government's policy goals simultaneously – one policy measure will bring it closer to some of its objectives, but take it further away from others. So, it really is not enough for a government – or in more general terms, a country – to decide which objectives are worth pursuing and which must be ignored for the time being. The country has effectively to decide on a 'rate of substitution' between them – it must decide how far it wishes to go towards one set of goals at the expense of another set of goals. Indeed, many economic controversies today concern the varying economic policies and goals open to a government. For instance, in the UK today almost everyone agrees that there is a need to reduce the level of unemployment *and* reduce inflation. However, there is considerable disagreement on the *relative* importance of these two goals. While some economists believe that there is a 'trade-off' between inflation and unemployment, others argue (particularly monetarists) that curing inflation is the prerequisite for curing unemployment (ie low inflation encourages job creation).

It might be possible to conduct a rational debate on the pros and cons of each approach – and remember each approach would entail the adoption of very different policy measures – but, in the final analysis, the ultimate decision is dependent on people's *value judgments* (normative judgments). The economist cannot decide policies based only on his economic knowledge.

The arguments for and against growth and the policies used to attain it are particularly dependent on value judgments. However, despite that serious warning, it should be remembered that economists agree on many things – even the non-monetarist economist still accepts that there is *some* relationship between the money supply and the level of prices within an economy, while the monetarist accepts that there may still be a need for strict fiscal and incomes policies in conjunction with the control of the money supply.

The need for intervention

A further point needs to be made in this connection. In the eighteenth century it was generally believed that the government should intervene as little as possible with the workings of the 'free market' economy (classical theory). In this way the public 'good' would be best served.

The depression of the 1930s led to the emergence of economic theories which urged government intervention to secure full employment and economic growth. The policies advocated by J M Keynes involved demand-management of the economy to secure growth (reflation). However, the high inflation and unemployment of the 1970s ('slumpflation') brought crisis to economic theories again, as the world went into depression. The emergence of monetarism and neo-classical economics moved ideaology back towards the theories of non-intervention followed in the eighteenth and nineteenth centuries. Monetarists argued that enterprise (and hence growth) would only flourish if the government created the right economic conditions for this growth. This meant reducing inflation, releasing resources to the private sector and de-regulating the economy. This would improve the economy's capability to grow, to supply more goods and services. Hence the observation that while Keynesians are 'demand side' economists, monetarists are concerned with the 'supply side'. Significantly, 'Keynesian' theories were abandoned in the UK in the late 1970s, and replaced with a more 'monetarist' approach.

Delivering the 1984 Mais Lecture, Nigel Lawson, the then Chancellor of the Exchequer, described the revolution that had taken place in economic policy since 1979:

> 'It is the conquest of inflation, and not the pursuit of growth and employment, which is or should be the objective of macroeconomic policy. And it is the creation of conditions conducive to growth and employment, and not the suppression of price rises, which is or should be the objective of micro-economic policy ... The most important point to emphasise is that this government is pursuing simultaneously both a macro and a micro policy, that the one complements the other, that the macro

policy is unequivocally directed at the continuing reduction in inflation with the ultimate objective of stable prices, and that the micro policy is equally wholeheartedly designed to make the economy work better and thus generate more jobs.' (18 June 1984)

This is the policy that the present government has pursued since taking office in 1979. By the late 1980s monetarism had evolved into 'supply side' economics. The 'crude' monetarism of the early 1980s did not survive the abandonment of strict monetary targets in 1985.

The economist – as a scientist – must always be prepared to admit that where observed fact comes into conflict with a neat theory, it is the theory which must give way.

De-industrialisation

Definition and evidence

De-industrialisation might be defined as *the absolute decline of employment in industrial activities*, particularly in manufacturing activity. In the United Kingdom there were 4 million jobs lost in industry between 1966 and 1981; 3 million of these were in manufacturing and the remaining 1 million were jobs lost in mining, construction and public utilities (gas, water, electricity supplies). The diagram below shows the changes in employment in the UK between 1950 and 1989.

Sector output as share of GDP

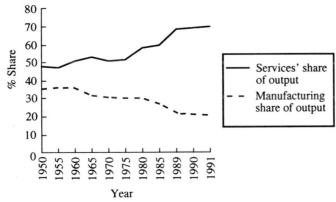

(Source: *National Income and Expenditure (Blue Book) 1992*, Table 2.1)

The worst-hit industries over this period were metal manufacturing, textiles, leather goods, clothing and footwear, and mining and quarrying. The decline of employment in manufacturing industry has continued throughout the 1980s but at a slower rate since 1985.

Another way of defining de-industrialisation might be to look at *industrial or manufacturing output as a proportion of Gross Domestic Product*. Manufacturing production was close to 40 per cent of GDP in 1950 and the long-term trend has been downward ever since. During the 1980s, the downward trend continued, reaching 21 per cent by 1991.

On the positive side, manufacturing output and productivity rose during the 1980s, but both from a very low base following the 1980–81 recession. The graph below shows manufacturing output and productivity from 1988 to 1992.

Output of manufacturing industries, 1988 to 1992

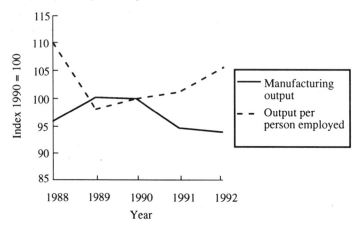

(Source: *Economic Trends*, June 1994, Table 2.1)

Importance of de-industrialisation

The natural course of development process in any economy is that resources shift first from agriculture into industry and then from industry into service-type activities. In the 1980s it was seen that service activities expanded their employment as production industry contracted. However, the impact of the 1990s recession has so far fallen very harshly on the service sector as well as manufacturing.

It is argued by some that manufacturing industry is the *engine of growth*. They argue that there is, for example, a strong relationship between the importance of manufacturing in the economy and per capita income, between increases in manufacturing output and growth of GDP, between increasing output of manufactures and productivity both in manufacturing and in non-manufacturing industry.

The decline of industry is important because of its impact on *international trade*. Traditionally, Britain has had to import raw materials and food, and has sold manufactured goods and services in order to pay for these essential imports. For this balance to work, there needed to be a large surplus of trade in manufactures. The problem is masked because of an expansion in service exports and particularly by net exports of North Sea oil. However, North Sea oil production will soon begin to fall and the market in services is becoming much more competitive worldwide. How are essential imports of food and raw material to be paid for when the oil runs out? Only in 1988 did manufacturing output overtake the 1979 level. The narrow industrial base of the UK is seen by many economists as a profound weakness in the economy. It can be argued that the UK has an underlying balance of payments problem because of its small manufacturing sector. Whenever the UK economy expands there is a danger that increased domestic demand merely increases imports because the home industry's production capacity is limited.

Causes of de-industrialisation

One argument is that employment in industry has declined because of *technological advance*. It may be true that a sudden technological breakthrough may destroy more jobs than it creates in the short run. However, in the long run technological progress creates employment.

Firstly, technological advance results in *higher incomes* which lead to higher consumer expenditures and therefore more demand for all goods and services. It may be that the demand for the products of industry may become satisfied (demand switching to higher-income-elastic products such as leisure and catering facilities), but this is far from the case world-wide.

Secondly, technological progress does not just raise productivity and increase demand for existing goods, it also *creates new goods and new demands*. For example, washing machines, vacuum cleaners, refrigerators, motor cars and aeroplanes are all new products whose development has provided many jobs. Currently, home and office computers, pocket calculators, video recorders and television games are all creating new jobs in manufacturing.

Finally, technological advance involves *investment*, which itself creates manufacturing jobs. Part of the UK's problem could be in under-investment in manufacturing industry. If technological progress were the explanation for falling employment in manufacturing, those countries with the most rapid technological advance would have the most rapidly declining manufacturing sectors. The opposite seems to be the case (eg Japan).

It might be argued that during the 1960s and 1970s the large public expenditure and a high and rising PSBR led to *higher interest rates* than would otherwise have been the case. The expansion of public sector borrowing perhaps crowded out private investment (with its long-term effects on productivity and competitiveness) and made the necessary cash flow borrowings more expensive, squeezing profits and constraining output. (This argument depends on an assumption of limited money supply. An expanding money supply could finance the PSBR without any effect on interest rates, though this would, of course, tend to be inflationary.)

The most convincing explanation for industrial decline is *the failure to compete successfully on world markets*. British manufactures have been less and less successful in foreign and domestic markets. Export sales are falling while the propensity to import manufactured goods increases. For example, the British car industry once supplied almost the whole of the domestic market and was very successful in export markets; now more foreign than British cars are sold on the domestic market. Since 1983 Britain has run a deficit on trade in manufactures with the rest of the world. High wages, trade union disruption of production, inept management, high interest rates, overmanning, insufficient innovation, and high exchange rates might all explain this failure to compete successfully.

Balance of trade (£ million, current prices)		
Year	Services	Manufactures
1980	3,653	5,428
1981	3,792	4,497
1982	3,022	2,094
1983	4,064	-2,733
1984	4,519	-4,527
1985	6,687	-3,765
1986	6,696	-6,125
1987	6,628	-8,112
1988	4,504	-15,100
1989	4,698	-16,822
1990	5,119	-10,883
1991	3,657	-11,492
1992	4,069	-14,893

(Source: *UK Balance of Payments (Pink Book)*, 1991 and 1993, Table 2.1)

Recent developments

It could be argued that de-industrialisation does not matter and must be accepted as a part of the natural process of economic change, and that services will provide the jobs and exports lost by manufacturing industry. This point is dealt with on pages 486–7.

It can also be argued that the manufacturing sector of the UK economy has seen a remarkable recovery in the last few years. Although employment has fallen sharply (less so of late) productivity has risen and even output has started to grow again. Undoubtedly, what is left of UK manufacturing is more competitive than ten years ago.

	Output per head of employed labour force, average % change (1990=100)			
	1964–73	1987–79	1980–88	1988–93
Manufacturing	3.8	0.7	5.25	3.2
Non-manufacturing	2.9	0.6	2.25	—
Whole economy	2.7	1.1	2.5	1.2

(Source: *Economic Trends*, June 1994, Table 4.7)

During the period 1988-1993, which covers the last recession, the output per worker in the manufacturing industries grew much more strongly than did the output for the economy as a whole. This is to some extent indicative of the continuing large-scale shakeouts from the manufacturing industries. Growth in output per worker has been achieved against a background of mass unemployment.

It is important to note that the UK sells 14 per cent more manufactured goods by volume in overseas markets than in 1979. The more worrying point, however, is that since 1983 the UK now imports more manufactured goods than it exports. It is of equal concern that the regions previously strong in manufacturing (the Midlands and North) have suffered disproportionately badly from the industrial decline of the late 1970s and early 1980s.

A strategy for de-industrialisation?

The present government would argue that any strategy designed to promote growth in manufacturing should revolve around creating the right conditions for enterprise, specifically:

a deregulation in factor markets;

b lower tax burdens and interest rates;

c advice to entrepreneurs;

d less direct government interference in industry.

It is argued by opponents of the 'enterprise culture' approach that more direct government action is required to boost manufacturing industry in the UK. Possible strategies involve:

a *Devaluation*, which makes exports cheaper on foreign markets and makes imports more expensive in the home market. This strategy was discussed in Chapter 18 and may well lead to more inflation and an even worse competitive situation.

b *Import controls.* The effect of import controls is discussed in Chapter 18. It is likely that our trading partners would retaliate, so the effect on our already weak export trade might be as serious as the effect of the controls on import penetration.

c *Reflation.* If the government increases public expenditure, particularly on capital projects, manufacturing industry would feel the benefits. Access to cheap funds for investment could also be provided by the government.

Whichever policy is used the UK does need to concentrate its resources into technologically dynamic industries, and into the manufacture of goods with a high income elasticity of demand. With the newly industrialised countries prominent in 'volume' manufactures, the UK needs to develop the manufacture of those goods at the quality end of the market. For many economists the decline in the UK's manufacturing sector has gone too far, leaving the country with too narrow an industrial base. During the early 1980s the UK lost many good names in manufacturing. Such a loss is impossible to quantify in purely financial terms.

Questions for review

1 What does a production possibility frontier represent?
2 If economic growth takes place in an economy, what will happen to its production possiblity frontier?
3 If resources are underutilised in an economy, how can this be shown on a production possibility diagram?
4 Explain the difference between technical efficiency and economic efficiency.
6 How does the rate of capital accumulation affect economic growth?
6 How may differing growth rates in different economies be explained?
7 What are the benefits of economic growth?
8 What are the costs of economic growth?
9 What does the term 'de-industrialisation' mean? Does de-industrialisation matter?
10 What are the causes of de-industrialisation?
11 What impact has it had on the UK?
12 What can be done about it?

Index

Accelerator process 177, 331
Activity rate 364
Advertising 49–50, 65, 71
Aggregate demand 315, 325
Average cost 87, 92
Average rate of tax 372, 377
Average propensity to consume 320

Balance of payments 431
Balance of trade 434
Balanced budget 367
Bank of England 262
Banks 254
Bretton Woods 458, 463, 465
British Gas 222
British Telecom 221
Budget 367
Buffer stocks 32–39
Business Expansion Scheme 211, 243
Business Improvement Scheme 211
Business rates 383

Capital 171
Capital gains tax 374
Capital goods 4, 147
Central Bank 262
Circular flow 295
Clearing system 251, 254
Co-operatives 101
Command economics 8–9
Commercial bills 257
Common Agricultural Policy 421
Community charge 383
Comparative advantage 409
Complementary goods 21
Concentration 137
Conglomerate integration 138
Consumer surplus 185
Consumer's demand 68–72

Consumption 315, 480
Consumption goods 4, 147
Corporation tax 375
Cost-push inflation 395, 403
Cost benefit analysis 183
Cost of living 271
Council tax 384
Credit creation 258, 261
Cross elasticity 66–67
Current account 436
Customs and Excise 370
Customs duties 412
Customs union 418
Cyclical unemployment 342

De-industrialisation 485
Deflationary gap 333, 335
Demand 17–23
Demand-pull inflation 394
Demand for investment 175–176
Demand for money 274
Demerit goods 45
Depression 344
Derived demand 147
Devaluation 440, 464
Developing countries 466
Diminishing returns 7, 85, 474
Direct taxes 369
Discount houses 266
Discounted cash flow 181
Diseconomies of scale 91–92
Dumping 415
Duopoly 129, 134

Earnings 192, 193–198, 397
Economic rent 157
Economies of scale 5, 90, 351
Effective demand 17
EFTA 418
Elasticity of demand 55–60
Elasticity of supply 77–78

Embargos 414
Employment training 243, 363
Enterprise allowance scheme 211, 244, 362
Enterprise zones 357
Equilibrium wages 166
Eurodollars 466
European Union 416
European Union competition law 142–143
Exchange rate 451
Exchange rate mechanism 423
Excise duties 370
External benefits 41, 72, 112, 123, 161, 235
External costs 45, 72, 112, 123, 161, 235

Factor cost 302
Fiduciary issue 251
Fiscal drag 377
Fiscal lag 378
Fiscal policy 346, 368
Fisher equation 285
Fixed costs 83
Fixed exchange rates 456
Floating exchange rates 454
Free market mechanism 111–114
Free trade 411
Free trade area 417
Frictional unemployment 341
Full employment GNP 323, 334
Funding 279

GATT 417
Giffen good 19
GNP 304
Gold standard 462
Goldsmiths 250
Government housing policies 236–240

Horizontal integration 138
Housing 228
Hyperinflation 273

Imperfect competition 114
Import controls 489
Import deposit scheme 414
Import quotas 412
Income 319, 403
Income elasticity 65–66
Income tax 372
Indirect taxes 369–375
Industrial policy 205
Industrial restructuring 207
Inferior goods 21, 42
Inflation 271, 393
Inflationary gap 333, 335
Inheritance tax 373
Injections 297, 301
Inland Revenue 371
Interest rate 283
International Bank for Reconstruction 469
International Monetary Fund 462, 464
Investment 5, 172, 300
Invisible trade 433, 435

J-curve 454
Job clubs 361

Keynes 327

Labour mobility 348
Labour supply 162
Land 159–162
Lateral integration 139
Liquidity 260
Liquidity preference 276
Loan guarantee scheme 209, 210, 244
Losses 89–90

Macroeconomics 3, 304, 313
Marginal cost pricing 217
Marginal costs 86, 217
Marginal efficiency of capital 174, 175
Marginal physical product 148
Marginal propensities 320
Marginal rate of tax 377
Marginal revenue 149

Market economics 9–11
Marshall-Lerner 453
Maximum pricing 46–48
Medium term financial strategy 288, 386
Medium of exchange 250
Merchant banks 264
Merit good 41, 226
Microeconomics 3
Minimum pricing 48–49
Minimum wage 200
Mixed economies 11–12
Mobility of workforce 348
Monetarism 285, 400–403
Monetary authorities 262
Monetary policy 346
Money 249
Money at call 266, 267
Money demand 274
Money supply 252, 277, 280
Monopolies and Mergers Commission 138
Monopolistic competition 125
Monopoly 118
Monopsony 136, 170–171
Multi-fibre agreement 413
Multiplier 261, 328

National debt 387
National income 326
National insurance 241
Nationalised industries 212
Non-price competition 130
Normative economics 3

Office of Fair Trading 138
Oligopoly 128
Open market operations 278
Opportunity cost 4, 174, 181
Ownership of resources 189–190

Partnership 99
Perfect competition 109
Perverse demand 19
Phillips curve 397–402
Point elasticity 60
Positive economics 3
Poverty trap 199
Price controls 403
Price discrimination 123
Price mechanism 26–32, 77
Price taker 149

Private company 100
Privatisation 219–226
Producer price index 272
Production possibility frontiers 473
Progressive tax 369, 371
Proportional tax 369
Protectionism 411
Public company 100
Public expenditure 379
Public goods 184, 226
Public Sector Borrowing requirement 386
Purchasing power 393
Purchasing power party 451

Quantity theory of money 285

Rate of interest 174, 283
Rate of return 173
Real income 157
Recession 345
Reflation 489
Regional policy 350, 353
Regressive tax 369
Restrictive practices 142
Retail Price Index 393

Savings 298, 319
Search costs 352
Seasonal unemployment 341
Shadow prices 187
Short-term excess profits 126
Single market 419
Small firm 116, 209–210
Social wage 382
Sole proprietor 99
Special deposits 257, 279
Special drawing rights 466
Stagflation 405
Standard of living 272, 478
Structural unemployment 341, 347
Subsidies 39–44
Subsistence economies 12
Substitutes 21, 30, 63
Supply 23–26, 158

Taxes 301, 368
Terms of trade 434
Third world 466
Trade cycles 343
Trade unions 166

Training 242–243
Transfer earnings 156
Transfer payments 382
Treasury bills 257, 267, 388

Unemployment 194, 339
Unemployment – types 194–195, 359

Unemployment trap 199
Unlisted securities market 210
Urban development corporations 357
Utility 4, 68

Value added tax 370
Variable costs 83, 87

Vertical integration 138
Visible trade 433

Wages councils 200
Water privatisation 223–224
Wealth 189–190
Withdrawals 297, 301
World Bank 468